Sylvia Johnson

ARCO

ACT

AMERICAN COLLEGE TESTING PROGRAM

EVE P. STEINBERG, M.A.

ARCO PUBLISHING, INC.
219 Park Avenue South, New York, N.Y. 10003

Eighth Edition, Fourth Printing, 1983

Published by Arco Publishing, Inc.
219 Park Avenue South, New York, N.Y. 10003

Library of Congress Cataloging in Publication Data

Steinberg, Eve P.
American college testing program (ACT)

1. American College Testing Program. I. Title.
LB2353.44.S7 378′.1664 81-2727
ISBN 0-668-05145-0 (Library Edition) AACR2
ISBN 0-668-05151-5 (Paper Edition)

Printed in the United States of America

TABLE OF CONTENTS

WHY YOU SHOULD USE THIS BOOK

Your high school career is about half over and college appears to you as a distant but appealing goal. The goal creeps slowly closer, and you must begin to prepare for it. Along with the classes, papers, exams, athletic contests, dramatic productions, parties and proms of your high school upperclass years, you must also apply to colleges, sit for interviews and take standardized tests.

If the colleges which you are considering recommend or require American College Testing Program (ACT) scores for admission, then this is the exam for which you must prepare. The ACT is a difficult exam. The more you know about the exam, the better your chances of being accepted by the college of your choice.

This book will introduce you to the ACT exam. It provides detailed descriptions of each type of question on the exam and demonstrates the best approach to answering each question type. This book will also show you how the exam is organized; how many questions of each variety you may expect and how much time you will have to answer the questions. As you study this book you will see where the test makers place their emphases and where your own weaknesses lie, so that you may plan a personal program of review of those subjects in which you are "rusty."

Included in this book are four full-length simulated ACT exams. These are not actual exams; the actual exams are copyrighted and cannot be reprinted. These exams are, however, based upon information gathered through research and experience. They are so similar to the "real thing" that they will give you excellent practice. By taking these exams you will learn to budget your study time to best advantage and to pace your test-taking time so that you answer every question yet have time to ponder the difficult ones. As you do the exams in this book you will build up your speed, accuracy and confidence. The answer to every question in each exam is fully explained so that you can learn from your successes as well as from your errors.

By the time you have completed this book you will be ready—ready to earn the best score of which you are capable, ready to merit serious consideration for the college of your choice, ready to apply for a scholarship which relies on ACT scores. And you will be able to take the ACT without the panic that accompanies the unknown.

HOW TO USE THIS BOOK

You will get the most benefit from this book if you use it with respect. By this we mean treat it seriously, follow instructions, observe time limits, and do not cheat. We also mean that you should read every chapter and answer every question.

Find yourself a quiet spot with good light and a clear work space. Eliminate as many distractions as possible. Set aside specified periods of at least an hour for your ACT preparation. In addition, reserve a number of three-hour stretches, because it is best to work straight through the nearly three-hour exams.

Start at the beginning of the book. Read through each chapter carefully so that you can appreciate why you are studying, how to use the book and how to take the exam. Be sure to reread the chapter on test-taking shortly before exam day.

Begin your active preparation by taking the Pretest in one three-hour sitting. Have your pencils sharpened beforehand so that you do not have to interrupt yourself. If you have a portable kitchen timer, bring it to your work area. If you have no timer, put a clock or watch in a clearly visible spot. Tear out the answer sheet. Then, before you begin to read the directions for Test 1, set the timer for 40 minutes, or write down the exact time. General instructions are given before the clock is started, but directions for answering the questions in each test must be read within the time limits. Allow yourself a short, untimed break to stand up and stretch between Tests 2 and 3.

If you finish a test before the time limit is up, check over your answers for that test. If the time runs out before you have completed a test, stop and mark the place where time ran out. Later on you will want to go back and answer the remaining questions so as to get all possible practice.

After you have devoted the full time allowed to each test, check your answers against the answer key. Calculate and enter your scores on the form provided on the back of your answer sheet. Concentrate first on the explanations for those questions which you answered incorrectly, for those which you answered hesitantly, and for the questions which you got right by virtue of a lucky guess. But be sure to read *all* of the explanations. By studying all the explanations, even for those questions you answered correctly, you may gain new insights into choosing the correct answers and you may pick up new and useful facts.

Proceed through the book. Study the chapters that teach you how to answer the questions. Give extra time to the chapters that deal with the types of questions on which you showed weakness. Answer the practice questions and study the explanations. If you discover that there are gaps in your education, subjects you never covered, seek out a teacher who is knowledgeable in that area and ask for recommendations for further study. Do not be shy. Your college career is at stake. If you find that you have forgotten much that you learned in a subject, go back to your notes, borrow a textbook, or approach a teacher for extra help. A review session with a student currently enrolled in that course might prove very beneficial.

There are no vocabulary questions on the ACT, but a good vocabulary is basic to a good score in English usage and on the reading tests. Work with a dictionary. Look up *every* unfamiliar word in this book. If you run across a word you do not know while doing the exams, circle the word and look it up later. Look up words you find in the reading passages, new words that appear in answer choices or explanations, words you meet in the study chapters. You are far more likely to remember a word which you have looked up for yourself than a word you have attempted to memorize from a long list. If you can understand every word used in this book, you have a broad-based vocabulary and can handle the verbal requirements of the exam.

Try another model exam. This time try to pace yourself so that you mark an answer for every question. Since there is no penalty for a wrong answer on the ACT exam, even blind guessing is worthwhile. Answer every question, putting a mark beside those that need more thought. If you have time you can go back and give those questions extra time and thought. After checking your answers, return to the study chapters that deal with the areas in which you still need help and go back to school books for more review as necessary.

We strongly suggest that you plan to take at least two of the model exams first thing in the morning. If you are not a "morning person," that is, if you are usually at your best late in the day, then you should try to take all four model exams in the morning. Set your alarm on a day when there is no school, eat a good breakfast and settle down to an exam. You'll have to train yourself to concentrate in the morning because that is when the actual exam is administered. Part of your preparation for the exam consists of gearing yourself to the early start.

Even if you feel that you have improved to the maximum of your ability, even if you are certain that you are ready, complete the book and read all of the explanations. More practice and more exposure can only do you more good. Perfection of your skills will make exam day less awesome and will improve your scores.

PART I

A FEW WORDS ABOUT THE *ACT*

LETS' TALK ABOUT *ACT*

What is ACT

The ACT Assessment is much more than an examination; it is a guidance service that seeks to assist students in their *choice* of college and career goal while giving assistance to colleges in their selection of candidates.

The ACT registration form includes a lengthy personal interest inventory and pages of questions requesting self-descriptive and self-evaluative information. If you supply this information and completely fill out all the forms, you will receive, along with your score report, an Interest Profile, college major suggestions, and career suggestions tailored to your interests. If at the time of registration you named colleges in which you are interested, and if those colleges have cooperated with ACT by supplying their figures, the ACT assessment report will predict your chances for success at those colleges and, by comparing your ACT exam scores with those of enrolled freshmen, give you a basis for assessing your own chances of admission.

The ACT examination is a 219-question (all multiple-choice), two hour and 40 minute test of your knowledge in English Usage, Mathematics, Social Studies and Natural Science. Your score on this exam is considered by the ACT assessment, along with your high school record, in predicting your success at the colleges you name. Your score on this exam is also considered by colleges, along with your high school record, personal factors, interview impression and numerous intangibles, in the admission decision-making process. The ACT examination score is also considered by many scholarship granting agencies—state, union, fraternal organization, etc.—in their appraisal of scholarship candidates.

When You Should Take the ACT

The ACT exam is administered five times a year in locations throughout the United States. The ACT registration packet indicates which test centers administer the exam on each date. The date on which you take the exam may be governed by the accessibility of test centers on certain dates.

Since the ACT exam is ordinarily taken only one time by each student, you want to be certain to choose a date on which you will feel well prepared. If you plan to study all summer, a fall date may be best for you. On the other hand, you may feel best prepared when you have just completed your study for school final exams. You must also check college and scholarship agency requirements. These institutions sometimes specify the date by which the ACT must be taken.

The proportion of questions on a recent ACT exam makes it clear that successful completion of American history and chemistry courses is presupposed. If you have not yet studied American history or chemistry, you should consider postponing the ACT exam, college and scholarship requirements permitting. If you completed American history, chemistry or biology some time ago, be prepared to review these subjects before taking the exam. The entire ACT exam must be taken in one sitting, so choose the time at which your overall preparation is best.

Format of the Examination

The ACT is divided into four separately timed tests.

Test 1. ENGLISH USAGE—*40 minutes, 75 questions.*
A series of prose reading passages with portions underlined. You are to choose the *best*—with consideration to spelling, punctuation, grammar, diction, sentence structure and logic—way of expressing each underlined portion.

Test 2. MATHEMATICS USAGE—*50 minutes, 40 questions.*
Mathematical problems testing your understanding and your ability to use elementary and intermediate algebra, geometry, percentages and multiple computations.

Test 3. SOCIAL STUDIES READING—*35 minutes, 52 questions.*
There are two types of questions in this test. About 75 percent of the questions are based upon four social studies reading passages. These passages may cover American history, economics, government, world history, psychology or sociology. Questions based upon these passages require not only that you understand the reading material, but also that you interpret the passage in light of your own knowledge. The remaining 25 percent of the questions is based strictly upon knowledge, with no accompanying reading passage.

Test 4. NATURAL SCIENCE READING—*35 minutes, 52 questions.*
This test is very similar to the Social Studies Reading test in that it measures both reading comprehension and general knowledge. The subjects covered by this test include biology, chemistry, physics, geology and meteorology. At least one of the reading passages is the description of an experiment. The questions based upon the experiment are designed to learn whether or not you can interpret experimental design and results.

You will be given a ten-minute break between Test 2 and Test 3.

Nature of the Questions

The following questions are typical of those which you may expect on this exam. The directions are typical of exam directions. Each series of questions is followed by an explanation to give you an idea of the thinking involved.

Test 1: English Usage

DIRECTIONS: In each of the following passages some portions are underlined and numbered. Corresponding to each numbered portion are three alternative ways of saying the same thing. Read through each passage quickly to determine the sense of the passage, then return to the underlined portions. If you feel that an underlined portion is correct and is stated as well as possible, mark NO CHANGE, A or F. If you feel that there is an error in grammar, sentence structure, punctuation or word usage, choose the correct answer. If an underlined portion appears to be correct, but you believe that one of the other choices would be more effective, mark that choice. Remember, you are to choose the *best* answer.

The coast of north Africa [1]

1. **A.** NO CHANGE
   B. north africa
   C. North Africa
   D. Northafrica

is allmost [2] as pleasant as

2. **F.** NO CHANGE
   G. almost
   H. all most
   J. mostly

southern California [3], with hot, dry summers and heavy

3. **A.** NO CHANGE
   B. Southern California
   C. southern California
   D. South California

rains in winter. The mountains of Morocco's and Algeria's [4] have a heavy winter snowfall and excellent

4. **F.** NO CHANGE
   G. Morocco and Algeria's
   H. Morocco's and Algeria
   J. Morocco and Algeria

ski grounds [5].

5. **A.** NO CHANGE
   B. skier grounds
   C. skiing ground
   D. grounds for skiing

1 Ⓐ Ⓑ Ⓒ Ⓓ   2 Ⓕ Ⓖ Ⓗ Ⓙ   3 Ⓐ Ⓑ Ⓒ Ⓓ   4 Ⓕ Ⓖ Ⓗ Ⓙ   5 Ⓐ Ⓑ Ⓒ Ⓓ

1. **C.** The points of the compass are capitalized when they are used to refer to a specific place, but not when they indicate direction. *North Africa* is the name of a specific place.

2. **G.** *Almost* is the correct spelling of the correct word. It means *nearly*. *Mostly* means *for the greatest part*. Use of *mostly* would imply that some parts are as pleasant, and others are not.

3. **A.** Southern California is a nonspecific area. The word *southern* serves as an adjective modifying *California*. As such it is not capitalized.

4. **J.** The preposition *of* serves to create the possessive. Adding an apostrophe and an "s" after Morocco and Algeria is incorrect in conjunction with the prepositional phrase.

5. **A.** *Ski grounds* is the correct term in common usage. D. is not incorrect but is unnecessarily wordy.

Test 2. Mathematics Usage

DIRECTIONS: Solve each problem and mark the letter of the correct answer on your answer sheet.

---

1. A square is changed into a rectangle by increasing its length 10% and decreasing its width 10%. Its area

   A. remains the same
   B. increases by 10%
   C. decreases by 10%
   D. increases by 1%
   E. decreases by 1%

2. A clerk can add 40 columns of figures an hour by using an adding machine and 20 columns of figures an hour without using an adding machine. What is the total number of hours it will take the clerk to add 200 columns of figures if $\frac{3}{5}$ of the work is done by machine and the rest without the machine?

   F. 6 hours
   G. 7 hours
   H. 8 hours
   J. 9 hours
   K. none of these

3. Which is the *least* of the following numbers?

A. $\frac{1}{5}$

B. $\sqrt{5}$

C. $\frac{1}{\sqrt{5}}$

D. $\frac{\sqrt{5}}{5}$

E. $\frac{1}{5\sqrt{5}}$

4. An office supply store buys 100 reams of special quality paper for $400. If one ream = 500 sheets of paper, how much must the store receive per 100 sheets to obtain a 20% gain on its cost?

F. 83¢
G. 85¢
H. 96¢
J. 98¢
K. none of these

5. The area of the right triangle is 24 square inches. The ratio of its legs is 2:3. Find the number of inches in the hypotenuse of the triangle.

A. $2\sqrt{13}$
B. $\sqrt{26}$
C. $4\sqrt{13}$
D. $\sqrt{13}$
E. $\sqrt{104}$

1 Ⓐ Ⓑ Ⓒ Ⓓ Ⓔ 3 Ⓐ Ⓑ Ⓒ Ⓓ Ⓔ 5 Ⓐ Ⓑ Ⓒ Ⓓ Ⓔ

2 Ⓕ Ⓖ Ⓗ Ⓙ Ⓚ 4 Ⓕ Ⓖ Ⓗ Ⓙ Ⓚ

1. **E.** Let side of original square = 10.

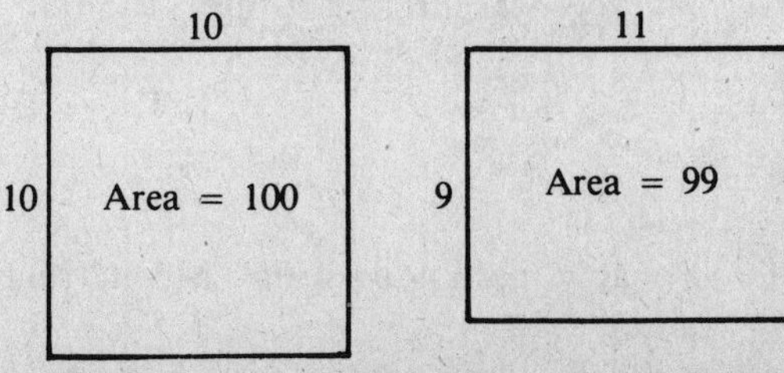

Hence, area decreases by 1, or a 1% decrease.

2. **G.** $\frac{3}{5}$ of 200 = 120 columns by machine @ 40 columns per hour = 3 hours
200 − 120 = 80 columns without machine @ 20 columns per hour = 4 hours
3 hours + 4 hours = 7 hours to complete the job.

3. **E.** A. $\frac{1}{5} = .2$
B. $\sqrt{5} = 2.2+$
C. $\frac{1}{\sqrt{5}} = \frac{\sqrt{5}}{5} = \frac{2.2}{5} = .4+$
C. and D. are same

E. $\frac{1}{5\sqrt{5}} = \frac{1}{5\sqrt{5}} \cdot \frac{\sqrt{5}}{\sqrt{5}} = \frac{\sqrt{5}}{25} = \frac{2.2}{25} = .09$ approx.

Hence $\frac{1}{5\sqrt{5}}$ is least value.

4. **H.** One ream = 500 sheets ∴ 100 reams = 50,000 sheets. To find the cost of 100 sheets, set up a proportion: $\frac{50,000}{100} = \frac{400}{x}$; 50,000x = 40,000; $x = \frac{40,000}{50,000} = 0.80$. The cost of 100 sheets is 80¢. To find the amount that the store must receive per 100 sheets to obtain a 20% gain on the 80¢ cost, first find 20% of 80¢ and then add this amount to the 80¢ cost: 80 + (0.20) (80) = 80 + 16 = 96¢.

5. **E.** Let legs be 2x and 3x
Then $(2x)^2 + (3x)^2 = \text{hypot.}^2$
But $\frac{1}{2} \cdot 2x \cdot 3x = 24$
$3x^2 = 24$
$x^2 = 8$
$x = \sqrt{8}$
Thus, $(2\sqrt{8})^2 + (3\sqrt{8})^2 = \text{hypot.}^2$
$32 + 72 = \text{hypot.}^2 = 104$
$\text{hypot.} = \sqrt{104}$

Test 3. Social Studies Reading

DIRECTIONS: Below each of the following reading passages is a series of questions. Choose the *best* answer to each question, interpreting what is stated or implied in the passage in the light of your own background in the subject. You may refer to the passage as often as necessary, though the answers to some questions may not be found expressly in the passage.

Unless you are a native of the Delmarva peninsula, you are probably unfamiliar with an American racial sub-group known as the *Moors*. The Moors have the dark olive skin of Mediterranean peoples, but they are not a recent immigrant group. The origin of the Moors is unclear, but one popular theory holds that they are descendants of shipwrecked Spanish and Portuguese sailors and native Indian women.

Since their origin is a mystery, the Moors have been subject to frequent controversy over their racial classification. South of the Mason-Dixon line, Moors are usually considered black and in past years were subject to Jim Crow laws. North of the Mason Dixon line, Moors have most often been considered white.

Because they do not have negroid features, many Moors have been able to assimilate into the northern white community. Those who have remained close to home have intermarried repeatedly, thus weakening their stock and limiting the growth of the group as a whole.

1. The Delmarva Moors are

A. descendants of refugees from the Spanish Inquisition
B. the Middle-Atlantic branch of the Black Muslims
C. probably descended from Mediterranean sailors
D. probably descendants of Indians and runaway slaves

2. The Mason-Dixon line is

F. the boundary between Delaware and Maryland
G. an imaginary line dividing the North from the South
H. the boundary between Pennsylvania and Maryland
J. the site of a famous Civil War battle line

3. Frequent intermarriage is

A. illegal
B. unhealthy
C. encouraged in Islam
D. a result of Jim Crow laws

DIRECTIONS: Questions 4 and 5 are not based upon a reading passage. Choose the *best* answer to each question in accordance with your background and understanding in the social studies.

4. Which of the following statements about the Homestead Act is NOT correct?

F. Much of the area available for homesteading consisted of arid and semiarid land.
G. The law made possible the acquisition of large blocks of land by speculators.
H. Credit was extended for homesteaders to enable them to acquire equipment.
J. Only a relatively small percentage of western settlers after the Civil War acquired their land under the terms of the Act.

5. The McCarran Internal Security Act of 1950

A. established a board to follow communist activities in the United States
B. virtually ended immigration to the United States
C. replaced the National Origins Act of 1924 with a more stringent act
D. discriminated against Asiatics

1 Ⓐ Ⓑ Ⓒ Ⓓ 2 Ⓕ Ⓖ Ⓗ Ⓙ 3 Ⓐ Ⓑ Ⓒ Ⓓ

4 Ⓕ Ⓖ Ⓗ Ⓙ 5 Ⓐ Ⓑ Ⓒ Ⓓ

---

1. **C.** The Delmarva Moors, the group described in this passage, are probably descended from shipwrecked sailors and native women. While some Spanish sailors may have been at sea to avoid the Inquisition, the majority were at sea to earn a living. The term *Moors* is also used to describe natives of Mauritania. In addition, the Berbers who overran Spain in the Eighth Century were called *Moors*.

2. **H.** The Mason-Dixon line was a line surveyed by Charles Mason and Jeremiah Dixon from 1763 to 1767 to settle a dispute between the Penn and Baltimore families and to establish the boundary between Pennsylvania and Maryland. In its later extension into Ohio, the line served as the boundary between slave and free states. An imaginary extension into Delaware separates those with northern sympathies from those with southern attitudes.

3. **B.** Frequent intermarriage leads to concentration of the gene pool, causing frequent appearance of undesirable recessive traits.

4. **H.** The Homestead Act of 1862 offered heads of household over twenty-one the opportunity to settle a 160-acre tract of land after living on it for five years or, alternately, at greater cost, after living on it for six months. No provision was made under the Act for credit to purchase equipment.

5. **A.** The McCarran Internal Security Act of 1950 barred the admission to the United States of anyone who had ever been a member of a totalitarian organization. It also established a Subversive Activities control board. The McCarran-Walter Immigration Act of 1952 was a highly restrictive immigration law enacted over the veto of President Truman.

Test 4. Natural Science Reading

DIRECTIONS: Below each of the following reading passages is a series of questions. Choose the *best* answer to each question, interpreting what is stated or implied by the passage in the light of your own background in the subject. You may refer to the passage as often as necessary, though the answers to some questions may not be found expressly in the passage.

Circulating blood is composed of two parts: (1) the solid cellular elements or blood corpuscles, and (2) the liquid portion or blood plasma. Within the blood vessels, the cells float freely in the fluid. Outside the body blood will coagulate unless clotting is prevented by artificial means.

The blood clot consists of blood cells packed onto fibrin. The fluid surrounding the clot is called blood serum. Serum differs from plasma by the latter's content of fibrinogen, the precursor of fibrin.

The blood cells, specifically the red blood corpuscles or erythrocytes, harbor substances known as antigens. Blood fluid, plasma as well as serum, contains reacting substances called antibodies. A reaction between antigens and antibodies will occur where corresponding substrate and reagent clash. Such antigen-antibody reaction may occur in vivo, in the body, or in vitro, in the glass test tube.

If one suspends blood cells of one person in the blood plasma or serum of another person, two possibilities arise: (1) The cells may be dispersed throughout the fluid—*the two individuals belong to the same blood group;* or (2) the red blood corpuscles clump—*the two persons have different blood groups.*

Excerpted from *Grouping, Typing and Banking of Blood,* Pollack, O.J., Springfield, Ill.: Charles C. Thomas. © 1951, with permission of the author.

1. A blood clot consists of

   A. blood plasma and fibrinogen
   B. blood cells and fibrin
   C. blood serum and fibrinogen
   D. blood corpuscles and blood plasma

2. The reason one might suspend the blood cells of one person in the blood plasma or serum of another person is to

   F. artificially prevent clotting
   G. see what will happen
   H. accelerate coagulation
   J. learn whether or not the two persons belong to the same blood group

3. The "test tube baby" born in England in 1979 was

   A. artificially inseminated
   B. fertilized in vivo
   C. fertilized in vitro
   D. a survivor of an abortion

DIRECTIONS: The following questions are not based upon a reading passage. Choose the *best* answer to each question on the basis of your scientific knowledge.

4. The symbol for two molecules of hydrogen is

F. H_2
G. 2H
H. $2H^-$
J. $2H_2$

5. If a precipitate was formed when a crystal of hypo was placed in a clear solution of hypo, the solution must have been

A. contaminated
B. saturated
C. supersaturated
D. unsaturated

1 Ⓐ Ⓑ Ⓒ Ⓓ 2 Ⓕ Ⓖ Ⓗ Ⓙ 3 Ⓐ Ⓑ Ⓒ Ⓓ

4 Ⓕ Ⓖ Ⓗ Ⓙ 5 Ⓐ Ⓑ Ⓒ Ⓓ

---

1. **B.** A blood clot consists of blood cells packed onto fibrin. The fluid surrounding the clot is called blood serum.

2. **J.** When the blood cells of one person are suspended in the blood plasma or serum of another person, the cells will either disperse themselves throughout the fluid or they will clump together. If the cells disperse, the two persons are of the same blood group; if the cells clump, the two persons have different blood groups. This information is vital to doctors administering transfusions. The body of one person will accept another's blood only if it is of the same group.

3. **C.** The "test tube baby" was in no way an artificial child. What made this baby unique was that she was fertilized *in vitro,* that is sperm and egg were united in a glass test tube and the resulting embryo was implanted in the mother's womb. The more usual locale of fertilization is *in vivo,* that is within the body.

4. **J.** Hydrogen is a diatomic molecule. It contains two atoms to the molecule, and the subscript 2 indicates two atoms. The coefficient 2 indicates that there are two molecules of hydrogen. Two molecules of hydrogen are expressed as $2H_2$.

5. **C.** A supersaturated solution is holding more solute than it can normally hold at a given temperature. The solution is unstable. The addition of a single crystal will cause all the excess solute to come out of solution.

Scoring and Reporting of Scores

Raw scores for each section of the ACT exam are determined by crediting one point for each question answered correctly. There is no penalty for any question which is answered incorrectly. In order to equalize for slight variations in difficulty for various editions of the exam, ACT scores are reported to you and the colleges not on the basis of the raw score, but rather on a specially devised scaled score, a *standard score.* The range within each test is scored follows:

English Usage	01—33
Mathematics Usage	01—36
Social Studies Reading	01—34
Natural Science Reading	01—35
Composite Score	01—35

The composite score is the average of the other four scores. In addition to the standard scores, your percentile ranking in comparison with college-bound students in the nation at large, with college-bound students in your state, and (if available) a comparison with students from your high school is also reported for each test score and for the composite score, as well.

About two months after you take the ACT, two copies of your student profile, including score reports and guidance information, will be sent to your high school principal. The principal will forward one copy to you. At that time copies of your scores will be sent to the colleges that you indicated at registration time. No one else will receive your scores without specific written authorization from you. On the ACT registration form, you are given the opportunity to authorize ACT to release information about you, your interests and your scores to colleges and scholarship agencies which are actively recruiting students with your characteristics. This service is free. If you choose to subscribe to it, you may find yourself deluged with literature. You may, however, learn about some less well-known colleges which meet all of your requirements. You must weigh the benefits against the relinquishing of your privacy.

CORRESPONDENCE ADDRESS

To request a registration packet, or to make inquiries about special testing for the handicapped, non-Saturday testing or testing outside of the United States, write to:

ACT Registration
P.O. Box 414
Iowa City, Iowa 52243

TEST-TAKING TECHNIQUES

Your last minute preparations for the ACT or for any exam are based strictly on common sense. They include assembling your materials the night before, getting a good night's sleep, awakening early enough so that you do not need to rush, and eating breakfast. The only materials you need to bring to the ACT are a few sharpened number two pencils with erasers, your admission ticket and positive identification. It is also very important to wear a watch, as the room clock may be behind you or out of order and it is ACT policy that you are *not* warned when time is almost up.

Enter the room early enough to be able to choose a seat where you want to sit. Relax. The first thing you will do is fill out the front of your answer form. You will be given detailed instructions for this procedure. Listen; read; follow the directions. Filling out forms is not timed. Do not rush. The exam will not begin until everyone has finished these preliminary steps.

The test proctor will then give you general instructions for taking the exam. You will be told how to recognize the stop and start signals. You will find out what to do if you have a problem, if all your pencils break or if a page is missing from your test booklet. Pay attention to the proctor's instructions. If you have any questions, ask them now.

When the signal is given, open your test booklet and READ.

•**READ** all directions carefully. The directions will probably be very similar to those in this book, but do not take anything for granted.

•**READ** every word of every question. Be alert for exclusionary words which might affect your answer—words like *not, most, all, every, except.*

•**READ** all the choices before you mark your answer. It is statistically true that the most errors are made when the correct answer is the last choice given. Too many people mark the first answer that seems correct without reading through all the choices to find out which answer is *best.*

If you read conscientiously, you are well on your way to mastering the exam.

If you answer every question, you are more likely to get a high score! The ACT is a heavily speeded exam. This means that you probably will not have time to do justice to every question. You may not even have time to read every question. We suggest the following strategy:

ENGLISH USAGE and MATHEMATICS USAGE

Start at the beginning and answer every question, marking in your test booklet those questions of which you are unsure. If you have no idea what might be the right answer, mark something anyway. You have nothing to lose. If you finish before time is up, return to the questions you marked and try to figure out the correct answer. Keep track of the time. If there is only one minute left and you still have a number of unanswered questions, pick a response other than the first and mark your answer sheet, straight down the line. The rationale for this procedure is that the correct answers are probably fairly evenly distributed through the four or five response choices, though the first response tends to be correct least often. Thus, by marking the same answer for all remaining English Usage questions, you will probably get 25 percent of them right. The same response mode should yield 20 percent correct answers on Mathematics.

SOCIAL STUDIES and NATURAL SCIENCE READING

The ease with which you answer the questions based on reading passages in these sections is closely related to how well you understand the subject matter of the passage. Thus, if a passage relates to the phases of stars and you know nothing at all about stars, you will have to read much more slowly and carefully and refer to the passage very often in order to answer the questions. If, on the other hand, you are a specialist on the American Revolution and find a passage on that subject, you may be able to answer the questions after just one reading to ascertain the point of view represented in the passage. Therefore, we suggest that within the Social Studies Reading Test and again within the Natural Science Reading Test you first skim rapidly over the four passages to find those which you will be able to answer most rapidly. Do those first, taking great care to mark your answers in the right place. Then go to the questions not based on a passage and answer those in the same manner that you answered English Usage and Mathematics. Finally, return to those reading passages which you skipped, reading as much as you can and answering all questions. Again, watch the time. When only one minute remains, pick a response and mark all unanswered questions, hoping for 25 percent accuracy.

The following suggestions are a comprehensive list of guidelines. Read them now before you attempt the practice exams in this book. Read them again before you take the ACT exam. All are useful and important.

1. Mark your answers by completely blackening the oval of your choice.
2. Mark only *one* answer for each question, even if you think that more than one answer is correct. You must choose only one. If you mark more than one answer, the scoring machine will consider you wrong.
3. If you change your mind, erase completely. Leave no doubt as to which answer you mean.
4. Every question must be answered in the right place. Check often to be sure that the answer number corresponds to the question number. If you do find that you have slipped "out of line," you must take the time to change your answers.
5. Do not dwell too long on any question, even if it poses an interesting challenge. Pick an answer and move on, but mark the question for later attention if time permits.
6. Answer *every* question, but be sure to note those questions which you answered hurriedly so that you may go back to them, time permitting.
7. Watch the clock. Use the last minute for answering every question.
8. Stay alert. Be aware of the risk of response errors, errors in which you mark the wrong answer because of a lapse in concentration. Example: The correct answer to a Mathematics question is **B.** d, and you mark **D.** instead of **B.**
9. Do not panic. If you do not have time to read and answer every question in a test before the time is called, do not worry. Many people do not finish, yet do very well on the questions they do read and answer and earn high scores. At any rate, do not let your performance on one test affect your performance on the next test.
10. Check and recheck. There is no bonus for leaving early. If you have completed the exam before the time is up, check the last test to be sure that each question is answered in the right space and that there is only one answer to each question. Return to the difficult questions and try them again.

Good luck!

PART II

PRETEST
MODEL EXAM I

TEST 1
ENGLISH USAGE

40 Minutes—75 Questions

DIRECTIONS: In each of the following passages, some portions are underlined and numbered. Corresponding to each numbered portion are three alternative ways of saying the same thing. Read through each passage quickly to determine the sense of the passage, then return to the underlined portions. If you feel that an underlined portion is correct and is stated as well as possible, mark NO CHANGE, A or F. If you feel that there is an error in grammar, sentence structure, punctuation or word usage, choose the correct answer. If an underlined portion appears to be correct, but you believe that one of the alternatives would be more effective, mark that choice. Remember, you are to choose the *best* answer.

Passage I

"My uncle John A. Quarles, (1) was a farmer, and his place was in the country four miles from Florida," Sam wrote. "I (2) was his guest for two or three months every year, from the fourth year after we removed to Hannibal, until the time (3) I was

1. A. NO CHANGE
   B. uncle, John A. Quarles,
   C. Uncle John A. Quarles
   D. uncle, John A. Quarles

2. F. NO CHANGE
   G. wrote, "I
   H. wrote: "I
   J. wrote. I

3. A. NO CHANGE
   B. Hannibal untill
   C. Hannibal until
   D. Hannibal, 'til

11 or 12 years of age old.
4
It was a heavenly place for a boy.

4. F. NO CHANGE
G. eleven or twelve.
H. 11 or 12 years old.
J. 11 or 12 years of age.

"The farmhouse standing in the middle of a very large
5
yard which was fenced on three sides with rails and on

5. A. NO CHANGE
B. was standing
C. stood
D. stands

the rear side with high pilings: against these stood the
6
smoke house; beyond the pilings was the orchard; beyond the orchard were the Negro quarters and the tobacco fields.

6. F. NO CHANGE
G. pilings. Against
H. pilings; against
J. pilings, against

Off in the distance stood a little log cabin, and their
7 8
the woody hill fell sharply away. A narrow footpath

7. A. NO CHANGE
B. Down a piece,
C. "Off in the distance
D. "Standing apart

8. F. NO CHANGE
G. they're
H. there
J. , there,

wound past the barns, the corncrib, the stables and the
9

9. A. NO CHANGE
B. passed
C. passing
D. passing by

tobacco-curing house, to a limpid brook which sang
10

10. F. NO CHANGE
G. tobaco curing house,
H. tobbaco curing-house
J. tobacco, curing-house,

along over it's gravelly bed and curved in and out of the
11

11. A. NO CHANGE
B. its gravelly
C. it's gravely
D. its gravely

deep shade of overhanging foliage and vines—a divine
12

12. F. NO CHANGE
G. vines a
H. vines. A
J. vines; a

place for wading, and it had swimming pools too, which
13

13. A. NO CHANGE
B. wading—and
C. wading. And
D. wading; and

were forbidden to us and therefore much frequented.
14

14. F. NO CHANGE
G. however
H. moreover,
J. also

"In the little log cabin lived a <u>bedridden white-headed</u> (15) slave <u>woman that</u> (16) we visited daily and looked upon with awe, for we believed she was <u>upward of</u> (17) a thousand years old and had talked with Moses. We believed that she had lost her health coming out of Egypt and had never been able to get <u>them back again.</u> (18) She had a <u>round bald place</u> (19) on the crown of her head, and we used to creep around and gaze at it in <u>reverent silence. And</u> (20) reflect that it was caused by her fright at seeing <u>Faro drowned.</u> (21)

15. **A.** NO CHANGE
    B. bed-ridden, white-headed
    C. bedridden, whiteheaded,
    D. bedridden, white-headed

16. **F.** NO CHANGE
    G. woman, which
    H. woman who
    J. woman, whom

17. **A.** NO CHANGE
    B. upward to
    C. nearly
    D. over and above

18. **F.** NO CHANGE
    G. any back again.
    H. her's back.
    J. it back.

19. **A.** NO CHANGE
    B. round-bald place
    C. round bald-place
    D. round, bald, place

20. **F.** NO CHANGE
    G. reverant silence, and
    H. reverant silence; and
    J. reverent silence and

21. **A.** NO CHANGE
    B. Pharaoh drowned.
    C. Pharohe drowned!"
    D. Pharaoh drowned."

Passage II

<u>There's</u> (22) a very sweet girl in our sorority <u>whose</u> (23) a real health addict. Her name is Ann O'Donohue. As you might guess, she's Irish. She is also the athletic type. Every night she opens the window wide "for a little <u>air," as</u> (24) she calls it. Now no one likes fresh air better

22. **F.** NO CHANGE
    G. There is
    H. Their's
    J. Theirs

23. **A.** NO CHANGE
    B. thats
    C. which is
    D. who is

24. **F.** NO CHANGE
    G. air", as
    H. air." As
    J. air"; as

than I; but air this fresh it belongs outside.
25 26

25. **A.** NO CHANGE
B. than I,
C. then me,
D. than me;

26. **F.** NO CHANGE
G. air this fresh
H. when its this fresh it
J. this air it

The other night I was laying in bed with the covers
27
up to my chin, listening to Ann getting ready for bed. I
could hear her turning on the water in the shower. As
28
the hot water faucet was broken, I knew it would be
29
freezing. I waited for Ann's reaction. What did she do?
She began singing. That was too much! She was actually
30 31
enjoying an ice cold shower.

27. **A.** NO CHANGE
B. was lieing
C. was lying
D. laid

28. **F.** NO CHANGE
G. her, turning
H. her; turning
J. her, she was turning

29. **A.** NO CHANGE
B. the water
C. the shower
D. she

30. **F.** NO CHANGE
G. begin
H. begins
J. begun

31. **A.** NO CHANGE
B. too much.
C. very much!
D. also much.

"Look Ann," I said when she returned to the
32
bedroom, its alright if you want to freeze yourself to
33
death and prove how healthy you are, but I for one need
34
some heat for comfort. If you want to freeze, why don't
you walk in the snow. It's almost midnight and I must
35

32. **F.** NO CHANGE
G. "Look, Ann
H. Look, "Ann
J. Look: "Ann

33. **A.** NO CHANGE
B. "it's all right
C. "Its allright
D. "It's alright

34. **F.** NO CHANGE
G. are
H. are;
J. are:

35. **A.** NO CHANGE
B. snow; it's
C. snow? It's
D. snow? it's

get some sleep." By this time Elaine Breen, who sleeps
36

36. F. NO CHANGE
G. sleep". By this time
H. sleep." (BEGIN new paragraph with "By this time . . .")
J. sleep." (OMIT "By this time" and BEGIN new paragraph with "Elaine Breen")

as sound as I do, woke up. "Shut up!" she demanded.
37

37. A. NO CHANGE
B. sound,
C. soundly
D. soundly,

"And as for you Ann," she said, "starting in with right
38 39
now, we're going to sleep with the window closed. At least we won't catch pneumonia."

38. F. NO CHANGE
G. you, Ann,"
H. you," Ann,
J. you Ann",

39. A. NO CHANGE
B. "starting out
C. "starting out from
D. "starting

Satisfied that the argument was settled. Elaine pulled
40
the blanket over her head and went back to sleep. At this point Ann, who had been standing by the open window doing breathing exercises, turned around and reached for her jacket. "You know, it really is a

40. F. NO CHANGE
G. the argument was settled,
H. the argument had been settled;
J. Ann and I were in agreement.

beautiful night for a walk," she said, "I believe I will go
41

41. A. NO CHANGE
B. said: "I
C. said. "I
D. said; I

out." What can you do???
42

42. F. NO CHANGE
G. What can you do?
H. What can I do?
J. OMIT

Passage III

The standardized educational or psychological tests, that are widely used to aid in selecting, classifying,
43

43. A. NO CHANGE
B. tests that are
C. tests, which are
D. tests; which are

assigning, or promoting students, employees, and
44
military personnel have been the target of recent attacks

44. F. NO CHANGE
G. promoting of students
H. promotion of students
J. promotion for students

in books, magazines, and newspapers that are printed
45
every day. The target is wrong, for in attacking the tests,
45
critics revert attention from the fault that lays with ill-
46 47
informed or incompetent users. The tests themselves are
47
merely tools; with characteristics that can be assessed
48 49
reasonably precise under specified conditions. Whether
49
the results will be valuable, meaningless, or even misleading are dependent partly upon the tool itself but
50
largely upon the user.

45. **A.** NO CHANGE
B. the daily press
C. newspapers that are published daily
D. the daily newspaper press

46. **F.** NO CHANGE
G. revert attention to
H. divert attention from
J. avert attention from

47. **A.** NO CHANGE
B. lies with poorly-informed
C. lays with poor-informed
D. lies with ill-informed

48. **F.** NO CHANGE
G. tools with
H. tools, possessed of
J. tools; whose

49. **A.** NO CHANGE
B. assessed as to its reasonable precision
C. assessed reasonably and with precision
D. assessed with reasonable precision

50. **F.** NO CHANGE
G. is dependant partly upon
H. depend partly upon
J. depends partly upon

Passage IV

The forces that generate conditions conducive to crime
and riots, are stronger in urban communities
51
then in rural areas. Urban living is more anonymous
52
living, it often releases the individual from community
53

51. **A.** NO CHANGE
B. rioting, are stronger
C. riots are more strong
D. riots are stronger

52. **F.** NO CHANGE
G. then in rural communities
H. than in rural areas
J. then they are in the country

53. **A.** NO CHANGE
B. living. It
C. living; which
D. living. Because it

restraints more common in tradition, oriented societies.
54

54. F. NO CHANGE
G. traditional oriented societies
H. traditionally, oriented societies
J. tradition-oriented societies

But more freedom from constraints and controls also
55
provides greater freedom to deviate. In the more imper-

55. A. NO CHANGE
B. Moreover
C. Therefore
D. Besides

sonalized, formally, controlled urban society regulatory
56
orders of conduct are often directed by distant bureau-

56. F. NO CHANGE
G. formally controlled
H. formalized controlled
J. formally-controlled

crats. The police are strangers which execute these
57
prescriptions on, at worst, an alien subcommunity and,

57. A. NO CHANGE
B. they execute
C. executing
D. who conduct executions of

at best, an anonymous and unknown set of subjects.
58
Minor offenses in a small town or village are often

58. F. NO CHANGE
G. anonymously unknown
H. anonymous
J. anonymous, unknown

handled without resort to official police action. As dis-
59

59. A. NO CHANGE
B. without their having to resort to
C. without needing
D. outside the limits of

putable as such action may seem to be, you will find
60
it results in fewer recorded violations of the law com-
60
pared to the city.

60. F. NO CHANGE
G. they say it results
H. you will say, "It results
J. it nonetheless results

Passage V

Human beings are born with a desire to communicate
61
with other human beings, they satisfy this desire in many
61 62

61. A. NO CHANGE
B. communicate to
C. communicate about
D. communicate

62. F. NO CHANGE
G. beings. They
H. beings, who
J. beings which

ways. A smile communicates <u>a friendly feeling,</u> (63) a clenched <u>fist anger;</u> (64) tears, sorrow. From the first days of life, <u>pain and hunger are expressed by baby's</u> (65) by cries and actions. Gradually they add expressions of pleasure and <u>smiling</u> (66) for a familiar face. Soon they begin to reach out <u>for picking up.</u> (67) <u>Those people who are human beings</u> (68) also use words to communicate. Babies eventually learn the language of <u>there</u> (69) parents. If the parents speak in English, the baby will learn to speak English. If the parents speak Spanish, <u>a Spanish-speaking baby will result.</u> (70) An <u>American baby</u> (71) who is taken from his natural parents and brought up by foster parents who speak Chinese,

63. A. NO CHANGE
B. a friendly, feeling;
C. friendship,
D. a friendly feeling;

64. F. NO CHANGE
G. fist an angry feeling,
H. fist, anger;
J. fist, angriness,

65. A. NO CHANGE
B. babies express pain or hunger
C. a baby's pain or hunger are expressed
D. pain and hunger is expressed by babies

66. F. NO CHANGE
G. smiled
H. smiles
J. he may smile

67. A. NO CHANGE
B. to pick up
C. and pick up
D. to be picked up

68. F. NO CHANGE
G. (BEGIN new paragraph) Those people who are human beings
H. (BEGIN new paragraph) Human being babies
J. (BEGIN new paragraph) Human beings

69. A. NO CHANGE
B. their
C. they're
D. OMIT

70. F. NO CHANGE
G. their baby will speak Spanish.
H. the baby will learn spanish.
J. there baby will speak Spanish.

71. A. NO CHANGE
B. American Baby
C. american baby
D. american-born baby

Urdu, Swahili, or any other language will talk the
72

72. F. NO CHANGE
G. will be speaking
H. will learn
J. will talk of

language of the people around them instead of English.
73

73. A. NO CHANGE
B. him
C. themselves
D. himself

Words are important tools of learning. It enables
74
children to ask questions and understand the answers;
74

74. F. NO CHANGE
G. It provides children with the means to
H. That makes it possible for children to
J. Once children learn to use language they can

they can tell about their discoveries and to express their
75
likes and dislikes.

75. A. NO CHANGE
B. use it to express
C. express
D. to talk about

END OF TEST

If you complete this test before the time limit is up, check back over the questions on this test. Do not proceed to the next test until you are told to do so.

TEST 2
MATHEMATICS USAGE

50 Minutes—40 Questions

DIRECTIONS: Solve each problem and mark the letter of the correct answer on your answer sheet.

DO YOUR FIGURING HERE

1. Which one of these quantities is the smallest?

A. $\frac{4}{5}$
B. $\frac{7}{9}$
C. .76
D. $\frac{5}{7}$
E. $\frac{9}{11}$

2. A girl earns twice as much in December as in each of the other months. What part of her entire year's earnings does she earn in December?

F. $\frac{2}{11}$
G. $\frac{2}{13}$
H. $\frac{3}{14}$
J. $\frac{1}{6}$
K. $\frac{1}{7}$

3. If $x = -1$, then $3x^2 + 2x^3 + x + 1 =$

A. -1
B. 1
C. -5
D. 5
E. 2

4. How many twelfths of a pound are equal to $83\frac{1}{3}\%$ of a pound?

F. 5
G. 10
H. 12
J. 14
K. 16

5. An equilateral triangle 3 inches on a side is cut up into smaller equilateral triangles one inch on a side. What is the greatest number of such triangles that can be formed?

DO YOUR FIGURING HERE

A. 3
B. 6
C. 9
D. 12
E. 15

6. If $\frac{a}{b} = \frac{3}{5}$, then 15a =

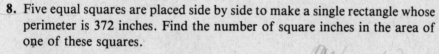

F. 3b
G. 5b
H. 6b
J. 9b
K. 15b

7. A square 5 units on a side has one vertex at the point (1, 1). Which one of the following points *cannot* be diagonally opposite the vertex?

A. (6, 6)
B. (− 4, 6)
C. (− 4, − 4)
D. (6, − 4)
E. (4, − 6)

8. Five equal squares are placed side by side to make a single rectangle whose perimeter is 372 inches. Find the number of square inches in the area of one of these squares.

F. 72
G. 324
H. 900
J. 961
K. 984

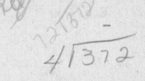

9. Which is the smallest of the following numbers?

A. $\sqrt{3}$

B. $\frac{1}{\sqrt{3}}$

C. $\frac{\sqrt{3}}{3}$

D. $\frac{1}{3}$

E. $\frac{1}{3\sqrt{3}}$

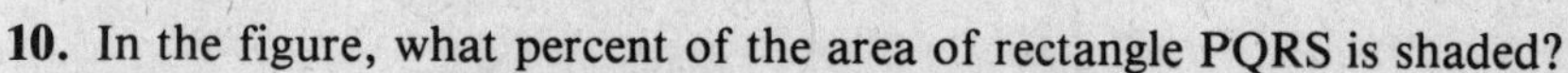

10. In the figure, what percent of the area of rectangle PQRS is shaded?

F. 20
G. 25
H. 30
J. $33\frac{1}{3}$
K. 40

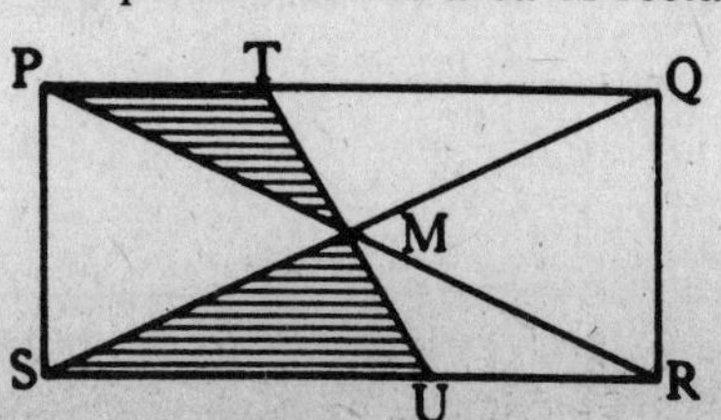

DO YOUR FIGURING HERE

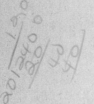

11. $\frac{1}{6}$ of an audience consisted of boys and $\frac{1}{3}$ of it consisted of girls. What percent of the audience consisted of children?

A. $66\frac{2}{3}$
B. 50
C. $37\frac{1}{2}$
D. 40
E. $33\frac{1}{3}$

12. One wheel has a diameter of 30 inches and a second wheel has a diameter of 20 inches. The first wheel traveled a certain distance in 240 revolutions. In how many revolutions did the second wheel travel the same distance?

F. 120
G. 160
H. 360
J. 420
K. 480

13. If x and y are two different real numbers and rx = ry, then r =

A. 0
B. 1
C. $\frac{x}{y}$
D. $\frac{y}{x}$
E. x − y

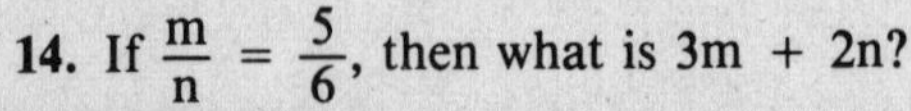

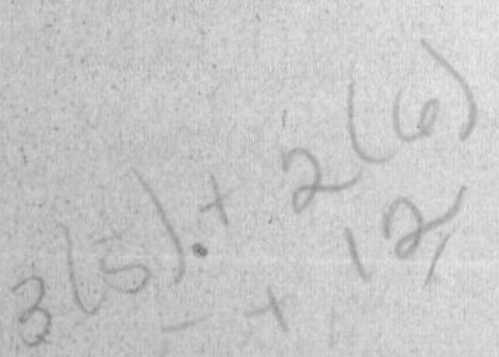

14. If $\frac{m}{n} = \frac{5}{6}$, then what is 3m + 2n?

F. 0
G. 2
H. 7
J. 10
K. cannot be determined from the information given

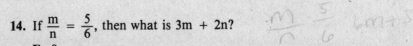

15. If x > 1, which of the following increase(s) as x increases?

I. $x - \frac{1}{x}$
II. $\frac{1}{x^2 - x}$
III. $4x^3 - 2x^2$

A. only I
B. only II
C. only III
D. only I and III
E. I, II, and III

DO YOUR FIGURING HERE

16. In the figure, PQRS is a parallelogram, and ST = TV = VR. What is the ratio of the area of triangle SPT to the area of the parallelogram?

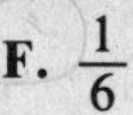

F. $\frac{1}{6}$

G. $\frac{1}{5}$

H. $\frac{1}{3}$

J. $\frac{2}{7}$

K. cannot be determined from the information given

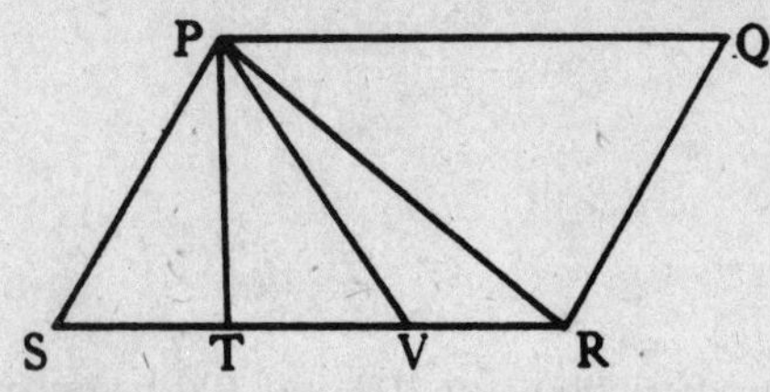

17. One angle of a triangle is 82°. The other two angles are in the ratio 2:5. Find the number of degrees in the smallest angle of the triangle.

A. 14
B. 25
C. 28
D. 38
E. 82

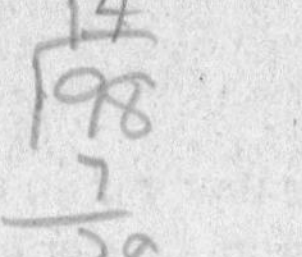

18. If a girl can mow a lawn in t minutes, what part can she do in 15 minutes?

F. t − 15

G. $\frac{t}{15}$

H. 15t

J. 15 − t

K. $\frac{15}{t}$

19. A typist uses lengthwise a sheet of paper 9 inches by 12 inches. He leaves a 1-inch margin on each side and a $1\frac{1}{2}$ inch margin on top and bottom. What fractional part of the page is used for typing?

A. $\frac{21}{22}$

B. $\frac{7}{12}$

C. $\frac{5}{9}$

D. $\frac{3}{4}$

E. $\frac{5}{12}$

20. It takes a girl 9 seconds to run a distance of 132 feet. What is her speed in miles per hour?

F. 8
G. 9
H. 10
J. 11
K. 12

DO YOUR FIGURING HERE

21. A rectangular sign is cut down by 10% of its height and 30% of its width. What percent of the original area remains?

A. 30
B. 37
C. 57
D. 70
E. 63

22. How many of the numbers between 100 and 300 begin or end with 2?

F. 20
G. 40
H. 180
J. 100
K. 110

23. If Mary knows that y is an integer greater than 2 and less than 7 and John knows that y is an integer greater than 5 and less than 10, then Mary and John may correctly conclude that

A. y can be exactly determined
B. y may be either of 2 values
C. y may be any of 3 values
D. y may be any of 4 values
E. there is no value of y satisfying these conditions

24. The area of a square is $49x^2$. What is the length of a diagonal of the square?

F. $7x$
G. $7x\sqrt{2}$
H. $14x$
J. $7x^2$
K. $\frac{7x}{\sqrt{2}}$

25. In the figure, MNOP is a square of area 1, Q is the mid-point of MN, and R is the mid-point of NO. What is the ratio of the area of triangle PQR to the area of the square?

A. $\frac{1}{4}$
B. $\frac{1}{3}$
C. $\frac{1}{16}$
D. $\frac{3}{8}$
E. $\frac{1}{2}$

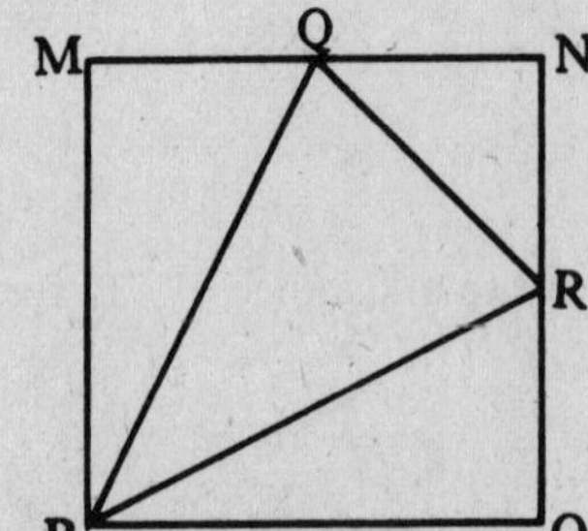

26. If a rectangle is 4 feet by 12 feet, how many two-inch tiles would have to be put around the outside edge to completely frame the rectangle?

DO YOUR FIGURING HERE

F. 32
G. 36
H. 192
J. 196
K. 200

27. One-tenth is what part of three-fourths?

A. $\frac{40}{3}$
B. $\frac{3}{40}$
C. $\frac{15}{2}$
D. $\frac{1}{8}$
E. $\frac{2}{15}$

28. The area of square PQRS is 49. What are the coordinates of Q?

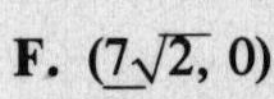

F. $(\frac{7\sqrt{2}}{2}, 0)$
G. $(0, \frac{7}{2}\sqrt{2})$
H. (0, 7)
J. (7, 0)
K. $(0, 7\sqrt{2})$

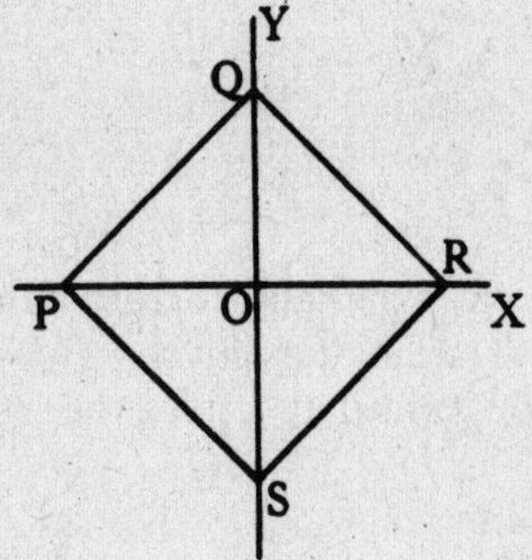

29. Village A has a population of 6800, which is decreasing at a rate of 120 per year. Village B has a population of 4200, which is increasing at a rate of 80 per year. In how many years will the population of the two villages be equal?

A. 9
B. 11
C. 13
D. 14
E. 16

DO YOUR FIGURING HERE

30. The average of 8 numbers is 6; the average of 6 other numbers is 8. What is the average of all 14 numbers?

F. 6
G. $6\frac{6}{7}$
H. 7
J. $7\frac{2}{7}$
K. $8\frac{1}{7}$

31. If x is between 0 and 1, which of the following increase(s) as x increases?

I. $1 - x^2$
II. $x - 1$
III. $\frac{1}{x^2}$

A. I and II
B. II and III
C. I and III
D. II only
E. I only

32. In the formula $T = 2\sqrt{\frac{L}{g}}$, g is a constant.

By what number must L be multiplied so that T will be multiplied by 3?

F. 3
G. 6
H. 9
J. 12
K. $\sqrt{3}$

33. Three circles are tangent externally to each other and have radii of 2 inches, 3 inches, and 4 inches respectively. How many inches are in the perimeter of the triangle formed by joining the centers of the three circles?

A. 9
B. 12
C. 15
D. 18
E. 21

34. If a circle of radius 10 inches has its radius decreased 3 inches, what percent is its area decreased?

F. 9
G. 49
H. 51
J. 70
K. 91

DO YOUR FIGURING HERE

35. If a beret costs \$4.20 after a 40% discount, what was its original price?

A. \$2.52
B. \$4.60
C. \$5.33
D. \$7.00
E. \$10.50

36. If r = 5x, how many tenths of r does $\frac{1}{2}$ of x equal?

F. 1
G. 2
H. 3
J. 4
K. 5

37. If $\frac{3}{7}$ of a bucket can be filled in 1 minute, how many minutes will it take to fill the rest of the bucket?

A. $\frac{4}{7}$

B. $\frac{4}{3}$

C. 1

D. $\frac{3}{4}$

E. $\frac{7}{3}$

38. In a right triangle, the ratio of the legs is 1:2. If the area of the triangle is 25 square units, what is the length of the hypotenuse?

F. $\sqrt{5}$
G. $5\sqrt{3}$
H. $10\sqrt{3}$
J. $5\sqrt{5}$
K. $25\sqrt{5}$

39. The ice compartment in a refrigerator is 8 inches deep, 5 inches high, and 4 inches wide. How many ice cubes will it hold if each cube is to be 2 inches on each edge?

A. 16
B. 20
C. 24
D. 80
E. 160

DO YOUR FIGURING HERE

40. QOR is a quadrant of a circle. PS = 6 and PT = 8. What is the length of arc QR?

F. 10π

G. 5π

H. 20π

J. 24

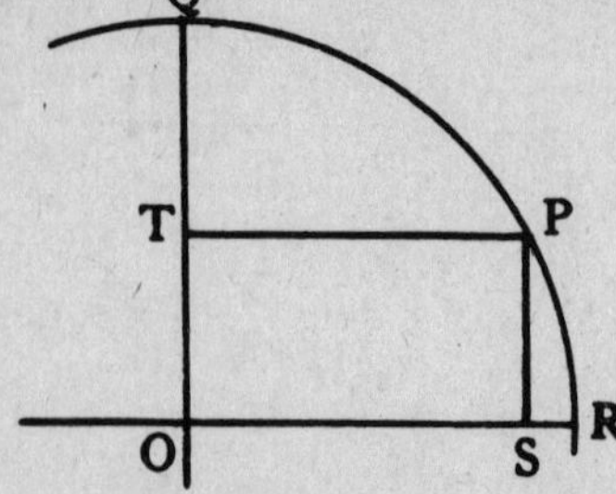

K. It cannot be determined from the information given

END OF TEST

If you complete this test before the time limit is up, go back over the questions on this test only. Do not return to the previous tests. Do not proceed to the next test until you are told to do so.

TEST 3
SOCIAL STUDIES READING

35 Minutes—52 Questions

DIRECTIONS: Below each of the following reading passages is a series of questions. Choose the *best* answer to each question, interpreting what is stated or implied by the passage in the light of your own background in the subject. You may refer to the passage as often as necessary, though the answers to some questions may not be found expressly in the passage.

"*To the Senate of the United States:*

"I regret that the bill, which has passed both Houses of Congress, entitled *An act to protect all persons in the United States in their civil rights and furnish the means of their vindication,* contains provisions which I cannot approve consistently with my sense of duty to the whole people and my obligations to the Constitution of the United States. I am therefore constrained to return it to the Senate, the House in which it originated, with my objections to its becoming a law.

"By the first section of the bill all persons born in the United States and not subject to any foreign power, excluding Indians not taxed, are declared to be citizens of the United States. The power to confer the right of State citizenship is just as exclusively with the several States as the power to confer the right of Federal citizenship is with Congress.

"The right of Federal citizenship thus to be conferred on the several excepted races before mentioned is now for the first time proposed to be given by law. If, as is claimed by many, all persons who are native born already are, by virtue of the Constitution, citizens of the United States, the passage of the pending bill can not be necessary to make them such. If, on the other hand, such persons are not citizens, as may be assumed from the proposed legislation to make them such, the grave question presents itself whether, when eleven of the thirty-six States are unrepresented in Congress at the present time, it is sound policy to make our entire colored population and all other excepted classes citizens of the United States . . . It may also be asked whether it is necessary that they should be declared citizens in order that they may be secured in the enjoyment of the civil rights proposed to be conferred by the bill. Those rights are, by Federal as well as State laws, secured to all domiciled aliens and foreigners, even before the completion of the process of naturalization; and it may safely be assumed that the same enactments are sufficient to give like protection and benefits to those for whom this bill provides special legislation. Besides, the policy of the Government from its origin to the present time seems to have been that persons who are strangers to and unfamiliar with our institutions and our laws should pass through a certain probation, at the end of which, before attaining the coveted prize, they must give evidence of their fitness to receive and to exercise the rights of citizens as contemplated by the Constitution of the United States. The bill in effect proposes a discrimination against large numbers of intelligent, worthy, and patriotic foreigners, and in favor of the negro, to whom, after long years of bondage, the avenues to freedom and intelligence have just now been suddenly opened. . ."

1. The document here quoted is a/an

   A. amendment to the Constitution
   B. commentary on the 14th Amendment
   C. justification of a veto
   D. part of a "State of the Union" message

2. The message opposes

   F. granting instant citizenship to Indians
   G. granting instant citizenship to blacks
   H. granting instant citizenship to foreigners
   J. naturalization procedures

3. The attitude of the author might best be characterized as

   A. cautiously conservative
   B. flamingly liberal
   C. highly intolerant
   D. intelligently constructive

4. Among the arguments advanced by the author are

   I. that the law is unnecessary
   II. that the law discriminates against immigrants
   III. that blacks are unready for citizenship

   F. I only
   G. I and II
   H. II and III
   J. I, II, and III

5. The writer claims that (at the time of his writing)

   A. blacks are already U.S. citizens
   B. the current status of blacks is unclear
   C. blacks are citizens only of their states
   D. under the Constitution, race plays no role in determining citizenship

6. Civil rights are granted to foreigners by

   I. executive order
   II. Constitutional guarantees
   III. Federal laws
   IV. State laws

   F. I and II
   G. II, III, and IV
   H. II only
   J. III and IV

7. The purpose of the naturalization process is to

   A. allow aliens time to learn English
   B. afford ample time for people to change their minds
   C. allow an opportunity for foreigners to learns the duties and privileges of citizenship
   D. be certain that all citizens have taken a course in American history

8. The writer states, in the second paragraph: "The power to confer the right of State citizenship is just as exclusively with the several States as the power to confer the right of Federal citizenship is with Congress." This statement is

   F. erroneous and entirely contrary to the Constitution
   G. in complete agreement with Article XIV, Section 1. of the Constitution
   H. partly in agreement and partly in disagreement with the Constitution
   J. an expression of wishful thinking on the part of the author

9. The author of this passage was

   A. impeached
   B. shot
   C. reelected
   D. removed from office

The communists' preoccupation with economic growth and their whole attitude toward economic progress have been shaped by Marx's theory of long-run development of human society. This theory places economic development at the center of the entire social philosophy and it is impossible to study the Marxists' political, social and economic views without referring to it. Without the knowledge of this theory it is difficult to understand the communists' dogmatic belief in the superiority of their system, whatever the observable facts are, and their faith in the final victory over capitalism. Economic development has to lead, sooner or later, to socialism and communism, and it is necessary to build socialism and, later, communism to make future economic growth possible. This principle is valid for all countries without an exception. They all have to proceed along the same path, although they may be placed at different points of it at present. Such is the logic of history.

This theory, which is usually referred to as "historical materialism," "the materialistic conception of history," or "Marx's historical determinism," is believed by the Marxists to be useful not only as the explanation of the past and the present but also as the basis for the prediction of the future course of history. As the final judgment on any prophecy has to be made in the light of the subsequent events, it is interesting to compare the developments since the theory was presented by Marx with the pattern which could have been expected on the basis of Marx's prediction. The purpose of this paper is to outline briefly such a comparison and to discuss the communist explanation of the disparity which has appeared between the actual and the predicted course of events. The paper does not attempt to evaluate the philosophical aspects of the theory, its materialism, one-sidedness and methodological oversimplification. Similarly, the value of the theory as a summary of the past historical events preceding the time when it was presented by Marx and its merits and weaknesses as one of numerous "stages of growth" theories are not discussed.

Marx's theory accepts as its basis that man's life is a conscious struggle with the natural environment, the struggle which takes the form of production as "life involves, before everything else, eating and drinking, a habitation, clothing, and many other things." The process of production is the interaction between man and nature and it takes the form of social labour. Man has to improve his instruments of production in order to master the natural environment but "the development of these instruments follows a definite sequence" as "each new improvement and invention can be made only on the basis of those that have preceded it, and must rest upon gradually accumulated production experience, the labour skills and knowledge of the people . . ." Production is carried on as a social process, because "in the process of producing material wealth, people, whether they like it or not, find themselves in some way linked with one another and the labour of each producer becomes a part of the social labour." These relationships among men are called the "relations of production." They exist independently of human consciousness and this gives them their materialistic character. They are determined by the level of development and the nature of productive forces.

10. The author indicates that the typical communist

- **F.** is more interested in the success of communism than in the welfare of his own family
- **G.** no longer adheres to the economic and/or philosophic principles set down by Marx
- **H.** has the same fundamental interests as the non-communist
- **J.** has an authoritative—if not arrogant—opinion about the advantages of communism over capitalism

11. A primary feature of Marxism is the stress on

- **A.** studying the lessons of history to formulate plans for the eventual victory of communism over capitalism
- **B.** the development and management of the material wealth of a government or community
- **C.** the need to move ahead with the implementation of the communist philosophy by violent means
- **D.** the eventual compromise between communism and the Western world

12. That a state of communism is to be preceded by socialism is

    F. contrary to Marxist theory
    G. considered by Marx to be just as feasible as the converse
    H. a phase of "relations of production"
    J. the doctrine of historical determinism

13. The writer states or implies that

    A. one cannot accurately appraise a proposed social or political philosophy until the results have been seen
    B. there is essentially no difference in practice between the communistic and the democratic form of government
    C. in the final analysis, man is an animal who cannot be guided by moral considerations
    D. the great majority of individuals are not intelligent enough to govern themselves—a dictator must always be present to make decisions for them

14. The writer's stated attitude toward the Communist Revolution is one of

    F. righteous indignation
    G. unnecessary oversimplification
    H. studied indifference
    J. scholarly objectivity

15. The writer's actual attitude toward communist theory is one of

    A. cynicism
    B. antipathy
    C. disbelief
    D. disgust

16. Marxist theory holds that man's primal struggle is against

    F. his superego
    G. the state
    H. nature
    J. supernatural forces

17. Karl Marx was

    A. the founder of Russian communism
    B. political editor of the New York *Tribune*
    C. a leading French political analyst
    D. a German socialist agitator

18. Technical progress is

    F. a necessary component in development toward socialism
    G. totally irrelevant to the progress of socialism
    H. a hindrance to socialism because it leads to unemployment
    J. an outgrowth of socialism

19. The selection does *not*

    A. refer to the importance of wealth in communistic philosophy
    B. detail the similarities between communist theory and that of capitalism
    C. define social labour
    D. quote Marx directly

Italy supposedly was more fortunate than its former allies, Germany and Austria-Hungary, because it was on the winning side when World War I ended. But many Italians felt that the war had cost Italy more than had been gained. An Italian at the close of the war might well have said: "We have poured out more blood and treasure to gain southern Tyrol and a few coast towns on the Adriatic than we did in all the wars for national liberty and union during the nineteenth century. Our allies begrudge us some of the territory we expected to acquire, such as the city of Fiume. Perhaps we would have done better to remain neutral. Perhaps a stronger government might have won for us richer spoils of victory."

Conditions within Italy were indeed discouraging. Trade and industry were in bad shape. Strikes and riots among workers were common and communist ideas were making headway among the poor. As in other European countries, there were many political parties, none of which was strong enough to remain in power for any length of time. Because one new cabinet followed another, the government was unable to enact laws that dealt effectively with the growing problems of depression and unemployment. Under these conditions, many Italians longed for a "man on horseback"—a strong leader who would restore order and prosperity.

The man who gave promise of being the strong leader so many Italians desired was Benito Mussolini. The son of a workingman, Mussolini had become a socialist and a newspaper writer before World War I. But when the Socialist Party opposed Italy's entrance into the war, Mussolini left it and served in the Italian army. After the fighting ceased, Mussolini organized bands of veterans called Fascisti. The Fascists wore black shirts and their emblem was the old Roman symbol of authority, the fasces or bundle of rods bound around an ax. The Fascists were a quarrelsome lot who often got into street fights with Italians holding other political ideas.

In 1922 the Fascists marched on Rome. The King and his ministers made no attempt to break up this parade of Mussolini's black-shirted followers. In fact, King Victor Emmanuel III appointed Mussolini Prime Minister. For a few years the outward forms of constitutional government were kept. All real power, however, was in the hands of Il Duce, or "The Leader," as Mussolini was called.

Soon the barrel-chested, square-jawed, loud-voiced Mussolini felt strong enough to do away with individual freedom and self-government altogether. He abolished all political parties except his own, the Fascist Party. From then on, Italy's voters were presented, as are the Russian voters, with a single list of candidates for office.

Mussolini built roads, drained marshes and expanded industry. He spent huge sums of money on the army, navy and air force. The average Italian felt pride in these national achievements. He also earned more money, but he paid more for what he bought, and taxes were higher. It may be doubted, then, that the average Italian was any better off for all Mussolini's efforts. And his freedom and importance had been lost.

20. During World War I Italy fought on the side of

F. the Axis
G. the Allies
H. Germany
J. Austria-Hungary

21. From this passage we may infer that as a dictator Mussolini

A. earned and kept the respect of his people
B. was opposed by democratic nations abroad
C. believed that his country should become a democracy as soon as possible
D. had as his first priority the freedom of Italy

22. What is the purpose of the first two paragraphs in this article?

F. to show how Italy had been mistreated
G. to show that Italy could not survive without a strong dictator
H. to indicate why Mussolini was able to take over the government
J. to present some of the weaknesses of a democratic government

23. The conditions described in paragraph two are in many ways similar to conditions which prevail in Italy today. A solution to which Italians might turn today in hopes of alleviating these conditions is

A. granting to the Pope secular power over all Italy
B. a new dictator
C. a rule of terror by the Red Brigades
D. Communism

24. The form of government Mussolini set up was similar to the dictatorship of Adolph Hitler in

F. Spain
G. Germany
H. Russia
J. Rome

25. The author of this article characterizes Mussolini as

A. a strong ruler who bettered the lot of the common people
B. a ruthless man who took what he wanted
C. a brilliant thinker who unfortunately was a poor leader
D. a cautious man concerned with history and tradition

26. What would be the best title for the third and fourth paragraphs of this article?

F. Mussolini's Rise to Power
G. Mussolini's Socialistic Beliefs
H. Mussolini's Dictatorial Methods
J. Mussolini's Reform Measures

27. In order to succeed, Mussolini seems to have relied strongly on appeal to Italians' sense of

A. pride
B. fair play
C. religion
D. freedom

28. Judging from this passage, Mussolini seems to have tried hardest to eliminate

F. poverty
G. religion
H. illiteracy
J. opposition

29. Within his own country, Mussolini's greatest opposition probably came from the

A. church
B. Fascists
C. common people
D. military

30. According to this article, Mussolini's greatest accomplishments probably came in his

F. domestic programs
G. military victories
H. foreign alliances
J. constitutional changes

DIRECTIONS: The following questions are not based upon reading passages. Read each question and mark the *best* answer, drawing upon your background in social studies.

31. In which one of the following situations did a President of the United States send troops to the scene despite the objections of the Governor of the state?

A. The railroad strike of 1877
B. The Haymarket riot of 1886
C. The Pullman strike of 1894
D. The steel strike of 1894

32. The Teapot Dome scandals of the 1920s involved

F. Presidential conduct
G. stock market fraud
H. the State Department
J. government oil wells

33. Which of the following groups of descriptive statements is generally characteristic of modern underdeveloped countries?

A. rising nationalism, population problems, middle class philosophy
B. low savings rate, inequality of wealth, need for land reform
C. poor endowment of national resources, failure of the wealthy to invest in manufacturing, security of foreign investments
D. overpopulation, full utilization of manpower, security of foreign investments

34. Before becoming President, Herbert Hoover had been all of the following *except*

F. a mining engineer
G. an administrator of relief activities
H. Secretary of Commerce
J. Vice President

35. The most fundamental concern of economics is

A. the problems of poverty
B. the control of goods and services produced
C. the reality of scarcity
D. the market structure of an economy

36. The Manhattan Project can be most accurately described as a

F. secret committee investigating security clearances during the early 1950s
G. pressure group seeking support for urban renewal projects after the Kerner report
H. group of physicists working at Los Alamos under J. Robert Oppenheimer
J. presidential advisory commission concerned with rehabilitation of victims of Hiroshima and Nagasaki

37. As compared to medieval times, which one of the following functions of the church has remained most constant today?

A. artistic functions
B. governmental functions
C. educational functions
D. ethical functions

38. Large families were desirable in the American colonies because

F. soldiers were needed to fight the Indians
G. the colonies were underpopulated and labor was scarce
H. school and college enrollments were small
J. most religious groups encouraged large families

39. One reason why Great Britain supported the Monroe Doctrine in 1823 was that she

A. had declared war on Spain
B. wished to support the Holy Alliance
C. had developed trade with the Latin American countries
D. followed a policy of supporting domestic revolutions

40. An important result of the Napoleonic Wars in Europe was the

F. success of the Continental system
G. rise of a spirit of nationalism
H. elimination of monarchies
J. military supremacy of France

41. In which pair of events is the first item a cause of the second?

A. Boston Tea Party—passage of the Intolerable Acts
B. meeting of the First Continental Congress—outbreak of the French and Indian War
C. Battle of Saratoga—adoption of the Declaration of Independence
D. adoption of the Articles of Confederation—Battle of Yorktown

42. A significant effect of the Dred Scott decision was that it

F. added to the powers of Congress
G. enhanced the reputation of the Supreme Court
H. lowered the prestige of the Supreme Court
J. antagonized the South

43. "Tippecanoe" refers specifically to

A. Martin Van Buren
B. John Tyler
C. an Indian battle
D. a racial stereotype of the American Indian

The first and most urgent task of our schools was to provide an enlightened citizenry in order that self-government might work. It is well to remember that democracy, which we take for granted, was an experiment—and largely an American experiment. It could not succeed with a people either corrupt or uninformed. People everywhere—as Jefferson and the spokesmen of the Age of Reason believed—were naturally good; but they were not naturally enlightened. To enlighten the people was the first duty of a democracy, and an enlightened people, in turn, saw to it that "schools and the means of education" were forever encouraged.

A second task imposed upon education and on the schools was that which we call Americanization. Each decade after 1840 saw from two to eight million immigrants pour into America. No other people had ever absorbed such large and varied racial stocks so rapidly or so successfully. It was the public school which proved itself the most efficacious of all agencies of Americanization—Americanization not only of the children but, through them, of the parents as well.

A third major service that the schools have rendered democracy is that of overcoming divisive forces in society and advancing understanding and equality. The most heterogeneous of modern societies, America might well have been a prey to ruinous class and religious divisons. The divisive forces did not, however, prevail, and one reason that they did not prevail is that the public school overcame them. In the classroom the nation's children learned and lived in equality. On the playground and the athletic field the same code obtained with rewards and applause going to achievements to which all could aspire equally, without regard to name, race and wealth.

44. The title of this selection should be

F. Education and the Immigrant
G. Society and the School
H. The School System and Democracy
J. The Public School

45. Democracy could not succeed if

A. the populace was corrupt or uninformed
B. there was no immigration
C. there was no Constitution
D. only half the population was educated

46. According to the author, the first duty of democracy was

F. to protect civil liberties
G. to enlighten the population
H. to promote equality for all
J. to provide higher education for all who wanted it

47. Americanization is

A. providing free public education for all
B. the requiring of all American citizens to speak English
C. keeping immigration to a minimum
D. creating unity out of diversity

48. The reason Americanization was needed was because of the

F. large emigration
G. large immigration
H. lack of patriotism among citizens
J. drop in population

49. America could have fallen prey to a religious or social class system because of the

A. heterogeneity of the populace
B. homogeneity of the populace
C. heritage of the Puritans
D. close attachment of America to Europe

50. The early public school stood for

F. liberalism
G. equality
H. conservatism
J. englightenment

51. The statement made in the last sentence

A. is not now true, but was once true
B. has recently become true
C. has always been true
D. has never been true

52. While much of what is stated in this passage has always applied to the Americanization of voluntary immigrants, the ideals were not realized until recent times with regard to the education of American blacks. This situation was finally rectified by

I. the case of *Brown* v. *Board of Education*
II. the Supreme Court
III. executive order
IV. legislation

F. I and II
G. II and IV
H. I, II, and IV
J. I, II, III, and IV

END OF TEST

If you complete this test before the time limit is up, go back over the questions on this test only. Do not return to the previous tests. Do not proceed to the next test until you are told to do so.

TEST 4
NATURAL SCIENCE READING

35 Minutes—52 Questions

DIRECTIONS: Below each of the following reading passages is a series of questions. Choose the *best* answer to each question, interpreting what is stated or implied by the passage in the light of your own background in the subject. You may refer to the passage as often as necessary, though the answers to some questions may not be found expressly in the passage.

The ear is indeed a remarkable mechanism; it is so complicated that its operation is not well understood. Certainly it is extremely sensitive. At the threshold of audibility, the power requirement is inconceivably tiny. If all the people in the United States were listening simultaneously to a whisper (20 decibels), the power received by all their collective eardrums would total only a few millionths of a watt—far less than the power generated by a single flying mosquito.

This aural organ is also remarkable for its ability to distinguish among various pitches and other qualities of sound. In the range of frequencies where the ear is most sensitive (between 500 and 4000 vibrations per second), changes in pitch of only .3 of a percent can be detected. Thus, if a singer trying to reach the octave above middle C (512 vibrations per second) is offkey by only 1.5 vibrations per second, the fault can be detected.

The normal ear can respond to frequencies ranging from 20 to 20,000 vibrations per second. In this range, it is estimated that the ear can distinguish more than half a million separate pure tones; that is, 500,000 differences in frequency or loudness. The range varies somewhat from ear to ear and becomes somewhat shorter for low-intensity sounds. Above the audible range, air vibrations similar to sound are called supersonic vibrations. These may be generated and detected by electrical devices and are useful particularly for depth sounding at sea. The time for the waves to travel from the generator to the bottom of the ocean and back again is a measure of the depth of that particular spot. Supersonic vibrations apparently can be heard by some animals—notably bats. It is believed that bats are guided during flight by supersonic sounds (supersonic only to humans) which they emit and which are reflected back to their ears in a kind of natural radar.

Humans can tell approximately where a sound comes from because we have two ears, not one. The sound arriving at one ear a split second before or after its arrival at the second ear gives the brain information, which the latter organ interprets to note the direction from which the sound originally came.

The ear is divided into three parts: the outer ear, the middle ear, and the inner ear. The outer ear consists of a canal closed at the inner end by a membrane, the eardrum. The middle ear contains a system of three bone levers, known as the hammer, the anvil, and the stirrup. These bones serve to transmit the sound vibration from the eardrum to the membrane-window covering the inner ear. The principal feature of the inner ear is the cochlea, a peculiar spiral bony enclosure that looks much like a snail shell. Contained in the cochlea is the vital organ of hearing, the basilar membrane of the organ of Corti.

Surrounding the basilar membrane is a liquid. The sound vibrations are transmitted to this liquid, and then, apparently, through the liquid for a distance which is dependent on the frequency of the sound vibration. Lower frequencies are transmitted to the farther end of the basilar membrane; higher frequencies are able to penetrate only a short distance through the liquid. Along the basilar membrane are located the auditory nerve endings. When a particular portion of the basilar membrane is stimulated by the sound vibrations, the brain records the disturbance as a certain pitch. More vigorous oscillation is interpreted as a louder sound.

1. A dog might be able to hear a whistle that a human ear cannot hear because the
   A. human can hear sounds of a lower frequency than the dog

B. dog can hear sounds of a lower frequency than the human
C. human can hear sounds of a higher frequency than the dog
D. dog can hear sounds of a higher frequency than the human

2. Ordinary sounds cause a wave-like vibration in bones of the
F. spinal column
G. auditory nerve
H. outer ear
J. middle ear

3. Which of the following statements about human hearing is true?
A. All ear vibrations occur at frequencies between 2000 and 20,000 vibrations per second.
B. All human beings can hear sounds if the vibrations are within a range of between 2 and 200,000 vibrations per second.
C. Vibrations below 20 or above 20,000 per second cannot be detected.
D. The cochlea is in the middle ear.

4. If a musical instrument had the ability to make a sound at 1000 vibrations per second, most people would consider the sound
F. inaudible
G. high pitched
H. medium pitched
J. low pitched

5. A sound coming from a person's left side would
A. hit both ears at the same time
B. hit the right ear first
C. hit the left ear first
D. not be perceived by a brain-damaged child

6. Which of the following would cause the most vigorous vibration in the human ear?
F. supersonic vibration
G. shot from a cannon
H. police whistle
J. loud bass drum

7. The auditory nerve allows the brain to
A. correctly interpret sounds
B. correctly hear sounds
C. correctly locate sounds
D. vibrate rapidly

8. Sound is transmitted immediately past the eardrum by
F. nerve endings
G. a series of bone levers
H. cochlea
J. basilar liquids

The genetic material is now known to be Deoxiribonucleic acid (DNA). The two general functions of DNA are (1) replication for the propagation of life, and (2) to serve as a template for protein synthesis. It is this second function that we shall outline here. The initial step is the assemblage of messenger ribonucleic acid (m–RNA) by DNA. This process is known as transcription. The m–RNA then acts as a complement of the genetic code in the DNA molecule that assembled it. The m–RNA then directs the assembly of a protein from an available pool of protein building blocks, amino acids. This process is known as translation. Therefore, we can summarize protein synthesis as transcription and translation. A second kind of RNA, known as transfer ribonucleic acid (t–RNA), is responsible for directing the correct amino acid to its correct place in the amino acid sequence that is to become the protein.

9. The title that best expresses the content of this passage is
A. The Mechanism of Protein Synthesis
B. The Structure and Function of DNA
C. Sexual and Asexual Reproduction
D. The Chemistry of Life

10. According to the passage
F. DNA is directly responsible for the synthesis of a protein
G. m–RNA makes DNA
H. transcription follows translation
J. proteins are assemblages of amino acids

11. Transcription can best be described as
A. the assembly of DNA from a protein model
B. m–RNA manufacture of a protein
C. DNA manufacture of m–RNA
D. replication

12. Relative to DNA, m–RNA could be considered a
F. nucleotide
G. duplicate of DNA
H. replicate of DNA
J. complement of DNA

The function of the heart is to discharge, with adequate force, an amount of blood sufficient for the metabolic needs of the body. The amount discharged in a unit of time is determined by the stroke, volume and rate of heartbeat. As the demand for blood by the body varies from momemt to moment, it is evident that the rate, force, and systolic output of the heart must be governed in accordance. This control is both neural and humoral.

The origin of the heartbeat is not dependent upon the central nervous system. But it is a fact, proved by everyday observation, that the state of mind or body can modify the action of the heart. The heart is connected with the central nervous system by means of two nerves, the vagus and the cervical sympathetic. From the brain there issue twelve pairs of cranial nerves; of these the vagus, or pneumogastric nerve, forms the tenth pair. The vagus springs from the lowest division of the brain, known as the medulla oblongata, which may be looked upon as the connection between the brain and the spinal cord. This nerve is very widely distributed, sending branches to the heart, lungs, trachea, esophagus, stomach, pancreas, gall bladder, intestines, etc.; it is, therefore, one of the most important nerves in the body. To the heart the vagus nerve sends both afferent and efferent fibers; the latter fibers belong to the autonomic nervous system. The efferent vagal fibers end in a peripheral ganglion lying in the heart; from this ganglion the impulses are carried by very short postganglionic fibers to the sino-auricular and the auriculo-ventricular nodes and the bundle of His.

In an animal the vagus nerve may be exposed without any great difficulty. Under the influence of an anesthetic the skin in the neck, a little to either side of the larynx, is slit open; the structures immediately below the skin are pushed aside, and the carotid artery is brought into view. Alongside this vessel lies a large nerve trunk, the vagus. When the vagus on one side is cut, there is usually little or no result, but when both vagi are severed, there is a marked cardiac acceleration. Stimulation of the vagus nerve may cause a decrease in the rate, or it may diminish the force without affecting the rate, or it may cause a complete cessation of the heartbeat in diastole. This slowing or stoppage of the heart, cardiac inhibition, is the result of a reduction in the irritability of the sino-auricular node and a decrease in the conductivity of the auriculo-ventricular bundle; upon the ventricular musculature the vagus is said to have no direct influence.

13. The statement that the vagus nerve is connected with involuntary action is

A. contrary to the paragraphs
B. neither made nor implied in the paragraphs
C. definitely stated by the author
D. not made, but implied in the paragraphs

14. Which of the following statements is *least* true of the vagus nerve? The vagus nerve

F. becomes the autonomic system
G. comes from the medulla oblongata
H. is one of the tenth pair of cranial nerves
J. serves the heart through both efferent and afferent fibers

15. Which of the following is true of the vagus nerve?

A. it completely controls heart action
B. it controls blood temperature
C. either branch of the vagus nerve can take over the functions of the other
D. it only accelerates the heart rate

16. Which of the phrases makes the following statement most nearly true? "The rate, force and systolic output of the heart are controlled by

F. neural connections
G. the sino-auricular node
H. the bundle of His
J. the vagus and cervical sympathetic systems

17. That the state of mind can modify heart action is

A. shown to operate through the vagus nerve
B. shown to operate through control from the brain
C. shown by cardiac inhibition
D. stated, but its mode of operation is not shown

18. The statement, "This control is both neural and humoral" means

F. both neural pathways and the mood control heartbeat
G. heartbeat is controlled by both efferent and afferent nerves
H. substances in the blood may affect heartbeat as well as the stimulation via neural pathways
J. both postganglionic fibers and the bundle of His are necessary to control the heartbeat

19. The function of the heart is to

A. clear impurities from the blood
B. pump blood throughout the body
C. regulate the emotions
D. stimulate the vagus nerve

20. Much is known about the operation of the vagus nerve because

F. it can be readily observed by fluoroscope
G. plastic models allow for manipulation of the nerve
H. experimentation with anesthesized opened frogs is common
J. the signals of the vagus nerve are easily recognized

DIRECTIONS: The following group of questions is not based upon a reading passage. Choose the *best* answer to each question according to your knowledge in the natural sciences.

21. Fluorine is the most active member of the halogen family because it

A. is a gas
B. has the smallest atomic radius
C. has no isotopes
D. combines with lithium

22. When strong acids are dissolved in water, a particle always formed is

F. NH_4^+
G. $SO_4^=$
H. NO_3^-
J. H_3O^+

23. Assimilation of lipids occurs in the

A. cilium
B. centriole
C. cytoplasm
D. lysosomes

24. The chemical responsible for phototropism is

F. ethylene
G. cytokinin
H. phytochrome
J. auxin

25. According to Kepler's third law, the period of a planet is proportional to some power of its mean distance from the sun. Which is the correct statement of this law?

A. $T \approx R^2$
B. $T \approx R^{2/3}$
C. $T \approx R^{1/3}$
D. $T \approx R^{3/2}$

26. Of the following, the most probable prediction concerning the compound formed between an alkali metal and a halogen is that it would

F. have a low melting point
G. be insoluble in water
H. conduct electricity in the solid state
J. conduct electricity when molten

27. A solution with pH = 2 is more acid than one with a pH = 6 by a factor of

A. 4
B. 12
C. 400
D. 10,000

28. The number of *ions* formed when $(NH_4)_3PO_4$ dissociates in water is

F. 20
G. 18
H. 7
J. 4

29. Occasionally, in some cases of overweight, a doctor may prescribe the use of thyroid extract along with a diet. The treatment causes a reduction in weight because the extract

A. increases the rate of general metabolism
B. increases the activity of the thyroid gland
C. decreases the patient's appetite
D. takes the place of starchy foods

30. The most likely reason that dinosaurs became extinct is that they

F. were killed by erupting volcanoes
G. were eaten as adults by the advancing mammalian groups
H. failed to adapt to a changing environment
J. killed each other in combat

31. Which of the following constitutes a chemical change?

A. magnetizing a rod of iron which weighs one kilogram
B. burning one pound of coal to determine its heat capacity
C. mixing flake graphite with oil
D. vaporizing one gram of mercury in a vacuum

32. Sodium is stored in

F. vacuum cans
G. hydrogen peroxide
H. ventilated cans
J. water

33. A *faraday* is a unit of quantity of electricity, the flow of which results in the

A. analysis of the constituents of an eutectic mixture
B. deposition of one gram-equivalent weight of metal on an electrode
C. determination of the isotopic structure of a compound
D. catalytic hydrogenation of organic compounds

34. If 22.5 ml of HCl are needed to neutralize 25 ml of 0.1N Na_2CO_3 solution, the normality of the acid is

F. 0.037
G. 0.056
H. 0.111
J. 0.167

35. The materials that would be most useful in demonstrating that germinating seeds give off carbon dioxide are a glass bottle, glass tubing,

A. limewater, a rubber stopper and lima beans
B. colchicine, test tubes and wheat
C. a rubber stopper, beaker and lima beans
D. a battery jar, limewater and sawdust

Sixty college freshmen volunteered to take part in a learning experiment. First, all sixty subjects completed a ten-question McQuarrie maze and were scored on the basis of both speed and accuracy. Below is a facsimile McQuarrie maze.

The subjects were then divided into six groups of ten each.

The subjects in Group I spent one-half hour practicing with more McQuarrie mazes;

Group II spent one-half hour working on the popular cul-de-sac variety of maze;

Group III spent the half-hour doing connect-the-dots;

Group IV spent a half-hour untangling a length of twine and unknotting the knots;

Group V spent their half-hour putting three dots into each circle on a page full of circles;

Group VI watched a half-hour situation comedy on TV.

All the subjects then took a ten minute break after which they completed a ten-question McQuarrie maze unfamiliar to them all.

The results were as follows:
Subjects in Group I showed a large and significant improvement in both the speed and the accuracy with which they completed McQuarrie mazes.
Subjects in Groups II, III and IV showed significant improvement in their performance, but significantly less improvement than the subjects in Group I.
Subjects in Groups V and VI showed slight improvement in their performance, but the improvement was not statistically significant.

36. The purpose of this experiment was to

- **F.** teach college freshmen to solve McQuarrie mazes
- **G.** learn how people solve McQuarrie mazes
- **H.** discover what kinds of practice are useful
- **J.** compare the effects of different types of practice

37. The function of Group IV was to

- **A.** get the knots out of the twine
- **B.** get practice following a strand from origin to conclusion
- **C.** get practice manipulating their fingers
- **D.** keep active but away from pencil and paper

38. The groups which received relevant practice were

- **F.** I only
- **G.** I, II, and III
- **H.** I, II, III, and IV
- **J.** I, II, III, IV, and V

39. The activity of Group V involved

- **A.** tracking
- **B.** eye-hand coordination
- **C.** steady nerves
- **D.** satisfaction upon completion

40. The subjects in Group VI all watched the same TV show because

- **F.** it is more sociable to watch TV in a group
- **G.** the experimenter wanted to reward them for their participation
- **H.** they were the control group
- **J.** keeping the subjects involved in the same controlled activity assured that they would not be engaged in any activity that might be construed as practice

41. The subjects in Groups V and VI improved slightly because they

- **A.** had already done one ten-question McQuarrie maze
- **B.** wanted to please the experimenters
- **C.** were intelligent people
- **D.** were older than they were when they did the maze the first time

42. Including a seventh group of subjects who did not take the first test at all and comparing their average speed and accuracy on the second maze with that of all other groups on the first maze would have

- **F.** substantially altered the experiment
- **G.** served to equate the difficulty of the initial and final mazes
- **H.** been useless because different people have different abilities
- **J.** made the results of groups V and VI statistically significant

43. This experiment was

- **A.** well designed because each group was carefully defined
- **B.** poorly designed because the ten minute break allowed for uncontrolled activity
- **C.** well designed because it proved its hypothesis
- **D.** poorly designed because it didn't take into account sex differences

44. An implication of these results is that

- **F.** practice is a good thing
- **G.** television hinders learning
- **H.** Boy Scout training in knot tying is worthwhile
- **J.** books offering relevant practice, such as this one, if properly used, should help students earn higher scores on the standardized exams for which the books were designed

"The general theory of organic evolution—the evolution model—finds that all living things have emerged by a materialistic, naturalistic, evolutionary process from a single source which itself arose by a similar process from a dead, inanimate world. This model is atheistic in nature and dogmatically asserts that chance alone is responsible for all that we see in our world.

"The creation model postulates that all basic animal and plant types were brought into existence by acts of a supernatural creator using special processes that are not operative today.

"Most scientists and teachers accept evolution not as a theory, but as an established fact. The late Theorosius Dobzhansky, geneticist and widely known evolutionist, former professor of Zoology at Columbia University, has stated, 'The occurrence of the evolution of life in the history of the earth is established about as well as events not witnessed by human observers can be.' Professor Goldschmidt, of the University of California, stated before his death, 'Evolution of the animal and plant world is considered by all entitled to judgment, to be a *fact* for which no further proof is needed.'

"Almost all science books and school texts present evolution as an established fact. These considerations alone convince most people that molecules-to-man evolution has actually occurred. The proponents of the evolutionary theory adamantly insist that special creation be excluded from any possible consideration as an explanation for origins on the basis that it does not qualify as a scientific theory. On the other hand, they would view as unthinkable the consideration of evolution as anything less than pure science.

"In reality, neither creation nor evolution qualifies as scientific theory. They are both axiomatic. Neither is supported by events, processes, or properties which can now be observed. In addition, a scientific theory must be subject to or capable of falsification. That is, it must be possible to conceive of an experiment, the failure of which would disprove the theory.

"In the rational, logical order of thinking it follows that neither theory is scientific in nature, but rather philosophical. Hence, neither theory is more than a postulate.

"In a recent book Pierre Grasse, one of France's best-known scientists, severely criticizes the modern theory of evolution. Grasse ends his book with the sentence, 'It is possible that in this domain, biology, impotent, yields the floor to metaphysics.'

"It is often claimed that there are no reputable scientists who do not accept the theory of evolution. This is just one more false argument used to win converts to the evolutionary model. There are literally thousands of qualified scientists all over the world who realize that the evidence in *every field* of science overwhelmingly supports the creation model, not the evolutionary model.

"The proponents of the creation model of origin are not asking for an 'Adam and Eve' story to be incorporated into the education syllabus. They do, however, propose that all the existing evidence be presented and the student be allowed the intellectual freedom to decide which model is best supported by the data. Students should be encouraged to study the data, think logically and demand verification.

"You will notice in the models that the evolution sub-models include the most common atheistic position first and also the deistic and theistic position. It must be emphasized that the two latter theories are equally unsupportable from existing evidence. . .

"No scientist questions the validity of variety, change and development within groups of living things. The works of Luther Burbank, Walter Lammerts, and others in California, have made it obvious that new forms can be bred, forms differing from the parents. But it is also obvious that this type of breeding is *limited* invariably and shows bounds beyond which it cannot go.

"After more than one hundred years of research in biology, evolution is without a sound foundation. The famous Dr. G. A. Kerkut states it this way, 'The evidence that supports general evolution is not sufficiently strong to allow us to consider it anything more than a working hypothesis. . .'

"If the first law of thermodynamics is valid, ordered complexity cannot simply increase. The law of biogenesis declares that life cannot develop from the inanimate. Such constraints, far from being mysterious, are observable, common-sense rules; one cannot get something from nothing.

"Dr. D.T. Gish, past biochemist at the University of California, Berkeley, and biomedical researcher at Cornell University Medical College argues, 'The refusal of the establishment within scientific and educational circles to consider creation as an alternative to evolution is thus based above all on the insistence upon a purely atheistic, materialistic, and mechanistic explanation for origins to the exclusion of an explanation based on theism. Restricting the teaching concerning origins to this one particular view thus constitutes indoctrination in a religious philosophy. Constitutional guarantees of separation of church and state are violated and true science is shackled in dogma.' "

This article was excerpted from an essay by Roy Slingo, a biology teacher at Scarsdale High School, Scarsdale, New York, and a member of the *Creation Research Society* and the *American Scientific Affiliation*. This essay appeared in the student newspaper *Maroon* and is excerpted with permission of the editor.

45. The theory of evolution is based on

- **A.** observation
- **B.** experimental proof
- **C.** experimental disproof of other theories
- **D.** postulation

46. Evolution has been established as a fact by

- **F.** dogmatic assertion
- **G.** Charles Darwin
- **H.** model builders
- **J.** Luther Burbank

47. All scientists agree that

I. both evolution and creation are valid theories

II. living things are capable of mutation and development

III. the first law of thermodynamics is true

IV. teaching the creation theory in the public schools would constitute a violation of the separation of church and state

- **A.** I and II

B. II only
C. II and III
D. II, III, and IV

48. Most public schools today

F. teach a theory of evolution
G. explain origins on the basis of creation
H. present both theories to students and allow them to choose
J. avoid the question of origins in order to sidestep controversy

49. The writings of Charles Darwin

A. were grounded in the established laws of science
B. were intended to spark the controversy between creationists and evolutionists
C. grew from his observations as a naturalist
D. were the writings of an atheist

50. The theory of special creation is

I. unscientific
II. true
III. accepted by some scientists
IV. taught in some schools

F. I and III
G. II and IV
H. I, III, and IV
J. II, III, and IV

51. The author of this article

A. believes in evolution
B. believes in special creation
C. is presenting the facts without bias
D. considers creation to be a scientific theory

52. The purpose of this article is to

F. plead for separation of church and state
G. convince the schools to stop teaching evolution
H. suggest that opposing theories of our origins be given equal time
J. bring God back to the classroom

END OF TEST

If you complete this test before the time limit is up, go back over the questions on this test only. Do not return to the previous tests.

CORRECT ANSWERS
PRETEST—MODEL EXAM I

TEST 1. ENGLISH USAGE

1. B.	11. B.	21. D.	31. A.	40. G.	49. D.	58. H.	67. D.
2. F.	12. F.	22. G.	32. G.	41. C.	50. J.	59. A.	68. J.
3. C.	13. B.	23. D.	33. B.	42. J.	51. D.	60. J.	69. B.
4. G.	14. F.	24. F.	34. F.	43. B.	52. H.	61. A.	70. G.
5. C.	15. B.	25. B.	35. C.	44. F.	53. B.	62. G.	71. A.
6. G.	16. J.	26. G.	36. H.	45. B.	54. J.	63. D.	72. H.
7. C.	17. A.	27. C.	37. C.	46. H.	55. A.	64. H.	73. B.
8. H.	18. J.	28. F.	38. G.	47. D.	56. G.	65. B.	74. J.
9. A.	19. A.	29. B.	39. D.	48. G.	57. C.	66. H.	75. C.
10. F.	20. J.	30. F.					

TEST 2. MATHEMATICS USAGE

1. D.	6. J.	11. B.	16. F.	21. E.	26. J.	31. D.	36. F.
2. G.	7. E.	12. H.	17. C.	22. K.	27. E.	32. H.	37. B.
3. A.	8. J.	13. A.	18. K.	23. A.	28. G.	33. D.	38. J.
4. G.	9. E.	14. K.	19. B.	24. G.	29. C.	34. H.	39. A.
5. C.	10. G.	15. D.	20. H.	25. D.	30. G.	35. D.	40. G.

TEST 3. SOCIAL STUDIES READING

1. C.	8. F.	15. A.	22. H.	29. A.	35. C.	41. A.	47. D.
2. G.	9. A.	16. H.	23. D.	30. F.	36. H.	42. H.	48. G.
3. A.	10. J.	17. D.	24. G.	31. C.	37. D.	43. C.	49. A.
4. J.	11. B.	18. F.	25. B.	32. J.	38. G.	44. H.	50. G.
5. B.	12. J.	19. B.	26. F.	33. B.	39. C.	45. A.	51. B.
6. J.	13. A.	20. G.	27. A.	34. J.	40. G.	46. G.	52. F.
7. C.	14. J.	21. A.	28. J.				

TEST 4. NATURAL SCIENCE READING

1. D.	8. G.	15. B.	22. J.	29. A.	35. A.	41. A.	47. C.
2. J.	9. A.	16. J.	23. D.	30. H.	36. J.	42. G.	48. F.
3. C.	10. J.	17. D.	24. J.	31. B.	37. B.	43. A.	49. C.
4. H.	11. C.	18. H.	25. D.	32. F.	38. H.	44. J.	50. H.
5. C.	12. J.	19. B.	26. J.	33. B.	39. B.	45. D.	51. B.
6. G.	13. D.	20. H.	27. D.	34. H.	40. J.	46. F.	52. H.
7. A.	14. F.	21. B.	28. J.				

EXPLANATORY ANSWERS
MODEL EXAMINATION I—PRETEST
TEST I: ENGLISH USAGE

1. **B.** *John A. Quarles* is an appositive which must be set off by commas.

2. **F.** A quoted sentence ends with *wrote* and a new sentence begins with *I.* There must, therefore, be a period after *wrote.*

3. **C.** There is no need for a comma after *Hannibal. Until* means "up to the time that," making the words *the time* unnecessary.

4. **G.** The original is redundant. Ordinarily, numbers under 100 should be spelled out.

5. **C.** The sentence calls for the past tense of the verb *to stand* which is *stood.*

6. **G.** While choice H. is technically correct, the clearest and therefore best choice of punctuation for this thought is to end the first sentence after *pilings* and start a new sentence with *Against.*

7. **C.** The paragraph is part of a quoted passage and must begin with quotation marks.

8. **H.** *Their* is the possessive of *they. They're* is the contraction for *they are.* Choice J. is incorrect because the commas are unnecessary.

9. **A.** *Passed* is the past tense of the verb *to pass.* The word needed here is *past*, meaning "in a course that goes close to and then beyond."

10. **F.** *Tobacco-curing* is used as a single adjective modifying *house* and must therefore be hyphenated.

11. **B.** *It's* is the contraction for *it is.* The correct possessive form for *it* is *its. Gravely* is an adverb meaning "seriously."

12. **F.** Dashes, commas or parentheses would all be correct here to set off the parenthetical expression *a divine place for wading.*

13. **B.** Unless the set-off expression ends a sentence, dashes must be used in pairs.

14. **F.** The frequenting of the swimming pools was a result of their being forbidden; hence, *therefore* is correct.

15. **B.** When a list of adjectives modifies a noun, all adjectives but the last must be followed by commas.

16. **J.** *Which* as a relative pronoun refers only to objects. *Who* and *whom* refer only to people. *That* may refer to either objects or people but it is used only with essential clauses. The pronoun required here is the object of the verb *visited*, thus *who* is incorrect. Because *whom we visited daily and looked upon with awe* is a nonrestrictive adjective clause, it must be set off by commas.

17. **A.** *Upward of* is correct and appropriate to the colloquial tone of this passage.

18. **J.** What is needed is simply a pronoun to refer to the singular noun *health*, namely *it.*

19. **A.** *Bald place* is considered a composite noun which is modified by the one adjective *round*; therefore, no punctuation is needed.

20. **J.** The correct spelling is *reverent.* Since the subject of the next clause is not restated, the clause cannot be a new sentence.

21. **D.** The ancient ruler of Egypt is spelled *Pharaoh.* The final sentence of this paragraph constitutes the end of a quoted passage. Quotation marks are always used at the end of a quotation.

22. **G.** *There's* is the correct contraction for *there is.* But it is considered poor form to begin a paragraph with a contraction.

23. **D.** The girl is a person, hence the personal relative pronoun *who.* The correct contraction for *who is* is *who's. Whose* is the possessive form.

24. **F.** *As she calls it* is a subordinate clause and cannot be a sentence by itself. For the same reason, it cannot be preceded by a semicolon. A comma is always contained within the quotation marks.

25. **B.** *Than* is acting here not as a preposition, but as a subordinate conjunction beginning the implied clause *than I do* in which *I* is the subject. A semicolon is not required.

26. **G.** The pronoun *it* is unnecessary in this sentence.

27. **C.** The only time the verb *to lay* is correct is when it can be replaced by the verb *to put*. At all other times use the verb *to lie*, of which the present participle is *lying*.

28. **F.** No punctuation is needed.

29. **B.** As the variety of answer choices implies, *it* is vague and as the sentence stands, the reference point is unclear. Technically, *it* refers to the nearest noun, which is *faucet*. The correct choice should make it clear that the *water*, not the faucet, would be freezing.

30. **F.** The passage is written in the past tense. *Began* is the correct past tense of the verb *to begin*.

31. **A.** The attitude expressed clearly justifies the emphasis represented by the exclamation point.

32. **G.** *Ann* is a noun of direct address; therefore, it should be set apart by commas. *Look* is part of the quote and must be enclosed in the quotation marks.

33. **B.** *It's* is the contraction for *it is*. Because this is a continuation of the quoted sentence, the first word should not begin with a capital letter.

34. **F.** A coordinating conjunction connecting two clauses of reasonable length should be preceded by a comma. A semicolon never precedes a coordinating conjunction.

35. **C.** A question must end with a question mark, even if the question does not encompass the entire sentence. The new sentence must begin with a capital letter.

36. **H.** A period is always placed within the quotation marks. A new paragraph is necessary because a new person and a new subject are being introduced. *By this time* provides an effective transition.

37. **C.** *Soundly* is an adverb which modifies the verb *sleeps*. No punctuation is needed.

38. **G.** A noun of direct address (*Ann*) must be set off by commas and commas are always placed within the quotation marks.

39. **D.** All other choices are unnecessarily wordy.

40. **G.** *Satisfied that the argument was settled* is a participial phrase, not a complete sentence. It should be set off from the rest of the sentence by a comma.

41. **C.** A quoted sentence ends with *walk* and a new one begins with *I*. There must, therefore, be a period after *said*.

42. **J.** This sentence is totally extraneous and breaks the flow of the passage.

43. **B.** The phrase following *tests* is an essential part of this sentence and should not be set off by commas.

44. **F.** This is correct.

45. **B.** The three words *the daily press* say everything that is said by the other, more wordy choices.

46. **H.** *Divert*, meaning "to turn from one course to another," is the most appropriate choice. *Revert* means "to return" and *avert* means "to turn away or prevent."

47. **D.** The present tense of the verb *to lie*, meaning "belonging to," is required here.

48. **G.** It is not necessary to separate the prepositional phrase from the rest of the sentence.

49. **D.** This is the clearest and least awkward choice.

50. **J.** The subject of the verb here is implied—the subject is actually the significance of the results. Thus, a singular verb is needed, and J. gives the only singular verb construction that is spelled correctly.

51. **D.** Do not use a comma to separate a subject and a verb (except when the subject contains a nonessential clause, an appositive or other phrase which is set off by two commas).

52. **H.** *Than*, a conjunction, is used after the comparative degree of an adjective or adverb. *Then*, an adverb, means "at that time" or "next."

53. **B.** To correct this run-on sentence, it is necessary to add a period after *living*. Beginning the next sentence with *Because* creates a sentence fragment, rather than a complete sentence.

54. **J.** Use a hyphen in unit modifiers immediately preceding the word or words modified. *Tradition-oriented* is a unit modifier.

55. **A.** *But* is correct to indicate a contrasting idea. *Moreover* and *besides* mean "in addition to what has been said." *Therefore* means "for that reason."

56. **G.** Do not use punctuation between the terms of a unit modifier when the first term is an adverb modifying the second term.

57. **C.** The participle *executing*, meaning "carrying out," not "putting to death," is the correct word for this sentence. *Which* refers to things, not to people. Choice B. creates a run-on sentence.

58. **H.** *Anonymous* means "unknown."

59. **A.** This is the most concise and correct way to make this statement.

60. **J.** As written, this sentence illustrates a needless shift in subject (from *action* to *you*) which results in a dangling modifier.

61. **A.** This is correct.

62. **G.** As written, this is a run-on sentence. To correct it, add a period after *beings* and start a new sentence with *They*.

63. **D.** Use a semicolon to separate sentence parts of equal rank if one or more of these parts is subdivided by commas.

64. **H.** Use a comma to indicate the omission of a word or words. This phrase actually means "a clenched fist (indicates) anger."

65. **B.** Avoid the shift from the active to the passive voice. The possessive *baby's* is incorrectly substituted for the plural *babies*.

66. **H.** *And* is used to connect similar grammatical elements, in this case the noun *expressions* and the noun *smiles*.

67. **D.** The present infinitive is correct because the action of the infinitive is present or future in relation to the action of the finite verb *begin*.

68. **J.** The introduction of a new topic—the use of words to communicate—indicates the need for a new paragraph. *Human beings* are people and so the phrase *Those people who are* is unnecessary.

69. **B.** The possessive pronoun needed here is *their*. *There* refers to place and *they're* is a contraction for *they are*.

70. **G.** A comparison is being drawn between English- and Spanish-speaking families. The two sentences that form the comparison should be parallel in structure. *Spanish* is a proper noun and must begin with a capital letter.

71. **A.** *American* is a proper noun and should be capitalized; *baby* is merely a noun and, therefore, needs no capital letter.

72. **H.** *Talk* means to use *language* for conversing or communicating.

73. **B.** The subject of this sentence, which is also the antecedent of the pronoun, is singular (*baby*); therefore, the pronoun must also be singular.

74. **J.** Avoid the indefinite use of *it*. In standard written English, *it* requires a stated antecedent for clarity.

75. **C.** Items presented in series should be parallel in structure.

TEST 2: MATHEMATICS USAGE

1. **D.** $\frac{4}{5} = .8$

$\frac{7}{9} = 9\overline{)7.00}$ = .78

$\frac{5}{7} = 7\overline{)5.00}$ = .71

$\frac{9}{11} = 11\overline{)9.00}$ = .82

Thus $\frac{5}{7}$ is the smallest quantity.

2. **G.** Let x = amount earned each month

2x = amount earned in December

Then 11x + 2x = 13x (entire earnings)

$\frac{2x}{13x} = \frac{2}{13}$

3. **A.** $3x^3 + 2x^2 + x + 1$

$= 3(-1)^3 + 2(-1)^2 + (-1) + 1$

$= 3(-1) + 2(1) - 1 + 1$

$= -3 + 2 + 0$

$= -1$

4. **G.** $\frac{x}{12} = \frac{83\frac{1}{3}}{100} = \frac{250}{300}$ or

$\frac{x}{12} = \frac{25}{30} = \frac{5}{6}$

$6x = 60$

$x = 10$

5. **C.** Since the ratio of the sides is 3:1, the ratio of the areas is 9:1.

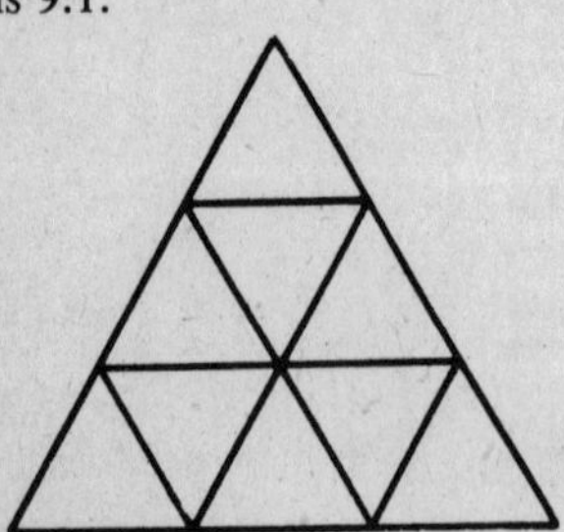

The subdivision into 9 triangles is shown.

6. **J.** $\frac{a}{b} = \frac{3}{5}$

$5a = 3b$

Multiply both sides by 3.

$15a = 9b$

7. **E.** The opposite vertices may be any of the number pairs $(1 \pm 5, 1 \pm 5)$ or (6, 6), (−4, −4), (−4, 6), (6, −4)

Thus, (4, −6) is not possible.

8. **J.**

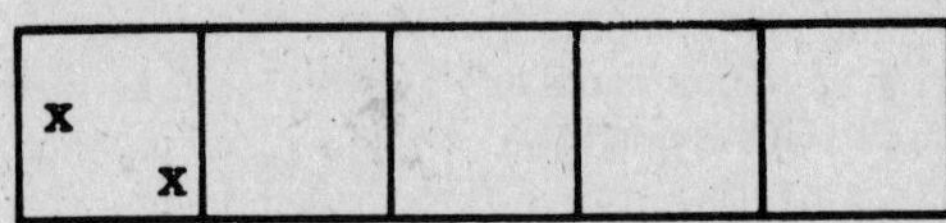

Perimeter of rectangle = x + 5x + x + 5x

Thus 12x = 372

x = 31

Area of square = $31^2 = 961$

9. **E.** $\sqrt{3} = 1.73$ (approx.)

$\frac{1}{\sqrt{3}} = \frac{\sqrt{3}}{3} = \frac{1.73}{3} = .57$

$\frac{\sqrt{3}}{3} = \frac{1.73}{3} = 5.7$

$\frac{1}{3} = .3333\ldots\ldots$

$\frac{1}{3\sqrt{3}} = \frac{\sqrt{3}}{3.3} = \frac{\sqrt{3}}{9} = \frac{1.73}{9} = .19$

Thus the smallest is $\frac{1}{3\sqrt{3}}$

10. **G.**

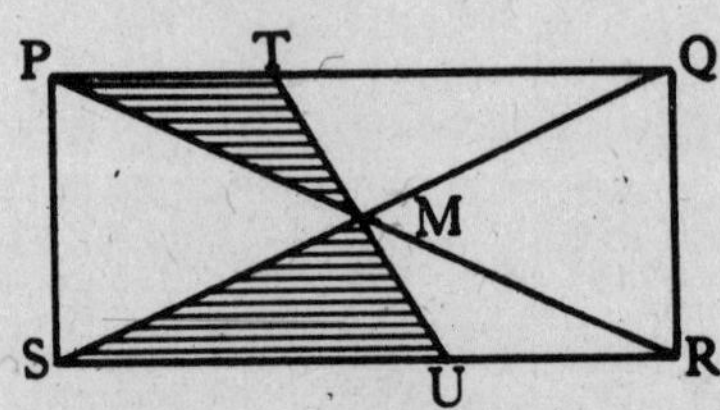

Since △ TQM ≅ △ SMU, it follows that the shaded area = △ PTM + △ TQM = △ PMQ. But △ PMQ = $\frac{1}{2}$ △ PQS = $\frac{1}{4}$ PQRS, $\frac{1}{4}$ = 25%

11. **B.** Let x = number of people in audience

Then, $\frac{1}{6}$x = no. of boys

$\frac{1}{3}x$ = no. of girls

$\frac{1}{6}x + \frac{1}{3}x = \frac{1}{6}x + \frac{2}{6}x = \frac{3}{6}x =$

$\frac{1}{2}x$ = no. of children

$\frac{1}{2} = 50\%$

12. **H.** The number of revolutions is inversely proportional to size of wheel.
Thus $\frac{30}{20} = \frac{n}{240}$
Where n = no. of revolutions for 2nd wheel,
$2n = 720$
$n = 360$

13. **A.** r cannot equal any number other than zero, for if we divided by r, x would equal y. Since $x \neq y$, it follows that $r = 0$.

14. **K.** $\frac{m}{n} = \frac{5}{6}$
$6m = 5n$
$6m - 5n = 0$
However, it is not possible to determine from this the value of $3m + 2n$.

15. **D.** I. As x increases, $\frac{1}{x}$ decreases and $x - \frac{1}{x}$ increases.

II. $\frac{1}{x^2 - x} = \frac{1}{x(x-1)}$ As x increases, both x and $(x - 1)$ increase, and $\frac{1}{x(x-1)}$ decreases.

III. $4x^3 - 2x^2 = 2x^2(2x - 1)$. As x increases, both $2x^2$ and $(2x - 1)$ increase, and their product increases.

Therefore, I and III increase.

16. **F.** $\triangle SPT = \frac{1}{3} \triangle PSR$ since they have common altitude and the base $ST = \frac{1}{3}SR$.

But $\triangle PSR = \frac{1}{2}$ [P] PQRS.

Hence $\triangle SPT = \frac{1}{3} \cdot \frac{1}{2}$ [P] $= \frac{1}{6}$ [P]

17. **C.** Let the other two angles be 2x and 5x.
Thus, $2x + 5x + 82 = 180$
$7x = 98$
$x = 14$
$2x = 28$
$5x = 70$
Smallest angle = 28°

18. **K.** Her rate is $\frac{1}{t}$ of the lawn per minute.
Hence, in 15 minutes she will do
$15 \cdot \frac{1}{t} = \frac{15}{t}$ of the lawn

19. **B.** Typing space is $12 - 3 = 9$ inches long and $9 - 2 = 7$ inches wide. Part used =
$\frac{9 \times 7}{9 \times 12} = \frac{7}{12}$

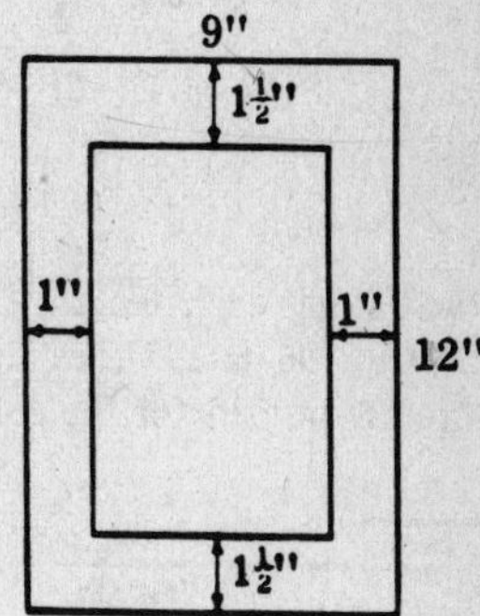

20. **H.** 132 feet in 9 seconds
$= 132 \times 400$ feet in $9 \times 400 = 3600$ seconds (1hr.)
$= \frac{132 \times 10}{132}$ miles per hr.
= 10 miles per hr.

21. **E.** Let the original sign be 10 by 10.

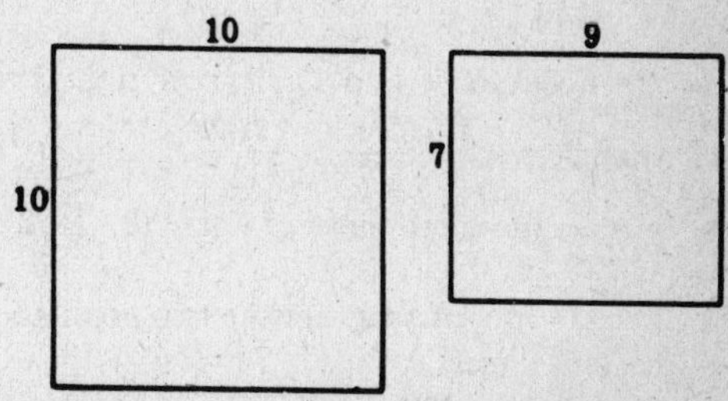

Then the new sign is 9 by 7
$\frac{63}{100} = 63\%$

22. **K.** All the numbers from 200 to 299 begin with 2. There are 100 of these. Then all numbers like 102, 112, ———, 192 end with 2. There are ten of these.
Hence, there are 110 such numbers.

23. **A.** If $2<y<7$ and $5<y<10$, then $5<y<7$ (intersection of 2 sets). Since y is an integer, it must be 6.

24. **G.** If the area is $49x^2$, the side of the square is 7x. Therefore, the diagonal of the square must be the hypotenuse of a right isosceles triangle of leg 7x.
Hence diagonal $= 7x\sqrt{2}$

25. **D.** Since MP = 1 and MQ = $\frac{1}{2}$, the area of
$\triangle$ PMQ = area of $\triangle$ POR $= \frac{1}{2} \cdot 1 \cdot \frac{1}{2} = \frac{1}{4}$
The area of $\triangle$ QNR $= \frac{1}{2} \cdot \frac{1}{2} \cdot \frac{1}{2} = \frac{1}{8}$
Area of $\triangle$ PQR $= 1 - 2(\frac{1}{4}) - \frac{1}{8} = 1 - \frac{5}{8}$
$= \frac{3}{8}$

26. **J.** 72 tiles along each length. 24 tiles along each width. 2 × 96 = 192 tiles along perimeter. But 4 more are needed for the corners of the frame.

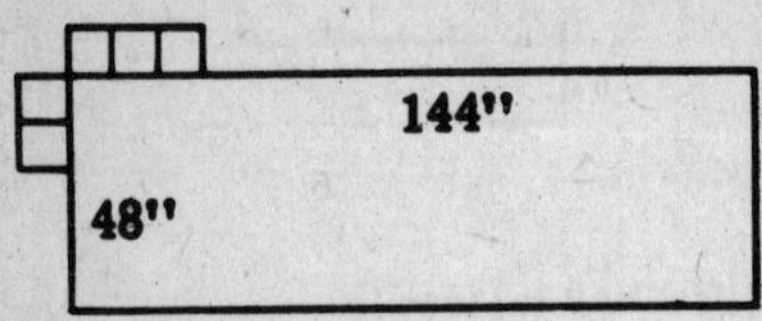

Hence, 196 tiles are needed.

27. **E.** $\frac{1}{10} = x \cdot \frac{3}{4} = \frac{3x}{4}$
Cross-multiplying, we obtain
$30x = 4$
$x = \frac{2}{15}$

28. **G.** Since QR = 7, and QOR is a right isosceles triangle, OQ $= \frac{7}{\sqrt{2}} = \frac{7\sqrt{2}}{2}$.
Hence, the coordinates of Q are $(0, \frac{7}{2}\sqrt{2})$.

29. **C.** Let x = no. of years for the two populations to become equal
Then $6800 - 120x = 4200 + 80x$
$2600 = 200x$
$x = 13$

30. **G.** $8 \times 6 = 48$
$6 \times 8 = \frac{48}{96}$ (sum of all 14 numbers)
Average $= \frac{96}{14} = 6\frac{6}{7}$

31. **D.** I. As x increases, $(1 - x^2)$ decreases.
II. As x increases, $(x - 1)$ increases.
III. As x increases, $\frac{1}{x^2}$ decreases.
Hence, only II increases.

32. **H.** $T = 2\pi\sqrt{\frac{L}{g}}$
In order for T to be tripled, L must be multiplied by 9, since the square root of this factor will be 3.

33. **D.** The line of center of two tangent circles passes through the point of tangency.
Hence, perimeter of
$\triangle = (2 + 3) + (3 + 4) + (4 + 2) =$
$5 + 7 + 6 = 18$

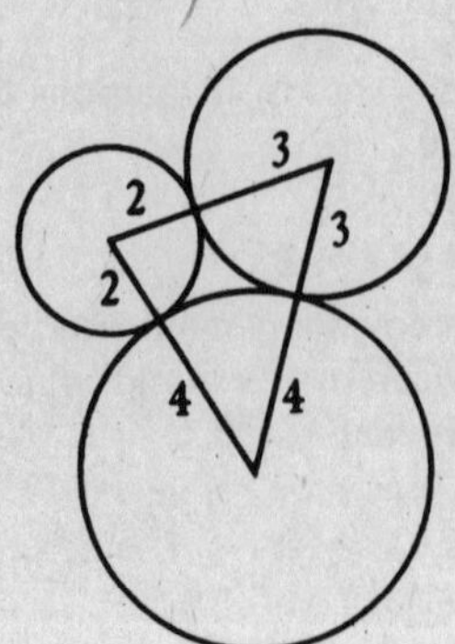

34. **H.** Area of outer circle $= 100\pi$
Area of inner circle $= 49\pi$
Decrease in area $= 51\pi$
% decrease $= \frac{51\pi}{100\pi} = 51\%$

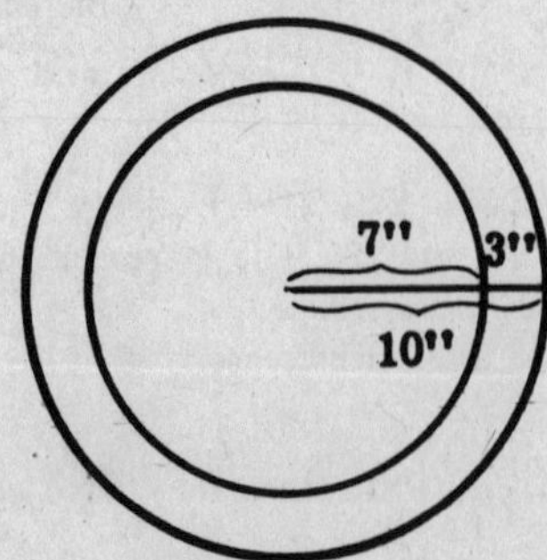

35. **D.** Let x = original price. Then
$.60x = \$4.20$
or $6x = \$42.00$
$x = \$7.00$

36. **F.** $r = 5x$
Divide both sides by 10
$\frac{r}{10} = \frac{5}{10}x$
or $\frac{1}{10}r = \frac{1}{2}x$
Hence, 1 is the answer.

37. **B.** Let x = no. of minutes to fill $\frac{4}{7}$ of bucket.

then $\frac{\frac{3}{7}}{1} = \frac{\frac{4}{7}}{x}$ or $\frac{3}{1} = \frac{4}{x}$

$3x = 4$

$x = \frac{4}{3}$

38. **J.** First solve for x, then y.

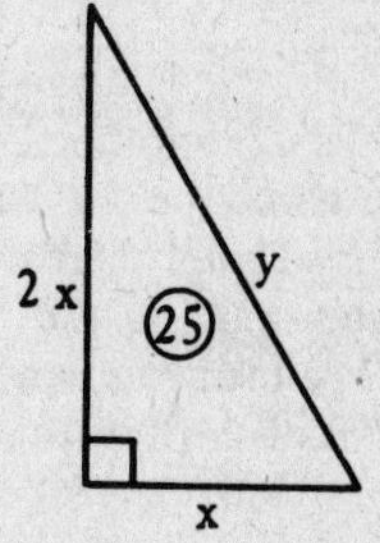

$$\frac{1}{2} \cdot x \cdot 2x = 25$$
$$x^2 = 25$$
$$x = 5$$
$$2x = 10$$

$$y^2 = 5^2 + 10^2$$
$$y^2 = 25 + 100$$
$$y^2 = 125$$
$$= \sqrt{125} = \sqrt{25 - 5}$$
$$= 5\sqrt{5}$$

39. **A.**

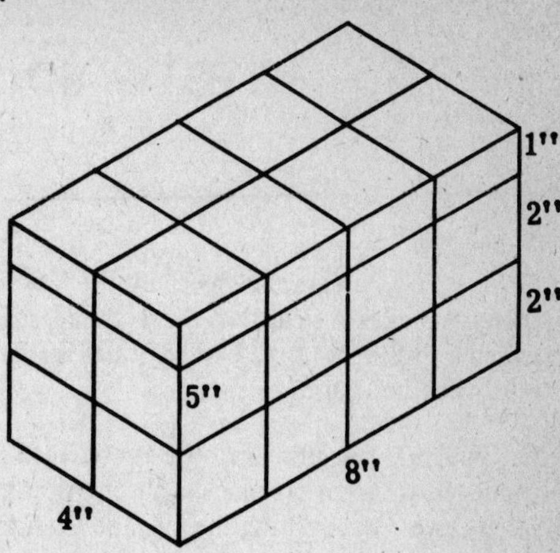

The 2-inch ice cube will fit only in the 8-inch by 4-inch by 4-inch part of the compartment. The upper inch cannot be used.

Hence, $\frac{8 \times 4 \times 4}{2 \times 2 \times 2} = 16$ cubes

40. **G.** Draw OP. Then in right triangle OPS,

$OP^2 = PS^2 + OS^2 = 6^2 + 8^2 = 10^2$

$OP = 10$

Then $QR = \frac{1}{4} \cdot 2\pi r = \frac{1}{4} \cdot 2\pi \cdot 10 = 5\pi$

TEST 3: SOCIAL STUDIES READING

1. **C.** The first paragraph, especially the last sentence thereof, makes it clear that this is the message with which a President of the United States is returning a bill which he refuses to sign.

2. **G.** Evidently the bill which the President is vetoing proposed to grant citizenship automatically to the freed slaves. In opposing the bill, the President also opposes the granting of citizenship to anyone without formal naturalization procedures.

3. **A.** The author is exceedingly cautious and conservative. He does not wish to rush into any legislation which might possibly be unnecessary. He fears the wrath of immigrants who might resent the special treatment being offered to the former slaves. He is loath to enact legislation affecting all the States while the Confederate States are still in self-imposed exile from Congress. His views may be intelligent, but in that portion quoted here they are only negative, not constructive.

4. **J.** In his veto message the President claims that the law is unnecessary because all residents of the United States are afforded equal protection under the laws, regardless of citizenship. He further claims that the law would discriminate against immigrants who must declare their intent, study, wait a number of years and then pass certain qualifying tests to attain citizenship. In addition, he feels that blacks, having been subjected and illiterate for so long, are truly not prepared to exercise the responsibilities of citizenship.

5. **B.** In discussing the need for this bill, the writer states on the one hand, that many persons interpret the Constitution to mean that all native-born persons are automatically citizens of the United States. By that test, many blacks would be citizens already. On the other hand, he says, the very fact that this bill is being proposed opens the above contention to doubt and thus casts doubt on the citizenship status of blacks.

6. **J.** The writer states, "Those rights [civil rights] are, by Federal as well as State laws, secured to all domiciled aliens and foreigners. . ."

7. **C.** The period between the filing of first papers and the citizenship oath is sufficient to allow for all four of the options, but the purpose of the process is to allow for education in citizenship.

8. **F.** Article XIV, Section 1 of the Constitution states: "All persons born or naturalized in the United States, and subject to the jurisdiction thereof, are citizens of the United States and of the State wherein they reside." The President must not be assumed to have been ignorant of the Constitution. The law of the land was as he stated it in 1866 when he vetoed this bill. The 14th Amendment was not adopted until 1868.

9. **A.** Since eleven of the thirty-six States were unrepresented in Congress at the time of the veto, it is clear that the President was Andrew Johnson. Johnson was impeached, but was aquitted at trial, so was not removed from office. This passage comes from Johnson's veto of the Civil Rights Act, March 27, 1866. The bill was passed over his veto on April 9, 1866.

10. **J.** The author states, ". . . it is difficult to understand the communists' dogmatic belief in the superiority of their system, whatever are the observable facts, and their faith in the final victory over capitalism."

11. **B.** The first paragraph opens with the clear statement that economic development is at the heart of the entire Marxist social philosophy. The remainder of the passage expands on that statement.

12. **J.** *Historical determinism* is the Marxist theory that all economic development must pass through socialism before it naturally moves on to communism.

13. **A.** The author states that ". . . the final judgment on any prophecy has to be made in the light of the subsequent events. . ."

14. **J.** The writer states that "The paper does not attempt to evaluate . . .," thus implying scholarly objectivity.

15. **A.** If one considers the entire *statement of objectivity,* one may instantly read into it cynicism and bias. The entire statement reads: "The paper does not attempt to evaluate the philosophical aspects of the theory, its materialism, onesidedness and methodological oversimplification."

16. **H.** Marxist theory holds that the basis of life is man's struggle against the natural environment in his search for the essentials of life—food, clothing and shelter.

17. **D.** Karl Marx (1818–1883) was a German socialist, political philosopher and social activist. He lived for some time in France, Belgium and England, but was never in Russia. His ideas were adapted in Russia long after his death. Marx was an economics correspondent of the New York *Tribune,* but was not an editor.

18. **F.** Technical progress is a necessary component in the communal drive to master the natural environment and to forge a better life for all members of the cooperative work force.

19. **B.** The selection deals at great length with socialism and to some extent with communism, but it does not compare communism with capitalism.

20. **G.** In 1882 Italy entered into the Triple Alliance with Germany and Austria-Hungary. However, since Austria-Hungary was the aggressor in World War I, Italy considered the Triple Alliance nonbinding and joined the war on the side of the Allies. Thus it is correctly stated in the first sentence that Germany and Austria-Hungary were Italy's former allies. In the Second World War Italy fought on side of the Axis.

21. **A.** While we may be aware that democratic nations decried Mussolini's fascist dictatorship, the passage gives us no reason to infer this. However, Mussolini's restoring of order and prosperity, his road building and business expansion must surely have earned him the respect of his people.

22. **H.** The first two paragraphs describe the physical conditions and the low national morale which made Italy ripe for a dictator.

23. **D.** Again today living conditions are hard for the Italians. Inflation is rampant, there is high unemployment and much poverty. Labor is volatile and the government is unstable. The Red Brigades with their kidnappings and murders are a symbol and symptom of the national malaise. The Communist Party is gaining adherents and seats in the government and might well rise to power in the near future if conditions do not improve.

24. **G.** Adolph Hitler was the Fascist dictator of Germany.

25. **B.** The author's attitude toward Mussolini can be seen in this characterization: "Soon the barrel-chested, square-jawed, loud-voiced Mussolini felt strong enough to do away with individual freedom and self-government altogether."

26. **F.** The third and fourth paragraphs of this article describe Mussolini's rise to power.

27. **A.** Despite the fact that individual freedom had been lost, the average Italian, according to the author, felt pride in Mussolini's national achievements.

28. **J.** In abolishing all political parties other than his own, Mussolini effectively eliminated organized opposition.

29. **A.** This answer may be derived through a process of elimination. The Fascists (B.) were Mussolini's own followers. The common people (C.) were imbued with national pride at Mussolini's accomplishments. The military (D.) were obviously pleased at the huge expenditures on army, navy and airforce. Opposition, therefore, could only have come from the church.

30. **F.** The article does not touch upon Mussolini's military victories (G.) nor his foreign alliances (H.). His constitutional changes (J.) are spoken of most disparagingly. Mussolini's domestic programs, however, were highly successful.

31. **C.** President Grover Cleveland sent federal troops to Illinois to guard the trains and protect the mail over the objection of Illinois Governor John P. Altgeld.

32. **J.** Teapot Dome was the Navy oil reserve that came to symbolize the political scandals of the Harding administration.

33. **B.** Answer (B.) contains three characteristics of modern underdeveloped countries. In each of the other answer choices there is at least one characteristic which does not apply to these countries. Some of these inapplicable characteristics are: middle class philosophy, poor endowment of national resources, security of foreign investments and full utilization of manpower.

34. **J.** Herbert Hoover was never Vice President.

35. **C.** Scarcity is fundamental to economics because human demands for goods will always exceed the supply of goods available. Thus, resources are scarce and must be rationally allocated to best satisfy human demands.

36. **H.** The Manhattan Project, a secret effort to develop a transportable atomic bomb, was initiated in

1942. The bomb was constructed at Los Alamos, New Mexico, under the direction of J. Robert Oppenheimer.

37. **D.** As compared with medieval times, all of the functions here have decreased in modern times, but ethical functions have clearly decreased less than the others because there are fewer secular institutions to take over this role.

38. **G.** Large families were desirable in the English colonies because of a perpetual labor shortage.

39. **C.** Britain's trade with the newly independent countries of Latin America was of great volume. She feared that the return of Spain would mean an end to her trade, so was happy to support the United States' declared intention to guarantee the independence of Latin American nations.

40. **G.** Nationalism was fostered as a device to defeat Napoleon by urging the subject peoples to demand their own government.

41. **A.** The Intolerable Acts of 1774 were a direct result of the Boston Tea Party of 1773. The Acts were intended to punish the people of Boston—by closing their harbor, altering their charter and enforcing the Quartering Act.

42. **H.** The Dred Scott decision, announced in 1857, lowered the prestige of the Supreme Court. The decision, delivered by Chief Justice Roger Taney, held that: Negroes are not citizens under the Constitution and so cannot claim the rights of a citizen to sue in a federal court, the status of a slave residing in a free state does not change, a slave cannot become free by residing in a northern territory because Congress has no right to deprive citizens of their property without due process of law. In other words, the Missouri Compromise was unconstitutional because Congress could not exclude slavery from the territories.

43. **C.** *Tippecanoe* refers to an Indian battle of 1811 in which William Henry Harrison, Governor of the Indiana Territory, repelled an Indian attack near Tippecanoe Creek. The Whigs nominated Harrison for President in 1840, along with Virginian John Tyler for Vice President. *Tippecanoe and Tyler too* was a Whig slogan during the 1840 campaign.

44. **H.** The *best* title for this selection should be *The School System and Democracy*. The thrust of the selection is that democracy itself could not survive if administered by an ignorant population.

45. **A.** It is stated in the first paragraph that "It [democracy] could not succeed with a people either corrupt or uninformed."

46. **G.** The last sentence of the first paragraph states, "To enlighten the people was the first duty of a democracy, and an enlightened people, in turn, saw to it that 'schools and the means of education' were forever encouraged." In other words, democracy's first task was to educate the first citizens, who then assumed the task of seeing to it that future generations were educated while democracy moved on to other tasks.

47. **D.** Americanization is, in effect, the creation of the *melting pot*, the training of immigrants to behave in conformity with the majority of Americans and to understand the rationale for that behavior.

48. **G.** A few immigrants can maintain their customs and habits without disrupting society as a whole, but the large numbers of immigrants who poured into America after 1840 required rapid assimilation.

49. **A.** The vast diversity of the populace might have easily permitted America to divide itself into a rigid religious or class system. Education in the principles and ideals of equality, along with the real opportunity to rise above the circumstances of one's birth through one's own efforts, have helped America to avoid such rigid stratification by class.

50. **G.** In the early public schools, all children who attended were treated equally and were taught principles of equality. Of course, early schooling was not compulsory, so in effect many children of the lower classes, those who could not be spared from the labor force, remained uneducated and unequal.

51. **B.** It has been only in recent years that the professional sports leagues have offered equal opportunity to all athletes. Excellence in the sports arena offers a quick route up the social and economic ladder to the minority athlete, but the opening of this avenue was a post-World War II development.

52. **F.** Equality of all schoolchildren has always existed in some schools of the United States, but in many areas of the country black children were segregated and were denied equal access to quality education until the case of *Brown* v. *Board of Education of Topeka* (Kansas) in 1954. The result of this case, which was affirmed by the Supreme Court, was the repudiation of the doctrine of *separate but equal* and the substitution of the premise that segregated education is by its nature discriminatory and unequal. Since that time, the Supreme Court has mandated that education be made equal in all respects.

TEST 4: NATURAL SCIENCE READING

1. **D.** Dogs can hear sounds at a higher frequency than man.

2. **J.** As stated in sentences 3 and 4 of paragraph 5, the middle ear contains a system of three bone levers which serve to transmit the sound vibration from the eardrum to the inner ear.

3. **C.** The human ear can respond to frequencies ranging from 20 to 20,000 vibrations per second as stated in the first sentence of paragraph 3.

4. **H.** The upper register would be above 2000 vibrations per second; therefore 1000 vibrations per second would produce a sound that is considered medium pitched.

5. **C.** A sound coming from a person's left would hit the left ear a split second before it hits the right ear, thus providing the brain with information that enables it to determine the direction from which the sound originally came.

6. **G.** The louder the sound, the more vigorous the vibration.

7. **A.** The brain does not hear sounds; it interprets them.

8. **G.** According to paragraph 5, sound is transmitted immediately past the eardrum by a system of bone levers known as the hammer, the anvil, and the stirrup.

9. **A.** The paragraph deals with a specific mechanism and not with reproduction, the structure of DNA, or life's chemistry in general.

10. **J.** DNA mediates protein synthesis through m-RNA which it makes; therefore, F and G are incorrect. Transcription leads to translation, the assembly of amino acids into a protein structure, thereby making answer J the correct one.

11. **C.** As defined in the passage, transcription is the process by which DNA makes m-RNA.

12. **J.** As stated in passage, m-RNA is a complement of DNA.

13. **D.** The author states (midway in the second paragraph) that the vagus nerve sends branches to specifically named organs. These organs are all concerned with vital involuntary functions. Therefore, it is suggested or implied that the vagus nerve is similarly concerned with involuntary regulation.

14. **F.** All of the other choices are directly true of the vagus nerve and are stated in the passage. However, only the efferent fibers of the vagus nerve belong to the autonomic nervous system. This is verified near the end of the second paragraph.

15. **B.** The vagus nerve regulates the rate of the heartbeat. When the heart beats faster, more blood reaches the muscles, causing them to expend more energy. Any increase in muscular activity is accompanied by a corresponding increase in temperature.

16. **J.** The second paragraph states that the heart is connected with the central nervous system by means of two nerves, the vagus and the cervical sympathetic. The last sentence in the first paragraph summarizes that the rate, force and systolic output of the heart is controlled by nerves and by chemicals that nerve endings or other structures produce.

17. **D.** This statement is made in the second sentence of the second paragraph, but not elaborated upon.

18. **H.** Neural control refers directly to nerves; humoral control refers to chemicals secreted into the blood stream (hormones, etc.) by various glands, structures, or organs.

19. **B.** The function of the heart is to discharge, with adequate force, an amount of blood sufficient for the metabolic needs of the body—that is, to pump blood. Impurities are cleared from the blood by the kidneys. Emotions have more effect upon the heart than the heart has upon emotions, despite popular misconceptions.

20. **H.** The procedure described in the last paragraph is often carried out on frogs because frogs are inexpensive and easy to obtain and their organs are easy to identify.

21. **B.** Nonmetallic elements gain electrons in a chemical reaction. The two factors that determine the activity of a nonmetal are the atomic radius and the number of electrons the nonmetal can gain. Fluorine has the smallest atomic radius of the halogens. Therefore, the nuclear pull on the electron will be greatest in the fluorine atom. Fluorine is

the most active of all the nonmetallic elements because it has the smallest atomic radius and requires only one electron to complete its valence shell.

22. **J.** According to the Brønsted definition, an acid is a proton donor. A strong acid donates a proton (H^+) to a base. When the water molecule takes on a proton, the molecule becomes the hydronium ion (H_3O^+). The H_2O molecule acts as a base or proton acceptor in such cases.

$$H^+ + H_2O \rightleftharpoons H_3O^+$$

23. **D.** One of the assimilative functions of lysosomes, saclike cellular organelles that contain various enzymes, is to break down lipids.

24. **J.** Phototropism, the movement of a plant toward light, is caused by auxin, a hormone that stimulates growth on the side of the plant *away* from the light, causing the plant to grow toward the light.

25. **D.** Kepler's Laws of Planetary Motion are:
    1. Each planet moves in a elliptical orbit with the sun at one focus.
    2. An imaginary line from the sun to any planet at any point in its orbit sweeps out equal areas in equal periods of time.
    3. The square of the time it takes for a planet to complete one revolution is proportional to the cube of its mean distance from the sun.

    Therefore, T^2 is proportional to R^3 or $T \approx R^{3/2}$.

26. **J.** An alkali metal and a halogen form a compound with an ionic bond. If the compound is melted, the ions become free-moving and the compound is able to conduct an electric current.

27. **D.** The pH scale is logarithmic, each unit representing a power of ten. The difference between four pH units then, is four powers of ten, 10^4, or 10,000.

28. **J.** There are 3 ammonium ions and 1 phosphate ion. The total number of ions is 4.

29. **A.** Thyroxin speeds up the oxidation or metabolic rate. This causes food to be burned more quickly, which, in turn, brings about a loss of weight.

30. **H.** Organisms can become extinct if they fail to adapt to their changing environment. The climate of the Mesozoic era became colder and more severe. These giant reptiles did not mutate favorably enough, and so were ill-equipped for survival.

31. **B.** Burning is a chemical activity that produces chemical change. When one pound of coal is burned, it releases heat, which may be measured in a calorimeter.

32. **F.** Sodium is a very active element. It must be stored in evacuated containers or under kerosene, to prevent the oxygen in the air from combining with it.

33. **B.** A faraday is equal to 96,500 coulombs. The coulomb measures a quantity of electricity. When a faraday is passed through a solution, one gram-equivalent weight of metal will be deposited on the electrode.

34. **H.** The volume of the acid times the normality of the acid is equal to the volume of the base times the normality of the base.

$$(22.5)x = (25)(.1)$$
$$x = .111$$

35. **A.** Colorless limewater turns milky-white or cloudy when carbon dioxide is bubbled through.

36. **J.** The purpose of this experiment was to learn of the efficacy of different types of practice—specific, related and unrelated—upon performance of a previously unfamiliar task.

37. **B.** The practice that group IV received consisted of tactilely following a strand from its point of origin to its end, a task similar to the paper and pencil McQuarrie maze (but in a different modality).

38. **H.** Group I received specific practice. Groups II, III and IV received related, relevant practice. The task of Group V, while involved with eye-hand coordination, was totally unrelated to the type of tracking required for the McQuarrie maze.

39. **B.** Group V had a task that required eye-hand coordination.

40. **J.** The subjects in Group VI constituted the control group. They were supervised as they watched the TV show to make certain that they did not participate in paper and pencil games while waiting, and to keep their minds off errors they might have made on the original mazes.

41. **A.** The original test constituted a certain amount of practice for all subjects.

42. **G.** Had a seventh group, a group with no previous practice with mazes, done substantially better or worse on the second set than the other six groups had done on the first set (before they had any exposure), it might have been concluded that the sec-

ond set was easier or more difficult than the first set. This information would be irrelevant to the results. The experiment compared subjects' improvement on the same two mazes with respect to the varying amounts of practice received.

43. **A.** This experiment was well designed in that it tested for the effects of carefully-designed practice upon the learning of a previously unfamiliar task.

44. **J.** Students who acquire practice and skill in answering the questions in this book should do substantially better on the ACT than they might have done with no such previous exposure or practice.

45. **D.** The author makes it quite clear that evolution cannot qualify as a scientific theory because it is not supported by events, processes or properties which can now be observed, and because it is not subject to scientific proof or disproof. Evolution is a philosophical theory, a scientific postulate.

46. **F.** Teachers and textbooks present the theory of evolution as if it were a fact, by pedagogic fiat.

47. **C.** Scientists are polarized into creation and evolution camps. Creationists feel that teaching evolution is teaching atheism, and adding creation to the school curriculum would support separation of church and state by presenting both sides. Mutation of living things is a documented observation with which all scientists concur. A scientific law admits of no exceptions, thus all scientists agree that the first law of thermodynamics is true.

48. **F.** Most public schools today teach a theory of evolution.

49. **C.** Charles Darwin was a naturalist who wrote about his observations and theories. The bulk of his writing had to do with survival of the fittest, of how species mutated in order to survive. The theory of evolution was a by-product of his writings. Darwin himself had studied for the ministry of the Church of England and had no desire to pit science against the church.

50. **H.** The theory of special creation is accepted by many scientists even though they are aware that it is unscientific. These scientists hold that the theory of evolution is no more scientific and feel that there is at least as much evidence for a theory of creation. The theory of creation is taught in non-public and parochial schools throughout the country and taught simultaneously with evolution in the public schools of Iowa, Mississippi, Georgia, Idaho, Indiana, Texas and California.

51. **B.** The downplay of evolution and defense of creation make it clear that the author believes in special creation.

52. **H.** The author states, ". . . propose that all the existing evidence be presented and the student be allowed the intellectual freedom to decide which model is best supported by the data," and, "restricting the teaching concerning origins to this one particular view thus constitutes indoctrination in a religious philosophy."

PART III

SKILLS REVIEW AND PRACTICE

ENGLISH USAGE

The English Usage test, like all the tests on the ACT exam, attempts to discover what you have learned about correct and effective use of the English language, and how well you apply your knowledge when faced with a novel testing situation.

The first step in tackling the English Usage test is to read through the passage quickly. It is important that you do this, for the meaning of the passage as a whole must be retained as you choose your answers. Once you are familiar with the passage, look at the questions. In each instance, read ahead a line or two, because what follows may well affect your choice of answer. For the most part, rely on instinct. Choose the response that *looks right* or *sounds right*. Subvocalizing may help you on this portion of the exam. If you do know which rule applies as you choose from among the response options, then, of course, you are in a good position to make a correct choice.

While it is impossible to present every aspect of English Usage at this time, we have, in the following pages, compiled some of the most important rules and some useful hints for your reference. You should be thoroughly familiar with all these rules and hints before exam day. If, as you work through the English Usage tests in this book, you discover a major deficiency in your preparation, try to pinpoint the specific weakness and return to a textbook or teacher for extra help and practice.

Rules You Must Know

The following list of rules is far from comprehensive. In fact, it has been purposely kept brief so that you can learn every rule and every hint. These are rules that you will find invaluable for all your writing.

CAPITALIZATION

1. The points of the compass are capitalized only when referring to a specific place or area.
   Example: Many retired persons spend the winter in the *South.*
   The points of the compass are not capitalized when they refer to a direction.
   Example: Many birds fly *south* in the winter.

2. The only school subjects which are regularly capitalized are languages and specific place names used as modifiers.
   Example: Next year I will study *French,* biology, *English* literature, mathematics, *European* history, and ancient philosophy.

3. A noun not regularly capitalized should be capitalized when it is used as part of a proper name.
   Example: Yesterday I visted *Uncle Charles,* my favorite *uncle.*

PUNCTUATION—QUOTATION MARKS

1. All directly quoted material must be enclosed by quotation marks. Words not quoted must remain outside the quotation marks.
   Example: "If it is hot on Sunday," she said, "we will go to the beach."

2. An indirect quote must not be enclosed by quotation marks.
   Example: She said that we might go to the beach on Sunday.

3. When a multiple-paragraph passage is quoted, each paragraph of the quotation must begin with quotation marks, but ending quotation marks are used only at the end of the last quoted paragraph.

4. A period ALWAYS goes inside the quotation marks, whether the quotation marks are used to denote quoted material, to set off titles, such as a book's chapter titles or titles of short stories, or to isolate words used in a special sense.
   Example: Jane explained: "The house is just around the corner."
   Example: The first chapter of *The Andromeda Strain* is entitled "The Country of Lost Borders."

5. A comma ALWAYS goes inside the quotation marks.
   Example: "We really must go home," said the dinner guests.
   Example: If your skills have become "rusty," you must study before you take the exam.
   Example: Three stories in Kurt Vonnegut's *Welcome to the Monkey House* are "Harrison Bergeron," "Next Door," and "Epicac."

6. A question mark goes inside the quotation marks if it is part of the quotation. If the whole sentence is a question, the question mark goes outside the quotation marks.
   Example: He asked, "Was the airplane on time?"
   Example: What did you really mean when you said "I do"?

7. An exclamation mark goes inside the quotation marks if the quoted words are an exclamation; outside if the entire sentence is an exclamation.
   Example: The sentry shouted, "Drop your gun!"
   Example: Save us from our "friends"!

8. A colon and a semicolon ALWAYS go outside the quotation marks.
   Example: He said, "War is destructive"; then added, "peace is constructive."

COMMAS

1. The salutation of a personal letter is followed by a comma, and the salutation of a business letter by a colon.
   Example: Dear Mary,
   Dear Leaders of Industry:

2. A noun of address is set apart by commas.
   Example: When you finish your homework, *Jeff*, please take out the garbage.

3. An appositive must be set off by commas.
   Example: Jim Rodgers, *my next-door neighbor,* is an excellent babysitter.

4. Parenthetical words are set off by commas.
   Example: I think, *however,* that a move might not be wise at this time.

5. When a list of adjectives modifies a noun, all adjectives but the last must be followed by commas.
   Example: The jolly, fat, ruddy man stood at the top of the stairs.
   Hint: If you can add the word *and* between the adjectives without changing the sense of the sentence, then use commas.

6. An introductory phrase of five or more words must be separated by a comma.
   Example: Because the prisoner had a history of attempted jailbreaks, he was put under heavy guard.

7. After a short introductory prepositional phrase, the comma is optional.
   Example: As a child she was a tomboy.

8. A comma is not generally used before a subordinate clause that ends a sentence, though in long, unwieldy sentences like this one, use of such comma is optional.

9. A comma precedes the coordinating conjunction unless the two clauses are very short.
   Example: The boy wanted to borrow a book from the library, but the librarian would not allow him to take it until he had paid his fines.
   Example: Roy washed the dishes and Helen dried.

10. A nonrestrictive adjective clause must be set off by commas.
    Example: Our new sailboat, which has bright orange sails, is very seaworthy. [nonrestrictive]
    Example: A sailboat without sails is useless. [restrictive]
    Hint: A nonrestrictive phrase or clause can be omitted without essentially changing the meaning of the sentence. A restrictive phrase or clause is vital to the meaning and cannot be omitted.

11. Where no other rule seems to apply, a comma must be used if the sentence might be subject to different interpretation without it.
    Example: The banks which closed yesterday are in serious financial difficulty. [Some banks closed yesterday and those banks are in trouble.]
    Example: The banks, which closed yesterday, are in serious financial difficulty. [All banks closed yesterday and all are in trouble.]
    Example: My brother Bill is getting married. [The implication is that I have more than one brother.]
    Example: My brother, Bill, is getting married. [Bill is an appositive. Presumably he is the only brother.]

12. If a pause would make the sentence clearer and easier to read, insert a comma.
    Example: Inside the people were dancing. [confusing]
    Example: Inside, the people were dancing. [clearer]
    Example: After all crime must be punished. [confusing]

Example: After all, crime must be punished. [clearer]

Hint: The pause rule is not infallible, but it is your best resort when all other rules governing use of the comma fail you.

SELECTED PUNCTUATION RULES

1. A question must end with a question mark even if the question does not encompass the entire sentence.
   Example: "Daddy, are we there yet?" the children asked.

2. Unless the set-off expression ends a sentence, dashes must be used in pairs.
   Example: The tools of his trade—probe, mirror, cotton swabs—were neatly arranged on the dentist's tray.

3. Two main clauses must be separated by a conjunction or by a semicolon or must be written as two sentences. A semicolon NEVER precedes a coordinating conjunction.
   Example: Autumn had come and the trees were almost bare.
   Example: Autumn had come; the trees were almost bare.
   Example: Autumn had come. The trees were almost bare.

4. In a contraction, the apostrophe is inserted in place of the omitted letter or letters.
   Examples: haven't = have not
   we're = we are
   let's = let us
   o'clock = of the clock
   class of '85 = class of 1985

5. Do NOT begin a paragraph with a contraction.

6. The apostrophe, when used to indicate possession, means *belonging to everything to the left of the apostrophe.*
   Example: lady's = belonging to the lady
   ladies' = belonging to the ladies
   children's = belonging to the children
   Hint: To test for correct placement of the apostrophe, read *of the.* Childrens' = *of the childrens* and therefore is obviously incorrect.

TROUBLESOME GROUPS OF WORDS

1. Their, They're, There
   Their is the possessive of *they.*
   They're is the contraction for *they are.*
   There is *that place.*
   Example: They're going to put *their* books over *there.*

2. Your, You're
   Your is the possessive of *you.*

You're is the contraction for *you are.*
Example: *You're* certainly planning to leave *your* muddy boots outside.

3. Whose, Who's
Whose is the possessive of *who.*
Who's is the contraction for *who is.*
Example: Do you know *who's* ringing the doorbell or *whose* car is in the street?

4. Its, It's
Its is the possessive of *it.*
It's is the contraction for *it is.*
Example: *It's* I who put *its* stamp on the letter.

5. Which, Who, That
Which as a relative pronoun refers only to *subjects.*
Who and *whom* refer only to *people.*
That may refer to *either objects or people.*
Example: This is the vase *which* the cat knocked over.
This is the vase *that* the cat knocked over.
The boy *who* won the prize is over there.
The boy *that* won the prize is over there.

6. Learn, Teach,
To *learn* is to acquire knowledge.
To *teach* is to impart knowledge.
Example: My *mother taught me* all that *I have learned.*

7. Between, among
Between commonly applies to only two people or things.
Among always implies that there are more than two.
Example: Let us keep this secret *between you and me.*
The knowledge is secure *among the members* of our club.
Hint: *Between* may be used with more than two objects to show the relationship of each object to the others, as in: The teacher explained the difference between adjective, adverb and noun clauses.

8. Beside, Besides
Beside is a preposition meaning *by the side of.*
Besides, an adverb, means *in addition to.*
Example: He sat *beside* his sick father. *Besides* his father, his mother also was not well.

CHOOSING THE RIGHT WORD

1. The verb *to lay,* except when referring to hens, may be used ONLY if you could replace it with the verb *to put.* At all other times use a form of the verb *to lie.*
Example: You may *lay* the books upon the table.
Example: Let sleeping dogs *lie.*

2. The use of *many/much, fewer/less, number/amount* is governed by a simple rule of thumb. If the object *can be counted,* use *many, fewer, number.* If the object *cannot be counted,* use *much, less, amount.*
   Example: *Many* raindrops make *much* water.
   Example: If you have *fewer* dollars, you have *less* money.
   Example: The *amount* of property you own depends upon the *number* of acres in your lot.

3. The choice of *I* or *me* when the first person pronoun is used in conjunction with one or more proper names may be confirmed by eliminating the proper names and by reading the sentence with the pronoun alone.
   Example: John, George, Marylou and (me or I) went to the movies last night. [By eliminating the names you can readily choose that *I went to the movies* is correct.]
   Example: It would be very difficult for Mae and (I or me) to attend the wedding. [Without *Mae* it is clear that it is *difficult for me* to attend.]

4. *As* is a conjunction introducing a subordinate clause, while *like* is a preposition. The object of a preposition is a noun or phrase.
   Example: Winston tastes good *as* a cigarette should. [*Cigarette* is the subject of the clause; *should* is its verb.]
   Example: He behaves *like* a fool.
   Example: The gambler accepts only hard currency *like* gold coins.

SERENDIPITOUS INFORMATION

1. Hardly, Scarcely
   Hardly, scarcely, barely, only and *but* (when it means *only*) are negative words. Do NOT use another negative in conjunction with any of these words.
   Examples: He *didn't have but* one hat. WRONG
   He had *but* one hat; or, He had *only* one hat.
   I *can't hardly* read the small print. WRONG
   I *can hardly* read the small print; or, I *can't* read the small print.

2. Agreement of Pronouns
   Each, either, neither, anyone, anybody, somebody, someone, somebody, everyone, one, no one and *nobody* are singular pronouns. Each of these words takes a singular verb.
   Examples: *Neither likes* the pets of the other.
   Everyone must wait his turn.
   Each of the patients *carries* insurance.

3. Correlative Conjunctions
   When the correlative conjunctions *either/or* and *neither/nor* are used, the number of the verb agrees with the number of the last subject.
   Example: Neither John nor *Greg eats* meat.
   Example: Either the cat or the *mice take* charge in the barn.

4. One or Two Words
   Per cent is never hyphenated. It maybe written as one (*percent*) or two (*per cent*) words.

Welcome is one word with one *l*.
All right is always two words. There is no such word as alright.
Already means *prior to some specified time.*
All ready means *completely ready.*

Example: By the time I was *all ready* to go to the play, the tickets were *already* all sold.

Altogether means *entirely.*
All together means *in sum* or *collectively.*

Example: There are *altogether* too many people to seat in this room when we are *all together.*

5. Numbers

All numbers under 100 should be spelled out and the numbers from twenty-one to ninety-nine are hyphenated.

It, when used as a relative pronoun, refers to the nearest noun. In your writing you must be certain that the grammatical antecedent is indeed the intended antecedent.

Example: Since the mouth of the cave was masked by underbrush, *it* provided an excellent hiding place. [Do you really mean that the underbrush is an excellent hiding place, or do you mean the cave?]

Which is another pronoun with which reference errors are often made. In fact, whenever using pronouns you must ask yourself whether or not the reference of the pronoun is clear.

Example: The first chapter awakens your interest in cloning, which continues to the end of the book. [What continues, cloning or your interest?]

Example: Jim told Bill that he was about to be fired. [Who is about to be fired? This sentence can be interpreted to mean that Jim was informing Bill about Bill's impending termination or about his, Jim's, own troubles.]

6. Abbreviations

Abbreviate Street, Road, Avenue, etc., only when addressing envelopes.

MODIFIERS

1. Phrases should be placed near the words they modify.

Example: The author says that he intends to influence your life *in the first chapter.* WRONG
The author, *in the first chapter,* says . . . or *In the first chapter,* the author . . .

Example: He played the part *in "Oklahoma"* of Jud. WRONG
He played the part of Jud *in Oklahoma.*

2. Adverbs should be placed near the words they modify.

Example: The man was *only* willing to sell one horse. WRONG
The man was willing to sell *only* one horse.

3. Clauses should be placed near the words they modify.

Example: *He* will reap a good harvest *who sows early.* WRONG
He who sows early will reap a good harvest.

4. A modifier must modify something.

   Example: Having excellent control, a no-hitter was pitched. WRONG
   Having excellent control does not modify anything.
   Having excellent control, the pitcher pitched a no-hitter. *Having excellent control* modifies the pitcher.

   Example: The day passed quickly, climbing the rugged rocks. WRONG
   The day passed quickly as we climbed the rugged rocks.

   Example: While away on vacation, the pipes burst. WRONG
   The pipes were not away on vacation.
   While we were away on vacation, the pipes burst.

   Example: To run efficiently, the serviceman should oil the lawnmower. WRONG
   The serviceman should oil the lawnmower to make it run efficiently.

   Hint: The best test for the placement of modifiers is to read the sentence literally. If you read a sentence literally and it is literally ridiculous it is WRONG. The meaning of a sentence must be clear to any reader. The words of the sentence *must make sense.*

The best course is to read and write carefully. Be aware of the rules which govern grammar, spelling, punctuation, sentence structure and choice of words or diction. The more rules you know, the easier it will be to earn a high score on the English Usage test and the easier it will be for you to write correctly. Beyond the rules, however, always ask "*Does it make sense?*" If the sentence does not make sense, and you are not certain of the governing rule, then you must be innovative. Look for a wrong choice of word. Look for faulty, misleading punctuation. Look for a misplaced modifier. Subvocalize, listen and do your best.

PRACTICE WITH ENGLISH USAGE QUESTIONS

On the actual examination, the English Usage questions appear as underlined portions within a number of passages. In order to give you more balanced practice, we have assembled here a representative selection of individual sentences.

DIRECTIONS: A portion of each of the following sentences is underlined. Corresponding to each underlined portion are three alternative ways of saying the same thing. If you feel that an underlined portion is correct and is stated as well as possible, mark NO CHANGE, A or F. If you feel that there is an error in grammar, sentence structure, punctuation or word usage, choose the correct answer from the remaining choices. If an underlined portion appears to be correct, but you believe that one of the alternative choices would be more effective, mark that choice. Remember, you are to choose the *best* answer.

---

1. He is not only famous in England but also in Russia.
1

2. Father asked Tom and I to help.
2

3. She is one of those girls who are always complaining.
3

1. A. NO CHANGE
B. famous not only in England but also in Russia.
C. not only famous in England but famous also in Russia
D. also famous in England and in Russia.

2. F. NO CHANGE
G. Tom and me to help.
H. for Tom and my help.
J. Tom's and my help.

3. A. NO CHANGE
B. whom are
C. who is
D. whom is

4. Making friends is more rewarding than to be antisocial.
4

4. F. NO CHANGE
G. being antisocial
H. being anti social
J. to be anti-social

5. Whoever the gods wish to destroy, they first make mad.
5

5. A. NO CHANGE
B. Who
C. Whom
D. Whomever

6. I would have loved to have seen you in the play.
6

6. F. NO CHANGE
G. love to have seen
H. have love to see
J. have loved to be seeing

7. There is a stain on my tie. Can you remove it?
7

7. A. NO CHANGE
B. tie—can you remove it?
C. tie; Can you remove it?
D. tie. Can you remove the spot?

8. Her brother never has and never will be dependable.
8

8. F. NO CHANGE
G. hardly never has
H. never has been
J. never ever has

9. Having raked the beach for hours, the search for the lost ring was abandoned.
9

9. A. NO CHANGE
B. Having the beach raked
C. After we had raked the beach
D. Having raked, the beach

10. After I had sucked the lemon, the apple tasted sweetly.
10

10. F. NO CHANGE
G. tasted sweet.
H. tasted sweetened.
J. tastes sweeter.

11. Nothing would satisfy him but that I bow to his wishes.
11

11. A. NO CHANGE
B. although that
C. when that
D. that

12. Was it really her who you saw last night?
12

12. F. NO CHANGE
G. she who you saw
H. she whom you saw
J. her whom you saw

13. Due to the mechanic's carelessness, forty lives were lost.
13

13. A. NO CHANGE
B. As to
C. In view to
D. Because of

14. Let's you and me settle the matter between ourselves.
14

14. F. NO CHANGE
G. Let's you and I
H. Let's
J. Let's me and you

15. The reason Frank is going to Arizona is because he needs a dry climate.
15

15. A. NO CHANGE
B. is that he needs
C. is the fact that he needs
D. is on account of he needs

16. If you would have been prompt, we might have arrived
16
in time for the first act.

16. F. NO CHANGE
G. If you were to have been prompt,
H. If you would've been prompt,
J. If you had been prompt,

17. Now kick your feet in the water like Gregory just did.
17

17. A. NO CHANGE
B. water, like Gregory just did.
C. water as Gregory just did.
D. water, as Gregory just did.

18. We can't assist but one of you at a time, so try to be
18
patient.

18. F. NO CHANGE
G. We can't assist only one
H. We can't only assist one
J. We can assist but one

19. Oliver Wendell Holmes decided to become a writer being that his father was a successful author.
19

19. A. NO CHANGE
B. being as how
C. since
D. in view of the fact that

20. My father is making chicken for dinner tonight, so I don't want to miss dinner.
20

20. F. NO CHANGE
G. tonight; so I don't want to miss dinner.
H. tonight and I don't want to miss chicken.
J. tonight, and I don't want to miss dinner.

21. "Are you absolutely certain, she asked, that you are right?"
21

21. A. NO CHANGE
B. certain", she asked, "that you are right"?
C. certain," she asked, "That you are right?"
D. certain," she asked, "that you are right?"

22. My parents don't approve of Tom's and my staying
22
out so late.

22. F. NO CHANGE
G. Tom and I
H. Tom and me
J. us

23. Andrea <u>Williams who is my cousin</u> also attends this school.
23

23. A. NO CHANGE
B. Williams, who is my Cousin,
C. Williams, he is also my cousin,
D. Williams, who is my cousin,

24. <u>After he graduated high school</u>, he went to Dartmouth.
24

24. F. NO CHANGE
G. When he graduated high school,
H. After graduating from high school,
J. After he graduated from High School,

25. The secret of happiness lies not in doing what you like but <u>to like what you do</u>.
25

25. A. NO CHANGE
B. in liking what you do.
C. to like what you are doing.
D. to like that which you do.

MARK YOUR ANSWERS HERE

1 Ⓐ Ⓑ Ⓒ Ⓓ	6 Ⓕ Ⓖ Ⓗ Ⓙ	11 Ⓐ Ⓑ Ⓒ Ⓓ	16 Ⓕ Ⓖ Ⓗ Ⓙ	21 Ⓐ Ⓑ Ⓒ Ⓓ
2 Ⓕ Ⓖ Ⓗ Ⓙ	7 Ⓐ Ⓑ Ⓒ Ⓓ	12 Ⓕ Ⓖ Ⓗ Ⓙ	17 Ⓐ Ⓑ Ⓒ Ⓓ	22 Ⓕ Ⓖ Ⓗ Ⓙ
3 Ⓐ Ⓑ Ⓒ Ⓓ	8 Ⓕ Ⓖ Ⓗ Ⓙ	13 Ⓐ Ⓑ Ⓒ Ⓓ	18 Ⓕ Ⓖ Ⓗ Ⓙ	23 Ⓐ Ⓑ Ⓒ Ⓓ
4 Ⓕ Ⓖ Ⓗ Ⓙ	9 Ⓐ Ⓑ Ⓒ Ⓓ	14 Ⓕ Ⓖ Ⓗ Ⓙ	19 Ⓐ Ⓑ Ⓒ Ⓓ	24 Ⓕ Ⓖ Ⓗ Ⓙ
5 Ⓐ Ⓑ Ⓒ Ⓓ	10 Ⓕ Ⓖ Ⓗ Ⓙ	15 Ⓐ Ⓑ Ⓒ Ⓓ	20 Ⓕ Ⓖ Ⓗ Ⓙ	25 Ⓐ Ⓑ Ⓒ Ⓓ

CORRECT ANSWERS TO ENGLISH USAGE PRACTICE QUESTIONS

1. **B.**	6. **G.**	11. **A.**	16. **J.**	21. **D.**
2. **G.**	7. **A.**	12. **H.**	17. **C.**	22. **F.**
3. **A.**	8. **H.**	13. **D.**	18. **J.**	23. **D.**
4. **G.**	9. **C.**	14. **H.**	19. **C.**	24. **H.**
5. **D.**	10. **G.**	15. **B.**	20. **F.**	25. **B.**

EXPLANATORY ANSWERS TO ENGLISH USAGE PRACTICE QUESTIONS

1. **B.** Words such as *only* (or *not only*) should be placed directly before the words they refer to. "He is not only famous in England" implies that he is something else in England as well. Also, structure with correlative conjunctions should be kept parallel. C. is verbose. D. implies that he is famous in still a third country.

2. **G.** *Tom* and *me* are both direct objects of the verb *asked.* A simple test for the correct form of the pronoun would be to try the sentence without *Tom.* ". . . for Tom's and my help" would be correct, but H. and J. are not.

3. **A.** *Who* refers to *those girls* and thus must take a plural verb. The object of the preposition *of* is "those girls who are always complaining." *Who* is the subject of the subordinate clause.

4. **G.** The gerund is needed to maintain parallelism. *Antisocial* is one word.

5. **D.** *Whomever* is the object of the verb *to destroy.*

6. **G.** Use of the past conditional, as in *would have loved,* implies that by this time the author would no longer love.

7. **A.** D. is technically correct but is unnecessarily repetitive, for the *it* clearly refers to the stain. C. would be correct if the *C* in *Can* were lower case. Use of dashes in this case is incorrect.

8. **H.** As implied, the main verb to complement the auxiliary verb *has* is *be.* However, the correct verb is *been,* and it must be stated. *Hardly never* is a double negative. *Never ever* is a childish form of emphasis.

9. **C.** This sentence contains a dangling modifier. The sentence implies that *the search* has been raking the beach.

10. **G.** *Tasted* is a linking verb, not an action verb. It therefore must be followed by an adjective, not an adverb. J. mixes tenses.

11. **A.** All other choices are meaningless.

12. **H.** *She* is a predicate nominative (it was she). *Whom* is the object of the verb *saw* (you saw whom).

13. **D.** *Due to* is a colloquial synonym for *because of. As to* changes the meaning of the sentence.

14. **H.** *Let's* is a contraction for *let us.* After the word *us, you and me* is redundant.

15. **B.** A subordinate clause beginning with a subordinate conjunction can serve only as an adverb. In the sentence as written, the clause "because of . . ." refers to the word *reason* and thus serves as a noun. A subordinate clause beginning with a relative pronoun, on the other hand, can serve as an adjective or a noun. C. is verbose.

16. **J.** There is no reason for the conditional.

17. **C.** The verb *did* is the clue that the second part of the sentence is a clause, not a phrase, and must begin with a conjunction such as *as.* A subordinate clause that ends a sentence need not be preceded by a comma.

18. **J.** All other choices contain double negatives.

19. **C.** *Being that, being as how,* and *in view of the fact that* are all colloquial or verbose synonyms for *because* or *since.*

20. **F.** *So* is a coordinating conjunction; it cannot be used with a semicolon. H. would be correct if a comma were to precede *and. So* is a better coordinating conjunction here than is *and,* for *so,* unlike *and,* implies a cause-effect relationship.

21. **D.** *She asked* is not part of the quote so must remain outside the quotation marks. The comma, as in *certain,"* must always be contained within the quotation marks. The second quoted portion within this sentence is not a new sentence, but rather the continuation of a quoted sentence; hence, it begins with a lower case, not a capital, letter.

22. **F.** *Staying* is a gerund and thus acts as a noun. Therefore it must be modified by adjectives, such as

Tom's and *my*. (The possessive form of a noun or pronoun is an adjective.)

23. **D.** *Who is my cousin* is a nonrestrictive appositive, so must be set off by commas. *Cousin* is capitalized only when it is part of a name, as in *Cousin Andy*.

24. **H.** *Graduate* is an intransitive verb and thus cannot take a direct object. J. would be correct if *High School* were in lower case, but *high school* is capitalized only when referring to a specific high school.

25. **B.** A., C. and D. destroy parallelism.

MATHEMATICS USAGE

The ACT exam's Mathematics Usage test checks your mastery of elementary and intermediate algebra, geometry, percentages and general mathematics. The questions are in the form of problems that you must read carefully. You must determine just what it is that the question asks, solve the problem and mark the letter of the correct answer.

You will find that some of the problems may be answered by inspection, that is, without any computation. Most of the questions, however, will require you to reason and calculate in the space provided on the page. In some instances, multiple calculations are called for. The computations are not so complicated that they require the use of a calculator or slide rule. If you find yourself involved with very "difficult" numbers or complex operations, you have probably made a mistake earlier in the problem. Look back and try to spot your error before you spend too much time on intricate computations.

A solid background in arithmetic, algebra and geometry is essential for success with the Mathematics Usage test. To renew your familiarity with the mathematics you have learned in past years, in the following pages we offer you a refresher course in the mathematics you need to know. If this chapter does not suffice and you still have difficulty with the Mathematics Usage tests in the latter part of this book, we urge you to seek specific instruction from your math teacher.

I. OPERATIONS WITH INTEGERS AND DECIMALS

In preparing for the mathematics section of the ACT, it is especially important to overcome any fear of mathematics. The level of this examination extends no further than simple geometry. Much of the material involves only basic arithmetic.

The four basic arithmetic operations are addition, subtraction, multiplication, and division. The results of these operations are called sum, difference, product, and quotient, respectively. Because these words are often used in problems, you should be thoroughly familiar with them.

When adding integers and/or decimals, remember to keep your columns straight and to write all digits in their proper column according to place value.

Example: Add 43.75, .631, and 5

Solution:

```
 43.75
   .631
  5.
------
 49.381
```

When subtracting integers and/or decimals, it is likewise important to put numbers in their proper columns. Be particularly careful in subtracting a longer decimal from a shorter one.

Example: Take .2567 from 3.8

Solution:

```
 3.8000
  .2567
-------
 2.5433
```

In order to perform this subtraction, zeros must be added to the top number to extend it to equal length with the bottom number. The zeros in this case are only place fillers and in no way change the value of the number.

When multiplying integers, pay particular attention to zeros.

Example: Find the product of 403 and 30.

Solution:

```
   403
    30
 -----
 12090
```

When multiplying decimals, remember that the number of decimal places in the product must be equal to the sum of the number of decimal places in the numbers being multiplied.

Example: Find the product of 4.03 and .3

Solution:

```
 4.03
   .3
-----
1.209
```

When dividing, it is also important to watch for zeros.

Example: Divide 4935 by 7

Solution:

```
   705
 7)4935
```

Since 7 divides evenly into 49, there is no remainder to carry to the next digit. When we divide 7 into 3, it cannot go, so we must put a 0 into the quotient. Carrying the 3, we then divide 7 into 35 evenly.

In dividing decimals, remember that we always wish to divide by an integer. If the divisor is a decimal, we must multiply by a power of ten in order to make it an integer. Multiplying by 10 moves a decimal point one place to the right. Multiplying by 100 moves it two places to the right, and so forth. However, remember to do the same to the number in the division sign. Since division can always be written as a fraction in which the number we are dividing by becomes the denominator, when we remove a decimal point from the divisor, we are really multiplying both parts of the fraction by the same number, which changes its form, but not its value.

Example: Divide 4.935 by .07

Solution:

$$.07\overline{)4.935}$$

$$\begin{array}{r} 70.5 \\ 7\overline{)493.5} \end{array}$$

PRACTICE EXERCISES I

Work out each problem in the space provided.

Add:

1. 6 + 37 + 42,083 + 125
2. .007 + 32.4 + 1.234 + 7.3
3. .37 + .037 + .0037 + 37

Subtract:

4. 3701 − 371
5. 1000 − 112
6. 40.37 − 6.983

Multiply:

7. 3147 by 206
8. 2.137 by .11
9. .45 by .06

Divide:

10. 12,894 by 42
11. 34.68 by 3.4
12. .175 by 25

SOLUTIONS TO PRACTICE EXERCISES I

1.
```
     6
    37
 42083
   125
 -----
 42251
```

2.
```
  .007
 32.4
  1.234
  7.3
 ------
 40.941
```

3.
```
    .37
    .037
    .0037
 37.
 -------
 37.4107
```

4.
```
 3701
  371
 ----
 3330
```

5.
```
 1000
  112
 ----
  888
```

6.
```
 40.370
  6.983
 ------
 33.387
```

7.
```
   3147
    206
 ------
  18882
 62940
 ------
 648282
```

8.
```
  2.137
    .11
 ------
   2137
  2137
 ------
 .23507
```

9.
```
   .45
   .06
 -----
 .0270
```

10.
```
      307
 42)12894
    126
    ----
      294
      294
      ---
```

11.
```
        10.2
 3.4)34.68
     34
     ----
       68
       68
       --
```

12.
```
      .007
 25).175
     175
     ---
```

II. OPERATIONS WITH FRACTIONS

In adding or subtracting fractions, you must remember that the numbers must have the same (common) denominator.

Example: Add $\frac{1}{3} + \frac{2}{5} + \frac{3}{4}$

The least number into which 3, 5, and 4 all divide evenly is 60. Therefore, we must use 60 as our common denominator. To add our fractions, we divide each denominator into 60 and multiply the result by the given numerator.

Solution: $\frac{20 + 24 + 45}{60} = \frac{89}{60}$, or $1\frac{29}{60}$

To add or subtract two fractions quickly, remember that a sum can be found by adding the two cross products and putting this answer over the denominator product.

$$\frac{a}{b} \times \frac{c}{d} = \frac{ad + bc}{bd}$$

A similar shortcut applies to subtraction.

$$\frac{a}{b} - \frac{c}{d} = \frac{ad - bc}{bd}$$

Example: $\frac{3}{4} - \frac{5}{7} = \frac{21 - 20}{28} = \frac{1}{28}$

All fractions should be left in their lowest terms. That is, there should be no factor common to both numerator and denominator. Often in multiple-choice questions you may find that the answer you have correctly computed is not among the choices but an equivalent fraction is. Be careful!

In reducing fractions involving large numbers, it is helpful to be able to tell whether a factor is common to both numerator and denominator before a lengthy trial division. Certain tests for divisibility help with this.

To test if a number is divisible by:	Check to see:
2	if it is even
3	if the sum of the digits is divisible by 3
4	if the last two digits are divisible by 4
5	if it ends in 5 or 0
6	if it is even *and* the sum of the digits is divisible by 3
8	if the last three digits are divisible by 8
9	if the sum of the digits is divisible by 9
10	if it ends in 0

Example: $\frac{3525}{4341}$

This fraction is reducible by 3, since the sum of the digits of the numerator is 15 and the denominator is 12, both divisible by 3.

$$\frac{3525}{4341} = \frac{1175}{1447}$$

The resulting fraction meets no further divisibility tests and therefore has no common factor listed above. Any higher divisors would be unlikely on an SAT test.

To add or subtract mixed numbers, it is again important to remember common denominators. In borrowing in subtraction, you must borrow in terms of the common denominator.

Addition:

$$\begin{array}{r} 43\frac{2}{5} \\ +\ 8\frac{1}{3} \\ \hline \end{array} \qquad \begin{array}{r} 43\frac{6}{15} \\ +\ 8\frac{5}{15} \\ \hline 51\frac{11}{15} \end{array}$$

Subtraction:

$$\begin{array}{r} 43\frac{2}{5} \\ -\ 6\frac{2}{3} \\ \hline \end{array} \qquad \begin{array}{r} 43\frac{6}{15} \\ -\ 6\frac{10}{15} \\ \hline \end{array} \qquad \begin{array}{r} 42\frac{21}{15} \\ -\ 6\frac{10}{15} \\ \hline 36\frac{11}{15} \end{array}$$

To multiply fractions, always try to cancel where possible before actually multiplying. In multiplying mixed numbers, always change them to improper fractions first.

Multiply: $\frac{2}{\cancel{5}} \cdot \frac{\overset{2}{\cancel{10}}}{\cancel{11}} \cdot \frac{\overset{9}{\cancel{99}}}{\underset{55}{\cancel{110}}} = \frac{18}{55}$

Multiply: $4\frac{1}{2} \cdot 1\frac{2}{3} \cdot 5\frac{1}{5}$

$\frac{\overset{3}{\cancel{9}}}{\cancel{2}} \cdot \frac{\cancel{5}}{\cancel{3}} \cdot \frac{\overset{13}{\cancel{26}}}{\cancel{5}} = 39$

To divide fractions or mixed numbers, remember to invert the divisor (the number after the division sign) and multiply.

Divide: $4\frac{1}{2} \div \frac{3}{4} = \frac{\overset{3}{\cancel{9}}}{\cancel{2}} \cdot \frac{\overset{2}{\cancel{4}}}{\cancel{3}} = 6$

Divide: $62\frac{1}{2} \div 5 = \frac{\overset{25}{\cancel{125}}}{2} \cdot \frac{1}{\cancel{5}} = 12\frac{1}{2}$

To simplify complex fractions (fractions within fractions), multiply every term by the lowest number needed to clear all fractions in the given numerator and denominator.

Example: $\dfrac{\frac{1}{2}+\frac{1}{3}}{\frac{1}{4}+\frac{1}{6}}$

The lowest number which can be used to clear all fractions is 12. Multiplying each term by 12, we have

$$\frac{6+4}{3+2}=\frac{10}{5}=2$$

Example: $\dfrac{\frac{3}{4}+\frac{2}{3}}{1-\frac{1}{2}}$

Again we multiply by 12.

$$\frac{9+8}{12-6}=\frac{17}{6}=2\frac{5}{6}$$

PRACTICE EXERCISES II

Work out each problem in the space provided.

Add:

1. $12\frac{5}{6}+2\frac{3}{8}+21\frac{1}{4}$
2. $\frac{1}{2}+\frac{1}{3}+\frac{1}{4}+\frac{1}{5}+\frac{1}{6}$

Subtract:

3. $5\frac{3}{4}$ from $10\frac{1}{2}$

4. $17\frac{2}{3}$ from 50

5. $25\frac{3}{5}$ from $30\frac{9}{10}$

Multiply:

6. $5\frac{1}{4}\cdot 1\frac{5}{7}$

7. $\frac{3}{4} \cdot \frac{3}{4} \cdot \frac{3}{4}$

8. $12\frac{1}{2} \cdot 16$

Divide:

9. $\frac{1}{5} \div 5$

10. $5 \div \frac{1}{5}$

11. $3\frac{2}{3} \div 1\frac{5}{6}$

Simplify:

12. $\dfrac{\frac{5}{6} - \frac{1}{3}}{2 + \frac{1}{5}}$

13. $\dfrac{3 + \frac{1}{4}}{5 - \frac{1}{2}}$

SOLUTIONS TO PRACTICE EXERCISES II

1.
$$\begin{array}{rl} 12\frac{5}{6} = & \frac{20}{24} \\ 2\frac{3}{8} = & \frac{9}{24} \\ 21\frac{1}{4} = & \frac{6}{24} \\ \hline 35 & \frac{35}{24} \\ 36\frac{11}{24} & \end{array}$$

2.
$$\begin{array}{l} \frac{1}{2} = \frac{30}{60} \\ \frac{1}{3} = \frac{20}{60} \\ \frac{1}{4} = \frac{15}{60} \\ \frac{1}{5} = \frac{12}{60} \\ \frac{1}{6} = \frac{10}{60} \\ \hline \end{array}$$
$$\frac{87}{60} = 1\frac{27}{60} = 1\frac{9}{20}$$

3.
$$\begin{array}{l} \overset{9}{\cancel{10}}\frac{1}{2} = \frac{2}{4} + \frac{4}{4} = \frac{6}{4} \\ 5\frac{3}{4} \\ \hline 4\frac{3}{4} \end{array}$$

4.
$$\begin{array}{l} \overset{49}{\cancel{50}}\frac{3}{3} \\ 17\frac{2}{3} \\ \hline 32\frac{1}{3} \end{array}$$

5.
$$\begin{array}{l} 30\frac{9}{10} \\ 25\frac{3}{5} = \frac{6}{10} \\ \hline 5\frac{3}{10} \end{array}$$

6. $\frac{\overset{3}{\cancel{21}}}{\cancel{4}} \cdot \frac{\overset{3}{\cancel{12}}}{\cancel{7}} = 9$

7. $\frac{3}{4} \cdot \frac{3}{4} \cdot \frac{3}{4} = \frac{27}{64}$

8. $\frac{25}{\cancel{2}} \cdot \overset{8}{\cancel{16}} = 200$

9. $\frac{1}{5} \cdot \frac{1}{5} = \frac{1}{25}$

10. $5 \cdot 5 = 25$

11. $\frac{\cancel{11}}{\cancel{3}} \cdot \frac{\overset{2}{\cancel{6}}}{\cancel{11}} = 2$

12. $\frac{25 - 10}{60 + 6} = \frac{15}{66} = \frac{5}{22}$

Each term was multiplied by 30.

13. $\frac{12 + 1}{20 - 2} = \frac{13}{18}$

Each term was multiplied by 4.

III. VERBAL PROBLEMS INVOLVING FRACTIONS

In dealing with fractional problems, we are usually dealing with a part of a whole.

Example: In a class there are 12 boys and 18 girls. What part of the class is boys?

Solution: 12 out of 30 students, or $\frac{12}{30} = \frac{2}{5}$

Be careful to read all the questions carefully. Often a problem may refer to a part of a previously mentioned part.

Example: $\frac{1}{4}$ of this year's seniors have averages above 90. $\frac{1}{2}$ of the remainder have averages between 80 and 90. What part of the senior class has a below 80 average?

Solution: $\frac{1}{4}$ have averages above 90.

$\frac{1}{2}$ of $\frac{3}{4}$ or $\frac{3}{8}$ have averages between 80 and 90.

$\frac{1}{4} + \frac{3}{8}$ or $\frac{5}{8}$ have averages above 80.

Therefore, $\frac{3}{8}$ of the class have averages below 80.

When a problem can easily be translated into an algebraic equation, remember that algebra is a very useful tool.

Example: 14 is $\frac{2}{3}$ of what number?

Solution: $14 = \frac{2}{3}x$

Multiply each side by $\frac{3}{2}$

$21 = x$

If a problem is given with letters in place of numbers, the same reasoning must be used as if numbers were given. If you are not sure how to proceed, replace the letters with numbers to determine the steps that must be taken.

Example: If John has p hours of homework and has worked for r hours, what part of his homework is yet to be done?

Solution: If John had 5 hours of homework and had worked for 3 hours, we would first find he had 5 − 3 hours, or 2 hours, yet to do. This represents $\frac{2}{5}$ of his work. Using letters, we have $\frac{p - r}{p}$.

PRACTICE EXERCISES III

Work out each problem in the space provided. Circle the letter that appears before your answer.

1. A team played 30 games of which it won 24. What part of the games played did it lose?

   (A) $\frac{4}{5}$ (B) $\frac{1}{4}$ (C) $\frac{1}{5}$ (D) $\frac{3}{4}$ (E) $\frac{2}{3}$

2. If a man's weekly salary is \$X and he saves \$Y, what part of his weekly salary does he spend?

   (A) $\frac{X}{Y}$ (B) $\frac{X - Y}{X}$ (C) $\frac{X - Y}{Y}$ (D) $\frac{Y-X}{X}$ (E) $\frac{Y - X}{Y}$

3. What part of an hour elapses between 11:50 a.m. and 12:14 p.m.?

   (A) $\frac{2}{5}$ (B) $\frac{7}{30}$ (C) $\frac{17}{30}$ (D) $\frac{1}{6}$ (E) $\frac{1}{4}$

4. One half of the employees of Acme Co. earn salaries above \$18,000 annually. One third of the remainder earn salaries between \$15,000 and \$18,000. What part of the staff earns below \$15,000?

   (A) $\frac{1}{6}$ (B) $\frac{2}{3}$ (C) $\frac{1}{2}$ (D) $\frac{1}{10}$ (E) $\frac{1}{3}$

5. David receives his allowance on Sunday. He spends $\frac{1}{4}$ of his allowance on Monday and $\frac{2}{3}$ of the remainder on Tuesday. What part of his allowance is left for the rest of the week?

   (A) $\frac{1}{3}$ (B) $\frac{1}{12}$ (C) $\frac{1}{4}$ (D) $\frac{1}{2}$ (E) $\frac{4}{7}$

6. 12 is $\frac{3}{4}$ of what number?

   (A) 16 (B) 9 (C) 36 (D) 20 (E) 15

7. A piece of fabric is cut into three sections so that the first is three times as long as the second and the second section is three times as long as the third. What part of the entire piece is the smallest section?

   (A) $\frac{1}{12}$ (B) $\frac{1}{9}$ (C) $\frac{1}{3}$ (D) $\frac{1}{7}$ (E) $\frac{1}{13}$

8. What part of a gallon is one quart?

   (A) $\frac{1}{2}$ (B) $\frac{1}{4}$ (C) $\frac{2}{3}$ (D) $\frac{1}{3}$ (E) $\frac{1}{5}$

9. A factory employs M men and W women. What part of its employees are women?

(A) $\frac{W}{M}$ (B) $\frac{M + W}{W}$ (C) $\frac{W}{M - W}$ (D) $\frac{W}{M + W}$ (E) W

10. A motion was passed by a vote of 5:3. What part of the votes cast were in favor of the motion?

(A) $\frac{5}{8}$ (B) $\frac{5}{3}$ (C) $\frac{3}{5}$ (D) $\frac{2}{5}$ (E) $\frac{3}{8}$

SOLUTIONS TO PRACTICE EXERCISES III

1. **(C)** The team lost 6 games out of 30. $\frac{6}{30} = \frac{1}{5}$

2. **(B)** The man spends X − Y out of X. $\frac{X - Y}{X}$

3. **(A)** 10 minutes elapse till noon, and another 14 after noon, making a total of 24 minutes. There are 60 minutes in an hour. $\frac{24}{60} = \frac{2}{5}$

4. **(E)** One half earn over $18,000. One third of the other $\frac{1}{2}$ or $\frac{1}{6}$ earn between $15,000 and $18,000. This accounts for $\frac{1}{2} + \frac{1}{6}$ or $\frac{3}{6} + \frac{1}{6} = \frac{4}{6} = \frac{2}{3}$ of staff, leaving $\frac{1}{3}$ to earn below $15,000.

5. **(C)** David spends $\frac{1}{4}$ on Monday and $\frac{2}{3}$ of the other $\frac{3}{4}$, or $\frac{1}{2}$, on Tuesday, leaving only $\frac{1}{4}$ for the rest of the week.

6. **(A)** $12 = \frac{3}{4}x$ Multiply each side by $\frac{4}{3}$.
   $16 = x$

7. **(E)** Let the third or shortest section = x. Then the second section = 3x. And the first section = 9x. The entire piece of fabric is then 13x, and the shortest piece represents $\frac{x}{13x}$, or $\frac{1}{13}$, of the entire piece.

8. **(B)** There are four quarts in one gallon.

9. **(D)** The factory employs M + W people, out of which W are women.

10. **(A)** For every 5 votes in favor, 3 were cast against. 5 out of every 8 votes cast were in favor of the motion.

IV. VARIATION

Two quantities are said to vary directly if they change in the same direction. As one increases, the other increases.

For example, the amount I must pay the milkman varies directly with the number of quarts of milk I buy. The amount of sugar needed in a recipe varies directly with the amount of butter used. The number of inches between two cities on a map varies directly with the number of miles between these cities.

Whenever two quantities vary directly, a problem can be solved by using a proportion. However, be very careful to compare the same units, in the same order in both fractions.

Example: If I pay 20¢ for a 2-ounce package of peanuts, how much should I pay for a pound?

Solution: Here we are comparing cents with ounces, so $\frac{20}{2} = \frac{x}{16}$

In solving a proportion, it is easiest to cross-multiply, remembering that the product of the means (the second and third terms of a proportion) is equal to the product of the extremes (the first and last terms of a proportion).

$2x = 320$

$x = 160$

Remembering that our units were cents, we pay $1.60.

When two fractions are equal, as in a proportion, it is sometimes easier to see what change has taken place in the given numerator or denominator and then to apply the same change to the missing term. In keeping fractions equal, the change will always involve multiplying or dividing by a constant. In the previous example, the denominator was changed from 2 to 16. This involved multiplication by 8; therefore, the numerator (20) must also be multiplied by 8, giving 160 as an answer without any written work necessary. Since time is a very important factor in this type of examination, shortcuts such as this could save critical time.

Example: If a truck can carry m pounds of coal, how many trucks are needed to carry p pounds of coal?

Solution: We are comparing trucks with pounds. This again is a direct variation, because the number of trucks increases as the number of pounds increases.

$$\frac{1}{m} = \frac{x}{p}$$

Solving for x, we have $mx = p$

$$x = \frac{p}{m}$$

Two quantities are said to vary inversely if they change in opposite directions. As one increases, the other decreases.

For example, the number of men I hire to paint my house varies inversely with the number of days the job will take. A doctor's stock of flu vaccine varies inversely with the number of patients he injects. The number of days a given supply of cat food lasts varies inversely with the number of cats being fed.

Whenever two quantities vary inversely, the problem is not solved by a proportion. Instead of dividing the first quantity by the second and setting the quotients equal as we did in direct variation, we multiply the first quantity by the second and set the products equal.

Example: If a case of cat food can feed 5 cats for 4 days, how long would it feed 8 cats?

Solution: Since this is a case of inverse variation (the more cats, the fewer days), we multiply the number of cats by the number of days in each instance and set them equal.

$5 \cdot 4 = 8 \cdot x$

$20 = 8x$

$2\frac{1}{2} = x$

PRACTICE EXERCISES IV

Work out each problem in the space provided. Circle the letter that appears before your answer.

1. If 60 ft. of uniform wire weighs 80 pounds, what is the weight of 2 yards of the same wire?

   (A) $2\frac{2}{3}$ (B) 6 (C) 2400 (D) 120 (E) 8

2. A gear 50 inches in diameter turns a smaller gear 30 inches in diameter. If the larger gear makes 15 revolutions, how many revolutions does the smaller gear make in that time?

   (A) 9 (B) 12 (C) 20 (D) 25 (E) 30

3. If x men can do a job in h days, how long would y men take to do the same job?

   (A) $\frac{x}{h}$ (B) $\frac{xh}{y}$ (C) $\frac{hy}{x}$ (D) $\frac{xy}{h}$ (E) $\frac{x}{y}$

4. If a furnace uses 40 gallons of oil in a week, how many gallons, to the nearest gallon, does it use in 10 days?

   (A) 57 (B) 4 (C) 28 (D) 400 (E) 58

5. A recipe requires 13 oz. of sugar and 18 oz. of flour. If only 10 oz. of sugar are used, how much flour, to the nearest ounce, should be used?

   (A) 13 (B) 23 (C) 24 (D) 14 (E) 15

6. If a car can drive 25 miles on two gallons of gasoline, how many gallons will be needed for a trip of 150 miles?

   (A) 12 (B) 3 (C) 6 (D) 7 (E) 10

7. A school has enough bread to last 30 children 4 days. If 10 more children are added, how many days will the bread last?

   (A) $5\frac{1}{3}$ (B) $1\frac{1}{3}$ (C) $2\frac{2}{3}$ (D) 12 (E) 3

8. At c cents per pound, what is the cost of a ounces of salami?

   (A) $\frac{c}{a}$ (B) $\frac{a}{c}$ (C) ac (D) $\frac{ac}{16}$ (E) $\frac{16c}{a}$

9. If 3 miles are equivalent to 4.83 kilometers, then 11.27 kilometers are equivalent to how many miles?

   (A) $7\frac{1}{3}$ (B) $2\frac{1}{3}$ (C) 7 (D) 5 (E) $6\frac{1}{2}$

10. If p pencils cost d dollars, how many pencils can be bought for c cents?

    (A) $\frac{100pc}{d}$ (B) $\frac{pc}{100d}$ (C) $\frac{pd}{c}$ (D) $\frac{pc}{d}$ (E) $\frac{cd}{p}$

SOLUTIONS TO PRACTICE EXERCISES IV

1. **(E)** We are comparing *feet* with pounds. The more feet the more pounds. This is DIRECT. Remember to change yards to feet: $\frac{60}{80} = \frac{6}{x}$. The numerator has been divided by 10, so we divide the denominator by 10.

2. **(D)** The larger a gear, the fewer times it revolves in a given period of time. This is INVERSE.
$50 \cdot 15 = 30 \cdot x$
$750 = 30x$
$25 = x$

3. **(B)** The more men, the fewer days. This is INVERSE.
$x \cdot h = y \cdot ?$
$\frac{xh}{y} = ?$

4. **(A)** The more days, the more oil. This is DIRECT. Remember to change a week to days.
$\frac{40}{7} = \frac{x}{10}$
$7x = 400$
$x = 57\frac{1}{7}$

5. **(D)** The more sugar, the more flour. This is DIRECT.
$\frac{13}{18} = \frac{10}{x}$
$13x = 180$
$x = 13\frac{11}{13}$

6. **(A)** The more miles, the more gasoline. This is DIRECT.
$\frac{25}{2} = \frac{150}{x}$
$25x = 300$
$x = 12$

7. **(E)** The more children, the less days. This is INVERSE.
$30 \cdot 4 = 40 \cdot x$
$120 = 4x$
$3 = x$

8. **(D)** The more salami, the more it will cost.
This is DIRECT. Remember to change a pound to 16 ounces.
$\frac{c}{16} = \frac{x}{a}$
$x = \frac{ac}{16}$

9. **(C)** The more miles, the more kilometers. This is DIRECT.

$$\frac{3}{4.83} = \frac{x}{11.27}$$
$$4.83x = 33.81$$
$$x = 7$$

10. **(B)** The more pencils, the more cost. This is DIRECT. Remember to change dollars to cents.

$$\frac{p}{100d} = \frac{x}{c}$$
$$x = \frac{pc}{100d}$$

V. PERCENT

"Percent" means "out of 100." Understanding this concept, it then becomes very easy to change a % to an equivalent decimal or fraction.

$$5\% = \frac{5}{100} = .05$$

$$2.6\% = \frac{2.6}{100} = .026$$

$$c\% = \frac{c}{100} \text{ or } \frac{1}{100} \cdot c = .01c$$

$$\frac{1}{2}\% = \frac{\frac{1}{2}}{100} = \frac{1}{100} \cdot \frac{1}{2} = \frac{1}{100} \cdot .5 = .005$$

To change a % to a decimal, we must remove the % sign and divide by 100. This has the effect of moving the decimal point two places to the LEFT.

Example: 37% = .37

To change a decimal to a %, we must put in the % sign and multiply by 100. This has the effect of moving the decimal point two places to the RIGHT.

Example: .043 = 4.3%

To change a % to a fraction, we must remove the % sign and divide by 100. This has the effect of putting the % over 100 and reducing the resulting fraction.

Example: $75\% = \frac{75}{100} = \frac{3}{4}$

To change a fraction to a %, we must put in the % sign and multiply by 100.

Example: $\frac{1}{8} = \frac{1}{8} \cdot 100\% = \frac{100}{8}\% = 12\frac{1}{2}\%$

Certain fractional equivalents of common percents occur frequently enough that they should be memorized. Learning the values in the following table will make your work with percent problems much easier.

PERCENT-FRACTION EQUIVALENT TABLE

$50\% = \frac{1}{2}$

$25\% = \frac{1}{4}$

$75\% = \frac{3}{4}$

$10\% = \frac{1}{10}$

$30\% = \frac{3}{10}$

$70\% = \frac{7}{10}$

$90\% = \frac{9}{10}$

$33\frac{1}{3}\% = \frac{1}{3}$

$66\frac{2}{3}\% = \frac{2}{3}$

$20\% = \frac{1}{5}$

$40\% = \frac{2}{5}$

$60\% = \frac{3}{5}$

$80\% = \frac{4}{5}$

$12\frac{1}{2}\% = \frac{1}{8}$

$37\frac{1}{2}\% = \frac{3}{8}$

$62\frac{1}{2}\% = \frac{5}{8}$

$87\frac{1}{2}\% = \frac{7}{8}$

$16\frac{2}{3}\% = \frac{1}{6}$

$83\frac{1}{3}\% = \frac{5}{6}$

Most percentage problems can be solved by using the following proportion:

$$\frac{\%}{100} = \frac{\text{part}}{\text{whole}}$$

Although this method works, it often yields unnecessarily large numbers that are difficult to compute. We will look at the three basic types of percent problems and compare methods for solving them.

A. To find a % of a number.
Example: Find 27% of 92.

PROPORTION METHOD

$$\frac{27}{100} = \frac{x}{92}$$
$$100x = 2484$$
$$x = 24.84$$

SHORT METHOD

Change the % to its decimal or fraction equivalent and multiply. Use fractions only when they are among the familiar ones given in the previous chart.

```
   92
  .27
 ----
  644
 184
 ----
24.84
```

Example: Find $12\frac{1}{2}\%$ of 96.

PROPORTION METHOD

$$\frac{12\frac{1}{2}}{100} = \frac{x}{96}$$
$$100x = 1200$$
$$x = 12$$

DECIMAL METHOD

```
    96
  .125
 -----
   480
  192
  96
 -----
12.000
```

FRACTION METHOD

$$\frac{1}{8} \cdot 96 = 12$$

Which method is easiest? It really pays to memorize those fractional equivalents.

B. To find a number when a % of it is given.

Example: 7 is 5% of what number?

PROPORTION METHOD

$$\frac{5}{100} = \frac{7}{x}$$
$$5x = 700$$
$$x = 140$$

SHORTER METHOD

Translate the problem into an algebraic equation. In doing this, the % must be written as a fraction or decimal.

$$7 = .05x$$
$$700 = 5x$$
$$140 = x$$

Example: 20 is $33\frac{1}{3}$% of what number?

PROPORTION METHOD

$$\frac{33\frac{1}{3}}{100} = \frac{20}{x}$$
$$33\frac{1}{3}x = 2000$$
$$\frac{100}{3}x = 2000$$
$$100x = 6000$$
$$x = 60$$

SHORTER METHOD

$$20 = \frac{1}{3}x$$
$$60 = x$$

Just think of the time you save and the number of extra problems you will get to solve if you know that $33\frac{1}{3}\% = \frac{1}{3}$.

C. To find what % one number is of another.

Example: 90 is what % of 1500?

PROPORTION METHOD

$$\frac{x}{100} = \frac{90}{1500}$$
$$1500x = 9000$$
$$15x = 90$$
$$x = 6$$

SHORTER METHOD

Put the part over the whole. Reduce the fraction and multiply by 100.

$$\frac{90}{1500} = \frac{9}{150} = \frac{3}{50} \cdot 100 = 6$$

Example: 7 is what % of 35?

PROPORTION METHOD

$$\frac{x}{100} = \frac{7}{35}$$
$$35x = 700$$
$$x = 20$$

SHORTER METHOD

$$\frac{7}{35} = \frac{1}{5} = 20\%$$

Example: 18 is what % of 108?

PROPORTION METHOD

$$\frac{x}{100} = \frac{18}{108}$$

$$108x = 1800$$

Time-consuming long division is necessary to get:

$$x = 16\frac{2}{3}$$

SHORTER METHOD

$$\frac{18}{108} = \frac{9}{54} = \frac{1}{6} = 16\frac{2}{3}\%$$

Once again, if you know your fraction equivalents of common percents, computation can be done in a few seconds.

D. When the percentage involved is over 100, the same methods apply.

Example: Find 125% of 64

PROPORTION METHOD

$$\frac{125}{100} = \frac{x}{64}$$

$$100x = 8000$$

$$x = 80$$

DECIMAL METHOD

```
    64
  1.25
 -----
   320
  128
  64
 -----
 80.00
```

FRACTION METHOD

$$1\frac{1}{4} \cdot 64$$

$$\frac{5}{\cancel{4}} \cdot \overset{16}{\cancel{64}} = 80$$

Example: 36 is 150% of what number?

PROPORTION METHOD

$$\frac{150}{100} = \frac{36}{x}$$

$$150x = 3600$$

$$15x = 360$$

$$x = 24$$

DECIMAL METHOD

$$36 = 1.50x$$

$$360 = 15x$$

$$24 = x$$

FRACTION METHOD

$$36 = 1\frac{1}{2}x$$

$$36 = \frac{3}{2}x$$

$$72 = 3x$$

$$24 = x$$

Example: 60 is what % of 50?

PROPORTION METHOD

$$\frac{x}{100} = \frac{60}{50}$$

$$50x = 6000$$

$$5x = 600$$

$$x = 120$$

FRACTION METHOD

$$\frac{60}{50} = \frac{6}{5} = 1\frac{1}{5} = 120\%$$

PRACTICE EXERCISES V (PART 1)

Work out each problem in the space provided. Circle the letter that appears before your answer.

1. Write .2% as a decimal.

   (A) .2 (B) .02 (C) .002 (D) 2 (E) 20

2. Write 3.4% as a fraction.

   (A) $\frac{34}{1000}$ (B) $\frac{34}{10}$ (C) $\frac{34}{100}$ (D) $\frac{340}{100}$ (E) $\frac{34}{10{,}000}$

3. Write $\frac{3}{4}$% as a decimal.

   (A) .75 (B) .075 (C) .0075 (D) .00075 (E) 7.5

4. Find 60% of 70.

   (A) 420 (B) 4.2 (C) $116\frac{2}{3}$ (D) 4200 (E) 42

5. What is 175% of 16?

   (A) $9\frac{1}{7}$ (B) 28 (C) 24 (D) 12 (E) 22

6. What percent of 40 is 16?

   (A) 20 (B) $2\frac{1}{2}$ (C) $33\frac{1}{3}$ (D) 250 (E) 40

7. What percent of 16 is 40?

   (A) 20 (B) $2\frac{1}{2}$ (C) 200 (D) 250 (E) 40

8. $4 is 20% of what?

   (A) $5 (B) $20 (C) $200 (D) $5 (E) $10

9. 12 is 150% of what number?

   (A) 18 (B) 15 (C) 6 (D) 9 (E) 8

10. How many sixteenths are there in $87\frac{1}{2}$%?

    (A) 7 (B) 14 (C) 3.5 (D) 13 (E) 15

SOLUTIONS TO PRACTICE EXERCISES V (PART 1)

1. **(C)** $.2\% = .002$ Decimal point moves to the LEFT two places.

2. **(A)** $3.4\% = \frac{3.4}{100} = \frac{34}{1000}$

3. **(C)** $\frac{3}{4}\% = .75\% = \frac{.75}{100} = \frac{75}{10{,}000}$

4. **(E)** $60\% = \frac{3}{5}$ $\quad \frac{3}{5} \cdot 70 = 42$

5. **(B)** $175\% = 1\frac{3}{4}$ $\quad \frac{7}{4} \cdot 16 = 28$

6. **(E)** $\frac{16}{40} = \frac{2}{5} = 40\%$

7. **(D)** $\frac{40}{16} = \frac{5}{2} = 2\frac{1}{2} = 250\%$

8. **(B)** $20\% = \frac{1}{5}$, so $4 = \frac{1}{5}x$ $\quad 20 = x$

9. **(E)** $150\% = 1\frac{1}{2}$ $\quad \frac{3}{2}x = 12$ $\quad 3x = 24$ $\quad x = 8$

10. **(B)** $87\frac{1}{2}\% = \frac{7}{8} = \frac{14}{16}$

VERBAL PROBLEMS INVOLVING PERCENT

Certain types of business situations are excellent applications of percent.

A. Percent of Increase or Decrease

The percent of increase or decrease is found by putting the amount of increase or decrease over the original amount and changing this fraction to a percent as explained in a previous section.

Example: Over a five-year period, the enrollment at South High dropped from 1,000 students to 800. Find the percent of decrease.

Solution: $\frac{200}{1000} = \frac{20}{100} = 20\%$

Example: A company normally employs 100 people. During a slow spell, it fired 20% of its employees. By what % must it now increase its staff to return to full capacity?

Solution: $20\% = \frac{1}{5}$ $\quad \frac{1}{5} \cdot 100 = 20$

The company now has $100 - 20 = 80$ employees. If it then increases by 20, the percent of increase is $\frac{20}{80} = \frac{1}{4}$ or 25%.

B. Discount

A discount is usually expressed as a percent of the marked price, which will be deducted from the marked price to determine the sale price.

Example: Bill's Hardware offers a 20% discount on all appliances during a sale week. How much must Mrs. Russell pay for a washing machine marked at $280?

LONG METHOD

$20\% = \frac{1}{5}$

$\frac{1}{5} \cdot 280 =$ $56 discount

$280 − $56 = $224 sale price

The danger inherent in this method is that $56 is sure to be among the multiple choice answers.

SHORTCUT METHOD

If there is a 20% discount, Mrs. Russell will pay 80% of the marked price.

$80\% = \frac{4}{5}$

$\frac{4}{5} \cdot 280 =$ $224 sale price

Example: A store offers a television set marked at $340 less discounts of 10% and 5%. Another store offers the same set with a single discount of 15%. How much does the buyer save by buying at the better price?

Solution: In the first store, the initial discount means the buyer pays 90% or $\frac{9}{10}$ of 340, which is $306. The additional 5% discount means the buyer pays 95% of $306, or $290.70. Note that the second discount must be figured on the first sale price. Taking 5% of $306 is a smaller amount than taking the additional 5% off $340. The second store will therefore have a lower sale price. In the second store, the buyer will pay 85% of $340, or $289, making the price $1.70 less than in the first store.

C. Commission

Many salesmen earn money on a commission basis. In order to inspire sales, they are paid a percentage of the value of goods sold. This amount is called a commission.

Example: Mr. Saunders works at Brown's Department Store, where he is paid $80 per week in salary plus a 4% commission on all his sales. How much does he earn in a week in which he sells $4,032 worth of merchandise?

Solution: Find 4% of $4,032 and add this amount to $80.

$$\begin{array}{r} 4032 \\ .04 \\ \hline \end{array}$$

$161.28 + $80 = $241.28

Example: Bill Olson delivers newspapers for a dealer and keeps 8% of all money collected. One month he was able to keep $16. How much did he forward to the newspaper?

Solution: First we find how much he collected by asking 16 is 8% of what number?

$$16 = .08x$$
$$1600 = 8x$$
$$200 = x$$

If Bill collected $200 and kept $16, he gave the dealer $200-$16 or $184.

D. Taxes

Taxes are a percent of money spent or money earned.

Example: Nassau County collects a 7% sales tax on automobiles. If the price of a new Ford is $5,832 before taxes, for what amount will Mrs. Behr have to write her check if she purchases this car?

Solution: Find 7% of $5,832 to find tax and then add it to $5,832. This can be done in one step by finding 107% of $5,832.

```
   5832
   1.07
 ------
  40824
 58320
 ------
$6240.24
```

Example: Mrs. Brady pays income tax at the rate of 10% for the first $10,000 of earned income, 15% for the next $10,000, 20% for the next $10,000 and 25% for all earnings over $30,000. How much income tax must she pay in a year in which she earns $36,500?

Solution:
10% of first $10,000 = $1,000
15% of next $10,000 = $1,500
20% of next $10,000 = $2,000
25% of $6,500 = $1,625
Total tax = $6,125

PRACTICE EXERCISES V (PART 2)

Work out each problem in the space provided. Circle the letter that appears before your answer.

1. A suit is sold for $68 while marked at $80. What is the rate of discount?

   (A) 15% (B) 12% (C) $17\frac{11}{17}$% (D) 20% (E) 24%

2. A man buys a radio for $70 after receiving a discount of 20%. What was the marked price?

   (A) $84 (B) $56 (C) $87.50 (D) $92 (E) $90

3. Willie receives r% commission on a sale of s dollars. How many dollars does he receive?

(A) rs (B) $\frac{r}{s}$ (C) 100rs (D) $\frac{r}{100s}$ (E) $\frac{rs}{100}$

4. A refrigerator was sold for $273, yielding a 30% profit on the cost. For how much should it be sold to yield only a 10% profit on the cost?

(A) $210 (B) $231 (C) $221 (D) $235 (E) $240

5. What single discount is equivalent to two successive discounts of 10% and 15%?

(A) 25% (B) 24% (C) 24.5% (D) 23.5% (E) 22%

6. The net price of a certain article is $306 after successive discounts of 15% and 10% have been allowed on the marked price. What is the marked price?

(A) $234.09 (B) $400 (C) $382.50 (D) $408 (E) none of these

7. If a merchant makes a profit of 20% based on the selling price of an article, what percent does he make on the cost?

(A) 20 (B) 40 (C) 25 (D) 80 (E) none of these

8. A certain radio costs a merchant $72. At what price must he sell it if he is to make a profit of 20% of the selling price?

(A) $86.40 (B) $92 (C) $90 (D) $144 (E) $148

9. A baseball team has won 40 games out of 60 played. It has 32 more games to play. How many of these must the team win to make its record 75% for the season?

(A) 26 (B) 29 (C) 28 (D) 30 (E) 32

10. If prices are reduced 25% and sales increase 20%, what is the net effect on gross receipts?
(A) They increase by 5%.
(B) They decrease by 5%.
(C) They remain the same.
(D) They increase by 10%.
(E) They decrease by 10%.

11. A saleswoman earns 5% on all sales between $200 and $600, and 8% on all sales over $600. What is her commission in a week in which her sales total $800?

(A) $20 (B) $46 (C) $88 (D) $36 (E) $78

12. If the enrollment at State U. was 3,000 in 1950 and 12,000 in 1975, what was the percent of increase in enrollment?

    (A) 125% (B) 25% (C) 300% (D) 400% (E) 3%

13. 6 students in a class failed algebra. This represents $16\frac{2}{3}\%$ of the class. How many students passed the course?

    (A) 48 (B) 36 (C) 42 (D) 30 (E) 32

14. 95% of the residents of Coral Estates live in private homes. 40% of these live in air-conditioned homes. What percent of the residents of Coral Estates live in air-conditioned homes?

    (A) 3% (B) 30% (C) 3.8% (D) 40% (E) 38%

15. Mr. Carlson receives a salary of $50 a month and a commission of 5% on all sales. What must be the amount of his sales in July so that his total monthly income is $240?

    (A) $4,800 (B) $3,800 (C) $760 (D) $380 (E) $2,500

SOLUTIONS TO PRACTICE EXERCISES V (PART 2)

1. **(A)** The amount of discount is \$12. Rate of discount is figured on the original price.
$\frac{12}{80} = \frac{3}{20} \quad \frac{3}{20} \cdot 100 = 15\%$

2. **(C)** \$70 represents 80% of the marked price.
$70 = .80x$
$700 = 8x$
$\$87.50 = x$

3. **(E)** $r\% = \frac{r}{100}$
Commission is $\frac{r}{100} \cdot s = \frac{rs}{100}$

4. **(B)** \$273 represents 130% of the cost.
$1.30x = 273$
$13x = 2730$
$x = \$210 = \text{cost}$
New price will add 10% of cost, or \$21, for profit.
New price = \$231

5. **(D)** Work with a simple figure, such as 100.
First sale price is 90% of \$100, or \$90.
Final sale price is 85% of \$90, or \$76.50
Total discount was \$100 − \$76.50 = \$23.50
$\%\text{ of discount} = \frac{23.50}{100}$ or 23.5%

6. **(B)** If marked price = m, first sale price = .85m and net price = .90(.85m) = .765m
$.765m = 306$
$m = 400$
In this case, it would be easy to work from the answers.
15% of \$400 is \$60, making a first sale price of \$340.
10% of this price is \$34, making the net price \$306.
Answers (A), (C), and (D) would not give a final answer in whole dollars.

7. **(C)** Use an easy amount of \$100 for the selling price. If profit is 20% of the selling price, or \$20, cost is \$80. Profit based on cost is $\frac{20}{80} = \frac{1}{4} = 25\%$

8. **(C)** If profit is to be 20% of selling price, cost must be 80% of selling price.
$72 = .80x$
$720 = 8x$
$90 = x$

9. **(B)** The team must win 75%, or $\frac{3}{4}$, of the games played during the entire season. With 60 games played and 32 more to play, the team must win $\frac{3}{4}$ of 92 games in all. $\frac{3}{4} \cdot 92 = 69$. Since 40 games have already been won, the team must win 29 additional games.

10. **(E)** Let original price = p, and original sales = s. Therefore, original gross receipts = ps. Let new price = .75p, and new sales = 1.20s. Therefore, new gross receipts = .90ps. Gross receipts are only 90% of what they were.

11. **(D)** 5% of sales between \$200 and \$600 is .05(400) = \$20. 8% of sales over \$600 is .08(200) = \$16. Total commission = \$20 + \$16 = \$36

12. **(C)** Increase is 9000. Percent of increase is figured on original. $\frac{9000}{3000} = 3$ $= 300\%$

13. **(D)** $16\frac{2}{3}\% = \frac{1}{6}$

$6 = \frac{1}{6}x$

$36 = x$

36 students in class. 6 failed. 30 passed.

14. **(E)** $40\% = \frac{2}{5}$

$\frac{2}{5}$ of 95% = 38%

15. **(B)** \$50 + .05s = \$240

.05s = 190

5s = 19,000

s = \$3,800

VI. AVERAGES

The concept of average is familiar to most students. To find the average of n numbers, simply add the numbers and divide by n.

Example: Find the average of 32, 50 and 47.

Solution:

$$\begin{array}{r} 32 \\ 50 \\ \underline{47} \\ 3\overline{)129} \\ 43 \end{array}$$

A more frequently encountered type of average problem will give the average and ask you to find a missing term.

Example: The average of three numbers is 43. If two of the numbers are 32 and 50, find the third number.

Solution: Using the definition of average, write the equation

$$\frac{32 + 50 + x}{3} = 43$$
$$32 + 50 + x = 129$$
$$82 + x = 129$$
$$x = 47$$

Another concept to be understood is the weighted average.

Example: Andrea has four grades of 90 and two grades of 80 during the spring semester of calculus. What is her average in the course for this semester?

Solution:

$$\begin{array}{r} 90 \\ 90 \\ 90 \\ 90 \\ 80 \\ \underline{80} \\ 6\overline{)520} \\ 86\frac{2}{3} \end{array}$$

or

$$\begin{array}{r} 90 \cdot 4 = 360 \\ 80 \cdot 2 = \underline{160} \\ 6\overline{)520} \\ 86\frac{2}{3} \end{array}$$

Be sure to understand that we cannot simply average 90 and 80, since there are more grades of 90 than 80.

The final concept of average that should be mastered is that of average rate. The average rate for a trip is the total distance covered, divided by the total time used.

Example: In driving from New York to Boston, Mr. Portney drove for 3 hours at 40 miles per hour and 1 hour at 48 miles per hour. What was his average rate for this portion of the trip?

Solution: $\text{Average rate} = \dfrac{\text{Total distance}}{\text{Total time}}$

$$\text{Average rate} = \frac{3\,(40) + 1\,(48)}{3 + 1}$$

$$\text{Average rate} = \frac{168}{4} = 42 \text{ miles per hour}$$

Since more of the trip was driven at 40 m.p.h. than at 48 m.p.h., the average should be closer to 40 than to 48, which it is. This will help you to check your answer, or to pick out the correct choice in a multiple-choice question.

PRACTICE EXERCISES VI

Work out each problem in the space provided. Circle the letter that appears before your answer.

1. Dan had an average of 72 on his first four math tests. After taking the next test, his average dropped to 70. Find his most recent test grade.

   (A) 60 (B) 62 (C) 64 (D) 66 (E) 68

2. Find the average of $\sqrt{.64}$, .85, and $\frac{9}{10}$.

   (A) $\frac{21}{25}$ (B) 3.25 (C) 2.55 (D) 85% (E) $\frac{4}{5}$

3. The average of two numbers is XY. If the first number is Y, what is the other number?

   (A) 2XY − Y (B) XY − 2Y (C) 2XY − X (D) X (E) XY − Y

4. 30 students had an average of X, while 20 students had an average of 80. The average for the entire group is

   (A) $\frac{X + 80}{50}$ (B) $\frac{X + 80}{2}$ (C) $\frac{50}{X + 80}$ (D) $\frac{3}{5}X + 32$ (E) $\frac{30X + 80}{50}$

5. What is the average of the first 15 positive integers?

   (A) 7 (B) 7.5 (C) 8 (D) 8.5 (E) 9

6. A man travels a distance of 20 miles at 60 miles per hour and then returns over the same route at 40 miles per hour. What is his average rate for the round trip in miles per hour?

   (A) 50 (B) 48 (C) 47 (D) 46 (E) 45

7. A number p equals $\frac{3}{2}$ the average of 10, 12, and q. What is q in terms of p?

   (A) $\frac{2}{3}p - 22$ (B) $\frac{4}{3}p - 22$ (C) $2p - 22$ (D) $\frac{1}{2}p + 11$ (E) $\frac{9}{2}p - 22$

8. Darren has an average of 86 in three examinations. What grade must he receive on his next test if he wants to raise his average to 88?

   (A) 94 (B) 90 (C) 92 (D) 100 (E) 96

9. The heights of the five starters on Redwood High's basketball team are 5′11″, 6′3″, 6′, 6′6″, and 6′2″. The average height of these boys is

   (A) 6′1″ (B) 6′2″ (C) 6′3″ (D) 6′4″ (E) 6′5″

10. Find the average of all numbers from 1 to 100 that end in 2.

   (A) 46 (B) 47 (C) 48 (D) 50 (E) none of these

SOLUTIONS TO PRACTICE EXERCISES VI

1. **(B)** $\frac{4(72) + x}{5} = 70$

   $288 + x = 350$

   $x = 62$

2. **(D)** In order to average these three numbers, they should all be expressed as decimals.

   $\sqrt{.64} = .8$

   $.85 = .85$

   $\frac{9}{10} = .9$

   $3\overline{)2.55}$

   $.85$ This is equal to 85%.

3. **(A)** $\frac{Y + x}{2} = XY$

   $Y + x = 2XY$

   $x = 2XY - Y$

4. **(D)** $\frac{30(X) + 20(80)}{50} = \text{Average}$

   $\frac{30X + 1600}{50} = \frac{3X + 160}{5} = \frac{3}{5}X + 32$

5. **(C)** Positive integers begin with 1.

   $\frac{1+2+3+4+5+6+7+8+9+10+11+12+13+14+15}{15}$

   Since these numbers are evenly spaced, the average will be the middle number, 8.

6. **(B)** Average rate $= \frac{\text{Total distance}}{\text{Total time}}$

   Total distance $= 20 + 20 = 40$

   Since time $= \frac{\text{distance}}{\text{rate}}$, time for first part of trip is $\frac{20}{60}$ or $\frac{1}{3}$ hour, while time for the second part of trip is $\frac{20}{40}$ or $\frac{1}{2}$ hour.

   Total time $= \frac{1}{3} + \frac{1}{2}$ or $\frac{5}{6}$ hour.

   Average rate $= \frac{40}{\frac{5}{6}} = 40 \cdot \frac{6}{5} = 48$

7. **(C)** $p = \frac{3}{2}\left(\frac{10 + 12 + q}{3}\right)$

   $p = \frac{10 + 12 + q}{2}$

   $2p = 22 + q$

   $2p - 22 = q$

8. **(A)** $\frac{3(86) + x}{4} = 88$

$258 + x = 352$

$x = 94$

9. **(B)**

5′11″
6′ 3″
6′
6′ 6″
6′ 2″

29′22″ = 5)30′10″

6′ 2″

10. **(B)** $\frac{2+12+22+32+42+52+62+72+82+92}{10}$

Since these numbers are evenly spaced, the average is the middle number. However, since there is an even number of addends, the average will be halfway between the middle two. Halfway between 42 and 52 is 47.

VII. SIGNED NUMBERS AND EQUATIONS

Basic to successful work in algebra is the ability to compute accurately with signed numbers.

Addition: To add signed numbers with the same sign, add the magnitudes of the numbers and keep the same sign. To add signed numbers with different signs, subtract the magnitudes of the numbers and use the sign of the number with the greater magnitude.

Subtraction: Change the sign of the bottom number and follow the rules for addition.

Multiplication: If there are an odd number of negative signs, the product is negative. An even number of negative signs gives a positive product.

Division: If the signs are the same, the quotient is positive. If the signs are different, the quotient is negative.

PRACTICE EXERCISES VII (PART 1)

Work out each problem in the space provided. Circle the letter that appears before your answer.

1. When $+3$ is added to -5, the sum is

   (A) -8 (B) $+8$ (C) -2 (D) $+2$ (E) -15

2. When -4 and -5 are added, the sum is

   (A) -9 (B) $+9$ (C) -1 (D) $+1$ (E) $+20$

3. Subtract $\begin{array}{r} +3 \\ \underline{-6} \end{array}$

   (A) -3 (B) $+3$ (C) $+18$ (D) -9 (E) $+9$

4. When -5 is subtracted from $+10$, the result is

   (A) $+5$ (B) $+15$ (C) -5 (D) -15 (E) -50

5. $(-6)(-3)$ equals

   (A) -18 (B) $+18$ (C) $+2$ (D) -9 (E) $+9$

6. The product of $(-6)(+\frac{1}{2})(-10)$ is

   (A) $-15\frac{1}{2}$ (B) $15\frac{1}{2}$ (C) -30 (D) $+30$ (E) $+120$

7. When the product of (-4) and $(+3)$ is divided by (-2), the quotient is

   (A) $\frac{1}{2}$ (B) $3\frac{1}{2}$ (C) 6 (D) $-\frac{1}{2}$ (E) -6

SOLUTIONS TO PRACTICE EXERCISES VII (PART 1)

1. **(C)** In adding numbers with opposite signs, subtract their magnitudes (5 − 3 = 2) and use the sign of the number with the greater magnitude (negative).

2. **(A)** In adding numbers with the same sign, add their magnitudes (4 + 5 = 9) and keep the same sign.

3. **(E)** Change the sign of the bottom number and follow the rules for addition.

$$\begin{array}{r} +3 \\ +\ominus 6 \\ \hline +9 \end{array}$$

4. **(B)** Change the sign of the bottom number and follow the rules for addition.

$$\begin{array}{r} +10 \\ +\ominus\ 5 \\ \hline +15 \end{array}$$

5. **(B)** The product of two negative numbers is a positive number.

6. **(D)** The product of an even number of negative numbers is positive.

$(\overset{3}{\cancel{6}})(\frac{1}{\cancel{2}})(10) = 30$

7. **(C)** $(-4)(+3) = -12$ Dividing a negative number by a negative number gives a positive quotient.

$$\frac{-12}{-2} = +6$$

The next step in gaining confidence in algebra is mastering linear equations. Whether an equation involves numbers or only letters, the basic steps are the same.

1. If there are fractions or decimals, remove them by multiplication.
2. Collect all terms containing the unknown for which you are solving on the same side of the equation. Remember that whenever a term crosses the equal sign from one side of the equation to the other, it must pay a toll. That is, it must change its sign.
3. Determine the coefficient of the unknown by combining similar terms or factoring when terms cannot be combined.
4. Divide both sides of the equation by this coefficient.

Example: Solve for x: $5x - 3 = 3x + 5$

Solution:

$$2x = 8$$
$$x = 4$$

Example: Solve for x: $ax - b = cx + d$

Solution:

$$ax - cx = b + d$$
$$x(a - c) = b + d$$
$$x = \frac{b + d}{a - c}$$

Example: Solve for x: $\frac{3}{4}x + 2 = \frac{2}{3}x + 3$

Solution: Multiply by 12: $9x + 24 = 8x + 36$

$$x = 12$$

Example: Solve for x: $.7x + .04 = 2.49$

Solution: Multiply by 100: $70x + 4 = 249$

$$70x = 245$$
$$x = 2.5$$

In solving equations with two unknowns, it is necessary to work with two equations simultaneously. The object is to eliminate one of the two unknowns, and solve the resulting single unknown equation.

Example: Solve for x: $2x - 4y = 2$

$$3x + 5y = 14$$

Solution: Multiply the first equation by 5:

$$10x - 20y = 10$$

Multiply the second equation by 4:

$$12x + 20y = 56$$

Since the y terms now have the same numerical coefficients, but with opposite signs, we can eliminate them by adding the two equations. If they had the same signs, we would eliminate them by subtracting the equations.

Adding, we have: $22x = 66$

$$x = 3$$

Since we were only asked to solve for x, we stop here. If we were asked to solve for both x and y, we would now substitute 3 for x in either equation and solve the resulting equation for y.

$$3(3) + 5y = 14$$
$$9 + 5y = 14$$
$$5y = 5$$
$$y = 1$$

Example: Solve for x: $ax + by = c$

$$dx + ey = f$$

Solution: Multiply the first equation by e:

$$aex + bey = ce$$

Multiply the second equation by b:

$$bdx + bey = bf$$

Since the y terms now have the same coefficient, with the same sign, we eliminate these terms by subtracting the two equations.

$$aex - bdx = ce - bf$$

Factor to determine the coefficient of x.

$$x(ae - bd) = ce - bf$$

Divide by the coefficient of x.

$$x = \frac{ce - bf}{ae - bd}$$

PRACTICE EXERCISES VII (PART 2)

Work out each problem in the space provided. Circle the letter that appears before your answer.

1. If $5x + 6 = 10$, then x equals

   (A) $\frac{16}{5}$ (B) $\frac{5}{16}$ (C) $-\frac{5}{4}$ (D) $\frac{4}{5}$ (E) $\frac{5}{4}$

2. Solve for x: $ax = bx + c$, $a \neq b$

   (A) $\frac{b + c}{a}$ (B) $\frac{c}{a - b}$ (C) $\frac{c}{b - a}$ (D) $\frac{a - b}{c}$ (E) $\frac{c}{a + b}$

3. Solve for k: $\frac{k}{3} + \frac{k}{4} = 1$

   (A) $\frac{11}{8}$ (B) $\frac{8}{11}$ (C) $\frac{7}{12}$ (D) $\frac{12}{7}$ (E) $\frac{1}{7}$

4. If $x + y = 8p$ and $x - y = 6q$, then x is

   (A) 7pq (B) $4p + 3q$ (C) pq (D) $4p - 3q$ (E) $8p + 6q$

5. If $7x = 3x + 12$, then $2x + 5 =$

   (A) 10 (B) 11 (C) 12 (D) 13 (E) 14

6. In the equation $y = x^2 + rx - 3$, for what value of r will $y = 11$ when $x = 2$?

   (A) 6 (B) 5 (C) 4 (D) $3\frac{1}{2}$ (E) 0

7. If $1 + \frac{1}{t} = \frac{t + 1}{t}$, what does t equal?

   (A) +1 only (B) +1 or −1 only (C) +1 or +2 only
   (D) no values (E) all values except 0

8. If $.23m = .069$, m =

   (A) .003 (B) .03 (C) .3 (D) 3 (E) 30

9. If $35rt + 8 = 42rt$, then rt =

   (A) $\frac{8}{7}$ (B) $\frac{8}{87}$ (C) $\frac{7}{8}$ (D) $\frac{87}{8}$ (E) $-\frac{8}{7}$

10. For what values of n is $n + 5$ equal to $n - 5$?

    (A) no value (B) 0 (C) all negative values
    (D) all positive values (E) all values

SOLUTIONS TO PRACTICE EXERCISES VII (PART 2)

1. **(D)** $5x = 4 \quad x = \frac{4}{5}$

2. **(B)** $ax - bx = c \quad x(a - b) = c \quad x = \frac{c}{a - b}$

3. **(D)** Multiply by 12: $4k + 3k = 12$
$$7k = 12$$
$$k = \frac{12}{7}$$

4. **(B)** Add equations to eliminate y:
$$2x = 8p + 6q$$
Divide by 2:
$$x = 4p + 3q$$

5 **(B)** Solve for x: $4x = 12$
$$x = 3$$
$$2x + 5 = 2(3) + 5 = 11$$

6. **(B)** Substitute given values: $11 = 4 + 2r - 3$
$$10 = 2r$$
$$r = 5$$

7. **(E)** Multiply by t: $t + 1 = t + 1$
This is an identity and therefore true for all values. However, since t was a denominator in the given equation, t may not equal 0, as we can never divide by 0.

8. **(C)** Multiply by 100 to make coefficient an integer.
$$23x = 6.9$$
$$x = .3$$

9. **(A)** Even though this equation has two unknowns, we are asked to solve for rt, which may be treated as a single unknown.
$$8 = 7rt$$
$$\frac{8}{7} = rt$$

10. **(A)** There is no number such that when 5 is added, we get the same result as when 5 is subtracted. Do not confuse choices (A) and (B). Choice (B) would mean that the number 0 satisfies the equation, which it does not.

In solving quadratic equations, remember that there will always be two roots, even though these roots may be equal. A complete quadratic equation is of the form $ax^2 + bx + c = 0$ and, in the SAT, can always be solved by factoring.

Example: $x^2 + 7x + 12 = 0$

Solution: $(x \quad)(x \quad) = 0$

Since the last term of the equation is positive, both factors must have the same sign, since the last two terms multiply to a positive product.

If the middle term is also positive, both factors must be positive, since they also add to a positive sum.

$$(x + 4)(x + 3) = 0$$

If the product of two factors is 0, each factor may be set equal to 0, yielding the values for x of −4 or −3.

Example: $x^2 + 7x - 18 = 0$

Solution: $(x \quad)(x \quad) = 0$

We are now looking for two numbers that multiply to −18; therefore, they must have opposite signs. To yield +7 as a middle coefficient, the numbers must be +9 and −2.

$$(x + 9)(x - 2) = 0$$

This equation gives the roots −9 and +2.

Incomplete quadratic equations are those in which b or c is equal to 0.

Example: $x^2 - 16 = 0$

Solution: $x^2 = 16$

$x = \pm 4$ Remember there must be 2 roots.

Example: $4x^2 - 9 = 0$

Solution: $4x^2 = 9$

$$x^2 = \frac{9}{4}$$

$$x = \pm\frac{3}{2}$$

Example: $x^2 + 4x = 0$

Solution: Never divide through an equation by the unknown, as this would yield an equation of lower degree having fewer roots than the original equation. Always factor this type of equation.

$$x(x + 4) = 0$$

The roots are 0 and −4.

Example: $4x^2 - 9x = 0$

Solution: $x(4x - 9) = 0$

The roots are 0 and $\frac{9}{4}$.

In solving equations containing radicals, always get the radical alone on one side of the equation, then square both sides to remove the radical and solve. Remember that all solutions to radical equations must be checked, as squaring both sides may sometimes result in extraneous roots.

Example: $\sqrt{x + 5} = 7$

Solution: $x + 5 = 49$

$x = 44$

Checking, we have $\sqrt{49} = 7$, which is true.

Example: $\sqrt{x} = -6$

Solution: $x = 36$

Checking, we have $\sqrt{36} = -6$ which is not true, as the radical sign means the positive, or principal, square root only. $\sqrt{36} = 6$, not −6, and therefore this equation has no solution.

Example: $\sqrt{x^2 + 6} - 3 = x$

Solution: $\sqrt{x^2 + 6} = x + 3$

$$x^2 + 6 = x^2 + 6x + 9$$
$$6 = 6x + 9$$
$$-3 = 6x$$
$$-\frac{1}{2} = x$$

Checking, we have $\sqrt{6\frac{1}{4}} - 3 = -\frac{1}{2}$

$$\sqrt{\frac{25}{4}} - 3 = -\frac{1}{2}$$
$$\frac{5}{2} - 3 = -\frac{1}{2}$$
$$2\frac{1}{2} - 3 = -\frac{1}{2}$$
$$-\frac{1}{2} = -\frac{1}{2}$$

This is a true statement. Therefore, $-\frac{1}{2}$ is a true root.

PRACTICE EXERCISES VII (PART 3)

Work out the problem in the space provided. Circle the letter that appears before your answer.

1. Solve for x: $x^2 - 2x - 15 = 0$

   (A) +5 or −3 (B) −5 or +3 (C) −5 or −3

   (D) +5 or +3 (E) none of these

2. Solve for x: $x^2 + 12 = 8x$

   (A) +6 or −2 (B) −6 or +2 (C) −6 or −2

   (D) +6 or +2 (E) none of these

3. Solve for x: $4x^2 = 12$

   (A) $\sqrt{3}$ (B) 3 or −3 (C) $\sqrt{3}$ or $-\sqrt{3}$

   (D) $\sqrt{3}$ or $\sqrt{-3}$ (E) 9 or −9

4. Solve for x: $3x^2 = 4x$

   (A) $\frac{4}{3}$ (B) $\frac{4}{3}$ or 0 (C) $-\frac{4}{3}$ or 0

   (D) $\frac{4}{3}$ or $-\frac{4}{3}$ (E) none of these

5. Solve for x: $\sqrt{x^2 + 7} - 2 = x - 1$

(A) no values (B) $\frac{1}{3}$ (C) $-\frac{1}{3}$

(D) -3 (E) 3

SOLUTIONS TO PRACTICE EXERCISES VII (PART 3)

1. **(A)** $(x - 5)(x + 3) = 0$
   $x = 5 \text{ or } -3$

2. **(D)** $x^2 - 8x + 12 = 0$
   $(x - 6)(x - 2) = 0$
   $x = 6 \text{ or } 2$

3. **(C)** $x^2 = 3$
   $x = \pm\sqrt{3}$

4. **(B)** $3x^2 - 4x = 0$
   $x(3x - 4) = 0$
   $x = 0 \text{ or } \frac{4}{3}$

5. **(E)** $\sqrt{x^2 + 7} = x + 1$
   $x^2 + 7 = x^2 + 2x + 1$
   $6 = 2x$
   $x = 3$
   Checking: $\sqrt{16} - 2 = 3 - 1$
   $4 - 2 = 3 - 1$
   $2 = 2$

VIII. LITERAL EXPRESSIONS

Many students who can compute easily with numbers become confused when they work with letters. The computational processes are exactly the same. Just think of how you would do the problem with numbers and do exactly the same thing with letters.

Example: Find the number of inches in 2 feet 5 inches.
Solution: Since there are 12 inches in a foot, we multiply 2 feet by 12 to change it to 24 inches and then add 5 more inches, giving an answer of 29 inches.

Example: Find the number of inches in f feet and i inches.
Solution: Doing exactly as we did above, we multiply f by 12, giving 12f inches, and add i more inches, giving an answer of $12f + i$ inches.

Example: A telephone call from New York to Chicago costs 85 cents for the first three minutes and 21 cents for each additional minute. Find the cost of an eight minute call at this rate.
Solution: The first three minutes cost 85 cents. There are five additional minutes above the first three. These five are billed at 21 cents each, for a cost of \$1.05. The total cost is \$1.90.

Example: A telephone call costs c cents for the first three minutes and d cents for each additional minute. Find the cost of a call which lasts m minutes if $m > 3$.
Solution: The first three minutes cost c cents. The number of *additional* minutes is $(m - 3)$. These are billed at d cents each, for a cost of $d(m - 3)$ or $dm - 3d$. Thus the total cost is $c + dm - 3d$. Remember that the first three minutes have been paid for in the basic charge, therefore you must subtract 3 from the total number of minutes to find the *additional* minutes.

PRACTICE EXERCISES VIII

Work out each problem in the space provided. Circle the letter that appears before your answer.

1. David had d dollars. After a shopping trip, he returned with c cents. How many cents did he spend?

   (A) $d - c$ (B) $c - d$ (C) $100d - c$ (D) $100c - d$ (E) $d - 100c$

2. How many ounces are there in p pounds and q ounces?

   (A) $\frac{p}{16} + q$ (B) pq (C) $p + 16q$ (D) $p + q$ (E) $16p + q$

3. How many passengers can be seated on a plane with r rows, if each row consists of d double seats and t triple seats?

(A) rdt (B) rd+rt (C) 2dr+3tr (D) 3dr+2tr (E) rd+t

4. How many dimes are there in 4x − 1 cents?

(A) 40x − 10 (B) $\frac{2}{5}x - \frac{1}{10}$ (C) 40x − 1 (D) 4x − 1 (E) 20x − 5

5. If u represents the tens' digit of a certain number and t represents the units' digit, then the number with the digits reversed can be represented by

(A) 10t + u (B) 10u + t (C) tu (D) ut (E) t + u

6. Joe spent k cents of his allowance and has r cents left. How many dollars was his allowance?

(A) k + r (B) k − r (C) 100(k + r) (D) $\frac{k + r}{100}$ (E) 100kr

7. If p pounds of potatoes cost $K, find the cost (in cents) of one pound of potatoes.

(A) $\frac{K}{p}$ (B) $\frac{K}{100p}$ (C) $\frac{p}{K}$ (D) $\frac{100K}{p}$ (E) $\frac{100p}{K}$

8. Mr. Rabner rents a car for d days. He pays m dollars per day for each of the first 7 days, and half that rate for each additional day. Find the total charge if d > 7.

(A) m + 2m(d − 7) (B) $m + \frac{m}{2}(d - 7)$ (C) $7m + \frac{m}{2}(d - 7)$

(D) $7m + \frac{md}{2}$ (E) 7m + 2md

9. A salesman earns 90 dollars per week plus a 4% commission on all sales over $1000. One month he sells $r worth of merchandise (r > 1000). How many dollars does he earn that month?

(A) 50 + .04r (B) .04r − 50 (C) .04r + 90

(D) r + 3.60 (E) .04(r − 90)

10. Elliot's allowance was just raised to k dollars per week. He gets a raise of c dollars per week every 2 years. How much will his allowance be per week y years from now?

(A) k + cy (B) k + 2cy (C) $k + \frac{1}{2}cy$ (D) k + 2c (E) ky + 2c

SOLUTIONS TO PRACTICE EXERCISES VIII

1. **(C)** Since the answer is to be in cents, we change d dollars to cents by multiplying by 100 and subtract the c cents he spent.

2. **(E)** There are 16 ounces in a pound. Therefore, we must multiply p pounds by 16 to change to ounces and then add q more ounces.

3. **(C)** Each double seat holds 2 people, so d double seats hold 2d people. Each triple seat holds 3 people, so t triple seats hold 3t people. Therefore, each row holds 2d + 3t people. If there are r rows, we must multiply the number of people in each row by r.

4. **(B)** To change cents to dimes, we must divide by 10.
$$\frac{4x - 1}{10} = \frac{4}{10}x - \frac{1}{10} = \frac{2}{5}x - \frac{1}{10}$$

5. **(A)** The original number would be 10u + t. The number with the digits reversed would be 10t + u.

6. **(D)** Joe's allowance was k + r cents. To change this to dollars, we must divide by 100.

7. **(D)** This can be solved by using a proportion. Remember to change $K to 100K cents.
$$\frac{p}{100K} = \frac{1}{x}$$
$$px = 100K$$
$$x = \frac{100K}{p}$$

8. **(C)** He pays m dollars for each of 7 days, for a total of 7m dollars. Then he pays $\frac{1}{2}$m dollars for (d − 7) days, for a cost of $\frac{m}{2}(d - 7)$.

   The total charge is $7m + \frac{m}{2}(d - 7)$.

9. **(A)** He gets a commission of 4% of (r − 1000), or .04(r − 1000), which is .04r − 40. Adding this to 90, we have .04r + 50.

10. **(C)** Since he gets a raise only every 2 years, in y years he will get $\frac{1}{2}y$ raises. Each raise is c dollars, so with $\frac{1}{2}y$ raises his present allowance will be increased by $c(\frac{1}{2}y)$.

IX. ROOTS AND RADICALS

Rules for addition and subtraction of radicals are much the same as for addition and subtraction of letters. The radicals must be exactly the same if they are to be added or subtracted and merely serve as a label that does not change.

Example: $4\sqrt{2} + 3\sqrt{2} = 7\sqrt{2}$
Example: $\sqrt{2} + 2\sqrt{3}$ cannot be added.
Example: $\sqrt{2} + \sqrt{3}$ cannot be added.

Sometimes, when the radicals are not the same, simplification of one or more radicals will make them the same. Remember that radicals are simplified by removing any perfect square factors.

Example: $\sqrt{27} + \sqrt{75}$
Solution: $\sqrt{9 \cdot 3} + \sqrt{25 \cdot 3}$
$3\sqrt{3} + 5\sqrt{3} = 8\sqrt{3}$

In multiplication and division, the radicals are again treated the same way as letters. They are factors and must be handled as such.
Example: $\sqrt{2} \cdot \sqrt{3} = \sqrt{6}$
Example: $2\sqrt{5} \cdot 3\sqrt{7} = 6\sqrt{35}$
Example: $(2\sqrt{3})^2 = 2\sqrt{3} \cdot 2\sqrt{3} = 4 \cdot 3 = 12$
Example: $\frac{\sqrt{75}}{\sqrt{3}} = \sqrt{25} = 5$
Example: $\frac{10\sqrt{3}}{5\sqrt{3}} = 2$

In simplifying radicals that contain a sum or difference under the radical sign, we must add or subtract first and then take the square root.

Example: $\sqrt{\frac{x^2}{9} + \frac{x^2}{16}}$

Solution: $\sqrt{\frac{16x^2 + 9x^2}{144}} = \sqrt{\frac{25x^2}{144}} = \frac{5x}{12}$

Had we taken the square root of each term before combining, we would have $\frac{x}{3} + \frac{x}{4}$, or $\frac{7x}{12}$, which is clearly not the same answer. Remember that $\sqrt{25}$ is 5. However if we write $\sqrt{25}$ as $\sqrt{16 + 9}$ we cannot say it is 4 + 3 or 7. *Always* combine the quantities within a radical sign into a single term before taking the square root.

To find the number of digits in the square root of a number, we must remember that the first step in the procedure for finding a square root is to pair off the numbers in the radical sign in each direction from the decimal point. Every pair of numbers under the radical gives one number in the answer.

Example: $\sqrt{\widehat{32}\ \widehat{14}\ \widehat{89}}$ will have 3 digits.

If we were given several choices for $\sqrt{321489}$, we would first look for a three digit number. If there were only one among the answers, that is the one we would select. If there were more than one, we would have to reason further. If a number ends in 9, such as in our example, its square root would have to end in a digit that would end in 9 when multiplied by itself. This might be either 3 or 7. Only one of these would probably be among the choices, as very few problems will call for much computation. This is an aptitude test, which tests your ability to reason.

Example: The square root of 61504 is exactly
(A) 245 (B) 246 (C) 247 (D) 248 (E) 249

Solution: The only answer among the choices which will end in 4 when squared is (D).

PRACTICE EXERCISES IX

Work out each problem in the space provided. Circle the letter that appears before your answer.

1. The sum of $\sqrt{12} + \sqrt{27}$ is

   (A) $\sqrt{29}$ (B) $3\sqrt{5}$ (C) $13\sqrt{3}$ (D) $5\sqrt{3}$ (E) $7\sqrt{3}$

2. The difference between $\sqrt{150}$ and $\sqrt{54}$ is

   (A) $2\sqrt{6}$ (B) $16\sqrt{6}$ (C) $\sqrt{96}$ (D) $6\sqrt{2}$ (E) $8\sqrt{6}$

3. The product of $\sqrt{18x}$ and $\sqrt{2x}$ is

   (A) $6x^2$ (B) $6x$ (C) $36x$ (D) $36x^2$ (E) $6\sqrt{x}$

4. If $\frac{1}{x} = \sqrt{.25}$, then x is equal to

   (A) 2 (B) .5 (C) .2 (D) 20 (E) 5

5. If n = 3.14, find $(3.14)^3$ to the nearest hundredth.

   (A) 3.10 (B) 30.96 (C) 309.59 (D) 3095.91 (E) 30959.14

6. The square root of 24336 is exactly

   (A) 152 (B) 153 (C) 155 (D) 156 (E) 158

7. The square root of 306.25 is exactly

   (A) .175 (B) 1.75 (C) 17.5 (D) 175 (E) 1750

8. Divide $6\sqrt{45}$ by $3\sqrt{5}$.

   (A) 9 (B) 4 (C) 54 (D) 15 (E) 6

9. Find $\sqrt{\frac{y^2}{25} + \frac{y^2}{16}}$

(A) $\frac{2y}{9}$ (B) $\frac{9y}{20}$ (C) $\frac{y}{9}$ (D) $\frac{y\sqrt{41}}{20}$ (E) $\frac{41y}{20}$

10. $\sqrt{a^2 + b^2}$ is equal to

(A) $a + b$ (B) $a - b$ (C) $(a+b)(a-b)$

(D) $\sqrt{a^2} + \sqrt{b^2}$ (E) none of these

SOLUTIONS TO PRACTICE EXERCISES IX

1. **(D)** $\sqrt{12} = \sqrt{4}\sqrt{3} = 2\sqrt{3}$
$\sqrt{27} = \sqrt{9}\sqrt{3} = 3\sqrt{3}$
$5\sqrt{3}$

2. **(A)** $\sqrt{150} = \sqrt{25}\sqrt{6} = 5\sqrt{6}$
$\sqrt{54} = \sqrt{9}\sqrt{6} = 3\sqrt{6}$
$2\sqrt{6}$

3. **(B)** $\sqrt{18x} \cdot \sqrt{2x} = \sqrt{36x^2} = 6x$

4. **(A)** $\sqrt{.25} = .5$
$$\frac{1}{x} = .5$$
$$1 = .5x$$
$$10 = 5x$$
$$2 = x$$

5. **(B)** $(3)^3$ would be 27, so we want an answer a little larger than 27.

6. **(D)** The only answer that will end in 6 when squared is (D).

7. **(C)** The square root of this number must have two digits before the decimal point.

8. **(E)** $\dfrac{6\sqrt{45}}{3\sqrt{5}} = 2\sqrt{9} = 2 \cdot 3 = 6$

9. **(D)** $\sqrt{\dfrac{y^2}{25} + \dfrac{y^2}{16}} = \sqrt{\dfrac{16y^2 + 25y^2}{400}}$
$$= \sqrt{\frac{41y^2}{400}} = \frac{y\sqrt{41}}{20}$$

10. **(E)** Never take the square root of a sum separately. There is no way to simplify $\sqrt{a^2 + b^2}$.

X. FACTORING AND ALGEBRAIC FRACTIONS

In reducing algebraic fractions, we must divide the numerator and denominator by the same factor, just as we do in arithmetic. We can never cancel terms, as this would be adding or subtracting the same number from the numerator and denominator, which changes the value of the fraction. When we reduce $\frac{6}{8}$ to $\frac{3}{4}$, we are really saying that $\frac{6}{8} = \frac{2 \cdot 3}{2 \cdot 4}$ and then dividing numerator and denominator by 2. We do not say $\frac{6}{8} = \frac{3+3}{3+5}$ and then say $\frac{6}{8} = \frac{3}{5}$. This is faulty reasoning in algebra as well. If we have $\frac{6t}{8t}$, we can divide numerator and denominator by 2t, giving $\frac{3}{4}$ as an answer. However, if we have $\frac{6 + t}{8 + t}$, we can do no more, as there is no factor that divides into the *entire* numerator as well as the *entire* denominator. Cancelling terms is one of the most frequent student errors. Don't get caught! Be careful!

Example: Reduce $\frac{3x^2 + 6x}{4x^3 + 8x^2}$ to its lowest terms.

Solution: Factoring the numerator and denominator, we have $\frac{3x(x + 2)}{4x^2(x + 2)}$. The factors common to both numerator and denominator are x and (x + 2). Dividing these out, we arrive at a correct answer of $\frac{3}{4x}$.

In adding or subtracting fractions, we must work with a common denominator and the same shortcuts we used in arithmetic.

Example: Find the sum of $\frac{1}{a}$ and $\frac{1}{b}$.

Solution: Remember to add the two cross products and put the sum over the denominator product. $\frac{b + a}{ab}$

Example: Add: $\frac{2n}{3} + \frac{3n}{2}$

Solution: $\frac{4n + 9n}{6} = \frac{13n}{6}$

In multiplying or dividing fractions, we may cancel a factor common to any numerator and any denominator. Always remember to invert the fraction following the division sign. Where exponents are involved, they are added in multiplication and subtracted in division.

Example: Find the product of $\frac{a^3}{b^2}$ and $\frac{b^3}{a^2}$

Solution: We divide a^2 into the first numerator and second denominator, giving $\frac{a}{b^2} \cdot \frac{b^3}{1}$.

Then we divide b^2 into the first denominator and second numerator, giving $\frac{a}{1} \cdot \frac{b}{1}$. Finally, we multiply the resulting fractions, giving an answer of ab.

Example: Divide $\frac{6x^2y}{5}$ by $2x^3$.

Solution: $\frac{6x^2y}{5} \cdot \frac{1}{2x^3}$. Divide the first numerator and second denominator by $2x^2$, giving $\frac{3y}{5} \cdot \frac{1}{x}$. Multiplying the resulting fractions, we have $\frac{3y}{5x}$.

Complex algebraic fractions are simplified by the same methods used in arithmetic. Multiply *each term* of the complex fraction by the lowest quantity that will eliminate the fraction within the fraction.

Example: $\dfrac{\frac{1}{a} + \frac{1}{b}}{ab}$

Solution: We must multiply *each term* by ab, giving $\frac{b + a}{a^2b^2}$. Since no reduction beyond this is possible, $\frac{b + a}{a^2b^2}$ is our final answer. Remember *never* to cancel terms.

Certain types of problems may involve factoring the difference of two squares. If an expression consists of two terms that are perfect squares separated by a minus sign, the expression can always be factored into two binomials, with one containing the sum of the square roots and the other the difference of the square roots. This can be expressed by the identity $a^2 - b^2 = (a + b)(a - b)$.

Example: If $x^2 - y^2 + 100$ and $x + y = 2$, find $x - y$.

Solution: Since $x^2 - y^2$ can be written as $(x + y)(x - y)$, these two factors must multiply to 100. If one is 2, the other must be 50.

Example: If $a + b = \frac{1}{2}$ and $a - b = \frac{1}{4}$, find $a^2 - b^2$.

Solution: $a^2 - b^2$ is the product of $(a + b)$ and $(a - b)$. Therefore, $a^2 - b^2$ must be equal to $\frac{1}{8}$.

PRACTICE EXERCISES X

Work out the problem in the space provided. Circle the letter that appears before your answer.

1. Find the sum of $\frac{n}{6} + \frac{2n}{5}$.

(A) $\frac{13n}{30}$ (B) 17n (C) $\frac{3n}{30}$ (D) $\frac{17n}{30}$ (E) $\frac{3n}{11}$

2. Combine into a single fraction: $1 - \frac{x}{y}$

(A) $\frac{1-x}{y}$ (B) $\frac{y-x}{y}$ (C) $\frac{x-y}{y}$ (D) $\frac{1-x}{1-y}$ (E) $\frac{y-x}{xy}$

3. Divide $\frac{x-y}{x+y}$ by $\frac{y-x}{y+x}$.

(A) 1 (B) -1 (C) $\frac{(x-y)^2}{(x+y)^2}$ (D) $-\frac{(x-y)^2}{(x+y)^2}$ (E) 0

4. Simplify: $\dfrac{1+\frac{1}{x}}{\frac{y}{x}}$

(A) $\frac{x+1}{y}$ (B) $\frac{x+1}{x}$ (C) $\frac{x+1}{xy}$ (D) $\frac{x^2+1}{xy}$ (E) $\frac{y+1}{y}$

5. Find an expression equivalent to $\left(\frac{2x^2}{y}\right)^3$.

(A) $\frac{8x^5}{3y}$ (B) $\frac{6x^6}{y^3}$ (C) $\frac{6x^5}{y^3}$ (D) $\frac{8x^5}{y^3}$ (E) $\frac{8x^6}{y^3}$

6. Simplify: $\dfrac{\frac{1}{x}+\frac{1}{y}}{3}$

(A) $\frac{3x+3y}{xy}$ (B) $\frac{3xy}{x+y}$ (C) $\frac{xy}{3}$ (D) $\frac{x+y}{3xy}$ (E) $\frac{x+y}{3}$

7. $\frac{1}{a} + \frac{1}{b} = 7$ and $\frac{1}{a} - \frac{1}{b} = 3$. Find $\frac{1}{a^2} - \frac{1}{b^2}$.

(A) 10 (B) 7 (C) 3 (D) 21 (E) 4

8. If $(a - b)^2 = 64$ and $ab = 3$, find $a^2 + b^2$.

(A) 61 (B) 67 (C) 70 (D) 58 (E) 69

9. If $c + d = 12$ and $c^2 - d^2 = 48$, then $c - d =$

(A) 4 (B) 36 (C) 60 (D) 5 (E) 3

10. The trinomial $x^2 + x - 20$ is exactly divisible by

(A) $x - 5$ (B) $x + 4$ (C) $x - 10$ (D) $x - 4$ (E) $x - 2$

SOLUTIONS TO PRACTICE EXERCISES X

1. **(D)** $\frac{n}{6} + \frac{2n}{5} = \frac{5n + 12n}{30} = \frac{17n}{30}$
2. **(B)** $\frac{1}{1} - \frac{x}{y} = \frac{y - x}{y}$
3. **(B)** $\frac{x - y}{x + y} \cdot \frac{y + x}{y - x}$
   Since addition is commutative, we may cancel x + y with y + x, as they are the same quantity. However, subtraction is not commutative, so we may not cancel x − y with y − x, as they are *not* the same quantity. We can change the form of y − x by factoring out a −1. Thus, y − x = (−1)(x − y). In this form, we can cancel x − y, leaving an answer of $\frac{1}{-1}$, or −1.
4. **(A)** Multiply every term in the fraction by x, giving $\frac{x + 1}{y}$.
5. **(E)** $\frac{2x^2}{y} \cdot \frac{2x^2}{y} \cdot \frac{2x^2}{y} = \frac{8x^6}{y^3}$
6. **(D)** Multiply every term of the fraction by xy, giving $\frac{y + x}{3xy}$.
7. **(D)** $\frac{1}{a^2} - \frac{1}{b^2}$ is equivalent to $\left(\frac{1}{a} + \frac{1}{b}\right)\left(\frac{1}{a} - \frac{1}{b}\right)$.
   We therefore multiply 7 by 3 for an answer of 21.
8. **(C)** $(a - b)^2$ is $(a - b)(a - b)$ or $a^2 - 2ab + b^2$, which is equal to 64.
   $a^2 - 2ab + b^2 = 64$
   $a^2 + b^2 = 64 + 2ab$
   Since ab = 3, 2ab = 6, and $a^2 + b^2 = 64 + 6$, or 70.
9. **(A)** $c^2 - d^2 = (c + d)(c - d)$
   $48 = 12(c - d)$
   $4 = c - d$
10. **(D)** The factors of $x^2 + x - 20$ are $(x + 5)$ and $(x - 4)$.

XI. PROBLEM SOLVING IN ALGEBRA

In solving verbal problems, the most important technique is to read accurately. Be sure you understand clearly what you are asked to find. Once this is done, represent what you are looking for algebraically. Write an equation that translates the words of the problem to the symbols of mathematics. Then solve that equation by the techniques reviewed previously.

We will review some of the frequently encountered types of algebra problems, although not every problem you may get will fall into one of these categories. However, thoroughly familiarizing yourself with the types of problems that follow will help you to translate and solve all kinds of verbal problems.

A. COIN PROBLEMS

In solving coin problems, it is best to change the value of all monies involved to cents before writing an equation. Thus, the number of nickels must be multiplied by 5 to give their value in cents; dimes must be multiplied by 10; quarters by 25; half dollars by 50; and dollars by 100.

Example: Richard has $3.50 consisting of nickels and dimes. If he has 5 more dimes than nickels, how many dimes does he have?

Solution: Let x = the number of nickels

$x + 5$ = the number of dimes

$5x$ = the value of the nickels in cents

$10x + 50$ = the value of the dimes in cents

350 = the value of the money he has in cents

$$5x + 10x + 50 = 350$$
$$15x = 300$$
$$x = 20$$

He has 20 nickels and 25 dimes.

In a problem such as this, you can be sure that 20 would be among the multiple-choice answers. You must be sure to read carefully what you are asked to find and then continue until you have found the quantity sought.

B. CONSECUTIVE INTEGER PROBLEMS

Consecutive integers are one apart and can be represented by x, $x+1$, $x+2$, etc. Consecutive even or odd integers are two apart and can be represented by x, $x+2$, $x+4$, etc.

Example: Three consecutive odd integers have a sum of 33. Find the average of these integers.

Solution: Represent the integers as x, $x+2$ and $x+4$. Write an equation indicating the sum is 33.

$$3x + 6 = 33$$
$$3x = 27$$
$$x = 9$$

The integers are 9, 11, and 13. In the case of evenly spaced numbers such as these, the average is the middle number, 11. Since the sum of the three numbers was given originally, all we really had to do was to divide this sum by 3, to find the average, without ever knowing what the numbers were.

C. AGE PROBLEMS

Problems of this type usually involve a comparison of ages at the present time, several years from now, or several years ago. A person's age x years from now is found by adding x to his present age. A person's age x years ago is found by subtracting x from his present age.

Example: Michelle was 12 years old y years ago. Represent her age b years from now.

Solution: Her present age is $12 + y$. In b years, her age will be $12 + y + b$.

D. INTEREST PROBLEMS

The annual amount of interest paid on an investment is found by multiplying the amount of principal invested by the rate (percent) of interest paid.

Principal · Rate = Interest income

Example: Mr. Strauss invests $4,000, part at 6% and part at 7%. His income from these investments in one year is $250. Find the amount invested at 7%.

Solution: Represent each investment.

Let x = the amount invested at 7%. Always try to let x represent what you are looking for.

$4000 - x$ = the amount invested at 6%

$.07x$ = the income from the 7% investment

$.06(4000 - x)$ = the income from the 6% investment

$.07x + .06(4000 - x) = 250$

$7x + 6(4000 - x) = 25000$

$7x + 24000 - 6x = 25000$

$x = 1000$

He invested $1,000 at 7%.

E. FRACTION PROBLEMS

A fraction is a ratio between two numbers. If the value of a fraction is $\frac{2}{3}$, it does not mean the numerator must be 2 and the denominator 3. The numerator and denominator could be 4 and 6 respectively, or 1 and 1.5, or 30 and 45, or any of infinitely many other combinations. All we know is that the ratio of numerator to denominator will be 2 : 3. Therefore, the numerator may be represented by 2x, the denominator by 3x and the fraction by $\frac{2x}{3x}$.

Example: The value of a fraction is $\frac{3}{4}$. If 3 is subtracted from the numerator and added to the denominator, the value of the fraction is $\frac{2}{5}$. Find the original fraction.

Solution: Let the original fraction be represented by $\frac{3x}{4x}$. If 3 is subtracted from the numerator and added to the denominator, the new fraction becomes $\frac{3x - 3}{4x + 3}$.

The value of the new fraction is $\frac{2}{5}$.

$$\frac{3x - 3}{4x + 3} = \frac{2}{5}$$

Cross multiply to eliminate fractions.

$$\begin{aligned} 15x - 15 &= 8x + 6 \\ 7x &= 21 \\ x &= 3 \end{aligned}$$

Therefore, the original fraction is

$$\frac{3x}{4x} = \frac{9}{12}$$

F. MIXTURE

There are two kinds of mixture problems with which you should be familiar. The first is sometimes referred to as dry mixture, in which we mix dry ingredients of different values, such as nuts or coffee. Also solved by the same method are problems such as those dealing with tickets at different prices. In solving this type of problem, it is best to organize the data in a chart of three rows and three columns, labeled as illustrated in the following problem.

Example: A dealer wishes to mix 20 pounds of nuts selling for 45 cents per pound with some more expensive nuts selling for 60 cents per pound, to make a mixture that will sell for 50 cents per pound. How many pounds of the more expensive nuts should he use?

Solution:

	No. of lbs. ·	Price/lb. =	Total Value
Original	20	.45	.45(20)
Added	x	.60	.60(x)
Mixture	20 + x	.50	.50(20+x)

The value of the original nuts plus the value of the added nuts must equal the value of the mixture. Almost all mixture problems require an equation that comes from adding the final column:

$.45(20) + .60(x) = .50(20 + x)$

Multiply by 100 to remove decimals.

$45(20) + 60(x) = 50(20 + x)$

$900 + 60x = 1000 + 50x$

$10x = 100$

$x = 10$

He should use 10 lbs. of 60 cent nuts.

In solving the second type, or chemical, mixture problem, we are dealing with percents rather than prices, and amounts instead of value.

Example: How much water must be added to 20 gallons of a solution that is 30% alcohol to dilute it to a solution that is only 25% alcohol?

Solution:

	No. of gals. ·	% alcohol =	Amt. alcohol
Original	20	.30	.30(20)
Added	x	0	0
New	20 + x	.25	.25(20 + x)

Note that the percent of alcohol in water is 0. Had we added pure alcohol to strengthen the solution, the percent would have been 100. The equation again comes from the last column. The amount of alcohol added (none in this case) plus the amount we had to start with must equal the amount of alcohol in the new solution.

$$.30(20) = .25(20 + x)$$
$$30(20) = 25(20 + x)$$
$$600 = 500 + 25x$$
$$100 = 25x$$
$$x = 4$$

G. MOTION PROBLEMS

The fundamental relationship in all motion problems is that Rate · Time = Distance. The problems at the level of this examination usually derive their equation from a relationship concerning distance. Most problems fall into one of three types.

1. *Motion in opposite directions.* When two objects start at the same time and move in opposite directions, or when two objects start at points at a given distance apart and move toward each other until they meet, then the distance the second travels will equal the total distance covered.

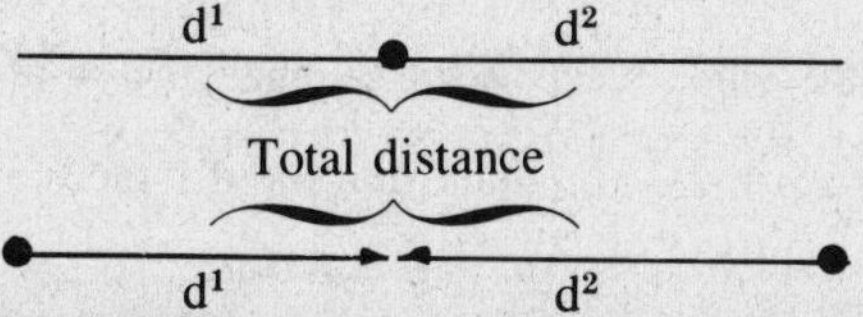

In either of the above cases, $d^1 + d^2$ = Total distance.

2. *Motion in the same direction*. This type of problem is sometimes called the "catch-up" problem. Two objects leave the same place at different times and different rates, but one "catches up" to the other. In such a case, the two distances must be equal.

3. *Round trip*. In this type of problem, the rate going is usually different from the rate returning. The times are also different. But if we go somewhere and then return to the starting point, the distances must be the same.

To solve any motion problem, it is helpful to organize the data in a box with columns for rate, time, and distance. A separate line should be used for each moving object. Remember that if the rate is given in *miles per hour,* the time must be in *hours* and the distance in *miles*.

Example: Two cars leave a restaurant at 1 p.m., with one car traveling east at 60 miles per hour and the other west at 40 miles per hour along a straight highway. At what time will they be 350 miles apart?

Solution:

	Rate ·	Time =	Distance
Eastbound	60	x	60x
Westbound	40	x	40x

Notice that the time is unknown, since we must discover the number of hours traveled. However, since the cars start at the same time and stop when they are 350 miles apart, their times are the same.

$$60x + 40x = 350$$
$$100x = 350$$
$$x = 3\frac{1}{2}$$

In $3\frac{1}{2}$ hours, it will be 4:30 p.m.

Example: Gloria leaves home for school, riding her bicycle at a rate of 12 m.p.h. Twenty minutes after she leaves, her mother sees Gloria's English paper on her bed and leaves to bring it to her. If her mother drives at 36 m.p.h., how far must she drive before she reaches Gloria?

Solution:

	Rate ·	Time =	Distance
Gloria	12	x	12x
Mother	36	$x - \frac{1}{3}$	$36(x - \frac{1}{3})$

Notice that 20 minutes has been changed to $\frac{1}{3}$ of an hour. In this problem the times are not equal, but the distances are.

$$12x = 36(x - \frac{1}{3})$$
$$12x = 36x - 12$$

$$12 = 24x$$
$$x = \frac{1}{2}$$

If Gloria rode for $\frac{1}{2}$ hour at 12 m.p.h., the distance covered was 6 miles.

Example: Judy leaves home at 11 a.m. and rides to Mary's house to return her bicycle. She travels at 12 miles per hour and arrives at 11:30 a.m. She turns right around and walks home. How fast does she walk if she returns home at 1 p.m.?

Solution:

	Rate ·	Time =	Distance
Going	12	$\frac{1}{2}$	6
Return	x	$1\frac{1}{2}$	$\frac{3}{2}x$

The distances are equal.

$$6 = \frac{3}{2}x$$
$$12 = 3x$$
$$x = 4$$

She walked at 4 m.p.h.

H. WORK PROBLEMS

In most work problems, a complete job is broken into several parts, each representing a fractional part of the entire job. For each fractional part, which represents the portion completed by one man, one machine, one pipe, etc., the numerator should represent the time actually spent working, while the denominator should represent the total time needed to do the entire job alone. The sum of all the individual fractions should be 1.

Example: John can wax his car in 3 hours. Jim can do the same job in 5 hours. How long will it take them if they work together?

Solution: If multiple-choice answers are given, you should realize that the correct answer must be smaller than the shortest time given, for no matter how slow a helper may be, he does do part of the job and therefore it will be completed in less time.

	John		Jim	
$\frac{\text{Time spent}}{\text{Total time needed to do job alone}}$	$\frac{x}{3}$	+	$\frac{x}{5}$	= 1

Multiply by 15 to eliminate fractions.

$$5x + 3x = 15$$
$$8x = 15$$
$$x = 1\frac{7}{8} \text{ hours}$$

PRACTICE EXERCISES XI

Work out the problem in the space provided. Circle the letter that appears before your answer.

1. Sue and Nancy wish to buy a gift for a friend. They combine their money and find they have $4.00, consisting of quarters, dimes, and nickels. If they have 35 coins and the number of quarters is half the number of nickels, how many quarters do they have?

   (A) 5 (B) 10 (C) 20 (D) 3 (E) 6

2. Three times the first of three consecutive odd integers is 3 more than twice the third. Find the third integer.

   (A) 9 (B) 11 (C) 13 (D) 15 (E) 7

3. Robert is 15 years older than his brother Stan. However, y years ago Robert was twice as old as Stan. If Stan is now b years old and $b > y$, find the value of $b - y$.

   (A) 13 (B) 14 (C) 15 (D) 16 (E) 17

4. How many ounces of pure acid must be added to 20 ounces of a solution that is 5% acid to strengthen it to a solution that is 24% acid?

   (A) $2\frac{1}{2}$ (B) 5 (C) 6 (D) $7\frac{1}{2}$ (E) 10

5. A dealer mixes a lbs. of nuts worth b cents per pound with c lbs. of nuts worth d cents per pound. At what price should he sell a pound of the mixture if he wishes to make a profit of 10 cents per pound?

   (A) $\frac{ab + cd}{a + c} + 10$ (B) $\frac{ab + cd}{a + c} + .10$ (C) $\frac{b + d}{a + c} + 10$

   (D) $\frac{b + d}{a + c} + .10$ (E) $\frac{b + d + 10}{a + c}$

6. Barbara invests $2,400 in the Security National Bank at 5%. How much additional money must she invest at 8% so that the total annual income will be equal to 6% of her entire investment?

   (A) $2,400 (B) $3,600 (C) $1,000 (D) $3,000 (E) $1,200

7. Frank left Austin to drive to Boxville at 6:15 p.m. and arrived at 11:45 p.m. If he averaged 30 miles per hour and stopped one hour for dinner, how far is Boxville from Austin?

   (A) 120 (B) 135 (C) 180 (D) 165 (E) 150

8. A plane traveling 600 miles per hour is 30 miles from Kennedy Airport at 4:58 p.m. At what time will it arrive at the airport?

   (A) 5:00 p.m. (B) 5:01 p.m. (C) 5:02 p.m. (D) 5:20 p.m. (E) 5:03 p.m.

9. Mr. Bridges can wash his car in 15 minutes, while his son Dave takes twice as long to do the same job. If they work together, how many minutes will the job take them?

(A) 5 (B) $7\frac{1}{2}$ (C) 10 (D) $22\frac{1}{2}$ (E) 30

10. The value of a fraction is $\frac{2}{5}$. If the numerator is decreased by 2 and the denominator increased by 1, the resulting fraction is equivalent to $\frac{1}{4}$. Find the numerator of the original fraction.

(A) 3 (B) 4 (C) 6 (D) 10 (E) 15

SOLUTIONS TO PRACTICE EXERCISES XI

1. **(B)** Let x = number of quarters

   2x = number of nickels

   35 − 3x = number of dimes

   Write all money values in cents.

   $25(x) + 5(2x) + 10(35 - 3x) = 400$

   $25x + 10x + 350 - 30x = 400$

   $5x = 50$

   $x = 10$

2. **(D)** Let x = first integer

   x + 2 = second integer

   x + 4 = third integer

   $3(x) = 3 + 2(x + 4)$

   $3x = 3 + 2x + 8$

   $x = +11$

   The third integer is 15.

3. **(C)** b = Stan's age now

   b + 15 = Robert's age now

   b − y = Stan's age y years ago

   b + 15 − y = Robert's age y years ago

   $b + 15 - y = 2(b - y)$

   $b + 15 - y = 2b - 2y$

   $15 = b - y$

4. **(B)**

	No. of oz. ·	% acid =	Amt. acid
Original	20	.05	1
Added	x	1.00	x
Mixture	20 + x	.24	.24(20 + x)

   $1 + x = .24(20 + x)$ Multiply by 100 to eliminate decimal.

   $100 + 100x = 480 + 24x$

   $76x = 380$

   $x = 5$

5. **(A)** The a lbs. of nuts are worth a total of ab cents. The c lbs. of nuts are worth a total of cd cents. The value of the mixture is ab + cd cents. Since there are a + c pounds, each pound is worth $\frac{ab + cd}{a + c}$ cents.

   Since the dealer wants to add 10 cents to each pound for profit, and the value of each pound is in cents, we add 10 to the value of each pound.

6. **(E)** If Barbara invests x additional dollars at 8%, her total investment will amount to 2400 + x dollars.

   $.05(2400) + .08(x) = .06(2400 + x)$

   $5(2400) + 8(x) = 6(2400 - x)$

   $12000 + 8x = 14400 + 6x$

   $2x = 2400$

   $x = 1200$

7. **(B)** Total time elapsed is $5\frac{1}{2}$ hours. However, one hour was used for dinner. Therefore, Frank drove at 30 m.p.h. for $4\frac{1}{2}$ hours, covering 135 miles.

8. **(B)** Time $= \frac{\text{Distance}}{\text{Rate}} = \frac{30}{600} = \frac{1}{20}$ hour, or 3 minutes.

9. **(C)** Dave takes 30 minutes to wash the car alone.

$$\frac{x}{15} + \frac{x}{30} = 1$$
$$2x + x = 30$$
$$3x = 30$$
$$x = 10$$

10. **(C)** Let $2x$ = original numerator
$5x$ = original denominator

$$\frac{2x - 2}{5x + 1} = \frac{1}{4} \text{ Cross multiply}$$
$$8x - 8 = 5x + 1$$
$$3x = 9$$
$$x = 3$$

Original numerator is 2(3), or 6.

XII. GEOMETRY

Numerical relationships from geometry should be reviewed thoroughly. A list of the most important formulas with illustrations follows.

A. Areas

1. Rectangle = bh

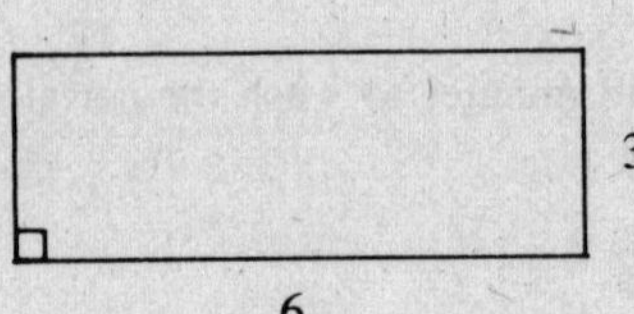

Area = 18

2. Parallelogram = bh

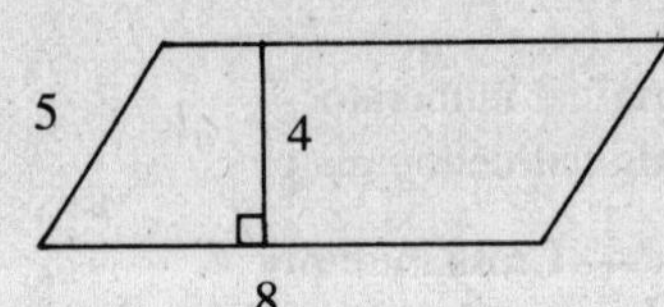

Area = 8 · 4 = 32

3. Rhombus = $\frac{1}{2}d_1d_2$

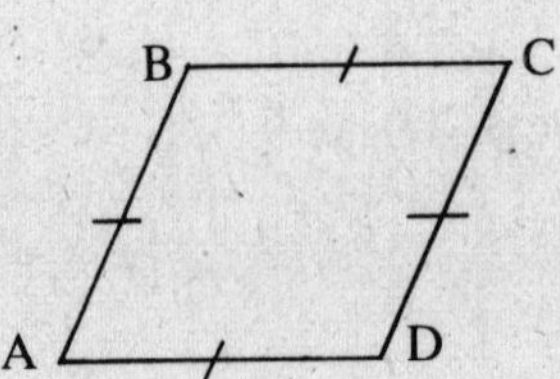

If AC = 10 and BD = 8,

then area is $\frac{1}{2}(10)(8) = 40$

4. Square = s^2 or $\frac{1}{2}d^2$

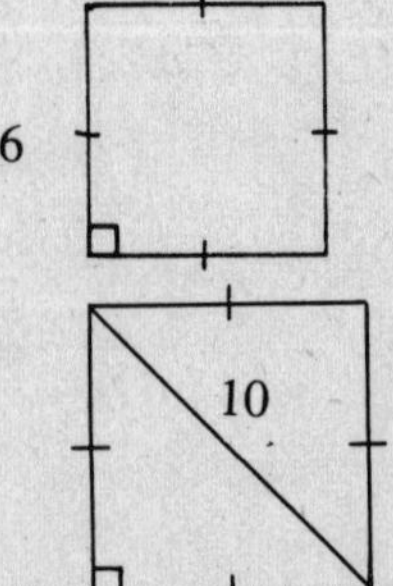

Area = $6^2 = 36$

Area = $\frac{1}{2}(10)(10) = 50$

5. Triangle = $\frac{1}{2}bh$

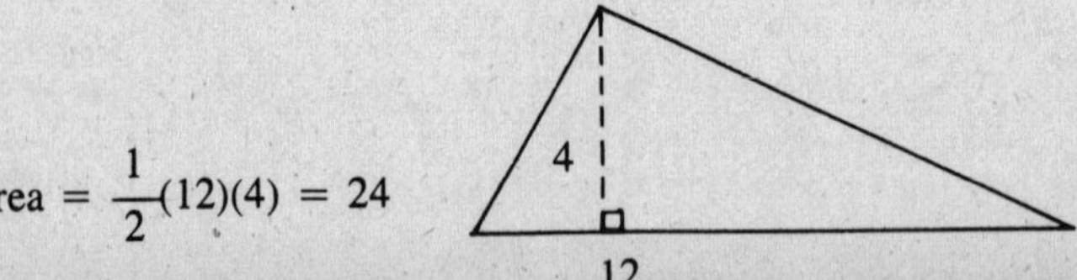

Area = $\frac{1}{2}(12)(4) = 24$

6. Equilateral triangle $= \frac{s^2}{4}\sqrt{3}$

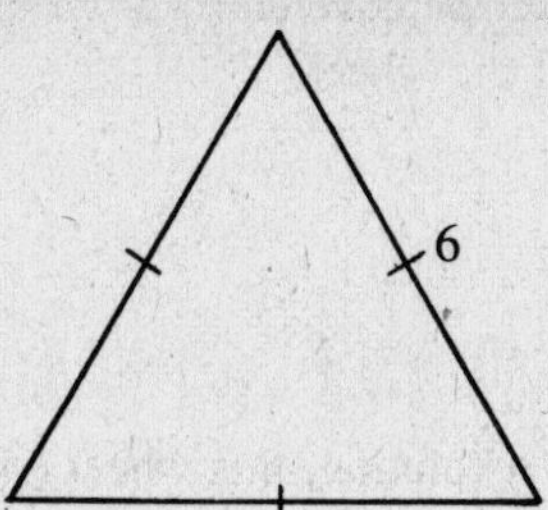

Area $= \frac{36}{4}\sqrt{3} = 9\sqrt{3}$

7. Trapezoid $= \frac{1}{2}h(b_1 + b_2)$

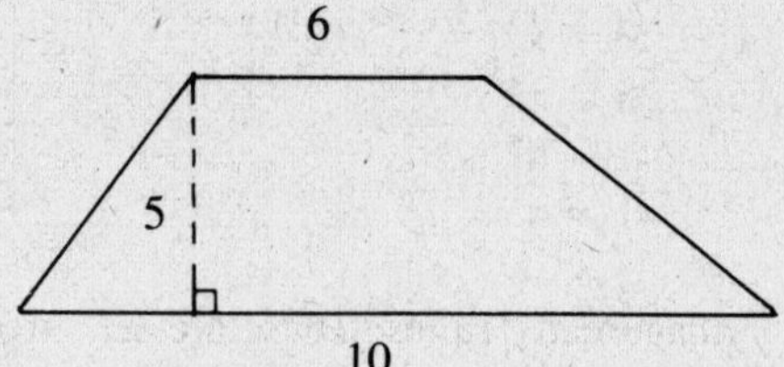

Area $= \frac{1}{2}(5)(16) = 40$

8. Circle $= \pi r^2$

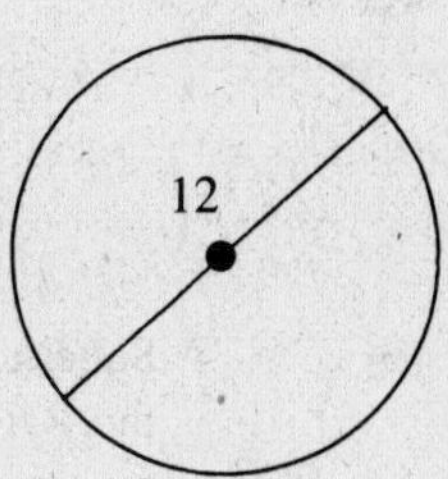

Area $= \pi (6)^2 = 36\pi$

B. Perimeter

1. Any polygon = simply add all sides

5

P = 24

11

2. Circle $= \pi d$
(called circumference)

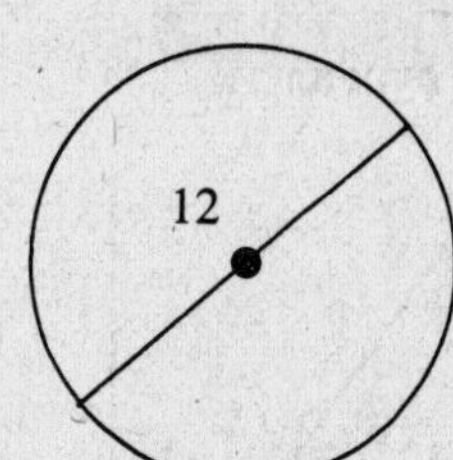

$C = \pi (12) = 12\pi$

3. The distance covered by a wheel in one revolution is equal to the circumference of the wheel.

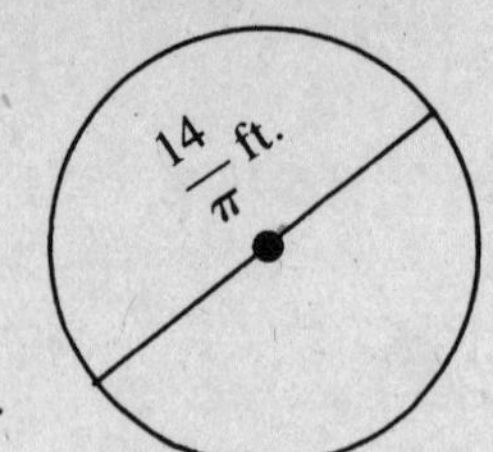

In one revolution, this wheel covers $\pi \cdot \frac{14}{\pi}$, or 14 feet.

C. Right Triangles

1. Pythagorean Theorem
$(\text{leg})^2 + (\text{leg})^2 = (\text{hypotenuse})^2$

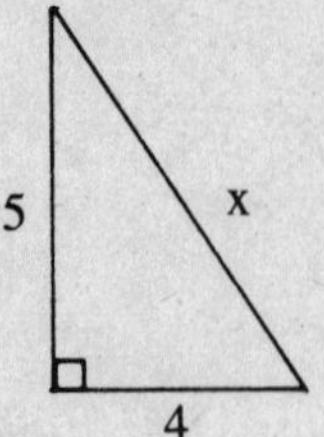

$$4^2 + 5^2 = x^2$$
$$16 + 25 = x^2$$
$$41 = x^2$$
$$\sqrt{41} = x$$

2. Pythagorean Triples: These are sets of numbers that satisfy the Pythagorean theorem. When a given set of numbers such as 3,4,5 form a Pythagorean triple ($3^2 + 4^2 = 5^2$), any multiples of this set such as 6,8,10 or 15,20,25 also form a Pythagorean triple. The most common Pythagorean triples, which should be memorized are:
3,4,5
5,12,13
8,15,17
7,24,25

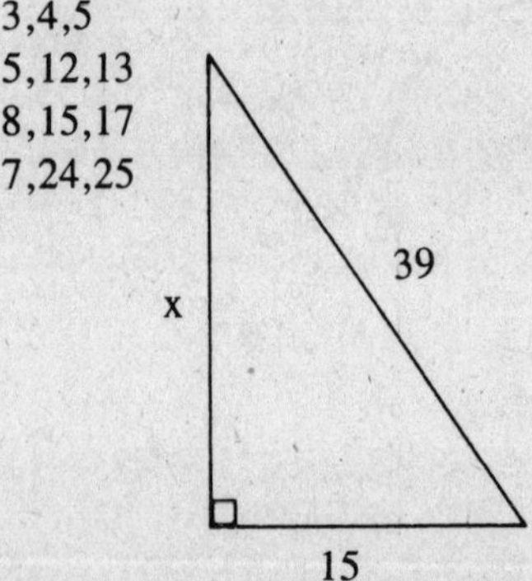

Squaring these numbers in order to apply the Pythagorean theorem would take too much time. Instead, recognize the hypotenuse as 3(13). Suspect a 5,12,13 triangle. Since the given leg is 3(5), the missing leg must be 3(12), or 36, with no computation and a great saving of time.

3. The 30°-60°-90° triangle

a) the leg opposite the 30° angle is $\frac{1}{2}$ hypotenuse.

b) The leg opposite the 60° angle is $\frac{1}{2}$ hypotenuse $\cdot \sqrt{3}$.

c) An altitude in an equilateral triangle forms a 30°-60°-90° triangle and is therefore equal to $\frac{1}{2}$ hypotenuse $\cdot \sqrt{3}$.

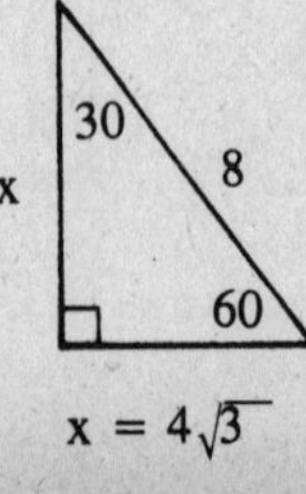

$x = 4\sqrt{3}$

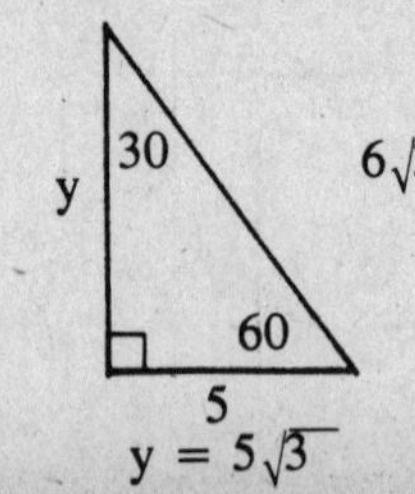

$y = 5\sqrt{3}$

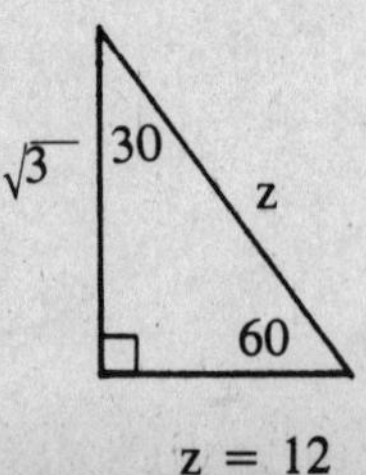

$z = 12$

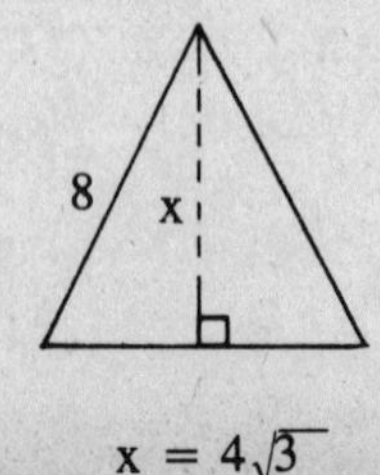

$x = 4\sqrt{3}$

4. 45°-45°-90° triangle (isosceles right triangle)
   a) Each leg is $\frac{1}{2}$ hypotenuse $\cdot \sqrt{2}$.
   b) Hypotenuse is leg $\cdot \sqrt{2}$.
   c) The diagonal in a square forms a 45°-45°-90° triangle and is therefore equal to a side $\cdot \sqrt{2}$.

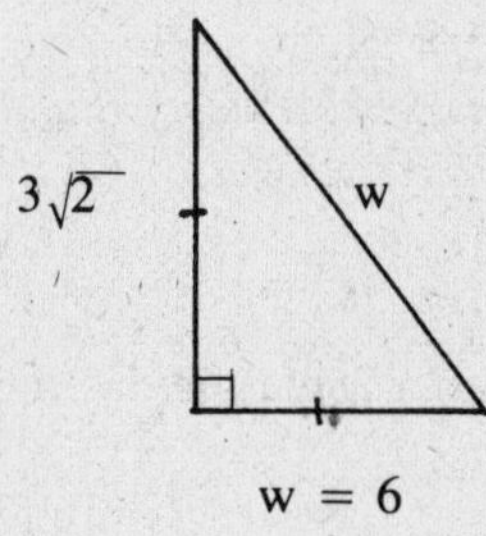

$w = 6$

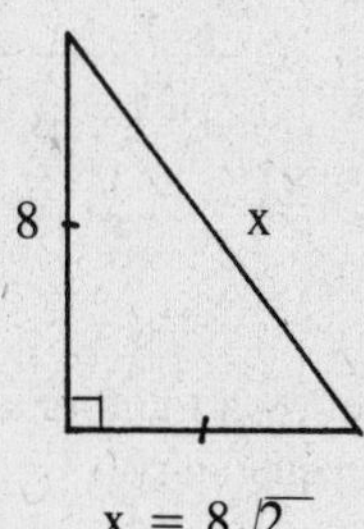

$x = 8\sqrt{2}$

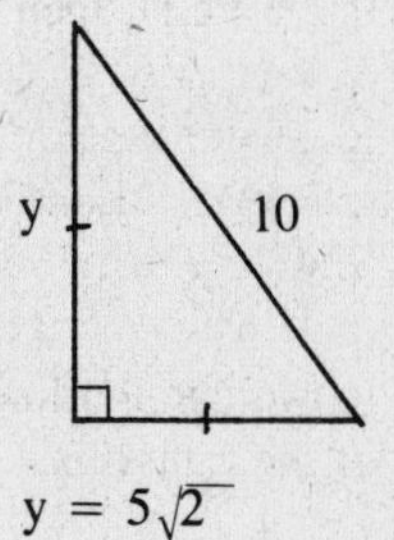

$y = 5\sqrt{2}$

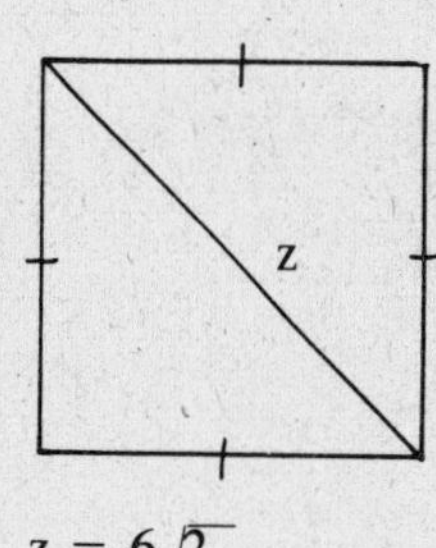

$z = 6\sqrt{2}$

D. Coordinate Geometry

1. Distance between two points
   $\sqrt{(x_2 - x_1)^2 + (y_2 - y_1)^2}$

   The distance from (−2,3) to (4,−1) is
   $\sqrt{[4 - (-2)]^2 + [-1 - (3)]^2}$

   $\sqrt{(6)^2 + (-4)^2} = \sqrt{36 + 16} = \sqrt{52}$

2. The midpoint of a line segment
   $\left(\frac{x_1 + x_2}{2}, \frac{y_1 + y_2}{2}\right)$

   The midpoint of the segment joining (−2,3) to (4, −1) is
   $\left(\frac{-2 + 4}{2}, \frac{3 + (-1)}{2}\right) = \left(\frac{2}{2}, \frac{2}{2}\right) = (1,1)$

E. Parallel Lines

1. If two parallel lines are cut by a transversal, the alternate interior angles are congruent.

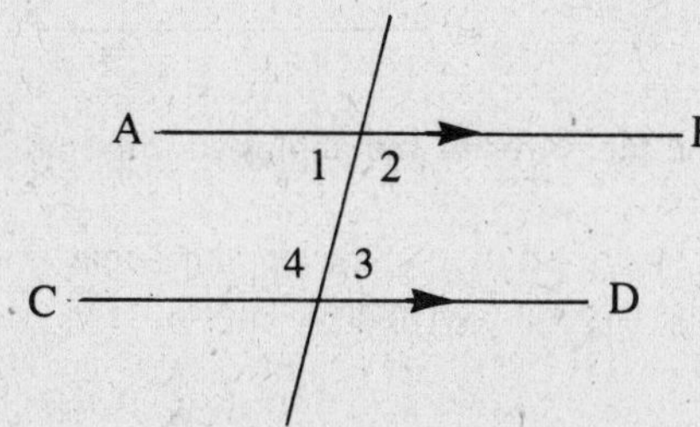

If $\overleftrightarrow{AB} \parallel \overleftrightarrow{CD}$, then
$\measuredangle 1 \cong \measuredangle 3$ and
$\measuredangle 2 \cong \measuredangle 4$.

2. If two parallel lines are cut by a transversal, the corresponding angles are congruent.

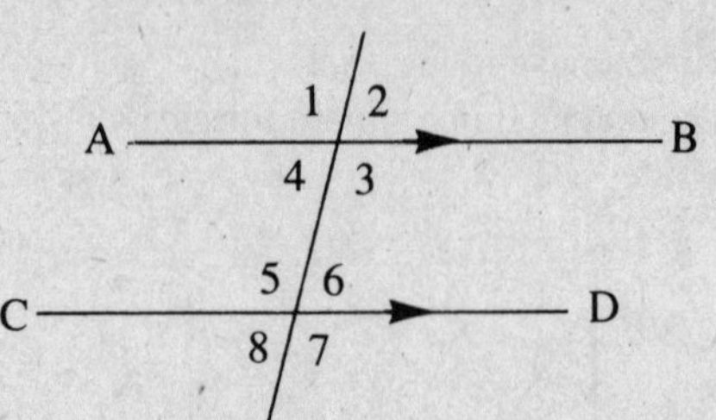

If $\overleftrightarrow{AB} \parallel \overleftrightarrow{CD}$, then
$\measuredangle 1 \cong \measuredangle 5$,
$\measuredangle 2 \cong \measuredangle 6$,
$\measuredangle 3 \cong \measuredangle 7$, and
$\measuredangle 4 \cong \measuredangle 8$.

3. If two parallel lines are cut by a transversal, interior angles on the same side of the transversal are supplementary.

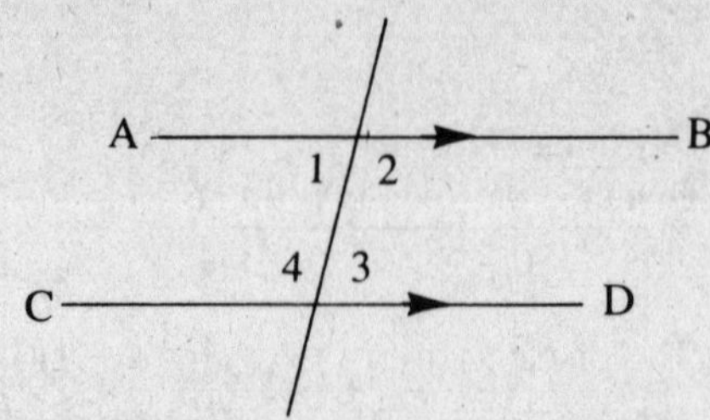

If $\overleftrightarrow{AB} \parallel \overleftrightarrow{CD}$, then
$\measuredangle 1$ is supplementary $\measuredangle 4$ and
$\measuredangle 2$ is supplementary $\measuredangle 3$.

F. Triangles

1. If two sides of a triangle are congruent, the angles opposite these sides are congruent.

If $\overline{AB} \cong \overline{AC}$, then
$\measuredangle B \cong \measuredangle C$.

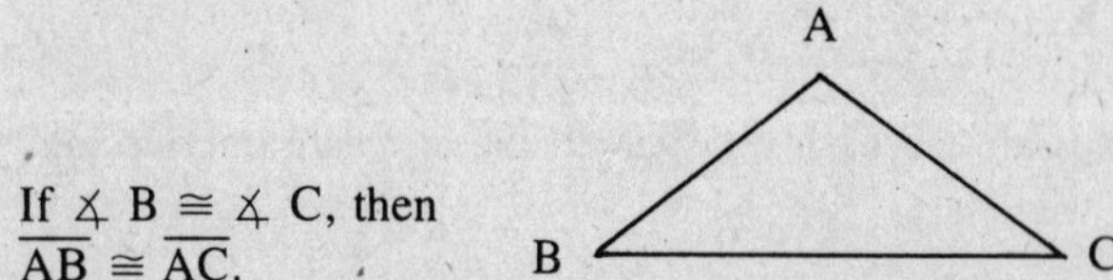

2. If two angles of a triangle are congruent, the sides opposite these angles are congruent.

If $\measuredangle B \cong \measuredangle C$, then
$\overline{AB} \cong \overline{AC}$.

3. The sum of the measures of the angles of a triangle is 180°.

4. The measure of an exterior angle of a triangle is equal to the sum of the measures of the two remote interior angles.

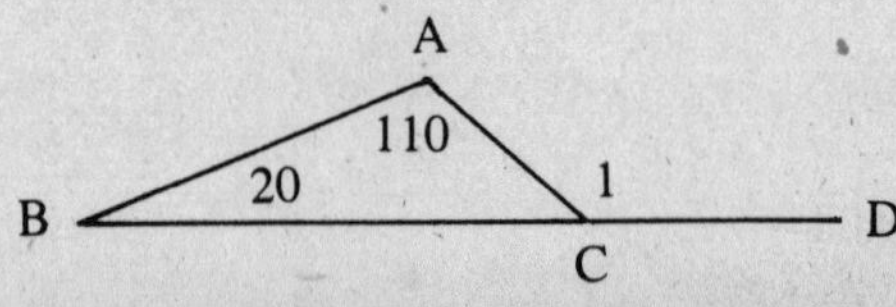

$\measuredangle 1 = 130°$

5. If two angles of one triangle are congruent to two angles of a second triangle, the third angles are congruent.

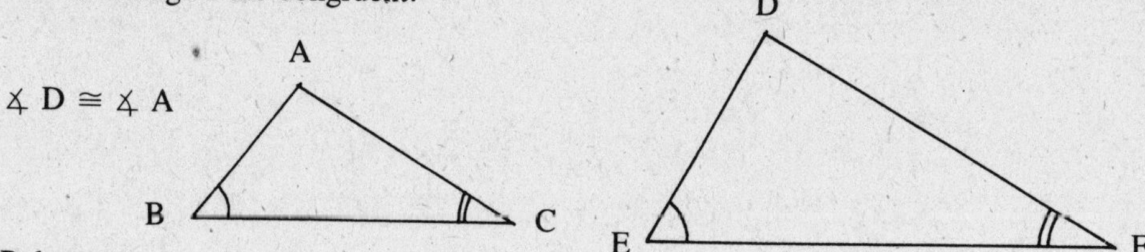

G. Polygons

1. The sum of the measures of the angles of a polygon of n sides is $(n - 2)180°$.

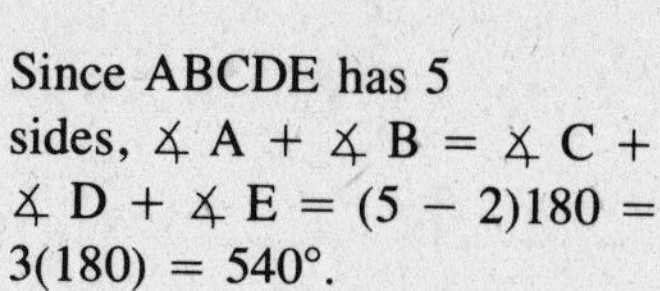
Since ABCDE has 5 sides, $\measuredangle A + \measuredangle B = \measuredangle C + \measuredangle D + \measuredangle E = (5 - 2)180 = 3(180) = 540°$.

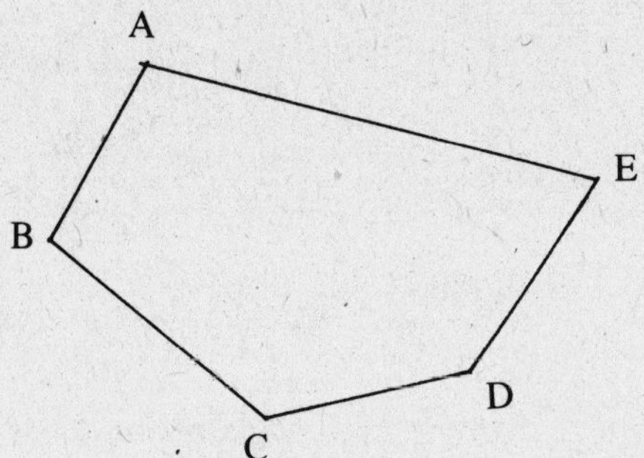

2. In a parallelogram:
   a) Opposite sides are parallel.
   b) Opposite sides are congruent.
   c) Opposite angles are congruent.
   d) Consecutive angles are supplementary.
   e) Diagonals bisect each other.
   f) Each diagonal bisects the parallelogram into two congruent triangles.

3. In a rectangle, in addition to the properties listed in (2) above:
   a) All angles are right angles.
   b) Diagonals are congruent.

4. In a rhombus, in addition to the properties listed in (2) above:
   a) All sides are congruent.
   b) Diagonals are perpendicular.
   c) Diagonals bisect the angles.

5. A square has *all* of the properties listed in (2), (3), and (4) above.

6. The apothem of a regular polygon is perpendicular to a side, bisects that side, and also bisects a central angle.

$\overline{OX}$ is an apothem. It bisects $\overline{AB}$, is perpendicular to $\overline{AB}$, and bisects $\measuredangle AOB$.

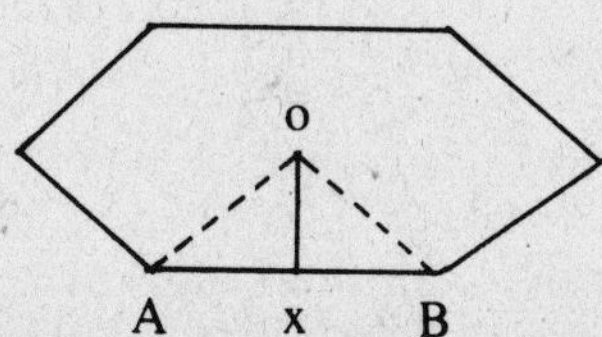

7. The area of a regular polygon is equal to one-half the product of its apothem and perimeter.

$$A = \frac{1}{2}(3)(30) = 45$$

H. Circles

1. A central angle is equal in degrees to its intercepted arc.

If AB = 80°, then
∡ AOB = 80°.

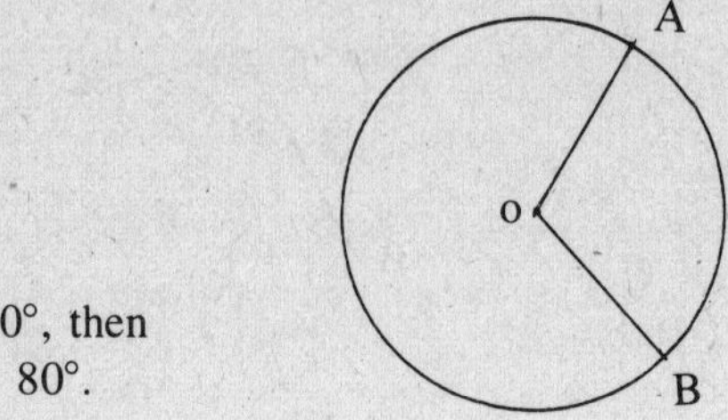

2. An inscribed angle is equal in degrees to one-half its intercepted arc.

If $\overset{\frown}{AC} = 120°$, then
∡ ABC = 60°.

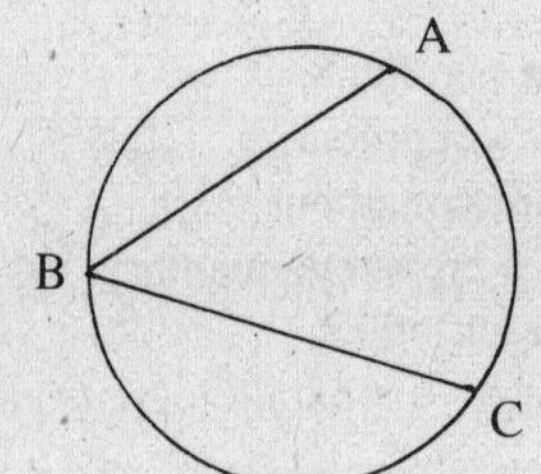

3. An angle formed by two chords intersecting in a circle is equal in degrees to one-half the sum of its intercepted arcs.

If $\overset{\frown}{AD} = 40°$ and $\overset{\frown}{CB} = 80°$,
then ∡ CEB = 60°.

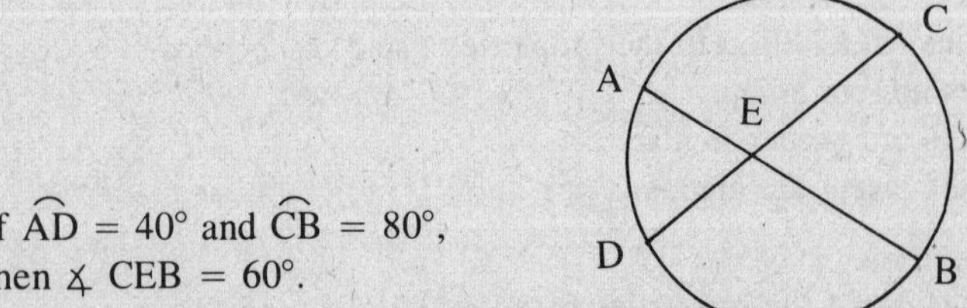

4. An angle outside the circle formed by two secants, a secant and a tangent, or two tangents is equal in degrees to one-half the difference of its intercepted arcs.

If $\overset{\frown}{AD} = 120°$ and
$\overset{\frown}{BD} = 70°$ then ∡ ACD = 25°.

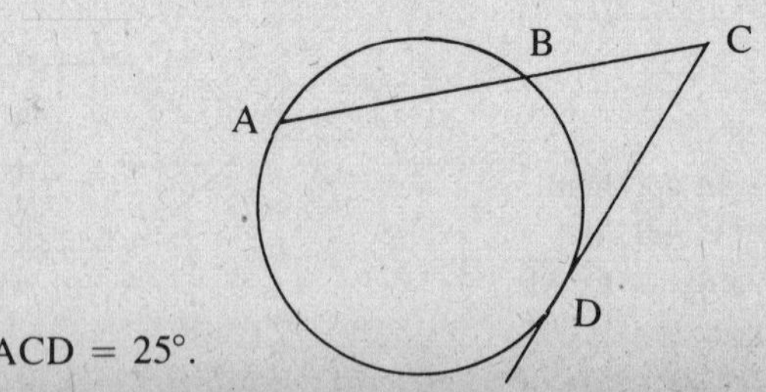

5. Two tangent segments drawn to a circle from the same external point are congruent.

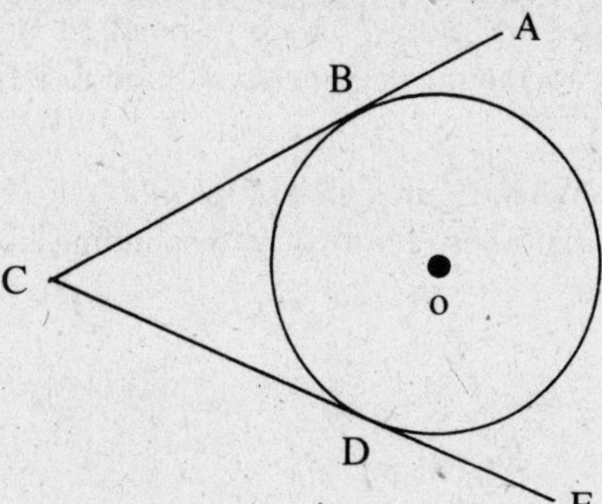

If $\overleftrightarrow{AC}$ and $\overleftrightarrow{CE}$ are tangent to circle O at B and D, then $\overline{CB} \cong \overline{CD}$.

I. Volumes

1. The volume of a rectangular solid is equal to the product of its length, width, and height.

$V = (6)(2)(4) = 48$

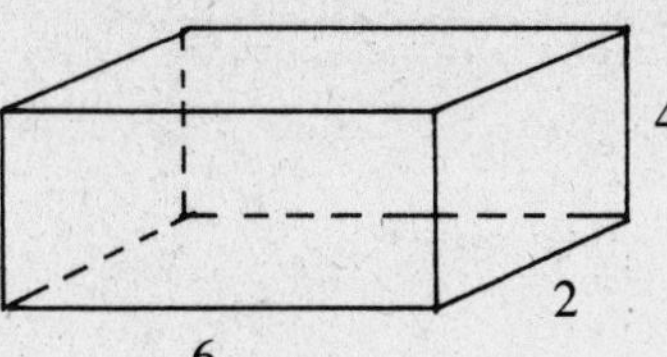

2. The volume of a cube is equal to the cube of an edge.

$V = (5)^3 = 125$

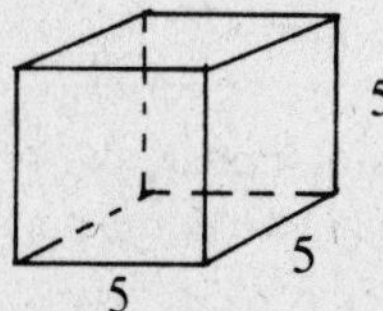

3. The volume of a cylinder is equal to π times the square of the radius of the base times the height.

$V = \pi(3)^2(10) = 90\pi$

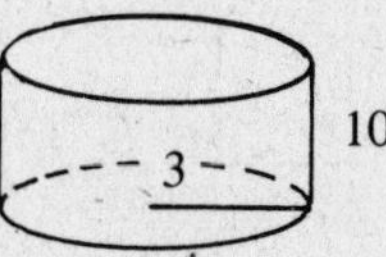

J. Similar Polygons

1. Corresponding angles of similar polyons are congruent.

2. Corresponding sides of similar polygons are in proportion.

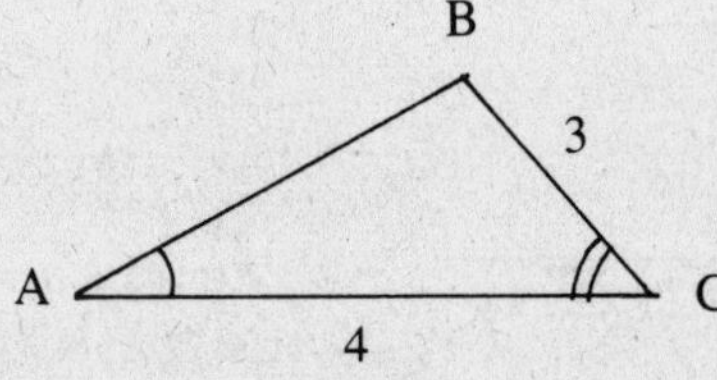

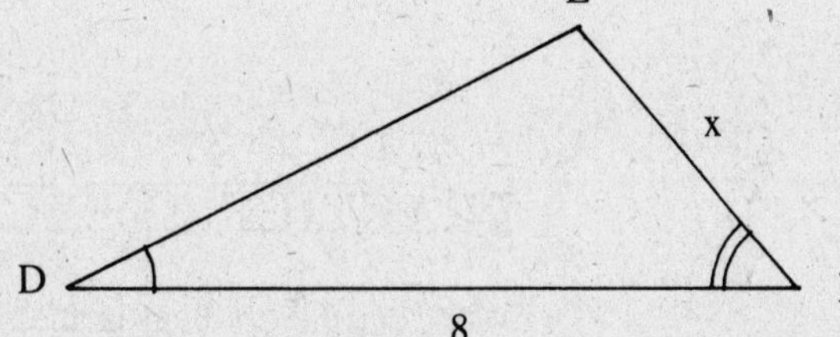

If triangle ABC is similar to triangle DEF, and the sides are given as marked, then EF must be equal to 6, as the ratio between corresponding sides is 4:8, or 1:2.

3. When figures are similar, all corresponding linear ratios are equal. The ratio of one side to its corresponding side is the same as perimeter to perimeter, apothem to apothem, altitude to altitude, etc.

4. When figures are similar, the ratio of their areas is equal to the square of the ratio between two corresponding linear quantities.

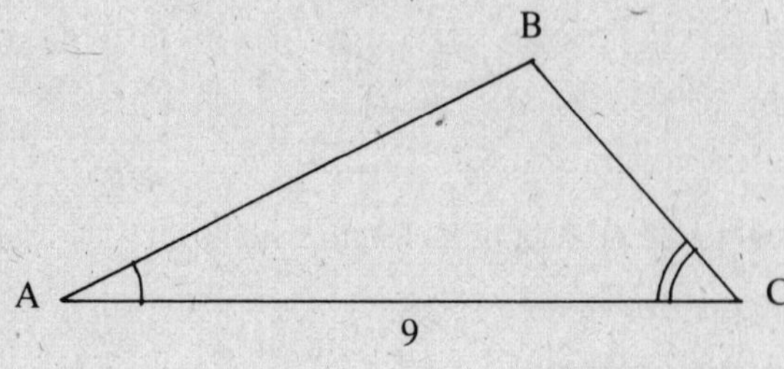

If triangle ABC is similar to triangle DEF, the area of triangle ABC will be 9 times as great as that of triangle DEF. The ratio of sides is 9:3 or 3:1. The ratio of areas will be the square of 3:1, giving 9:1.

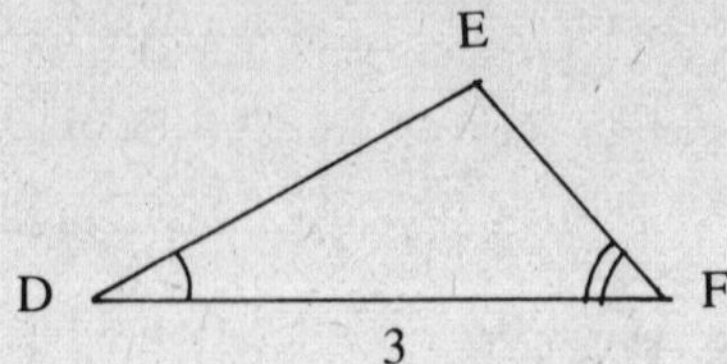

5. When figures are similar, the ratio of their volumes is equal to the cube of the ratio between two corresponding linear quantities.

The volume of the larger cube is 8 times as large as the volume of the smaller cube. If the ratio of sides is 3:6, or 1:2, the ratio of volumes becomes the cube of this, or 1:8.

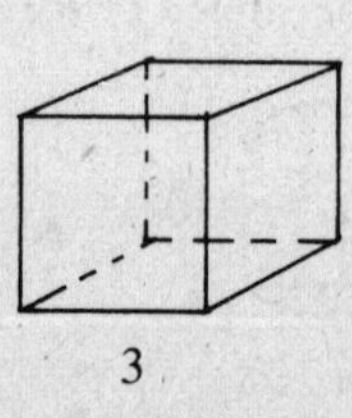

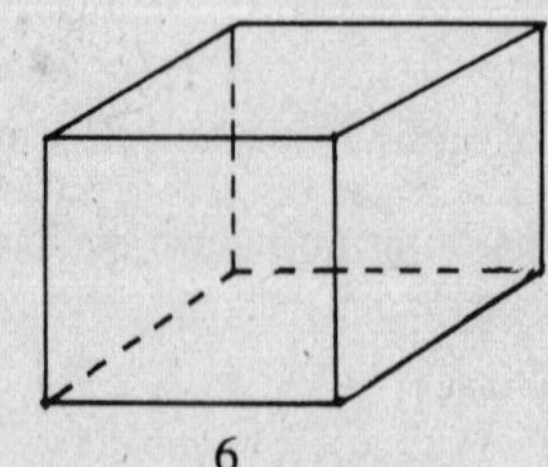

PRACTICE EXERCISES XII

Work out the problem in the space provided. Circle the letter that appears before your answer.

1. If the angles of a triangle are in the ratio 2:3:7, the triangle is

   (A) acute (B) isosceles (C) obtuse (D) right (E) equilateral

2. If the area of a square of side x is 5, what is the area of a square of side 3x?

(A) 15 (B) 45 (C) 95 (D) 75 (E) 225

3. If the radius of a circle is decreased by 10%, by what percent is its area decreased?

(A) 10 (B) 19 (C) 21 (D) 79 (E) 81

4. A spotlight is 5 feet from one wall of a room and 10 feet from the wall at right angles to it. How many feet is it from the intersection of the two walls?

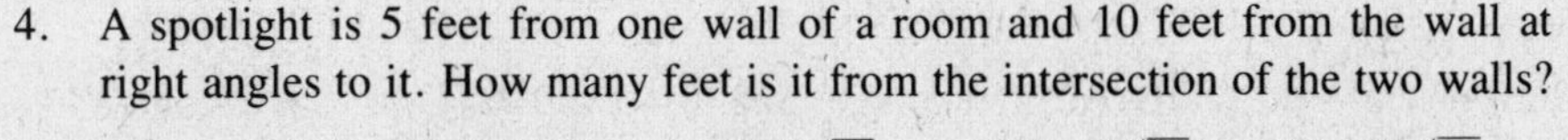

(A) 15 (B) $5\sqrt{2}$ (C) $5\sqrt{5}$ (D) $10\sqrt{2}$ (E) $10\sqrt{5}$

5. A dam has the dimensions indicated in the figure. Find the area of this isosceles trapezoid.

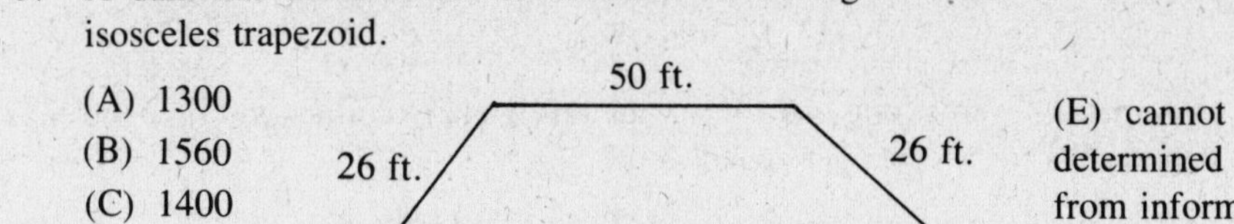

(A) 1300
(B) 1560
(C) 1400
(D) 1440
(E) cannot be determined from information given

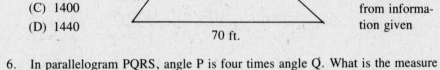

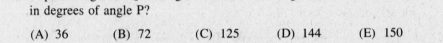

6. In parallelogram PQRS, angle P is four times angle Q. What is the measure in degrees of angle P?

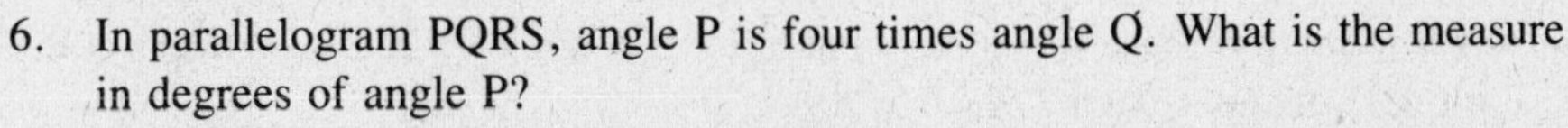

(A) 36 (B) 72 (C) 125 (D) 144 (E) 150

7. If $\overline{PQ} \cong \overline{QS}$, $\overline{QR} \cong \overline{RS}$ and angle PRS = 100°, what is the measure, in degrees, of angle QPS?

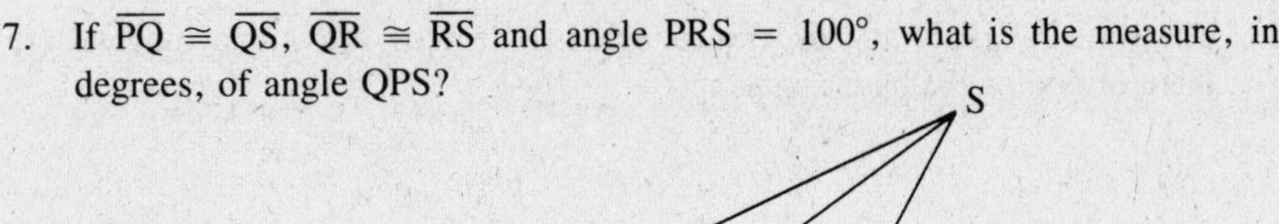

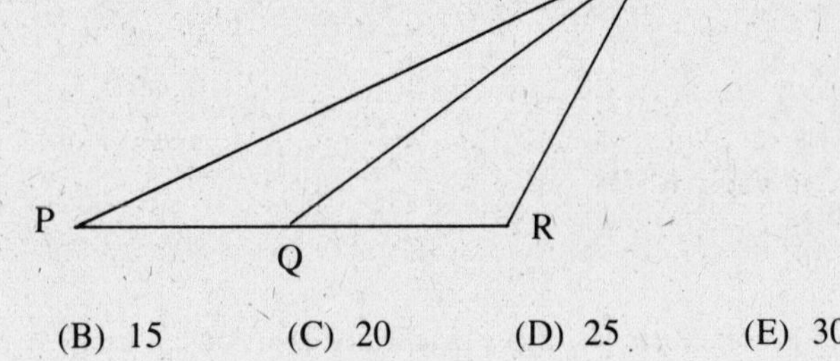

(A) 10 (B) 15 (C) 20 (D) 25 (E) 30

8. A line segment is drawn from the point (3,5) to the point (9,13). What are the coordinates of the midpoint of this line segment?

(A) (3,4) (B) (12,18) (C) (6,8) (D) (9,6) (E) (6,9)

9. A rectangular box with a square base contains 6 cubic feet. If the height of the box is 18 inches, how many feet are there in each side of the base?

(A) 1 (B) 2 (C) $\sqrt{3}$ (D) $\frac{\sqrt{3}}{3}$ (E) 4

10. The surface area of a cube is 150 square feet. How many cubic feet are there in the volume of the cube?

(A) 30 (B) 50 (C) 100 (D) 125 (E) 150

11. Peter lives 12 miles west of school and Bill lives north of the school. Peter finds that the direct distance from his house to Bill's is 6 miles shorter than the distance by way of school. How many miles north of the school does Bill live?

    (A) 6 (B) 9 (C) 10 (D) $6\sqrt{2}$ (E) None of these

12. A square is inscribed in a circle of area 18π. Find a side of the square.

    (A) 3 (B) 6 (C) $3\sqrt{2}$ (D) $6\sqrt{2}$ (E) cannot be determined from the information given

13. A carpet is y yards long and f feet wide. How many dollars will it cost if the carpet sells for x cents per square foot?

    (A) xyf (B) 3xyf (C) $\frac{xyf}{3}$ (D) $\frac{.03yf}{x}$ (E) .03xyf

14. If a triangle of base 6 has the same area as a circle of radius 6, what is the altitude of the triangle?

    (A) 6π (B) 8π (C) 10π (D) 12π (E) 14π

15. The vertex angle of an isosceles triangle is p degrees. How many degrees are there in one of the base angles?

    (A) $180 - p$ (B) $90 - p$ (C) $180 - 2p$ (D) $180 - \frac{p}{2}$ (E) $90 - \frac{p}{2}$

16. In a circle with center O, arc RS = 132 degrees. How many degrees are there in angle RSO?

    (A) 66 (B 20 (C) 22 (D) 24 (E) 48

17. The ice compartment of a refrigerator is 8 inches long, 4 inches wide, and 5 inches high. How many ice cubes will it hold if each cube is 2 inches on an edge?

    (A) 8 (B) 10 (C) 12 (D) 16 (E) 20

18. In the figure, PSQ is a straight line and $\overline{RS}$ is perpendicular to $\overline{ST}$. If angle RSQ = 48°, how many degrees are there in angle PST?

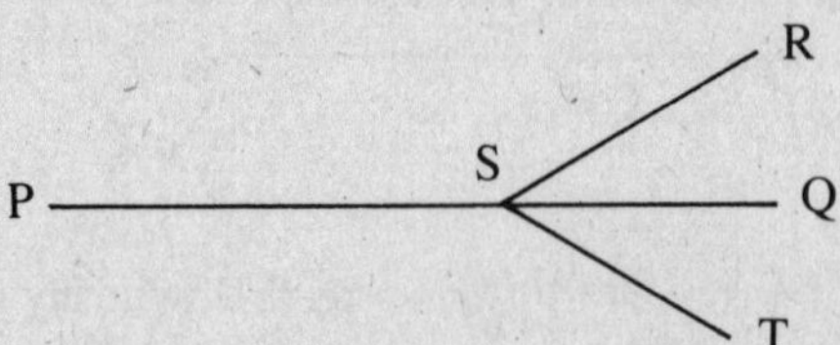

    (A) 48 (B) 132 (C) 90 (D) 136 (E) 138

19. A cylindrical pail has a radius of 7 inches and a height of 9 inches. If there are 231 cubic inches to a gallon, approximately how many gallons will this pail hold?

(A) 6 (B) $\frac{12}{7}$ (C) 7.5 (D) 8.2 (E) 9

20. In triangle PQR, $\overline{QS}$ and $\overline{SR}$ are angle bisectors and angle P = 80°. How many degrees are there in angle QSR?

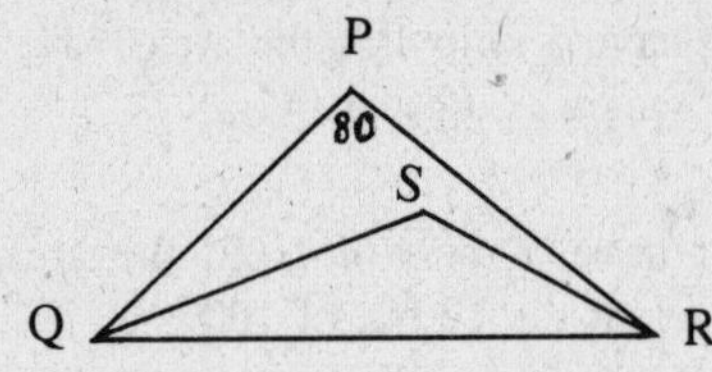

(A) 115 (B) 120 (C) 125 (D) 130 (E) 135

SOLUTIONS TO PRACTICE EXERCISES XII

1. **(C)** Represent the angles as 2x, 3x, and 7x.

$$2x + 3x + 7x = 180$$
$$12x = 180$$
$$x = 15$$

The angles are 30°, 45°, and 105°. Since one angle is between 90° and 180°, the triangle is called an obtuse triangle.

2. **(B)** If the sides have a ratio 1:3, the areas have a ratio 1:9. Therefore, the area of the large square is 9(5), or 45.

3. **(B)** If the radii have a ratio of 10:9, the areas have a ratio of 100:81. Therefore, the decrease is 19 out of 100, or 19%.

4. **(C)**

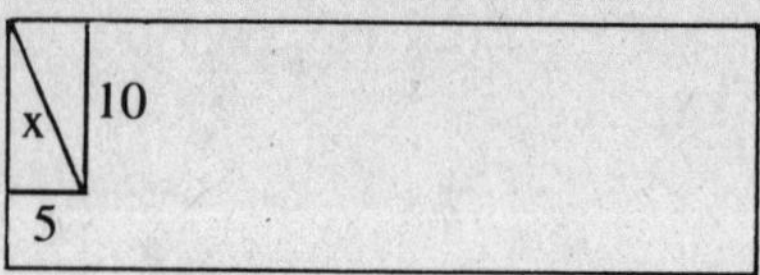

$$5^2 + 10^2 = x^2$$
$$25 + 100 = x^2$$
$$x^2 = 125$$
$$x = \sqrt{125} = \sqrt{25}\,\sqrt{5} = 5\sqrt{5}$$

5. **(D)**

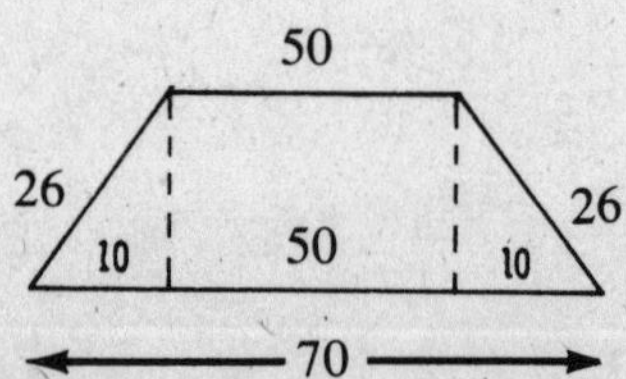

When altitudes are drawn from both ends of the upper base in an isosceles trapezoid, the figure is divided into a rectangle and two congruent right triangles. The center section of the lower base is equal to the upper base, and the remainder of the lower base is divided equally between both ends. The altitude can then be found using the Pythagorean theorem. In this case, we have a 5,12,13 triangle with all measures doubled, so the altitude is 24. The area is $\frac{1}{2}(24)(120)$, or 1440.

6. **(D)** The consecutive angles of a parallelogram are supplementary, so

$$x + 4x = 180$$
$$5x = 180$$
$$x = 36$$

Angle P is 4(36), or 144°.

7. **(C)**

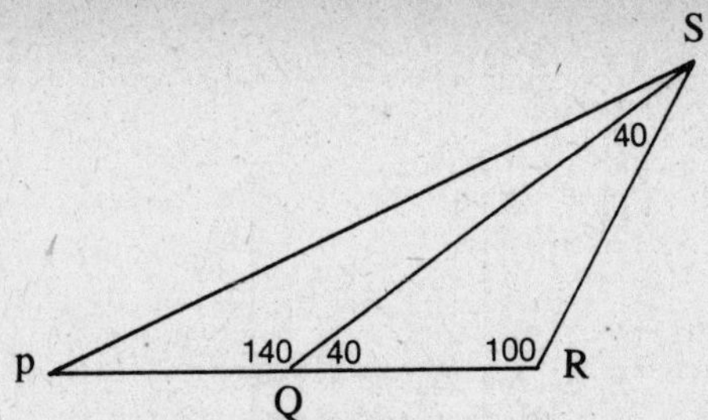

Since $\overline{QR} \cong \overline{RS}$, angle RQS ≅ angle RSQ. There are 80° left in the triangle, so each of these angles is 40°. Angle SQP is supplementary to angle SQR, making it 140°. Since $\overline{QP} \cong \overline{QS}$, angle QPS ≅ angle QSP. There are 40° left in the triangle, so each of these angles is 20°.

8. **(E)** Add the x values and divide by 2. Add the y values and divide by 2.

9. **(B)** Change 18 inches to 1.5 feet. Letting each side of the base be x, the volume is $1.5x^2$.

$1.5x^2 = 6$
$15x^2 = 60$
$x^2 = 4$
$x = 2$

10. **(D)** The surface area of a cube is made up of 6 equal squares. If each edge of the cube is x, then,

$6x^2 = 150$
$x^2 = 25$
$x = 5$
Volume = $(\text{edge})^3 = 5^3 = 125$

11. **(B)**

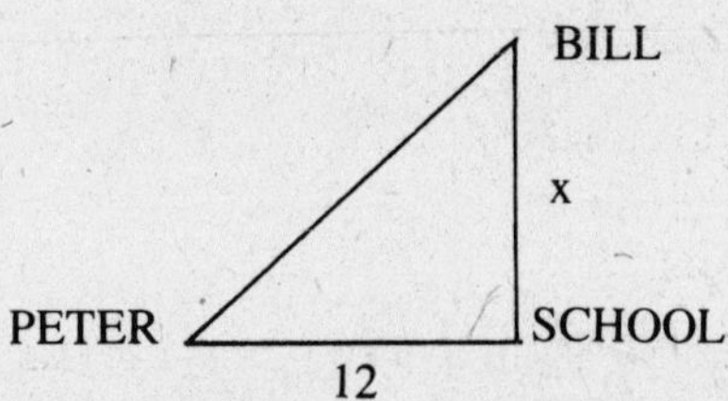

The direct distance from Peter's house to Bill's can be represented by means of the Pythagorean theorem as $\sqrt{144 + x^2}$. Then

$\sqrt{144 + x^2} = (12 + x) - 6$
$\sqrt{144 + x^2} = x + 6$
Square both sides.
$144 + x^2 = x^2 + 12x + 36$
$144 = 12x + 36$
$108 = 12x$
$9 = x$

12. **(B)**

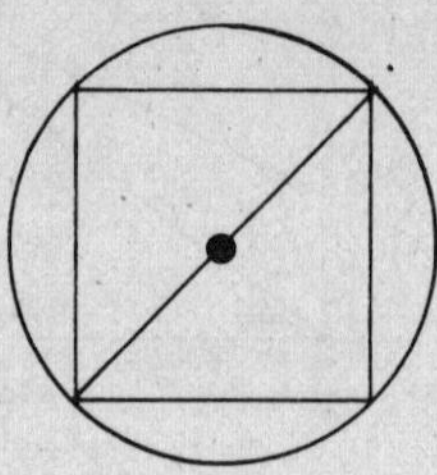

The diagonal of the square will be a diameter of the circle.

$\pi r^2 = 18\pi$

$r^2 = 18$

$r = \sqrt{18} = \sqrt{9}\sqrt{2} = 3\sqrt{2}$

Then the diameter is $6\sqrt{2}$ and, since the triangles are 45° − 45° − 90°, a side of the square is 6.

13. **(E)** We want the area in square feet, so change y yards to 3y feet. The area is then (3y)(f), or 3yf square feet. If each square yard costs x cents, we change this to dollars by dividing x by 100. Thus, each square yard costs $\frac{x}{100}$ dollars. The cost of 3yf square yards will be $(3yf)\left(\frac{x}{100}\right)$, or $\frac{3xyf}{100}$.

Since $\frac{3}{100} = .03$, the correct answer is (E).

14. **(D)** The area of the circle is $\pi\,(6)^2$, or 36π.

In the triangle $\frac{1}{2}(6)(h) = 36\pi$

$3h = 36\pi$

$h = 12\pi$

15. **(E)** There are (180 − p) degrees left, which must be divided between 2 congruent angles. Each angle will contain $\frac{180 - p}{2}$ or $90 - \frac{p}{2}$ degrees.

16. **(D)**

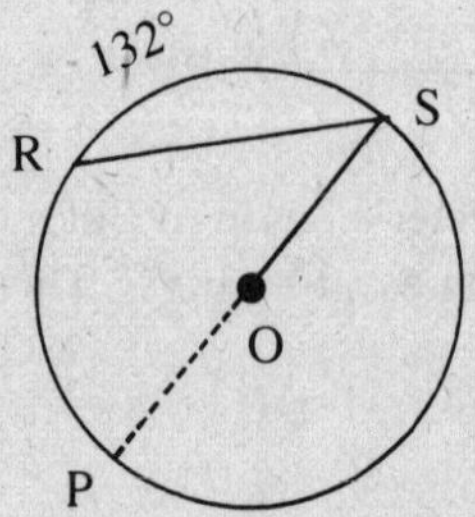

By extending $\overline{SO}$ until it hits the circle at P, arc PRS is a semicircle. Therefore, arc PR = 48°, and inscribed angle RSO = 24°.

17. **(D)**

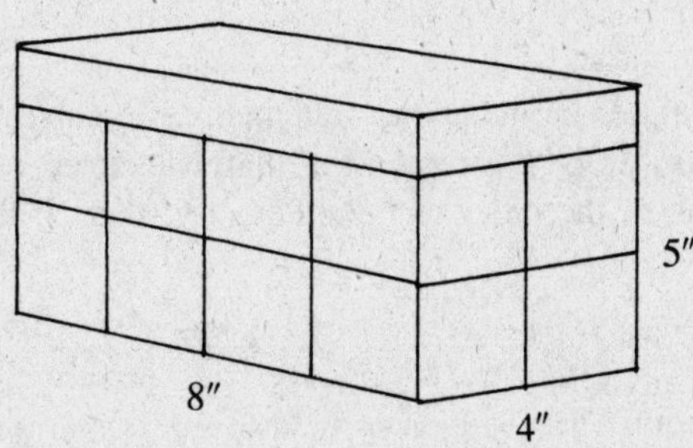

To fill the bottom layer, we can fit two rows of 4 cubes each. We can fit another layer above this, leaving a height of 1 inch on top empty. Therefore, the compartment can hold 16 cubes.

18. **(E)**

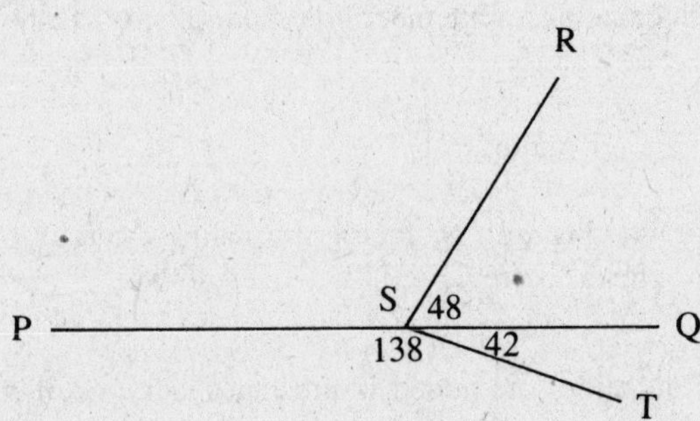

Since $\measuredangle$ RST is a right angle, 42° are left for $\measuredangle$ QST. Since PSQ is a straight angle of 180°, $\measuredangle$ PST contains 138°.

19. **(A)** The volume of the pail is found using the formula $V = \pi r^2h$. Since our answers are not in terms of π, it is best to use $\frac{22}{7}$ as a value for π, since the 7 will cancel with r^2, $V = \frac{22}{7} \cdot \overset{7}{\cancel{49}} \cdot 9$. Rather than multiply this out, which will take unnecessary time, we divide by 231 and cancel wherever possible.

$$\frac{\overset{2}{\cancel{22}} \cdot 7 \cdot \overset{3}{\cancel{9}}}{\underset{\underset{\cancel{3}}{\cancel{33}}}{\cancel{231}}} = 6$$

20. **(D)** If $\measuredangle$ P = 80°, there are 100° left between angles PQR and PRQ. If they are both bisected, there will be 50° between angles SQR and SRQ, leaving 130° in triangle SRQ for angle QSR.

XIII. INEQUALITIES

In solving algebraic inequality statements, we solve them as we would an equation. However, we must remember that whenever we multiply or divide by a negative number, the order of the inequality, that is, the inequality symbol, must be reversed.

Example: Solve for x: $3 - 5x > 18$
Solution: Add -3 to both sides:

$$-5x > 15$$

Divide by -5, remembering to reverse the inequality:

$$x < -3$$

Example: $5x - 4 > 6x - 6$
Solution: Collect all x terms on the left and numerical terms on the right. As with equations, remember that if a term crosses the inequality symbol, the term changes sign.

$$-x > -2$$

Divide (or multiply) by -1:

$$x < 2$$

In working with geometric inequalities, certain postulates and theorems should be reviewed. The list follows.

1. If unequal quantities are added to unequal quantities of the same order, the result is unequal quantities in the same order.

2. If equal quantities are added to, or subtracted from, unequal quantities, the results are unequal in the same order.

3. If unequal quantities are subtracted from equal quantities, the results are unequal in the opposite order.

4. Doubles, or halves, of unequals are unequal in the same order.

5. If the first of three quantities is greater than the second, and the second is greater than the third, then the first is greater than the third.

6. The sum of two sides of a triangle must be greater than the third side.

7. If two sides of a triangle are unequal, the angles opposite these sides are unequal, with the larger angle opposite the larger side.

8. If two angles of a triangle are unequal, the sides opposite these angles are unequal, with the larger side opposite the larger angle.

9. An exterior angle of a triangle is greater than either remote interior angle.

Example:

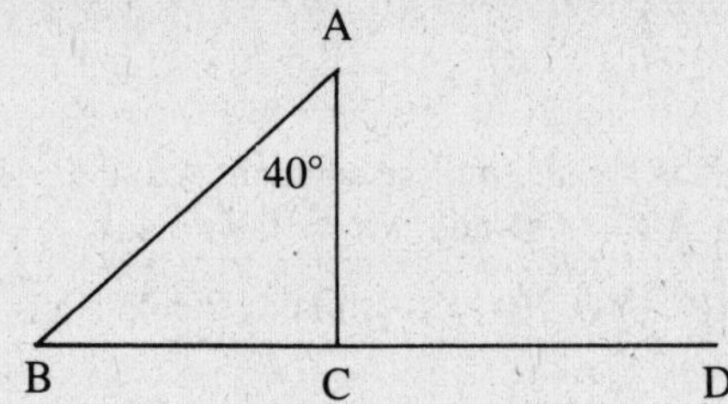

If BCD is a straight line and ∡ A = 40°, then angle ACD contains
(A) 40° (B) 140° (C) less than 40°
(D) more than 40° (E) 100°

Solution: The correct answer is (D), since an exterior angle of a triangle is always greater than either of the remote interior angles.

Example:

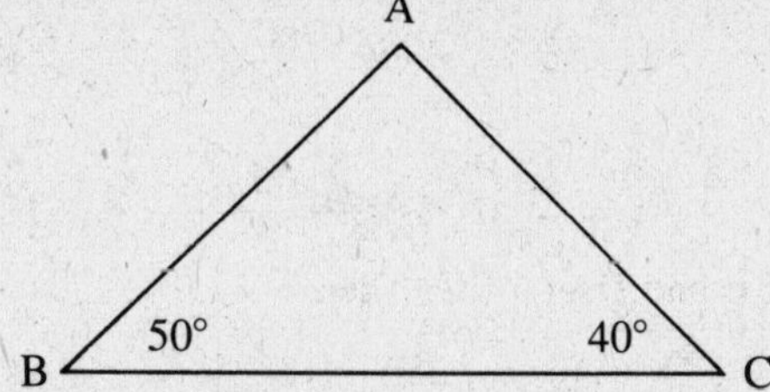

Which of the following statements is true regarding the above triangle?
(A) $\overline{AB} > \overline{AC}$ (B) $\overline{AC} > \overline{BC}$ (C) $\overline{AB} > \overline{BC}$
(D) $\overline{AC} > \overline{AB}$ (E) $\overline{BC} > \overline{AB} + \overline{AC}$

Solution: The correct answer is (D), since a comparison between two sides of a triangle depends upon the angles opposite these sides. The larger side is always opposite the larger angle. Since angle A contains 90°, the largest side of this triangle is BC, followed by AC and then AB.

PRACTICE EXERCISES XIII

Work out the problem in the space provided. Circle the letter that appears before your answer.

1. If $x < y$, $2x = A$, and $2y = B$, then

   (A) $A = B$ (B) $A < B$ (C) $A > B$ (D) $A < x$ (E) $B < y$

2. If $a > b$ and $c > d$, then

   (A) $a = c$ (B) $a < d$ (C) $a + d = b + c$

   (D) $a + c < b + d$ (E) $a + c > b + d$

3. If $ab > 0$ and $a < 0$, which of the following is negative?

   (A) b (B) $-b$ (C) $-a$ (D) $(a - b)^2$ (E) $-(a + b)$

4. If $4 - x > 5$, then

(A) $x > 1$ (B) $x > -1$ (C) $x < 1$ (D) $x < -1$ (E) $x = -1$

5. Point X is located on line segment AB and point Y is located on line segment CD. If AB = CD and AX > CY, then

(A) XB>YD (B) XB<YD (C) AX>XB (D) AX<XB (E) AX>AB

6. In triangle ABC, AB = BC. D is any point on side AB. Which of the following statements is always true?

(A) AD<DC (B) AD=DC (C) AD>DC (D) AD≤DC (E) AD≥DC

7. In the diagram at the right,

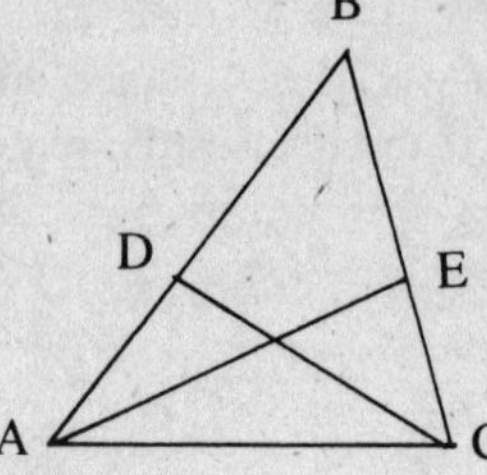

BD = BE and DA > EC. Then

(A) AE > DC (B) ∡ BCA > ∡ BAC (C) ∡ DCA > ∡ EAC

(D) AB < BC (E) AD < BD

8. In the diagram at the right, which of the following is always true?
   I. a > b
   II. c > a
   III. d > a

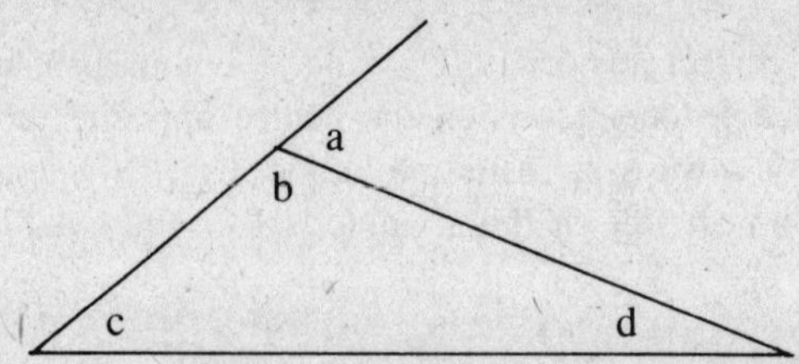

(A) I only (B) II and III only (C) I, II, and III

(D) II only (E) none of these

9. If point X is on line segment AB, all of the following may be true except

(A) AX = XB (B) AX > XB (C) AX < XB

(D) AB > XB (E) AX + XB < AB

10. If $x > 0$, $y > 0$, and $x - y < 0$, then

(A) $x > y$ (B) $x < y$ (C) $x+y < 0$ (D) $y-x < 0$ (E) $x = -y$

SOLUTIONS TO PRACTICE EXERCISES XIII

1. **(B)** Doubles of unequals are unequal in the same order.

2. **(E)** If unequal quantities are added to unequal quantities of the same order, the results are unequal in the same order.

3. **(A)** If the product of two numbers is > 0 (positive), then either both numbers are positive or both are negative. Since $a < 0$ (negative), b must also be negative.

4. **(D)** $4 - x > 5$
   $-x > 1$ Divide by -1. Change inequality sign.
   $x < -1$

5. **(B)**

A ——————●—————— B
X

C ——●—————————— D
Y

If unequal quantities are subtracted from equal quantities, the results are unequal in the same order.

6. **(A)**

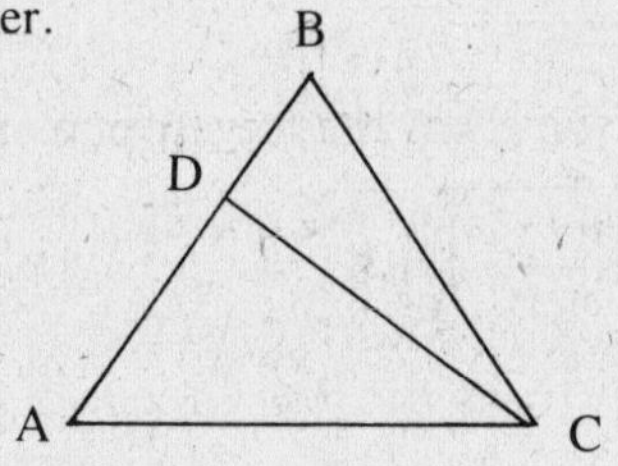

Since AB = BC, ∡ BAC = ∡ BCA. Since ∡ BCA > ∡ DCA, it follows that ∡ BAC is also greater than ∡ DCA. Then DC > DA. If two angles of a triangle are unequal, the sides opposite these angles are unequal, with the larger side opposite the larger angle.

7. **(B)** BA > BC. If equal quantities are added to unequal quantities, the sums are unequal in the same order. It follows in triangle ABC, that the angle opposite BA will be greater than the angle opposite BC.

8. **(E)** An exterior angle of a triangle must be greater than either remote interior angle. There is no fixed relationship between an exterior angle and its adjacent interior angle.

9. **(E)** Point X could be so located to make each of the other choices true, but the whole segment AB will always be equal to the sum of its parts AX and XB.

10. **(B)** If x and y are both positive, but $x - y$ is negative, then y must be a larger number than x.

XIV MATHEMATICS USAGE QUESTIONS

DIRECTIONS: Solve each problem and mark the letter of the correct answer on your answer sheet.

DO YOUR FIGURING HERE

1. If the outer diameter of a cylindrical oil tank is 54.28 inches and the inner diameter is 48.7 inches, the thickness of the wall of the tank, in inches, is

A. 5.58
B. 2.29
C. 2.79
D. 6.42
E. 3.21

2. Which of the following has the largest numerical value?

F. $\frac{3}{5}$
G. $(\frac{2}{3})(\frac{3}{4})$
H. $\sqrt{.25}$
J. $(.9)^2$
K. $\frac{2}{.3}$

3. $\frac{1}{4}\%$ written as a decimal is

A. 25
B. 2.5
C. .25
D. .025
E. .0025

4. 53% of the 1000 students at Jackson High are girls. How many boys are there in the school?

F. 470
G. 53
H. 47
J. 530
K. 540

DO YOUR FIGURING HERE

5. How many digits are there in the square root of a perfect square of 12 digits?

A. 4
B. 6
C. 10
D. 12
E. 24

6. The value of $\dfrac{\frac{1}{2}}{\frac{1}{3} - \frac{1}{4}}$ is

F. 6
G. $\frac{1}{6}$
H. 1
J. 3
K. $\frac{3}{2}$

7. The sum of Alan's age and Bob's age is 40. The sum of Bob's age and Carl's age is 34. The sum of Alan's age and Carl's age is 42. How old is Bob?

A. 18
B. 24
C. 20
D. 16
E. 12

8. On a map having a scale of $\frac{1}{4}$ inch = 20 miles, how many inches should there be between towns 325 miles apart?

F. $4\frac{1}{16}$
G. $16\frac{1}{4}$
H. $81\frac{1}{4}$
J. $32\frac{1}{2}$
K. $6\frac{1}{4}$

9. In Simon's General Store, there are *m* male employees and *f* female employees. What part of the staff is male?

A. $\frac{m + f}{m}$
B. $\frac{m + f}{f}$
C. $\frac{m}{f}$
D. $\frac{m}{m + f}$
E. $\frac{f}{m}$

DO YOUR FIGURING HERE

10. If the angles of a triangle are in the ratio 2:3:4, the triangle is

F. acute
G. isosceles
H. right
J. equilateral
K. obtuse

11. If the length and width of a rectangle are each multiplied by 2, then

A. the area and perimeter are both multiplied by 4
B. the area is multiplied by 2 and the perimeter by 4
C. the area is multiplied by 4 and the perimeter by 2
D. the area and perimeter are both multiplied by 2
E. the perimeter is multiplied by 4 and the area by 8

12. Paul needs m minutes to mow the lawn. After working for k minutes, what part of the lawn is still unmowed?

F. $\frac{k}{m}$
G. $\frac{m}{k}$
H. $\frac{m - k}{k}$
J. $\frac{m - k}{m}$
K. $\frac{k - m}{m}$

13. Mr. Marcus earns $250 per week. If he spends 20% of his income for rent, 25% for food, and 10% for savings, how much is left each week for other expenses?

A. $112.50
B. $125
C. $137.50
D. $132.50
E. $140

14. Find the value of $(3\sqrt{2})^2$

F. $9\sqrt{2}$
G. $6\sqrt{2}$
H. 18
J. 36
K. 24

15. How far is the point $(-4, -3)$ from the origin?

A. 2
B. 2.5

DO YOUR FIGURING HERE

C. $4\sqrt{2}$
D. $4\sqrt{3}$
E. 5

16. The product of 3456 and 789 is exactly

F. 2726787
G. 2726785
H. 2726781
J. 2726784
K. 2726786

17. Susan got up one morning at 7:42 A.M. and went to bed that evening at 10:10 P.M. How much time elapsed between her getting up and going to bed that day?

A. 18 hrs. 2 min.
B. 14 hrs. 18 min.
C. 15 hrs. 18 min.
D. 9 hrs. 22 min.
E. 14 hrs. 28 min.

18. Find the perimeter of right triangle ABC if the area of square AEDC is 100 and the area of square BCFG is 36.

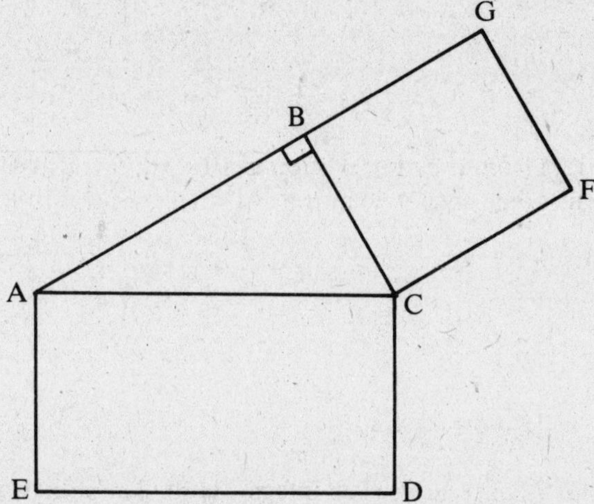

F. 22
G. 24
H. $16 + 6\sqrt{3}$
J. $16 + 6\sqrt{2}$
K. cannot be determined from information given

DO YOUR FIGURING HERE

19. Find the number of degrees in angle 1 if AB = AC, DE = DC, angle 2 = 40° and angle 3 = 80°.

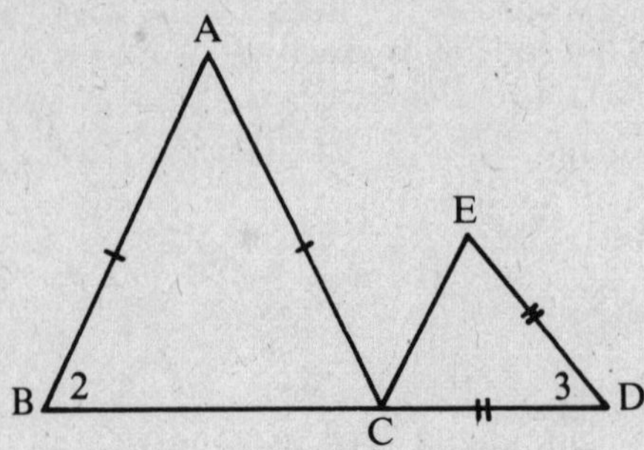

A. 60
B. 40
C. 90
D. 50
E. 80

20. If p pencils cost 2D dollars, how many pencils can be bought for c cents?

F. $\frac{pc}{2D}$

G. $\frac{pc}{200D}$

H. $\frac{50pc}{D}$

J. $\frac{2Dp}{c}$

K. 200pcD

21. Two trains start from the same station at 10 A.M., one traveling east at 60 m.p.h. and the other west at 70 m.p.h. At what time will they be 455 miles apart?

A. 3:30 P.M.
B. 12:30 P.M.
C. 1:30 P.M.
D. 1 P.M.
E. 2 P.M.

22. The average of 7 consecutive even integers is 14. The sum of the first 2 integers is

F. 18
G. 23
H. 14
J. 20
K. cannot be determined

DO YOUR FIGURING HERE

23. If 12 inches = 1 foot and 3 feet = 1 yard, what part of a yard is 54 inches?

A. $\frac{2}{3}$
B. $\frac{5}{4}$
C. $\frac{6}{5}$
D. $\frac{3}{2}$
E. $\frac{7}{6}$

24. If a classroom contains 20 to 24 students and each corridor contains 8 to 10 classrooms, what is the minimum number of students on one corridor at a given time, if all classrooms are occupied?

F. 200
G. 192
H. 160
J. 240
K. 210

25. If the area of each circle enclosed in rectangle ABCD is 9π, the area of ABCD is

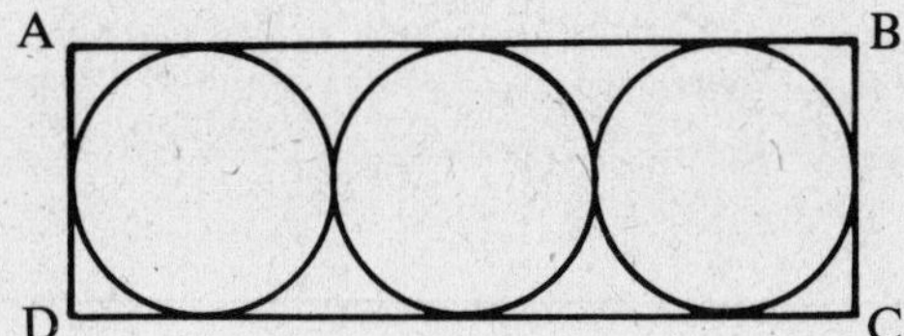

A. 108
B. 27
C. 54
D 54π
E. 108π

MARK YOUR ANSWERS HERE

1 Ⓐ Ⓑ Ⓒ Ⓓ Ⓔ	6 Ⓕ Ⓖ Ⓗ Ⓙ Ⓚ	11 Ⓐ Ⓑ Ⓒ Ⓓ Ⓔ	16 Ⓕ Ⓖ Ⓗ Ⓙ Ⓚ	21 Ⓐ Ⓑ Ⓒ Ⓓ Ⓔ
2 Ⓕ Ⓖ Ⓗ Ⓙ Ⓚ	7 Ⓐ Ⓑ Ⓒ Ⓓ Ⓔ	12 Ⓕ Ⓖ Ⓗ Ⓙ Ⓚ	17 Ⓐ Ⓑ Ⓒ Ⓓ Ⓔ	22 Ⓕ Ⓖ Ⓗ Ⓙ Ⓚ
3 Ⓐ Ⓑ Ⓒ Ⓓ Ⓔ	8 Ⓕ Ⓖ Ⓗ Ⓙ Ⓚ	13 Ⓐ Ⓑ Ⓒ Ⓓ Ⓔ	18 Ⓕ Ⓖ Ⓗ Ⓙ Ⓚ	23 Ⓐ Ⓑ Ⓒ Ⓓ Ⓔ
4 Ⓕ Ⓖ Ⓗ Ⓙ Ⓚ	9 Ⓐ Ⓑ Ⓒ Ⓓ Ⓔ	14 Ⓕ Ⓖ Ⓗ Ⓙ Ⓚ	19 Ⓐ Ⓑ Ⓒ Ⓓ Ⓔ	24 Ⓕ Ⓖ Ⓗ Ⓙ Ⓚ
5 Ⓐ Ⓑ Ⓒ Ⓓ Ⓔ	10 Ⓕ Ⓖ Ⓗ Ⓙ Ⓚ	15 Ⓐ Ⓑ Ⓒ Ⓓ Ⓔ	20 Ⓕ Ⓖ Ⓗ Ⓙ Ⓚ	25 Ⓐ Ⓑ Ⓒ Ⓓ Ⓔ

CORRECT ANSWERS TO PRACTICE MATHEMATICS USAGE QUESTIONS XIV

1. **C.**	6. **F.**	11. **C.**	16. **J.**	21. **C.**
2. **K.**	7. **D.**	12. **J.**	17. **E.**	22. **F.**
3. **E.**	8. **F.**	13. **A.**	18. **G.**	23. **D.**
4. **F.**	9. **D.**	14. **H.**	19. **C.**	24. **H.**
5. **B.**	10. **F.**	15. **E.**	20. **G.**	25. **A.**

EXPLANATORY ANSWERS TO PRACTICE MATHEMATICS USAGE QUESTIONS

1. **C.** The difference of 5.58 must be divided between both ends. The thickness on each side is 2.79.

2. **K.** $\frac{3}{5} = .6$

   $(\frac{2}{3})(\frac{3}{4}) = \frac{1}{2} = .5$

   $\sqrt{.25} = .5$

   $(.9)^2 = .81$

   $\frac{2}{.3} = \frac{20}{3} = 6.6$

3. **E.** $\frac{1}{4} = .25$

   $\frac{1}{4} = .25\% = .0025$

4. **F.** 47% of 1000 are boys

   $(.47)(1000) = 470$ boys

5. **B.** For every pair of digits in a number, there will be one digit in the square root.

6. **F.** Multiply every term by 12.

   $\frac{6}{4 - 3} = 6$

7. **D.** $A + B = 40$

   $B + C = 34$

   $A + C = 42$

   Subtract the second equation from the third.

   $A - B = 8$

   Subtract this from the first equation.

   $2B = 32$

   $B = 16$

8. **F.** Use a proportion comparing inches to miles.

   $\frac{\frac{1}{4}}{20} = \frac{x}{325}$

   $20x = \frac{325}{4}$

   $x = \frac{325}{4} \cdot \frac{1}{20} = \frac{325}{80}$

   $= 4\frac{5}{80} = 4\frac{1}{16}$

9. **D.** There are m + f people on the staff. Of these, m are male.

   $\frac{m}{m + f}$ of the staff is male.

10. **F.** Represent the angles as 2x, 3x, and 4x.

    $9x = 180$

    $x = 20$

    The angles are 40°, 60°, and 80°, all acute.

11. **C.** The linear ratio stays constant, so the perimeter is also multiplied by 2. The area ratio is the square of the linear ratio, so the area is multiplied by 2^2 or 4.

12. **J.** In k minutes, $\frac{k}{m}$ of the lawn is mowed.

    Still undone is $1 - \frac{k}{m}$ or $\frac{m - k}{m}$.

13. **A.** 55% of his salary is spent. 45% is left. There is only one answer among the choices less than $\frac{1}{2}$ of his salary.

14. **H.** $(3\sqrt{2})(3\sqrt{2}) = 9 \cdot 2 = 18$

15. **E.** Plotting the point shows a 3, 4, 5, triangle.

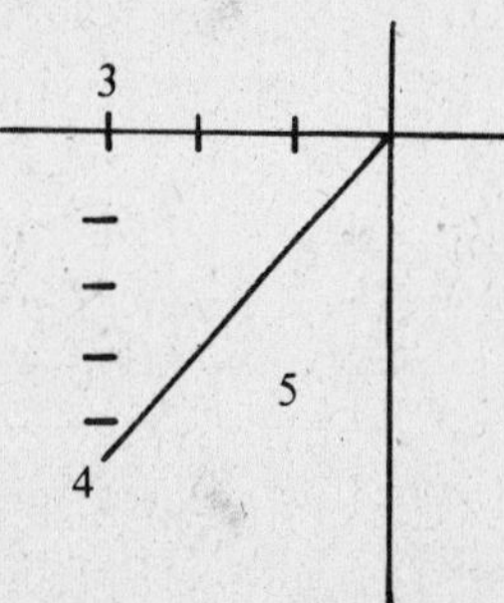

16. **J.** Since 6 times 9 is 54, the product must end in 4.

17. **E.** Figure the time elapsed on either side of 12 noon. From 7:42 A.M. to 12 noon is 4 hrs. 18 min. From 12 noon to 10:10 P.M. is 10 hrs. 10 min. The sum of the two is 14 hrs. 28 min.

18. **G.** Each side of AEDC is 10.
Each side of BCFG is 6.
Triangle ABC is a 6, 8, 10 triangle, making the perimeter 24.

19. **C.**

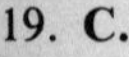

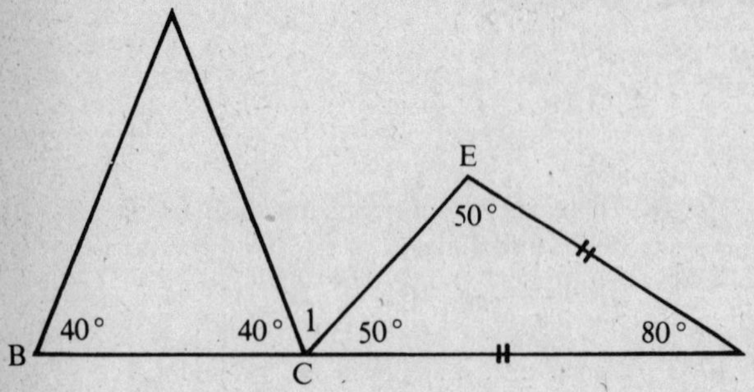

There are 90° left for angle 1 if BCD is a straight angle.

20. **G.** Use a proportion comparing pencils to cents.
Change 2D dollars to 200D cents.

$$\frac{p}{200D} = \frac{x}{c}$$

$$\frac{pc}{200D} = x$$

21. **C.** Distance of first train = 60x
Distance of second train = 70x

$$60x + 70x = 455$$
$$130x = 455$$
$$x = 3\tfrac{1}{2}$$

In $3\frac{1}{2}$ hours, the time will be 1:30 p.m.

22. **F.** The average will be the middle integer, since they are evenly spaced. If 14 is the middle or fourth consecutive even integer, the third is 12, second is 10, first is 8. The sum of the first two is 18.

23. **D.** There are 36 inches in 1 yard.

$$\frac{54}{36} = \frac{3}{2}$$

24. **H.** The minimum is 20 students in 8 classrooms.

25. **A.** The radius of each circle is 3, making the dimensions of the rectangle 18 by 6, and the area (18) (6), or 108.

SOCIAL STUDIES READING and NATURAL SCIENCE READING

The two Reading tests of the ACT exam serve double functions. Each test is a test of your knowledge in the subject area. In addition, each is a test of your reading ability. Reading is, of course, basic to scholarship. Proficiency in reading serves as proof of achievement and as prediction of future achievement. The questions based on reading passages test not only how well you know the subject but also how well you understand what you read and how well you can interpret the meaning of the passage and the intent of the author.

Reading speed is vital for success with questions based upon reading. You cannot answer the questions intelligently if you have not had time to read the passage. What follows is a short course in improving your reading speed.

Read, Read, Read! The best way to increase your reading speed is to read. Read everything in sight between now and the test. Newspaper reading is an especially good way to improve your reading skills. Don't be satisfied with just the opening paragraph of each article. Push yourself to read the whole story and give it your full attention as you read. If your mind wanders, you will not comprehend what you read.

Expand Your Peripheral Vision. You have probably heard about speed readers who can race down a page, consuming it almost instantaneously. Unfortunately, that technique works for very few people. To read with understanding your eyes must fixate (i.e., stop). Most people fixate on each word because that is the way reading is taught. However, this method wastes a great deal of time.

The key to increasing your reading speed is to take in more words each time your eyes stop. If a line has ten words in it and you are able to read the line by stopping only twice instead of ten times, you would be reading five times as fast as you do now. For example, if you are now reading about 200 words per minute, by stopping only twice per line you would increase your speed to 1000 words per minute.

Don't Subvocalize. If you can hear every word you read, you are subvocalizing. No matter how fast you can talk, you can read faster if you stop subvocalizing. Reading teachers have employed many tricks to stop people from subvocalizing. They may ask students to put pebbles in their mouths or to chew on pencils. We ask only that you be aware that you may be subvocalizing. Reading is a very psychological thing; if you become aware of your bad habits, you may be able to correct them.

Become Aware of Words. You cannot build a good vocabulary in a day or even a week. However, you can increase your knowledge of words by stopping to look up each new word you run across and by systematic study of those prefixes, suffixes and roots which make up the greater part of the English language.

Use Your Hand. Here is a simple technique for you to try; when you read, move your hand or your pen underneath the line you are reading. Because your eyes tend to move as quickly as your pen, you will not stop on every word, you will not regress, and you probably will not subvocalize. However, what you may do is concentrate on your pen and not on the reading passage. That is why you must practice this technique before using it on your test.

Start your pen at the second or third word in the line and stop it before the last word in the line. Your peripheral vision will pick up the first and last words in the lines and you will save time by not having to focus on them.

Try the SQ2R Method. The SQ2R method of reading was developed by the government during World War II in an attempt to advance men to officer rank as quickly as possible. The method used may be helpful to you and so it is presented here.

1. SCAN—Before you read, scan the material (S). Once you have scanned the passage, you should be aware of the type of passage you are about to read and the logical structure of the passage.
2. QUESTION—Scanning the passage should bring questions to mind (Q).
3. READ—Now read the passage (R1), trying to answer your own questions. By using this question and answer method you will become involved in what you are reading and consequently you will remember more of it. As you read, stop briefly at the end of each paragraph and think about what you have read. If you cannot remember what you have read, reread the paragraph immediately. Don't wait until the end of the passage expecting that understanding will come later.
4. REREAD—After you have read the passage, reread it quickly (R2). In other words, scan it a second time. This second scanning should give you additional information and allow you to fill in gaps in your understanding of the passage.

Keep Track of Your Time. Timing is an essential element of this test. That is why it is important that you wear a watch while taking the exam. You may think the suggestions given here will slow you down. On the contrary, if you practice these techniques before taking the test, you will actually finish the readings faster and your score will be higher.

Speed Reading Tests

DIRECTIONS: Read the following passage as quickly as possible, timing yourself as you read. When you are finished, divide the number of minutes it took you to read the passage into the number of words in the passage (435). This will give you the number of words you are reading per minute. Next, answer the questions following the reading passage. Multiply the number of words you are reading per minute by the number of questions which you answered correctly and divide by the number of questions in the test (5). This will give you your Real Reading Speed. To illustrate, if you read 200 words per minute and answered three questions correctly, your Real Reading Speed would be:

$$\frac{\text{200 words per minute} \times \text{3 correct answers}}{\text{5 questions}} = \text{120 words per min.}$$

Sample Reading Passage

The supernatural world was both real and awesome to early man, as it still is in primitive societies, and heavy dependency was put upon it in worshiping and propitiating the gods. It is more than likely that the degree to which our ancestral homo sapiens relied upon telepathic communication instead of articulate speech would today fill us with both amazement and disbelief. Certainly human beings who populated the earth prior to the fourteenth century are well documented as having had a keen interest in the spirit world, thought transference, witches, premonitions, and so forth. In order to conjure up departed spirits, make predictions or go into a trance, a variety of drugs existing since antiquity (many of which are now classed as hallucinogens) were used by witch doctors, alchemists, shaman and cultist tribesmen throughout the world, and seemed to buttress natural powers. Yage, a drug related to LSD and known under several different names (including "telepathine"), is from a vine native to the Amazon Basin and is identical with harmine, an alkaloid from the seeds of wild rice. Both are reputed to aid in locating missing objects, in transporting users to distant lands and times, and in communicating with the dead. Greatly favored in Europe at witches' sabbaths are bufotenin (related to serotonin and first obtained from toad skins), scopolamine and henbane.

However, by the fifteenth century the church itself had declared magic and witchcraft evil. After the witch-hunts and witch burnings that continued for three centuries, the supernatural world with its ghosts, demons and human emissaries, was in a state of subjugation. It was not until the ninteenth century that there was any open revival of interest in "seers" and "spooks" or acceptance of their possible validity.

Those who pioneered the re-exploration of what is now called "psi phenomena," or all things pertaining to the psychic world, were considered crazy, pathetic, eccentric and ridiculous. They were sneered at for their sacrilegious superstition and made to feel uncomfortable among their fellow men. Sir Oliver Lodge and a handful of others did succeed, however, in establishing the Society for Psychical Research in London in 1882, and gradually interest in spiritualism, clairvoyance and mental telepathy seeped out of its small confines and spread elsewhere. The American Society for Psychic Research was founded in 1906; however, the psi subject did not gain much public ground until the 1930s and it is still far from respected despite the efforts of such men as Drs. J.B. Rhine and Gardner Murphy, who have approached it scientifically and have been steadily working at it in conjunction with their European colleagues.

Adapted from LAW SCHOOL ADMISSION TEST, Candrilli & Slawsky, ARCO Publishing, Inc.: New York, NY. © 1978, by permission of the authors.

1. The author's attitude toward telephathic communication is one of

A. disbelief
B. skepticism
C. acceptance
D. inquisitiveness

2. All of the following groups were mentioned by the author as using drugs of ancient origin except

I. witch doctors
II. voodooists
III. alchemists
IV. shamen
V. cultist tribesmen

F. I only
G. I and II only
H. II, III, and IV only
J. II only

3. Another name for the drug known as telepathine is

A. marijuana
B. LSD
C. wild rice
D. yage

4. Harmine is reputed to have the ability to

F. transport users to distant lands and aid in communication with the dead
G. enable one to communicate with spirits
H. help the user find his directions
J. transport the users to distant lands, aid in locating missing objects, and help the user communicate with the dead

5. During what period of time, approximately, did the church declare magic and witchcraft evil?

A. 1400s
B. 1500s
C. 1600s
D. 1900s

Answers To Speed Reading Test

1. **C.** 2. **J.** 3. **D.** 4. **J.** 5. **A.**

The same reading techniques apply to all types of reading passages. However, due to the nature of the passage, some may have to be read more slowly than others. The reading passages may be very general or they may be highly specific and full of detail. Some of these readings may be self-contained; that is, all the information on which you will be questioned is stated in the passage. Others are idea oriented and may require that you draw conclusions from the information given in order to answer the questions. Still others require you to go beyond the passage and to answer on the basis of your related knowledge.

Types of Questions You May be Asked

1. *General Question.* These questions are usually based on the main idea of the passage, its purpose or the best title for it. To answer this type of question, look for the choice which takes in the greatest amount of information. Wrong answers are usually too limited or too vague.
2. *Inclusive Question.* These questions often contain the phrase "all of the following EXCEPT" and are best answered by attempting to eliminate all the alternatives that do not fit first. This narrows the field considerably, increasing your chances for choosing the right answer.
3. *Comparison Question.* If the passage mentions both nineteenth- and twentieth-century authors, for example, you can expect to be quizzed on comparisons between the two. Try to spot these obvious sources of comparison as you read.
4. *Detail Question.* These questions refer to a fact or statistic given in the reading. Don't try to memorize these specifics. A glance back at the reading will enable you to answer. The greater your familiarity with the subject, the easier it will be for you to answer this type of question.

How to Answer Questions Based Upon Reading Passages

1. Skim the passage to get a general idea of the subject matter and of the point that is being made. If the subject material is totally foreign to you, skip that passage

and leave it for last. If you skip a passage for the time being, be certain to skip *all* the answer spaces for questions relating to that passage.

2. Reread the passage, giving attention to details and point of view. Be alert for the author's hints as to what he or she thinks is important. Phrases such as *note that, of importance is* and *do not overlook* give clues to what points the writer is stressing.

3. If the author has quoted material from another source, be sure that you understand for what purpose. Does the author agree or disagree? If the passage cites more than one opinion on a subject, do you recognize the juxtaposition of the opinions?

4. Read and answer one question at a time. Read the question or incomplete statement. Determine exactly what is being asked. Watch for negatives or all-inclusive words such as *always, never, all, only, every, absolutely, completely, none, entirely, no.* These words can affect your choice of answer.

5. Read all four answer choices. Eliminate those which are obviously incorrect. Reread the remaining options and refer to the passage, if necessary, to determine the *best* answer.

6. Do not allow yourself to spend too much time on any one question. If looking back at the passage does not help you find or figure out the answer, it may be that the question is related to but not directly based upon the passage. If the related facts do not come readily to mind, guess at an answer and put a mark beside the question so that you can come back to it later if there is time.

7. Once you have decided to read a passage and answer the questions based upon it, do not leave any blanks. Answer every question. Remember that you want to answer correctly as many questions as possible. You are unlikely to have time to reread a whole passage after you have completed the remainder of the test.

8. If you have skipped a reading passage, be sure to read it when you have completed the other questions, or, at the very least, be sure to fill in all the answer spaces at the last minute.

How to Answer Questions Not Based Upon Reading Passages

We cannot give you much help with answering questions which depend entirely upon what you know. We can suggest that as you work your way through this book you take careful note of the areas of knowledge in which you most often miss questions. Study in those specific areas is your best preparation. Otherwise, our advice is as before—answer every question, eliminating ridiculous answers, selecting accurately where you know the answer, guessing where you are not sure, and filling blanks rapidly when time runs out.

PRACTICE WITH SOCIAL STUDIES READING QUESTIONS

DIRECTIONS: Below each of the following reading passages is a series of questions. Choose the *best* answer to each question, interpreting what is stated or implied by the passage in the light of your own background in the subject. You may refer to the passage as often as necessary, though the answers to some questions may not be found expressly in the passage.

You tell me that law is above freedom of utterance. And I reply that you can have no wise laws nor free enforcement of wise laws until there is free expression of the wisdom of the people —and, alas, their folly with it. But if there is freedom, folly will die of its own poison. That is the history of the race. You say that freedom of utterance is not for time of stress, and I reply with the sad truth that only in time of stress is freedom of utterance in danger. No one questions it in calm days, because it is not needed. And the reverse is true also; only when free utterance is suppressed is it needed, and when it is needed, it is most vital to justice. Peace is good. But if you are interested in peace through force and without discussion, that is to say, without free utterance decently and in order—your interest in justice is slight. And peace without justice is tyranny. This state today is in more danger from suppression than from violence, because, in the end, suppression leads to violence. Violence is the child of suppression. Whoever pleads for justice helps to keep the peace; and whoever tramples upon the plea for justice, temperately made in the name of peace, only outrages peace and kills something fine in the heart of man which was put there when we got our manhood. When that is killed, brute meets brute on each side of the line.

1. Wise laws are dependent upon

A. judicious legislators
B. an enlightened population
C. freedom of expression
D. the amount of corruption in government

2. The greatest threat to free expression is during

F. a depression
G. a critical period
H. an election campaign
J. prosperity

3. Just as clouds precede the rain, suppression leads to

A. prejudice
B. violence
C. dictatorship
D. anarchy

4. When times are peaceful
   - **F.** there is bound to be graft in government
   - **G.** people don't care about freedom of speech
   - **H.** freedom of expression is never questioned
   - **J.** freedom of speech is in serious danger

5. When peace is brought about with the use of force
   - **A.** it will last a long time
   - **B.** it is lacking justice
   - **C.** it won't be democratic
   - **D.** there will be the need for a constant police force

6. "With freedom of expression, there will be much folly as well as wisdom." According to the author
   - **F.** this statement is not true
   - **G.** only with true freedom will wisdom survive and folly be exposed.
   - **H.** censorship is needed to weed out the folly
   - **J.** this statement is true only in times of stress

7. Our freedom is protected in the
   - **A.** first amendment to the Constitution
   - **B.** Declaration of Independence
   - **C.** Magna Carta
   - **D.** thirteenth amendment to the Constitution

8. A point being made by the author is that
   - **F.** man has animal instincts
   - **G.** he is unhappy over the death of folly
   - **H.** the ends justify the means
   - **J.** the ends do not justify the means

9. The group which would concur *most* heartily with this statement is the
   - **A.** American Legion
   - **B.** Daughters of the American Revolution
   - **C.** American Civil Liberties Union
   - **D.** Lions Club International

"He has refused his Assent to Laws, the most wholesome and necessary for the public good.

"He has forbidden his Governors to pass Laws of immediate and pressing importance, unless suspended in their operation till his Assent should be obtained; and when so suspended, he has utterly neglected to attend to them.

"He has refused to pass other Laws for the accommodation of large districts of people, unless those people would relinquish the right of Representation in the Legislature, a right inestimable to them and formidable to tyrants only.

"He has called together legislative bodies at places unusual, uncomfortable, and distant from the depository of their Public Records, for the sole purpose of fatiguing them into compliance with his measures.

"He has dissolved Representative Houses repeatedly, for opposing with manly firmness his invasions on the rights of the people.

"He has refused for a long time, after such dissolutions, to cause others to be elected; whereby the Legislative Powers, incapable of Annihilation, have returned to the People at large for their exercise; the State remaining in the mean time exposed to all the dangers of invasion from without, and convulsions within.

"He has endeavoured to prevent the population of these States; for that purpose obstructing the Laws of Naturalization of Foreigners; refusing to pass others to encourage their migration hither, and raising the conditions of new Appropriations of Lands.

"He has obstructed the Administration of Justice, by refusing his Assent to Laws for establishing Judiciary Powers.

"He has made Judges dependent on his Will alone, for the tenure of their offices, and the amount and payment of their salaries.

"He has erected a multitude of New Offices, and sent hither swarms of Officers to harass our People, and eat out their substance.

"He has kept among us, in times of peace, Standing Armies without the Consent of our legislature.

"He has affected to render the Military independent of and superior to the Civil Power . . .

"He has abdicated Government here, by declaring us out of his Protection and waging War against us.

"He has plundered our seas, ravaged our Coasts, burnt our towns, and destroyed the lives of our people.

"He is at this time transporting large armies of foreign mercenaries to compleat the works of death, desolation and tyranny, already begun with circumstances of Cruelty & perfidy scarcely paralleled in the most barbarous ages, and totally unworthy the Head of a civilized nation.

"He has constrained our fellow Citizens taken Captive on the High Seas to bear Arms against their Country, to become the executioners of their friends and Brethren, or to fall themselves by their Hands.

"He has exicted domestic insurrections amongst us, and has endeavoured to bring on the inhabitants of our frontiers, the merciless Indian Savages, whose known rule of warfare, is an undistinguished destruction of all ages, sexes and conditions."

10. The term *He* as used in this document refers to

F. the royal house of England in an adaptive use of the royal *We*
G. Parliament
H. specifically King George III
J. all kings of England, past and present

11. One of the objections raised in this document arises from

A. a manpower shortage
B. imposition of a state religion
C. the anti-slavery movement
D. complaints by the Indians

12. Among the complaints listed are a number of "sins of omission." These include

I. neglecting to Assent to laws passed in the colonies
I. refusing to protect the colonies
III. withholding tea from the American people
IV. not paying Judges

F. I only
G. I and II
H. I, II, and III
J. I, II, and IV

13. The foreign mercenaries referred to are the

A. Huguenots
B. prisoners released from jail
C. Hessians
D. Poles

14. A complaint against the large number of bureaucrats sent to govern appears to be that

F. their luxurious living conditions incited envy
G. they create too much red tape in government
H. they destroy public records
J. they eat too much

15. Among the "sins of commission" listed in the quoted portion are

I. suspension of self-government
II. murder
III. creation of a powerful, independent military
IV. taxation without representation

A. I and II
B. I and III
C. I, II, and III
D. I, II, III, and IV

16. A form of harassment complained about is

F. denial of the right to emigrate
G. capricious changes of the locale of government
H. high protective tariffs
J. restrictions on the planting of certain crops

17. The passage is quoted from the

A. Mayflower Compact
B. Articles of Confederation
C. Declaration of Independence
D. Constitution

18. The document was

F. repudiated by the southern colonies
G. vetoed by the King
H. signed by representatives of the thirteen colonies
J. signed by representatives of the thirteen colonies and Vermont

DIRECTIONS: The following questions are not based upon a reading passage. Read each question and choose the *best* answer, drawing on your background in social studies.

19. Under the United States Constitution no state may, without the consent of Congress,

A. tax business enterprise
B. regulate public utilities
C. enter into agreements or compacts with another state
D. establish a militia

20. The effect of pre-election polls on election results which is the opposite of the underdog effect is the

F. halo effect
G. bandwagon effect
H. Doppler effect
J. top-dog effect

21. On which issue did Thomas Jefferson reverse his opinion as to strict construction of the Constitution? The

A. Bank of the United States
B. purchase of the Louisiana Territory
C. moving of the capital to Washington, D.C.
D. appointment of the "midnight judges"

22. The chief reason for the opposition of the South to the election of Abraham Lincoln in 1860 was his

F. resistance to slavery
G. demand for the immediate abolition of slavery
H. hostility to the extension of slavery
J. insistence on equal education for blacks and whites

23. Which one of the following did *not* break with the Roman Catholic Church during the Protestant Reformation?

A. John Calvin
B. Desiderius Erasmus
C. John Knox
D. Huldreich Zwingli

24. Samuel Gompers attempted to win gains for labor by

F. uniting skilled and unskilled workers into one union
G. organizing industrial or vertical unions
H. forming craft unions of skilled workers
J. urging civil disobedience as a means to win public support

25. Which one of the following does *not* require the President's signature? A

A. joint resolution
B. private bill
C. public bill
D. proposed amendment to the Constitution

MARK YOUR ANSWERS HERE

1 Ⓐ Ⓑ Ⓒ Ⓓ	6 Ⓕ Ⓖ Ⓗ Ⓙ	11 Ⓐ Ⓑ Ⓒ Ⓓ	16 Ⓕ Ⓖ Ⓗ Ⓙ	21 Ⓐ Ⓑ Ⓒ Ⓓ
2 Ⓕ Ⓖ Ⓗ Ⓙ	7 Ⓐ Ⓑ Ⓒ Ⓓ	12 Ⓕ Ⓖ Ⓗ Ⓙ	17 Ⓐ Ⓑ Ⓒ Ⓓ	22 Ⓕ Ⓖ Ⓗ Ⓙ
3 Ⓐ Ⓑ Ⓒ Ⓓ	8 Ⓕ Ⓖ Ⓗ Ⓙ	13 Ⓐ Ⓑ Ⓒ Ⓓ	18 Ⓕ Ⓖ Ⓗ Ⓙ	23 Ⓐ Ⓑ Ⓒ Ⓓ
4 Ⓕ Ⓖ Ⓗ Ⓙ	9 Ⓐ Ⓑ Ⓒ Ⓓ	14 Ⓕ Ⓖ Ⓗ Ⓙ	19 Ⓐ Ⓑ Ⓒ Ⓓ	24 Ⓕ Ⓖ Ⓗ Ⓙ
5 Ⓐ Ⓑ Ⓒ Ⓓ	10 Ⓕ Ⓖ Ⓗ Ⓙ	15 Ⓐ Ⓑ Ⓒ Ⓓ	20 Ⓕ Ⓖ Ⓗ Ⓙ	25 Ⓐ Ⓑ Ⓒ Ⓓ

ANSWER KEY FOR PRACTICE SOCIAL STUDIES READING QUESTIONS

1. **C.**	6. **G.**	11. **A.**	16. **G.**	21. **B.**
2. **G.**	7. **A.**	12. **J.**	17. **C.**	22. **H.**
3. **B.**	8. **J.**	13. **C.**	18. **H.**	23. **B.**
4. **H.**	9. **C.**	14. **J.**	19. **C.**	24. **H.**
5. **B.**	10. **H.**	15. **C.**	20. **G.**	25. **D.**

EXPLANATIONS TO PRACTICE SOCIAL STUDIES READING QUESTIONS

1. **C.** In the second sentence the author tells us that we can have no wise laws until there is free expression of the wisdom of the people.

2. **G.** The author regrets that in times of stress, when free speech is most needed, it tends to be in the greatest danger. Especially at times of national danger, freedom of speech tends to be somewhat suppressed in the 'interests of national security.'

3. **B.** "Violence is the child of suppression."

4. **H.** The author's point is that freedom of speech is a necessity at all times which in peacetime is taken for granted. While freedom of speech is always desirable and desired, no thought is given it when no one is actively seeking to suppress it.

5. **B.** Peace through force and without discussion is said to be peace without justice. "And," the author claims, "peace without justice is tyranny."

6. **G.** The author freely admits, in the second sentence, that with freedom of expression folly will be expressed along with wisdom. However, he goes on to say, in the third sentence, that with freedom, wisdom will prevail over folly.

7. **A.** The first ten amendments to the Constitution, which are known as the *Bill of Rights,* guarantee certain rights to Americans. The first amendment specifically guarantees free speech.

8. **J.** In his statement ". . . whoever tramples upon the plea for justice, temperately made in the name of peace, only outrages peace . . ." the author is claiming that no worthwhile goal can justify undemocratic or violent means.

9. **C.** The American Civil Liberties Union is dedicated to the preservation of freedom of speech, even to the extent that the freedom of one group may at times be injurious to another group. The American Legion and the Daughters of the Revolution have at times espoused the curtailment of certain liberties in the interest of "patriotism." The Lions Club International is a service organization which makes no political statements.

10. **H.** The behavior about which the colonists are complaining is specific to the reign of George III, hence no prior monarchs are subjects of wrath. When they complain of cruelty and perfidy unworthy the Head of a civilized nation, it is clear that they are pointing at a single individual, rather than at the government as a whole. Furthermore, it was the King personally who had reserved to himself the right to assent to the laws passed in the colonies, hence the complaint that he ignored these laws is a complaint directly against the King, George III.

11. **A.** In colonial times a large family was a blessing and greatly to be desired because the cost of living was low, but there was a severe shortage of labor. The complaint that "He has endeavoured to prevent the population of these States" arises from the King's thwarting of immigration and thereby limiting growth of the labor force from without.

12. **J.** Tea is nowhere mentioned. All the other complaints are voiced.

13. **C.** The Hessians were mercenaries recruited by the English from Germany. The French were allies of the colonists, and a number of Polish officers also assisted the colonial effort.

14. **J.** "He has erected a multitude of New Offices, and sent hither swarms of Officers to harass our People, and eat out their substance." This is a general complaint against the imposed bureaucracy which contributed nothing to the economy of the colonies, but only consumed that which was needed by the local population.

15. **C.** While "taxation without representation" was one of the major complaints of the colonists, that portion of the document is not quoted here.

16. **G.** One complaint reads, "He has called together legislative bodies at places unusual, uncomfortable, and distant . . . for the sole purpose of fatiguing them into compliance with his measures." Emigration is not mentioned. The complaint in that area has to do with immigration restrictions.

17. **C.** The complaints listed are some of the justifications for declaring independence from England.

18. **H.** Representatives of all thirteen original colonies signed the Declaration. Vermont was to be the fourteenth state, but was not involved at the time of the

Declaration. The King rejected the statement by the colonists, but he had no power of veto over such a document.

19. **C.** Article I, Section 10, of the U.S. Constitution specifically forbids a state to "enter into any agreement or compact with another State" without the consent of Congress.

20. **G.** Whereas the underdog effect would encourage a voter to feel sorry for and favor a candidate with seemingly little support or chance of winning, the bandwagon effect would operate to encourage the voter to support the most favored candidate for the sake of being on the winning side. The halo effect is the aura projected by an idolized person, so that the admirers believe their idol is perfect in all judgments. The Doppler effect is a physical phenomenon having to do with changes in perceived sound wave frequencies as a function of distance from the observer.

21. **B.** The need for prompt action to confirm the Louisiana Purchase made a constitutional amendment impractical. Therefore, Jefferson had to reverse his position and accept a loose interpretation of the Constitution.

22. **H.** Lincoln had steadfastly maintained that he would not interfere with slavery in the states, but he opposed its extension into the territories.

23. **B.** Desiderius Erasmus believed that the Roman Catholic Church could be reformed from within; therefore, he did not break with the Church. John Calvin was a French theologian and reformer, whose ideas formed the foundation of Calvinism in England. John Knox was a Scottish reformer, and Huldreich Zwingli a Swiss reformer.

24. **H.** Gompers learned from the earlier failures in union organizing and limited himself to working with skilled workers.

25. **D.** The amending process is entirely a legislative process. The President is in no way involved in this procedure except as he influences opinion by the prestige of his position and his public statements.

NATURAL SCIENCE GLOSSARY

This glossary was created to help you master some of the key words you may meet in the Natural Science section of the test. Generally, the test deals with four natural sciences: astronomy, biology, chemistry, and physics. You should know that astronomy is the study of celestial bodies, biology the study of living things, chemistry the study of the composition of different kinds of matter and the changes that happen to them, and physics the study of the actions of objects and the reasons behind their actions.

In the glossary, you will usually find a science in parenthesis after the word. This means that the word is by and large identified with that science. That does not mean that the word might not be used in other sciences, though. The word *element* refers to a chemical element and is used, of course, in connection with chemistry. But uranium is an element which is most important in nuclear fission, which is usually considered part of the field of physics.

[A]

absolute zero (physics) The lowest temperature to which a gas can get. This is 460 degrees below zero on the Fahrenheit scale and 273 degrees below zero on the centigrade scale.

acceleration (physics) A change in the speed of an object. If the object goes faster, this is called positive acceleration. If the object goes slower, it is called negative acceleration.

acid (chemistry) A compound that dissolves in water, has a sour taste, and changes blue litmus paper to red.

alchemy (chemistry) The theory that less valuable metals can be transformed into gold or silver. This idea, popular during the Middle Ages, was false, but the experiments of alchemists laid the foundation of modern chemistry.

alkali (chemistry) A base that dissolves in water, has a bitter taste, and changes red litmus paper to blue.

alkaline (chemistry) The adjective form of alkali.

ampere (physics) A measurement of the velocity of electric current. It was named after a French scientist, André Marie Ampére.

Ampére, André Marie (physics) A French scientist (1775–1836) whose work and theory laid the foundation for the science of electrodynamics. His name lives on in the electrical measurement ampere, and its abbreviation, amp.

amphipods (biology) A crustacean group that includes sand fleas.

anatomy (biology) The study of the structure of living things. Usually anatomy refers to the structure of the human body.

anemone (biology) A sea animal that resembles the flower of the same name.

aphid (biology) A small insect which is destructive to crops. A fluid produced by aphids is eaten by ants.

aquatic (biology) An adjective referring to water, such as "aquatic sports" (diving, swimming, etc.).

Aristotle (biology) An ancient Greek philosopher whose active mind pondered all aspects of life and its processes. He is often called the "Father of Biology."

asteroids (astronomy) Small planet-like bodies that orbit around the sun.

astrology (astronomy) A theory that the position of the stars, sun, moon and planets influence people's lives. Although this is false, the study of astrology was most helpful to the development of astronomy.

astronomer (astronomy) A person who studies the movements of celestial bodies.

astronomy The study of the movements of celestial bodies. This is a major science.

atmosphere (general) The air mass surrounding the earth.

atom (physics and chemistry) A small particle of matter. See atomic energy. Once it was thought that the atom was the smallest particle of matter that existed, but now it is known that atoms are made up of protons, neutrons and electrons.

atomic energy (physics) Power released when atoms are split or united. This is also called nuclear energy. Also see nuclear fission and nuclear fusion.

[B]

bacteria (biology) Tiny organisms with one cell.

bacteriology (biology) The study of bacteria. Bacteriology is a branch of biology.

base (chemistry) A compound that can combine with an acid to make a salt.

biochemistry (biology and chemistry) The study of the chemical makeup of organisms. This science is a branch of both chemistry and biology.

biology The study of living things. This is a major science.

botany (biology) The study of plant life. Botany is a branch of biology.

Brahe, Tycho (astronomy) A Danish astronomer (1546–1601) who made the first systematic study of the movement of celestial bodies. He is often referred to only as Tycho.

[C]

carbohydrate (biology) A food substance made up of carbon, hydrogen and oxygen.

carbon (chemistry) An important chemical element.

carbon dioxide (chemistry) A gas made up of carbon and oxygen.

celestial (astronomy) An adjective referring to the sky.

cell (biology) The basic and smallest part of living things.

centigrade (physics) A system of measurement of temperature. On the centigrade scale, the freezing point of water is zero degrees. The boiling point of water is 100 degrees. Another generally used temperature measurement is the Fahrenheit scale.

chemistry The study of the composition of different kinds of matter and the changes that happen to them. This is a major science.

chlorophyll (biology) The green coloring matter in the cells of living plants, caused by sunlight. Chlorophyll is the means by which all regular absorption and digestion of plant food is made.

chromosome (biology) The part of cells that determines heredity. Chromosomes contain genes.

colloid (chemistry) A substance that does not pass through membranes very quickly and may not pass through them at all.

compound (chemistry) The combining of two or more elements into a single unit.

conduction (physics) The process by which heat is carried from molecule to molecule.

conservation of energy (chemistry) The idea that energy changes its form but cannot be created or destroyed.

conservation of matter (chemistry) The idea that matter can change its form but cannot be created or destroyed.

constellation (astronomy) A particular grouping of stars.

copepod (biology) A small crustacean which is in the plankton family.

Copernicus, Nicholas (astronomy) A Polish astronomer (1473–1543) who put forth the idea that the earth moved through space. It was generally believed in this time that the earth was the center of the universe and did not move through space at all.

cosmic year (astronomy) The time it takes the sun to go around its galaxy.

crop rotation (biology) A method by which crops in an area are changed each year. This helps maintain the fertility of the soil.

crustacean (biology) A group of aquatic animals with a hard covering. They are often called shellfish.

crystal (chemistry) The form many inanimate objects take.

[D]

Dalton, John (physics) An English scientist (1766–1844) who set forth the idea that matter was made up of atoms.

Darwin, Charles (biology) The English scientist (1809–1883) who developed a theory of evolution.

deforestation (biology) The process by which land is cleared of forests.

dorso-ventral (biology) An adjective referring to the dorsal vertebrae. These are a set of bones which are found in the spinal column of the human body near the chest.

[E]

eclipse (astronomy) The blotting out of light when one celestial object moves in front of another. When the moon comes between the earth and the sun it casts a shadow on part of the earth. During this time, the sun cannot be seen from that part of the earth. This is known as a solar eclipse. When the earth comes between the sun and the full moon, it casts a shadow on the moon. The moon cannot be seen during this time. This is a lunar eclipse.

Einstein, Albert (physics) A German-Jewish scientist (1879–1955) who escaped WWII and lived the last years of his life in the United States. His theories changed the field of physics. He, more than any other scientist, was responsible for nuclear fission.

electron (physics) One of the smallest electrical charges known. It is part of every atom. See proton and neutron.

electronics (physics) The study of the motion of electrons.

element (chemistry) One of 102 known basic substances. These substances, or combinations of them, make up all matter as far as is known.

embryology (biology) The study of the early development of organisms, ususally plant and animal.

energy (physics) The capacity to do work.

enzyme (biology) An organic substance that acts as an agent of change within cells.

eugenics (biology) A system that is thought will improve the human race by mating so-called superior men and women.

evolution, theory of (biology) Usually refers to Darwin's theory that living things change from generation to generation. Furthermore, the living things that survive, according to Darwin, manage to do so because they have acquired certain characteristics that make them more powerful or adaptable than others of their kind.

evaporation (biology and chemistry) The process by which liquids and solids change to gases.

experiment (general) A test to see if an idea or theory is true or false.

[F]

Fahrenheit (physics) The system of measurement of temperature which is generally used in the United States. It was developed by Gabriel Fahrenheit (1686–1736), a German scientist. On the Fahrenheit scale, 32 degrees is the freezing point of water and 98.6 degrees is the average temperature of the human body. Another widely used temperature measurement is the centigrade scale.

Faraday, Michael (physics) An English scientist (1791–1867) who discovered electricity could move through metal by the use of a magnet.

fertility (biology) The ability to reproduce. See reproduction.

force (physics) That which stops or creates motion, or changes the velocity of motion.

friction (physics) The resistance objects have when they are moved across other objects.

fungi (biology) A group of simple plants. Fungi do not have any leaves, flower or color. Because they have no chlorophyll, they must feed on plants, animals or decaying matter.

fungicides (biology) Chemicals which kill fungi.

[G]

galaxy (astronomy) A grouping of stars. Our sun is a star in the galaxy called the Milky Way.

Galileo (astronomy and physics) An Italian scientist (1564–1642) who made many contributions to science. He discovered that objects of different weights and shapes fall to the ground at the same rate of speed, attracted by gravity. He was a strong believer in Copernicus' theory that the earth moved in space and was persecuted for this belief.

gene (biology) A part of the cell found in the chromosome. Genes determine the traits of heredity.

genetics (biology) The study of the differences and similarities between living things and those living things that have reproduced them. See reproduction.

geology (general) The study of how the earth has changed since its beginning.

gravitation (physics and astronomy) The property of objects to attract each other.

gravity (physics and astronomy) Usually the tendency of smaller objects at or near the surface to move towards the earth.

[H]

Harvey, William (biology) An English scientist (1578–1657) who discovered the way blood moves through the body.

heat (physics) The measurement of kinetic energy.

hemoglobin (biology) A substance that gives blood its red color.

heredity (biology) The way traits are carried from generation to generation.

hormone (biology) An organic substance produced by the body. Hormones are responsible for many bodily functions.

hydrogen (chemistry) One of the most important chemical elements.

hypothesis (general) An unproved explanation of something that has happened or might happen.

[I]

inorganic (biology) An adjective meaning "not organic." See organic.

insecticides (biology) Chemical combinations used to destroy harmful insects.

interstellar (astronomy) An adjective meaning "between the stars."

isotopes (physics) Atoms that belong to the same chemical element, but are different in weight or mass.

[K]

Kepler, Johannes (astronomy) A German astronomer (1571–1630) who made important discoveries about the orbits of planets.

kinetic energy (physics) Energy that is in motion. The motion of the baseball between the pitcher's hand and the catcher's glove is an example of kinetic energy. See potential energy.

Koch, Robert (biology) A German doctor (1843–1910) who studied bacteria. He and Louis Pasteur are considered the founders of the science of bacteriology.

[L]

Lamarck, Chevalier de (biology) A French scientist (1744–1829) who developed a theory of evolution. See Darwin.

Lavoisier, Antoine (chemistry) A French scientist (1743–1794) who made important discoveries concerning fire and conservation of matter.

light year (astronomy) The distance light travels in a vacuum in one year. Roughly 5,878,000,000,000 miles.

Linnaeus, Carolus (biology) A Swedish scientist (1707–1778) best known for developing a system to name animals and plants.

litmus paper (chemistry) A special paper used by chemists to test for acid and alkalies.

lunar (astronomy) An adjective referring to the moon. A lunar eclipse is an eclipse of the moon. See solar.

[M]

marine (biology) An adjective meaning "of the sea." Example: "Fish are a form of marine life."

molecule (physics and chemistry) A basic unit of matter made up of atoms.

mechanics (physics) The study of the effect force has on moving or motionless bodies. This is a branch of physics.

membrane (biology) Soft, thin sheet of tissue in an organism. A membrane acts as a wall between two different parts of the organism, or it covers a particular part of the organism.

Mendel, Gregor Johann (biology) An Austrian monk and scientist (1822–1844) who made important discoveries concerning heredity.

metabolism (biology) The process used by all living organisms to change food into tissue and energy.

mercury (chemistry) An important chemical element.

meteorology (general) A science that studies the weather and the atmosphere.

mollusks (biology) A family of animals usually found in water. Mollusks have no bones. Examples of mollusks are snails, oysters, and octopuses.

mutation (biology) A change from the parents in an offspring. If a rat was born with no tail although its parents had tails, this change would be a mutation.

[N]

nebula (astronomy) A cloudy and gaseous mass found in interstellar space.

neutron (physics and chemistry) A small particle that is part of the atom and has no electrical charge. See electron and proton.

Newton, Isaac (physics and astronomy) An English scientist (1642–1727) who made major discoveries in astronomy and physics. His most important work was in his study of gravitation and optics.

nuclear (physics) An adjective referring to the nucleus of the atom.

nuclear fission (physics) The splitting of an atom in order to produce energy.
nuclear fusion (physics) The joining together of light weight atoms resulting in the release of energy.
nucleus (physics and chemistry) The center or core of an object, necessary to maintain human life.

[O]

observatory (astronomy) A specially constructed building containing one or more telescopes for observation of the heavens.
optics (physics) The study of light and its effect. Optics is a branch of physics.
orbit (astronomy) The route that an object in space (such as the moon) takes around another body (such as the earth).
organic ((biology) An adjective referring to living things. See inorganic.
organism (biology) Living things, such as people, plants or animals.
oxide (chemistry) A compound made up of oxygen and another element. Water, for example, is a compound made up of two atoms of hydrogen for each atom of oxygen.
oxygen (chemistry) A very important chemical element. Oxygen, a gaseous element, makes up about 20% of air and is the supporter of ordinary combustion.

[P]

Pasteur, Louis (biology) A French scientist (1822–1895) who made major discoveries in chemistry and biology, especially in the control of many diseases. He and Robert Koch were the founders of the science of bacteriology.
physics The study of the action of objects and the reasons behind these actions.
phytogeographic map (biology) A map showing plant life.
Planck, Max (physics) A German scientist (1858–1947) who did notable work in thermodynamics.
planet (astronomy) A large body that moves around the sun. The earth is a planet.
plankton (biology) A group of sea life—both plant and animal—which drifts with tides and currents. Jellyfish are an example of plankton.
potential energy (physics) Energy that is available for use. The baseball in the pitcher's hand is an example of potential energy. It becomes kinetic energy when it is thrown.
Priestley, Joseph, (chemistry) The English chemist (1738–1804) who discovered oxygen.
primeval (general) An adjective meaning "the first" or "early."
protein (biology) A class of food necessary for life. Proteins build tissues and provide energy.
proton (physics) An electrically charged particle found in all atoms. See electron and neutrons.
protoplasm (biology) A substance necessary for life found in the cells of all organisms.

[R]

radio astronomy (astronomy) The study of radio waves received from outer space.
regeneration (biology) The capacity of an organism to create new parts of itself.
reproduction (biology) The process by which organisms create offspring of their own species.

[S]

salinity (chemistry) The degree of salt present. Usually refers to the amount of salt in a fluid.
salt (biology) A substance that is formed when an acid is mixed with a base.
satellite (astronomy) An object that orbits around a planet, such as a moon. In recent years, the earth has had artificial satellites.
soluble (chemistry) Able to be dissolved in a fluid. See solute, solvent and solution.
solar (astronomy) An adjective referring to the sun. A solar eclipse is an eclipse of the sun. See lunar.
solar system (astronomy) The sun, the planets, satellites, and the asteroids.
solute (chemistry) What is dissolved in a fluid to form a solution. See solution, soluble, and solvent.
solution (chemistry) A solution occurs when a liquid, solvent or gas mixes completely in a fluid. For example, when sugar is completely dissolved in hot water, the result is a solution. See solute, solvent, and soluble.
solvent (chemistry) The fluid in which a solute is dissolved to form a solution. Also see soluble.
sonic (physics) An adjective referring to sound.
spawn (biology) A noun referring to the eggs of certain aquatic animals, such as fish. Also a verb meaning to lay eggs, usually used in connection with fish.
stimulus (general) That which brings a response. If a person is hungry, the sight of food might cause salivation. The stimulus is food, and the response, the watering of the mouth.
substratum (geology) A layer lying beneath the top layer.
supersonic (physics) An adjective meaning "faster than sound."

[T, U]

theory (general) An unproved explanation of something that has happened or might happen.
thermodynamics (physics) The study of the actions of heat.
ultrasonic (physics) An adjective referring to sound no person can hear because of its high frequency.
unicellular (biology) An adjective meaning "one-celled." See cell.
universe (astronomy) All things that exist in space taken as a whole.

[V]

velocity (physics) The rate of motion.

Vesalius, Andreas (biology) An Italian scientist (1514–1564) who studied the body. His discoveries were so important that he is often referred to as "The Father of Anatomy." See anatomy.

virus (biology) A tiny germ that attacks body cells and causes disease.

vitamins (biology) Name for many special substances found in food which are necessary for the operation of particular functions of the body and to maintain health.

[W, X, Y, Z]

water table (general) The level nearest to the surface of the ground where water is found.

work (physics) In science, work is what occurs when a force moves an object.

zoology (biology) The study of animals. This science is a branch of biology.

PRACTICE WITH NATURAL SCIENCE READING QUESTIONS

DIRECTIONS: Below each of the following reading passages is a series of questions. Choose the *best* answer to each question, interpreting what is stated or implied by the passage in the light of your own background in the subject. You may refer to the passage as often as necessary, though the answers to some questions may not be found expressly in the passage.

Some time ago, a set of experiments was done on grass coleoptiles. A coleoptile is a rigid, sheathed blade of grass.

Experiment 1: The coleoptile tip was covered by an opaque cap. Another coleoptile tip was covered by a transparent cap. A coleoptile bottom was covered by an opaque cylinder.
Results: The plants with the transparent cap and the opaque cylinder exhibited positive phototropism to sunlight. The coleoptile with the opaque cap did not bend toward the light.

Experiment 2: A coleoptile tip was cut off and replaced, but with an agar block separating it from the stump.
Result: The plant grew in the direction of sunlight.

Experiment 3: A number of coleoptile tips were cut off. Some were put back on one side of the stump, while the others remained separate from the stumps. No light was present.
Result: The stumps with no tip replaced grew straight up. Those with tips on one side grew in the direction opposite to that which the tips were on.

Experiment 4: Coleoptile tips were cut off and were placed atop agar blocks for one hour. Other agar blocks remained untreated. The treated and the untreated blocks were placed on different stumps, one block per stump. Some blocks were placed off-center on the shoot; others covered the entire diameter of the stump.
Results: The plants with the untreated agar blocks grew very little, and showed no phototropic tendencies. The plants with the treated blocks grew well for a time. Those with the blocks centered on the stump grew towards a light source. Those with the block on one side of the stump, as in *Experiment 3,* grew in the direction opposite to that which the block was on.

1. The experiments indicate that

A. the sun induces synthesis of a growth substance
B. the coleoptile tip produces a substance causing a phototropic response
C. the shoot releases a substance causing a phototropic response
D. agar blocks contain a plant growth substance

2. The opaque cap in *Experiment 1*

F. inhibited formation of the growth substance
G. stimulated a phototropic response
H. blocked all visible light
J. blocked all the sun's radiation

3. The substance responsible for the phototropic responses observed in these experiments is classed as a

A. protein
B. amino acid
C. nucleic acid
D. hormone

4. An hypothesis not tested by these experiments is that

F. roots produce a substance necessary for phototropism
G. sunlight can cause differential growth in parts of the plant
H. plants can grow in the dark
J. cutting a coleoptile in half prevents the plant from growing

5. The experiment that showed phototropism to have a chemical stimulus is

A. 1
B. 2
C. 3
D. 4

6. A phototropism is the tendency of an organism to

F. grow toward the sun
G. grow away from artificial light
H. grow irrespective of sunlight
J. be influenced by light

7. All green plants show positive phototropism because

A. light is the source of their energy
B. they are negatively geotropic
C. they are not phototactic
D. green plants require sunlight for photosynthesis

"One of the duties of the Director of a Hospital Blood Bank is to educate physicians, nurses and also lay members of the community. It is impossible for the practicing physician to follow the advancements in the field of serology. It is not at all surprising that some physicians do not understand the principle of blood grouping and especially of blood typing or that they misunderstand the working of the Blood Bank. It is up to the Director of the Blood Bank to impress upon the physician, who has the most intimate contact with the patient and the patient's family, that the practitioner is the person most likely to succeed in the solicitation of blood for the patient. It is far easier for the family physician to ask Joan or Bill to donate a pint of blood for their sick father who has to undergo a major surgical operation, than it is for the Blood Bank technician or nurse to negotiate with the family on the phone. The family's blood is always preferred because of the familial incidence of the same blood group and type. An *rh* person must have at least one *rh* parent and might have an *rh* sibling. The attending physician knows the number of children and other relatives and often knows the religious affiliations of his patients. Frequently organizations such as the Rotary Club, the Lions Club, the Knights of Columbus and others can be approached to solicit blood donations for one of their members among the membership. The family physician can do what a Blood Bank nurse or technician cannot.

"A surprisingly large number of physicians and a very large number of lay people have to be told over and over again that *the term 'Bank' implies a well-balanced economic unit with a surplus available for loan.* This is *the principle of banking of money* and *must be the principle of banking of blood:* You cannot withdraw money without first depositing some, and you cannot borrow money unless you guarantee repayment of the loan. *The differences between banking of money and banking of blood are:* (1) a monetary institution handles money while the Blood Bank handles blood; (2) money can be stored indefinitely while blood can be stored for a comparatively short period of time only, and, (3) while money of different currencies may be traded according to established rates of exchange, blood of one variety cannot be substituted with blood of another group and type. . .

"In order to establish a blood reserve great effort has to be made to stimulate blood donations. Various methods have been recommended to this end. The whole community has to share in this effort. Hospital as well as Community Blood Banks must adopt the motto that, 'insurance be taken out before a catastrophe and not after,' and spread the word that similarly, '*blood donations should be made before the actual need for blood arises.*' Voluntary donations are to be preferred to professional solicitation of blood. The public must be educated to the fact that *dollars cannot be transfused,* that *blood must be again replaced with blood.* Principally, it is wrong to charge a patient for blood transfused. This is recognized by all parties concerned. Still, it is widely practiced. This is done not to cover the costs of operation of the Blood Bank but to force people into blood replacement. The more 'expensive' the blood is made, the higher its 'price,' the more people might try to replace blood by donations instead of paying with money . . . Practically all hospitals will credit this sum (the charge for blood) where two pints of blood were deposited in advance of a pint administered. They will refund the fee where two pints of blood are donated in replacement of a pint transfused. *Commonly, minimum replacement of each pint of blood given with two pints of blood donated is required to establish a blood reserve . . . Actually, the number of donors should not be limited to two, but the largest possible number of donations should be encouraged.* To promote blood donations, some hospitals refund the administration charge for blood donated in excess of the required replacement."

Excerpted from GROUPING, TYPING and BANKING OF BLOOD, Pollak, O.J., Springfield, Ill.: Charles C. Thomas. © 1951, with permission of the author.

8. In order to have *rh* blood, a person must have

F. an *rh sibling*
G. an *rh* child
H. an *rh* parent
J. a large family

9. The principle of Blood Banking is most readily understood by a

A. banker
B. physician
C. sick person
D. sick person's family

10. Charging large sums of money for blood is justified because

F. blood is absolutely essential to life
G. blood is priceless
H. running a Blood Bank is expensive
J. high costs encourage people to donate needed blood as a means of avoiding the fees

11. Even if blood is replaced, a charge is generally made. This charge covers

A. expenses of operating the Blood Bank
B. cost of administering the transfusion
C. insurance against future blood requirements
D. educational programs for the community

12. An analogy is drawn between a Blood Bank and a commercial bank. This analogy is valid because both types of banks

I. can store their assets indefinitely
II. require that one make deposits in order to have an account
III. charge interest on loans

F. I and II
G. II only
H. II and III
J. I, II, and III

13. The reason that many physicians do not

understand the principles of blood grouping and typing is that they are

A. too busy to keep up with rapid advances in specialized fields
B. willing to abdicate this aspect of medicine to technicians
C. bad businessmen
D. uneducated

14. Aside from the analogy with a commercial bank, an analogy is also drawn between a Blood Bank and a/an

F. educational institution
G. insurance company
H. fraternal organization
J. reservoir

15. The *main* reason voluntary donations are preferred to solicitation of professional donors is that

A. voluntarily donated blood is free
B. professional donors may not reveal disease which renders their blood dangerous
C. voluntarily donated blood is more likely to be of the correct group and type
D. organized donation of blood creates community spirit

16. A relationship idealized in the selection, but one which does not necessarily exist today, is that between

F. family physician and patient's family
G. sons and fathers
H. fraternal organizations and their members
J. lay people and banks

17. Serology is

A. a technical aspect of banking
B. a less-known branch of psychology
C. the art of persuasion
D. the science which deals with the reactions and properties of serums

18. It is especially important for a Blood Bank to have a large reserve because

I. emergencies may require great quantities of blood
II. the supplies must include ample amounts of blood of each group and type
III. blood must not be withheld even if a person is unable to replace it
IV. sometimes bankers need blood

F. I, II, and III
G. I, III, and IV
H. II, III, and IV
J. I, II, III, and IV

DIRECTIONS: The following questions are not based upon a reading passage. Use your knowledge in the natural sciences to choose the *best* answer to each question.

19. The equation: $3H_2 + N_2 \rightarrow 2NH_3$ takes place in a closed container. The reactions would move to the right if

A. the volume of the container were increased
B. the pressure on the system were decreased
C. the gases were heated
D. some of the gas were removed

20. A gas which will turn dampened red litmus paper blue is

F. CO_2
G. O_2
H. NH_3
J. PO_4

21. A dog breeder can determine that a "hairless" dog is a mutation if the dog

A. is still "hairless" after five years
B. shows no change in its "hairless" condition after its diet is changed
C. develops other conspicuous differences from its parents
D. is bred and produces "hairless" offspring

22. If X is an element of group 3A of the Periodic Table, the formula for its oxide would be

F. XO_2
G. X_3O_4
H. X_2O
J. X_2O_3

23. The heaviest of the following particles is

A. S^{-2}
B. S^{+4}
C. S^{+6}
D. S^{-4}

24. A test tube containing a molasses solution and yeast is kept in a warm place overnight. The gas collected from this mixture would

F. burst into flame when ignited
G. cause a glowing splint to burst into flame
H. cause red litmus paper to turn blue
J. turn limewater milky

25. Which one of the following terms is not related to the other three?

A. isogloss
B. isotope
C. isotherm
D. isohel

MARK YOUR ANSWERS HERE

1 Ⓐ Ⓑ Ⓒ Ⓓ	6 Ⓕ Ⓖ Ⓗ Ⓙ	11 Ⓐ Ⓑ Ⓒ Ⓓ	16 Ⓕ Ⓖ Ⓗ Ⓙ	21 Ⓐ Ⓑ Ⓒ Ⓓ
2 Ⓕ Ⓖ Ⓗ Ⓙ	7 Ⓐ Ⓑ Ⓒ Ⓓ	12 Ⓕ Ⓖ Ⓗ Ⓙ	17 Ⓐ Ⓑ Ⓒ Ⓓ	22 Ⓕ Ⓖ Ⓗ Ⓙ
3 Ⓐ Ⓑ Ⓒ Ⓓ	8 Ⓕ Ⓖ Ⓗ Ⓙ	13 Ⓐ Ⓑ Ⓒ Ⓓ	18 Ⓕ Ⓖ Ⓗ Ⓙ	23 Ⓐ Ⓑ Ⓒ Ⓓ
4 Ⓕ Ⓖ Ⓗ Ⓙ	9 Ⓐ Ⓑ Ⓒ Ⓓ	14 Ⓕ Ⓖ Ⓗ Ⓙ	19 Ⓐ Ⓑ Ⓒ Ⓓ	24 Ⓕ Ⓖ Ⓗ Ⓙ
5 Ⓐ Ⓑ Ⓒ Ⓓ	10 Ⓕ Ⓖ Ⓗ Ⓙ	15 Ⓐ Ⓑ Ⓒ Ⓓ	20 Ⓕ Ⓖ Ⓗ Ⓙ	25 Ⓐ Ⓑ Ⓒ Ⓓ

ANSWER KEY FOR PRACTICE NATURAL SCIENCE READING QUESTIONS

1. **B.**	6. **J.**	11. **B.**	16. **F.**	21. **D.**
2. **H.**	7. **A.**	12. **H.**	17. **D.**	22. **J.**
3. **D.**	8. **H.**	13. **A.**	18. **J.**	23. **D.**
4. **F.**	9. **A.**	14. **G.**	19. **C.**	24. **J.**
5. **D.**	10. **J.**	15. **B.**	20. **H.**	25. **B.**

EXPLANATORY ANSWERS TO PRACTICE NATURAL SCIENCE READING QUESTIONS

1. **B.** Experiments 3 and 4 show that the stumps did not grow toward light without the tip or a substance from the tip, whereas the tip or agar containing a substance from the tip was associated with phototropism. The tip must, then, release a substance necessary for phototropism.

2. **H.** By definition, opaque objects prevent all visible light from passing through. Opaque objects are permeable to other forms of the electromagnetic radiation the sun produces.

3. **D.** A hormone is a diffusable substance causing a particular response in the target organ. Auxin, the substance causing phototropism, meets those specifications.

4. **F.** Since the grass' roots were not removed in any experiment, any possible contribution they made was not observed or measured.

5. **D.** Experiment 4 showed that something from the tip diffused into the agar block and then diffused down the stump giving the stump the capacity for a phototropic response.

6. **J.** A *tropism* is a tendency to turn in response to a stimulus. The prefix *photo* means *light*. The source of the light is irrelevant. A tropism can be either positive, toward the stimulus, or negative, away from the stimulus.

7. **A.** A green plant turns toward the light which is the source of the energy involved in its food-manufacturing processes. The mechanism of the tropism is not fully understood. Either the light blocks the action of auxin on the light side or the light causes excess auxin to migrate to the dark side. At any rate, concentration of auxin on the dark side causes elongation on the dark side, with further turning toward the light. The roots of green plants are positively geotropic, B., that is they grow to the stimulus of gravity. A taxis, C., involves moving the whole body under the influence of the stimulus. Animals may be phototactic, but not plants. Any light will suffice for photosynthesis, D.

8. **H.** A blood type must be inherited from a parent.

9. **A.** The fundamental operating principles of a Blood Bank are very similar to those of a commercial bank. Once they were explained in such terms, the banker would readily comprehend them.

10. **J.** It is imperative that a Blood Bank be constantly replenished. The high price tag on blood is meant to encourage replacement donations. The high cost of blood is not immoral because one can always avoid paying the huge sums by obtaining donors.

11. **B.** Administration of a transfusion requires the full attention of a highly trained nurse or technician and the use of accurate, new instruments for each transfusion. Even so, most hospitals will absorb the monetary cost and accept excess donation of blood in lieu of cash payment.

12. **H.** To withdraw from one's bank account, one must first deposit money in that account; to withdraw blood from a Blood Bank (without charge) one must first donate or arrange donations from others into that account. Banks charge interest on loans; Blood Banks require replacement at, most commonly, a rate of two for one. Unfortunately, blood cannot be stored indefinitely.

13. **A.** Knowledge in all branches of medicine is expanding at a very rapid rate. A physician with an active private practice hopefully keeps abreast of new developments within a particular area or specialty, but cannot be expected to be current with advancements made in other specialized areas.

14. **G.** The author suggests that the concept of insurance be applied to Blood Banking. Since the writing of the book from which this selection is excerpted, this concept has been widely adopted. It is now possible to donate a pint of blood with the expectation of coverage for unlimited blood in time of need in the same way that one pays an insurance premium in return for full restitution in case of loss.

15. **B.** A *professional donor* sells blood. Unfortunately, the person who chooses to sell blood instead of donating it is usually desperate for money. Such a person may withhold information about a history of

hepatitis or syphilis for fear of being rejected as a donor. Transfusion of the blood of a person who has had hepatitis, syphilis, or a number of other diseases, may transmit the disease to the recipient.

16. **F.** The kindly old family doctor who knows the whole family and everything about it exists today more in fiction than in impersonal reality. However, the patient's physician is still a highly respected person and is still in the most strategic position to solicit donations from family members.

17. **D.** The second and third sentences of the selection make it clear that serology has to do with blood grouping and typing, hence with the properties and reactions of serums.

18. **J.** The need for blood is unpredictable in terms of time of need, amount needed and the specific group and type needed at any given moment. Hence, a large reserve must be on hand at all times.

19. **C.** If the gases were heated, the volume of the gases would increase, causing the equation to shift to the side of least volume (Le Chatelier's principle). The right side of the equation produces two moles of gas for every four on the left side.

20. **H.** NH_3 will react with water to form NH_4^+ and OH^-. The presence of the OH^- will make the water solution on the litmus basic, turning it blue.

21. **D.** Mutations breed true; that is, a mutation is a permanent gene change which is then passed on to succeeding generations as part of the gene heritage.

22. **J.** An element from group 3A has three valence electrons to donate. Oxygen requires two in order to complete its outer shell. Two atoms of the element from group 3A would donate six electrons, and three oxygen atoms would accept six electrons.

23. **D.** The sulfur nucleus is identical in each of the particles and only the number of electrons differs. S^{-4} has the most electrons and hence is the heaviest.

24. **J.** The yeast plants cause fermentation to occur. During this process carbon dioxide is given off as a waste gas and liquid alcohol is produced. The presence of carbon dioxide can be verified by bubbling the gas through limewater. The colorless chemical will turn milky.

25. **B.** *Isotope* is a term from chemistry. It is the term applied to a variation of an atomic element which has a different number of neutrons and, hence, different mass. The other three terms all refer to imaginary lines drawn on a map. *Isogloss* is the boundary line between places or regions that differ in a particular linguistic feature. *Isotherm* is the line connecting points having the same temperature at a given time or the same mean temperature for a given period. *Isohel* is the line connecting places with equal duration of sunshine.

PART IV

MODEL EXAM II

ANSWER SHEET—MODEL EXAM II

ENGLISH USAGE

1 Ⓐ Ⓑ Ⓒ Ⓓ	12 Ⓕ Ⓖ Ⓗ Ⓙ	23 Ⓐ Ⓑ Ⓒ Ⓓ	34 Ⓕ Ⓖ Ⓗ Ⓙ	45 Ⓐ Ⓑ Ⓒ Ⓓ	56 Ⓕ Ⓖ Ⓗ Ⓙ	67 Ⓐ Ⓑ Ⓒ Ⓓ
2 Ⓕ Ⓖ Ⓗ Ⓙ	13 Ⓐ Ⓑ Ⓒ Ⓓ	24 Ⓕ Ⓖ Ⓗ Ⓙ	35 Ⓐ Ⓑ Ⓒ Ⓓ	46 Ⓕ Ⓖ Ⓗ Ⓙ	57 Ⓐ Ⓑ Ⓒ Ⓓ	68 Ⓕ Ⓖ Ⓗ Ⓙ
3 Ⓐ Ⓑ Ⓒ Ⓓ	14 Ⓕ Ⓖ Ⓗ Ⓙ	25 Ⓐ Ⓑ Ⓒ Ⓓ	36 Ⓕ Ⓖ Ⓗ Ⓙ	47 Ⓐ Ⓑ Ⓒ Ⓓ	58 Ⓕ Ⓖ Ⓗ Ⓙ	69 Ⓐ Ⓑ Ⓒ Ⓓ
4 Ⓕ Ⓖ Ⓗ Ⓙ	15 Ⓐ Ⓑ Ⓒ Ⓓ	26 Ⓕ Ⓖ Ⓗ Ⓙ	37 Ⓐ Ⓑ Ⓒ Ⓓ	48 Ⓕ Ⓖ Ⓗ Ⓙ	59 Ⓐ Ⓑ Ⓒ Ⓓ	70 Ⓕ Ⓖ Ⓗ Ⓙ
5 Ⓐ Ⓑ Ⓒ Ⓓ	16 Ⓕ Ⓖ Ⓗ Ⓙ	27 Ⓐ Ⓑ Ⓒ Ⓓ	38 Ⓕ Ⓖ Ⓗ Ⓙ	49 Ⓐ Ⓑ Ⓒ Ⓓ	60 Ⓕ Ⓖ Ⓗ Ⓙ	71 Ⓐ Ⓑ Ⓒ Ⓓ
6 Ⓕ Ⓖ Ⓗ Ⓙ	17 Ⓐ Ⓑ Ⓒ Ⓓ	28 Ⓕ Ⓖ Ⓗ Ⓙ	39 Ⓐ Ⓑ Ⓒ Ⓓ	50 Ⓕ Ⓖ Ⓗ Ⓙ	61 Ⓐ Ⓑ Ⓒ Ⓓ	72 Ⓕ Ⓖ Ⓗ Ⓙ
7 Ⓐ Ⓑ Ⓒ Ⓓ	18 Ⓕ Ⓖ Ⓗ Ⓙ	29 Ⓐ Ⓑ Ⓒ Ⓓ	40 Ⓕ Ⓖ Ⓗ Ⓙ	51 Ⓐ Ⓑ Ⓒ Ⓓ	62 Ⓕ Ⓖ Ⓗ Ⓙ	73 Ⓐ Ⓑ Ⓒ Ⓓ
8 Ⓕ Ⓖ Ⓗ Ⓙ	19 Ⓐ Ⓑ Ⓒ Ⓓ	30 Ⓕ Ⓖ Ⓗ Ⓙ	41 Ⓐ Ⓑ Ⓒ Ⓓ	52 Ⓕ Ⓖ Ⓗ Ⓙ	63 Ⓐ Ⓑ Ⓒ Ⓓ	74 Ⓕ Ⓖ Ⓗ Ⓙ
9 Ⓐ Ⓑ Ⓒ Ⓓ	20 Ⓕ Ⓖ Ⓗ Ⓙ	31 Ⓐ Ⓑ Ⓒ Ⓓ	42 Ⓕ Ⓖ Ⓗ Ⓙ	53 Ⓐ Ⓑ Ⓒ Ⓓ	64 Ⓕ Ⓖ Ⓗ Ⓙ	75 Ⓐ Ⓑ Ⓒ Ⓓ
10 Ⓕ Ⓖ Ⓗ Ⓙ	21 Ⓐ Ⓑ Ⓒ Ⓓ	32 Ⓕ Ⓖ Ⓗ Ⓙ	43 Ⓐ Ⓑ Ⓒ Ⓓ	54 Ⓕ Ⓖ Ⓗ Ⓙ	65 Ⓐ Ⓑ Ⓒ Ⓓ	
11 Ⓐ Ⓑ Ⓒ Ⓓ	22 Ⓕ Ⓖ Ⓗ Ⓙ	33 Ⓐ Ⓑ Ⓒ Ⓓ	44 Ⓕ Ⓖ Ⓗ Ⓙ	55 Ⓐ Ⓑ Ⓒ Ⓓ	66 Ⓕ Ⓖ Ⓗ Ⓙ	

MATHEMATICS USAGE

1 Ⓐ Ⓑ Ⓒ Ⓓ Ⓔ	7 Ⓐ Ⓑ Ⓒ Ⓓ Ⓔ	13 Ⓐ Ⓑ Ⓒ Ⓓ Ⓔ	19 Ⓐ Ⓑ Ⓒ Ⓓ Ⓔ	25 Ⓐ Ⓑ Ⓒ Ⓓ Ⓔ	31 Ⓐ Ⓑ Ⓒ Ⓓ Ⓔ	37 Ⓐ Ⓑ Ⓒ Ⓓ Ⓔ
2 Ⓕ Ⓖ Ⓗ Ⓙ Ⓚ	8 Ⓕ Ⓖ Ⓗ Ⓙ Ⓚ	14 Ⓕ Ⓖ Ⓗ Ⓙ Ⓚ	20 Ⓕ Ⓖ Ⓗ Ⓙ Ⓚ	26 Ⓕ Ⓖ Ⓗ Ⓙ Ⓚ	32 Ⓕ Ⓖ Ⓗ Ⓙ Ⓚ	38 Ⓕ Ⓖ Ⓗ Ⓙ Ⓚ
3 Ⓐ Ⓑ Ⓒ Ⓓ Ⓔ	9 Ⓐ Ⓑ Ⓒ Ⓓ Ⓔ	15 Ⓐ Ⓑ Ⓒ Ⓓ Ⓔ	21 Ⓐ Ⓑ Ⓒ Ⓓ Ⓔ	27 Ⓐ Ⓑ Ⓒ Ⓓ Ⓔ	33 Ⓐ Ⓑ Ⓒ Ⓓ Ⓔ	39 Ⓐ Ⓑ Ⓒ Ⓓ Ⓔ
4 Ⓕ Ⓖ Ⓗ Ⓙ Ⓚ	10 Ⓕ Ⓖ Ⓗ Ⓙ Ⓚ	16 Ⓕ Ⓖ Ⓗ Ⓙ Ⓚ	22 Ⓕ Ⓖ Ⓗ Ⓙ Ⓚ	28 Ⓕ Ⓖ Ⓗ Ⓙ Ⓚ	34 Ⓕ Ⓖ Ⓗ Ⓙ Ⓚ	40 Ⓕ Ⓖ Ⓗ Ⓙ Ⓚ
5 Ⓐ Ⓑ Ⓒ Ⓓ Ⓔ	11 Ⓐ Ⓑ Ⓒ Ⓓ Ⓔ	17 Ⓐ Ⓑ Ⓒ Ⓓ Ⓔ	23 Ⓐ Ⓑ Ⓒ Ⓓ Ⓔ	29 Ⓐ Ⓑ Ⓒ Ⓓ Ⓔ	35 Ⓐ Ⓑ Ⓒ Ⓓ Ⓔ	
6 Ⓕ Ⓖ Ⓗ Ⓙ Ⓚ	12 Ⓕ Ⓖ Ⓗ Ⓙ Ⓚ	18 Ⓕ Ⓖ Ⓗ Ⓙ Ⓚ	24 Ⓕ Ⓖ Ⓗ Ⓙ Ⓚ	30 Ⓕ Ⓖ Ⓗ Ⓙ Ⓚ	36 Ⓕ Ⓖ Ⓗ Ⓙ Ⓚ	

SOCIAL STUDIES READING

1 Ⓐ Ⓑ Ⓒ Ⓓ	8 Ⓕ Ⓖ Ⓗ Ⓙ	15 Ⓐ Ⓑ Ⓒ Ⓓ	22 Ⓕ Ⓖ Ⓗ Ⓙ	29 Ⓐ Ⓑ Ⓒ Ⓓ	36 Ⓕ Ⓖ Ⓗ Ⓙ	43 Ⓐ Ⓑ Ⓒ Ⓓ Ⓔ	50 Ⓕ Ⓖ Ⓗ Ⓙ Ⓚ
2 Ⓕ Ⓖ Ⓗ Ⓙ	9 Ⓐ Ⓑ Ⓒ Ⓓ	16 Ⓕ Ⓖ Ⓗ Ⓙ	23 Ⓐ Ⓑ Ⓒ Ⓓ	30 Ⓕ Ⓖ Ⓗ Ⓙ	37 Ⓐ Ⓑ Ⓒ Ⓓ	44 Ⓕ Ⓖ Ⓗ Ⓙ Ⓚ	51 Ⓐ Ⓑ Ⓒ Ⓓ Ⓔ
3 Ⓐ Ⓑ Ⓒ Ⓓ	10 Ⓕ Ⓖ Ⓗ Ⓙ	17 Ⓐ Ⓑ Ⓒ Ⓓ	24 Ⓕ Ⓖ Ⓗ Ⓙ	31 Ⓐ Ⓑ Ⓒ Ⓓ	38 Ⓕ Ⓖ Ⓗ Ⓙ	45 Ⓐ Ⓑ Ⓒ Ⓓ Ⓔ	52 Ⓕ Ⓖ Ⓗ Ⓙ Ⓚ
4 Ⓕ Ⓖ Ⓗ Ⓙ	11 Ⓐ Ⓑ Ⓒ Ⓓ	18 Ⓕ Ⓖ Ⓗ Ⓙ	25 Ⓐ Ⓑ Ⓒ Ⓓ	32 Ⓕ Ⓖ Ⓗ Ⓙ	39 Ⓐ Ⓑ Ⓒ Ⓓ	46 Ⓕ Ⓖ Ⓗ Ⓙ Ⓚ	
5 Ⓐ Ⓑ Ⓒ Ⓓ	12 Ⓕ Ⓖ Ⓗ Ⓙ	19 Ⓐ Ⓑ Ⓒ Ⓓ	26 Ⓕ Ⓖ Ⓗ Ⓙ	33 Ⓐ Ⓑ Ⓒ Ⓓ	40 Ⓕ Ⓖ Ⓗ Ⓙ	47 Ⓐ Ⓑ Ⓒ Ⓓ Ⓔ	
6 Ⓕ Ⓖ Ⓗ Ⓙ	13 Ⓐ Ⓑ Ⓒ Ⓓ	20 Ⓕ Ⓖ Ⓗ Ⓙ	27 Ⓐ Ⓑ Ⓒ Ⓓ	34 Ⓕ Ⓖ Ⓗ Ⓙ	41 Ⓐ Ⓑ Ⓒ Ⓓ	48 Ⓕ Ⓖ Ⓗ Ⓙ Ⓚ	
7 Ⓐ Ⓑ Ⓒ Ⓓ	14 Ⓕ Ⓖ Ⓗ Ⓙ	21 Ⓐ Ⓑ Ⓒ Ⓓ	28 Ⓕ Ⓖ Ⓗ Ⓙ	35 Ⓐ Ⓑ Ⓒ Ⓓ	42 Ⓕ Ⓖ Ⓗ Ⓙ	49 Ⓐ Ⓑ Ⓒ Ⓓ Ⓔ	

NATURAL SCIENCE READING

1 Ⓐ Ⓑ Ⓒ Ⓓ	8 Ⓕ Ⓖ Ⓗ Ⓙ	15 Ⓐ Ⓑ Ⓒ Ⓓ	22 Ⓕ Ⓖ Ⓗ Ⓙ	29 Ⓐ Ⓑ Ⓒ Ⓓ	36 Ⓕ Ⓖ Ⓗ Ⓙ	43 Ⓐ Ⓑ Ⓒ Ⓓ Ⓔ	50 Ⓕ Ⓖ Ⓗ Ⓙ Ⓚ
2 Ⓕ Ⓖ Ⓗ Ⓙ	9 Ⓐ Ⓑ Ⓒ Ⓓ	16 Ⓕ Ⓖ Ⓗ Ⓙ	23 Ⓐ Ⓑ Ⓒ Ⓓ	30 Ⓕ Ⓖ Ⓗ Ⓙ	37 Ⓐ Ⓑ Ⓒ Ⓓ	44 Ⓕ Ⓖ Ⓗ Ⓙ Ⓚ	51 Ⓐ Ⓑ Ⓒ Ⓓ Ⓔ
3 Ⓐ Ⓑ Ⓒ Ⓓ	10 Ⓕ Ⓖ Ⓗ Ⓙ	17 Ⓐ Ⓑ Ⓒ Ⓓ	24 Ⓕ Ⓖ Ⓗ Ⓙ	31 Ⓐ Ⓑ Ⓒ Ⓓ	38 Ⓕ Ⓖ Ⓗ Ⓙ	45 Ⓐ Ⓑ Ⓒ Ⓓ Ⓔ	52 Ⓕ Ⓖ Ⓗ Ⓙ Ⓚ
4 Ⓕ Ⓖ Ⓗ Ⓙ	11 Ⓐ Ⓑ Ⓒ Ⓓ	18 Ⓕ Ⓖ Ⓗ Ⓙ	25 Ⓐ Ⓑ Ⓒ Ⓓ	32 Ⓕ Ⓖ Ⓗ Ⓙ	39 Ⓐ Ⓑ Ⓒ Ⓓ	46 Ⓕ Ⓖ Ⓗ Ⓙ Ⓚ	
5 Ⓐ Ⓑ Ⓒ Ⓓ	12 Ⓕ Ⓖ Ⓗ Ⓙ	19 Ⓐ Ⓑ Ⓒ Ⓓ	26 Ⓕ Ⓖ Ⓗ Ⓙ	33 Ⓐ Ⓑ Ⓒ Ⓓ	40 Ⓕ Ⓖ Ⓗ Ⓙ	47 Ⓐ Ⓑ Ⓒ Ⓓ Ⓔ	
6 Ⓕ Ⓖ Ⓗ Ⓙ	13 Ⓐ Ⓑ Ⓒ Ⓓ	20 Ⓕ Ⓖ Ⓗ Ⓙ	27 Ⓐ Ⓑ Ⓒ Ⓓ	34 Ⓕ Ⓖ Ⓗ Ⓙ	41 Ⓐ Ⓑ Ⓒ Ⓓ	48 Ⓕ Ⓖ Ⓗ Ⓙ Ⓚ	
7 Ⓐ Ⓑ Ⓒ Ⓓ	14 Ⓕ Ⓖ Ⓗ Ⓙ	21 Ⓐ Ⓑ Ⓒ Ⓓ	28 Ⓕ Ⓖ Ⓗ Ⓙ	35 Ⓐ Ⓑ Ⓒ Ⓓ	42 Ⓕ Ⓖ Ⓗ Ⓙ	49 Ⓐ Ⓑ Ⓒ Ⓓ Ⓔ	

SCORE SHEET

	NUMBER CORRECT								
ENGLISH USAGE	____	÷	75	=	____	× 100	=	____%
MATHEMATICS USAGE	____	÷	40	=	____	× 100	=	____%
SOCIAL STUDIES READING	____	÷	52	=	____	× 100	=	____%
Questions based on reading	____	÷	39	=	____	× 100	=	____%
Questions not based on reading	____	÷	13	=	____	× 100	=	____%
NATURAL SCIENCE READING	____	÷	52	=	____	× 100	=	____%
Questions based on reading	____	÷	40	=	____	× 100	=	____%
Questions not based on reading	____	÷	12	=	____	× 100	=	____%
TOTAL SCORE	____	÷	219	=	____	× 100	=	____%

PROGRESS CHART

	Exam I	Exam II
ENGLISH USAGE	%	%
MATHEMATICS USAGE	%	%
SOCIAL STUDIES READING	%	%
NATURAL SCIENCE READING	%	%
TOTAL	%	%

TEST 1
ENGLISH USAGE

40 Minutes—75 Questions

DIRECTIONS: In each of the following passages, some portions are underlined and numbered. Corresponding to each numbered portion are three alternative ways of saying the same thing. Read through each passage quickly to determine the sense of the passage, then return to the underlined portions. If you feel that an underlined portion is correct and is stated as well as possible, mark NO CHANGE, **A** or **F.** If you feel that there is an error in grammar, sentence structure, punctuation or word usage, choose the correct answer. If an underlined portion appears to be correct, but you believe that one of the alternative choices would be more effective, mark that choice. Remember, you are to choose the *best* answer.

Passage I

There is such a voluble hue and cry about the abysmal state of culture in the United States by well-meaning sincere criticizers (1) that I would like to strongly present (2)

1. **A.** NO CHANGE
   B. well-meant, sincere critiques
   C. well-meaning, sincere critics
   D. well-meaning sincere critics

2. **F.** NO CHANGE
   G. to present strongly
   H. to boldy present
   J. to present in strong language

some evidence for the contrary. Are none of us tempted
3 4
to remind these disapprovers that no country to date

3. A. NO CHANGE
B. on the opposite side
C. of the contrary
D. to the contrary

4. F. NO CHANGE
G. Are there none of us
H. Are none of you
J. Is none of us

ever achieved the complete integration of *haute culture*
5

5. A. NO CHANGE
B. has ever achieved
C. has achieved ever
D. never achieved

into the warp and woof of its everyday life. In the wish-
6

6. F. NO CHANGE
G. it's everyday life,
H. its everyday life?
J. its every day life.

ful memories of those who moon over the passed glories
7

7. A. NO CHANGE
B. them who woom
C. those which mourn
D. mourners

of Shakespeares England, it is seldom called to mind
8
that bearbaiting was far more popular than any Shakespearian production. Who cares to remember that the same Rome that found a Juvenal proclaiming *mens sana in corpore sano* could also watch Emperor Trajan celebrate his win over Decebalus with no less than 5,000
9 10
pairs of gladiators matched to the death? This was in the name of amusement!

8. F. NO CHANGE
G. Shakespeare's England,
H. Shakespeare's England.
J. Shakespeares England;

9. A. NO CHANGE
B. celebrating his win
C. celebrate his winning
D. celebrate his victory

10. F. NO CHANGE
G. no more then
H. no fewer than
J. no less then

Passage II

The most serious threatening to modern man it would
11 12
seem is not physical annihilation but the alleged mean-
12

11. A. NO CHANGE
B. most seriously threatening
C. most serious threat
D. seriously threatening

12. F. NO CHANGE
G. man; it would seem that
H. man. It would seem that
J. man, it would seem,

inglessness of life. This latent vacuum becomes manifest (13) in a state of boredom. Automation will lead to more and more freer time (14) and many will not know how to use their liesure hours, this (15) is evidenced today by what a prominent psychiatrist refers to as Sunday Neurosis the (16) depression that inflicts people who (17) become conscious of the lack of content in their lives when the rush of the busy week stops. Nothing in the world helps man to keep healthy so much as (18) the knowledge of a life task. Nietzsche wisely said "he who (19) knows a Why of living surmounts over (20) every How."

13. **A.** NO CHANGE
    B. latent vacuum become
    C. latent vacuum have become
    D. latent vacuole becomes

14. **F.** NO CHANGE
    G. more freer time
    H. more and more free time
    J. more or less free-time

15. **A.** NO CHANGE
    B. liesure hours, that
    C. leisure hours, that
    D. leisure hours. This

16. **F.** NO CHANGE
    G. Neurosis, the
    H. neurosis. The
    J. Neurosis. The

17. **A.** NO CHANGE
    B. inflicts people whom
    C. afflicts people who
    D. afflicts people whom

18. **F.** NO CHANGE
    G. so much so
    H. so much that
    J. so much as that

19. **A.** NO CHANGE
    B. said "He who
    C. said, "he whom
    D. said, "He who

20. **F.** NO CHANGE
    G. surmounted over
    H. surmounts
    J. surmount

Passage III

The cynical some times (21) are critical. But I do not know of no more (22) worthy motive or purpose that a

21. **A.** NO CHANGE
    B. some of the times
    C. sometimes
    D. at sometimes

22. **F.** NO CHANGE
    G. I know of no more worthy
    H. I don't know of no more worthy
    J. I can't know of any more worthy

human being can have had than to try to lie out as her
23 24

23. **A.** NO CHANGE
B. human being could have had
C. human being could be going to have
D. human being can have

24. **F.** NO CHANGE
G. to try to layout
H. trying to lie out
J. trying to lay out

goal a Program that will educate the mind, that will con-
25

25. **A.** NO CHANGE
B. a "Program" that will
C. a program, that will
D. a program that will

quer disease in the body. That will permit your children
26

26. **F.** NO CHANGE
G. in the body; that
H. in the body, but
J. in the body, and that

and you're people to live in an atmosphere and
27

27. **A.** NO CHANGE
B. and Your People to
C. and you are people to
D. and your people to

an environment of beauty and culture—and enjoy the
28
better things of life.

28. **F.** NO CHANGE
G. environs of
H. the environs of
J. environments of

We cannot conquer disease nor we cannot educate all
29

29. **A.** NO CHANGE
B. or we cannot
C. nor we can
D. nor can we

humanity. We can't not have a symphony in every town
30 31

30. **F.** NO CHANGE
G. We can not
H. We can't
J. When can we

31. **A.** NO CHANGE
B. Symphony in
C. symphony, in
D. Symphony, in

and we cannot have a mellon art gallery in every capitol.
32 33

32. **F.** NO CHANGE
G. a "mellon art gallery"
H. a Mellon "Art" gallery
J. a Mellon Art Gallery

33. **A.** NO CHANGE
B. every capitol?
C. every capital.
D. every capital?

But we can hope for these amenities and be working for them, and we can give what we have to them. And we can urge them and provide leadership and ideas
(34: "But we"; 35: "be working for them"; 36: "to them. And we can"; 37: "urge them")

34. F. NO CHANGE
G. Therefore we
H. Moreover we
J. Since we

35. A. NO CHANGE
B. work for them
C. have them work
D. keep them working

36. F. NO CHANGE
G. to them; and we can
H. to them. We can also
J. to them. Also we can

37. A. NO CHANGE
B. encourage them
C. urge it
D. encourage development of the arts

and try to move along.
(38: "and try to move along")

38. F. NO CHANGE
G. and try to move up.
H. and try to move them up.
J. OMIT

Passage IV

The Dictionary defines the word, gadfly as a "fly that
(39: "Dictionary"; 40: "word,"; 41: "gadfly")

39. A. NO CHANGE
B. dictionary
C. dictionery
D. dictionary,

40. F. NO CHANGE
G. "word
H. word—
J. word

41. A. NO CHANGE
B. "gadfly"
C. *gadfly*
D. Gadfly"

bites. But the word also applies to a person that knows how to use biting words to jostle others into thinking
(42: "bites. But"; 43: "that")

42. F. NO CHANGE
G. bites." But
H. bites", but
J. bites;" but

43. A. NO CHANGE
B. who
C. which
D. whom

and debate. Its the second type that is being sought by
44 45 46

44. **F.** NO CHANGE
G. toward debating
H. into debate
J. debating

45. **A.** NO CHANGE
B. It's
C. Its'
D. 'Tis

46. **F.** NO CHANGE
G. the second definition
H. the second type of gadfly
J. a gadfly of the second type

the Great Books foundation to train volunteer leaders
47 48

47. **A.** NO CHANGE
B. Foundation
C. foundation,
D. Foundation,

48. **F.** NO CHANGE
G. to volunteer to train
H. to enter a training class for volunteer
J. to be trained by volunteer

of their discussion groups. Training will be offered in a
49 50

49. **A.** NO CHANGE
B. to lead their
C. of the
D. of

50. **F.** NO CHANGE
G. They will offer training
H. It will be offered
J. The Foundation will offer training

series of 10 Thursday evenings meetings beginning at
51 52

51. **A.** NO CHANGE
B. ten
C. 10-
D. ten,

52. **F.** NO CHANGE
G. evening
H. Evening
J. Evenings

8 P.M. at Teachers College on 123 rd St. in
53 54

53. **A.** NO CHANGE
B. P.M.,
C. PM
D. p.m.

54. **F.** NO CHANGE
G. 123 rd. St.
H. 123rd St.
J. 123rd Street

New York city. Dr. Paul Daniels associate Professor at
55 56

oriental college will direct the program. He is co-leader
57 58
also of Great Books groups in Meadow Lane.
58

In each group, he explains, we have two leaders. They
59 60

are intended to balance each other, he adds. "One is
61

nice and one is nasty, the gadfly. Hes the one who
62 63

prods people and gets them in a corner so they think for
64 65
themselves and fight back."

55. A. NO CHANGE
    B. New York City
    C. N.Y. City
    D. N.Y.C.

56. F. NO CHANGE
    G. Daniels, associate
    H. Daniels, Associate
    J. Daniels Associate

57. A. NO CHANGE
    B. Oriental College
    C. Oriental college,
    D. Oriental College,

58. F. NO CHANGE
    G. He also is co-leader
    H. He is also co-leader
    J. Also, he is co-leader

59. A. NO CHANGE
    B. "In each group",
    C. "In each group,"
    D. "In each group,

60. F. NO CHANGE
    G. "we have two leaders.
    H. "we have two leaders."
    J. we have two leaders."

61. A. NO CHANGE
    B. other," he adds.
    C. other", he adds.
    D. other, he adds."

62. A. NO CHANGE
    B. nasty the gadfly.
    C. nasty; the gadfly.
    D. nasty—the gadfly.

63. F. NO CHANGE
    G. —he's
    H. He's
    J. "He's

64. A. NO CHANGE
    B. corners them
    C. gets them into a corner
    D. gets them into corners

65. F. NO CHANGE
    G. so that they think
    H. forcing them to think
    J. so that they have to think

Passage V

A high school diploma by itself is not sufficient preparation for many occupations. But neither is a college degree. [66] Different fields of work require different types of training. Just as there are occupations that require college degrees, so to there are [67] occupations for which technical training or work experience are the most important [68] entry requirement. Employers always wish to hire the best qualified applicants, but this does not mean that the jobs always go to those applicants which are most educated. [69] The type of education and training an individual has had is as important [70] as the amount. For this reason, a vital part of the career planning process is deciding what kind as well as how much [71] education and training to pursue.

Persons who have definite career goals may not find this decision difficult, many [72] occupations have specific education requirements. Physicians, for example, must generally complete at least 3 years of college, 4 years of Medical School, [73] and in most states 1 year of residency. Cosmetologists are required to complete a state-approved cosmetology course that generally lasts 18 months.

66. **A.** NO CHANGE
B. Nor a college degree.
C. No more a college degree.
D. Nor a degree from a four-year college.

67. **F.** NO CHANGE
G. so to are there
H. so too there are
J. there are to

68. **A.** NO CHANGE
B. is the most important
C. are more important
D. are of the utmost importance as an

69. **F.** NO CHANGE
G. that are most educated of all
H. that have the most years of school
J. who have the most education.

70. **A.** NO CHANGE
B. has had are as important
C. have had is as important
D. had had was as important

71. **F.** NO CHANGE
G. what kind of as well as how much of
H. what kind of as well as how much
J. what and how much

72. **A.** NO CHANGE
B. difficult. Many
C. difficult many
D. difficult being that many

73. **F.** NO CHANGE
G. four years of Medical School
H. 4 years in Medical School
J. 4 years of medical school

<u>For most people, however</u>, the decision is more difficult.
74
Either they have yet to choose a field of work, or the field they have selected may be entered in a variety of ways. Making career decisions requires not only specific information about the types of education and training preferred for various occupations, but also <u>to know one's</u>
75
<u>own</u> abilities and aspirations.
75

74. **A.** NO CHANGE
B. However, for most people
C. Begin new paragraph
D. For most persons, however,

75. **F.** NO CHANGE
G. a knowledge of one's own
H. the knowing of ones' own
J. you must know your own

END OF TEST

If you complete this test before the time limit is up, check back over the questions on this test only. Do not proceed to the next test until you are told to do so.

TEST 2
MATHEMATICS USAGE

50 Minutes—40 Questions

DIRECTIONS: Solve each problem and mark the letter of the correct answer on your answer sheet.

DO YOUR FIGURING HERE

1. Which of the following fractions is more than $\frac{3}{4}$?

A. $\frac{35}{71}$

B. $\frac{13}{20}$

C. $\frac{71}{101}$

D. $\frac{19}{24}$

E. $\frac{15}{20}$

2. If $820 + R + S - 610 = 342$, and if $R = 2S$, then $S =$

F. 44
G. 48
H. 132
J. 184
K. 192

3. What is the cost in dollars to carpet a room x yards long and y yards wide, if the carpet costs two dollars per square foot?

A. xy
B. 2xy
C. 3xy
D. 6xy
E. 18xy

4. If $7M = 3M - 20$, then $M + 7 =$

F. 0
G. 2
H. 5
J. 12
K. 17

5. In circle O, AB is a diameter, angle BOD contains 15°, and angle EOA contains 85°. Find the number of degrees in angle ECA.

DO YOUR FIGURING HERE

A. 15
B. 35
C. 50
D. 70
E. 85

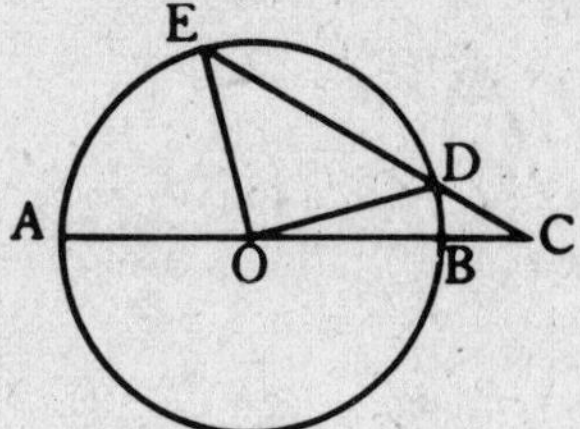

6. The diagonal of a rectangle is 10. The area of the rectangle

F. must be 24
G. must be 48
H. must be 50
J. must be 100
K. cannot be determined from the data given

7. In triangle PQR in the figure below, angle P is greater than angle Q and the bisectors of angle P and angle Q meet in S. Then

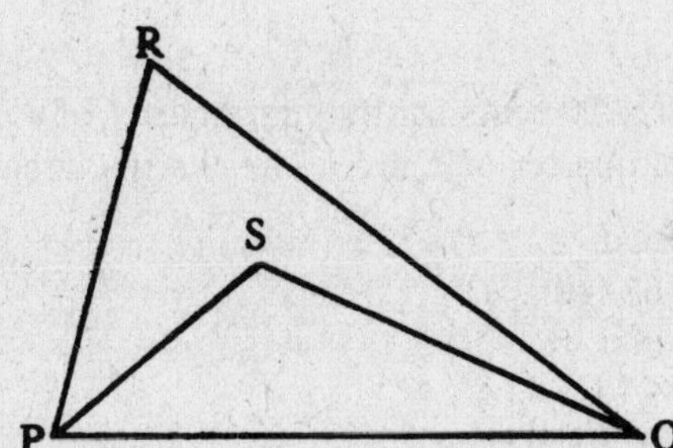

A. SQ > SP
B. SQ = SP
C. SQ < SP
D. SQ ≥ SP
E. no conclusion concerning the relative lengths of SQ and SP can be drawn from the data given

8. The coordinates of vertices X and Y of equilateral triangle XYZ are (−4, 0) and (4, 0), respectively. The coordinates of Z may be

F. $(0, 2\sqrt{3})$
G. $(0, 4\sqrt{3})$
H. $(4, 4\sqrt{3})$
J. (0, 4)
K. $(4\sqrt{3}, 0)$

9. Given: All men are mortal. Which statement expresses a conclusion that logically follows from the given statement?

A. All mortals are men.
B. If X is a mortal, then X is a man.
C. If X is not a mortal, then X is not a man.
D. If X is not a man, then X is not mortal.
E. Some mortals are not men.

DO YOUR FIGURING HERE

10. In the accompanying figure, ACB is a straight angle and DC is perpendicular to CE. If the number of degrees in angle ACD is represented by x, the number of degrees in angle BCE is represented by

F. 90 − x
G. x − 90
H. 90 + x
J. 180 − x
K. 45 + x

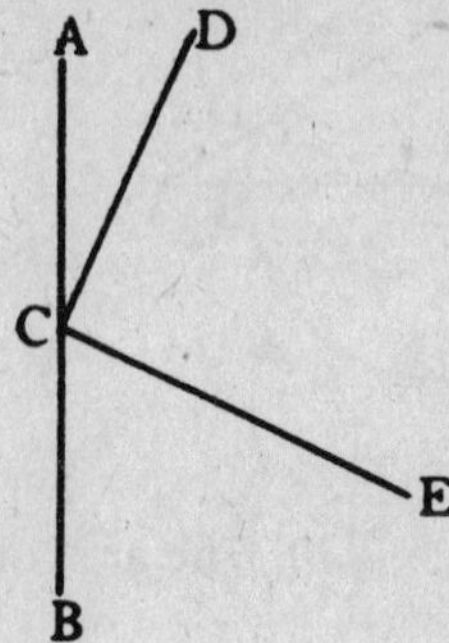

11. What is the smallest positive number which, when divided by 3, 4, or 5, will leave a remainder of 2?

A. 22
B. 42
C. 62
D. 122
E. 182

12. Taxis charge 90 cents for the first quarter of a mile and 65 cents for each additional quarter of a mile. The charge, in cents, for a trip of d miles is

F. 90 + 65d
G. 90 + 65 (4d − 1)
H. 90 + 90d
J. 90 + 4 (d − 1)
K. 90 + 90 (d − 1)

13. In a certain army post, 30% of the draftees are from New York State, and 10% of these are from New York City. What percent of the draftees in the post are from New York City?

A. 3
B. .3
C. .03
D. 13
E. 20

14. From 9 AM to 2 PM, the temperature rose at a constant rate from −14 °F to +36 °F. What was the temperature at noon?

F. −4°
G. +6°
H. +16°
J. +26°
K. +31°

DO YOUR FIGURING HERE

15. There are just two ways in which 5 may be expressed as the sum of two different positive (non-zero) integers; namely, $5 = 4 + 1 = 3 + 2$. In how many ways may 9 be expressed as the sum of two different positive (non-zero) integers?

A. 3
B. 4
C. 5
D. 6
E. 7

16. A board 7 feet 9 inches long is divided into three equal parts. What is the length of each part?

F. 2 ft. 7 in.
G. 2 ft. $6\frac{1}{3}$ in.
H. 2 ft. $8\frac{1}{3}$ in.
J. 2 ft. 8 in.
K. 2 ft. 9 in.

17. In the figure below, the largest possible circle is cut out of a square piece of tin. The area of the remaining piece of tin is approximately (in square inches)

A. .75
B. 3.14
C. .14
D. .86
E. 1.0

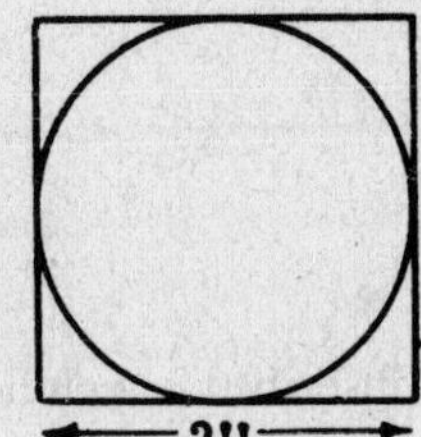

18. Which of the following is equal to 3.14×10^6?

F. 314
G. 3,140
H. 31,400
J. 314,000
K. 3,140,000

19. $\dfrac{36}{29 - \dfrac{4}{0.2}} =$

A. $\frac{4}{3}$
B. 2
C. 4
D. $\frac{3}{4}$
E. 18

DO YOUR FIGURING HERE

20. In terms of the square units in the figure below, what is the area of the semicircle?

F. 32π
G. 16π
H. 8π
J. 4π
K. 2π

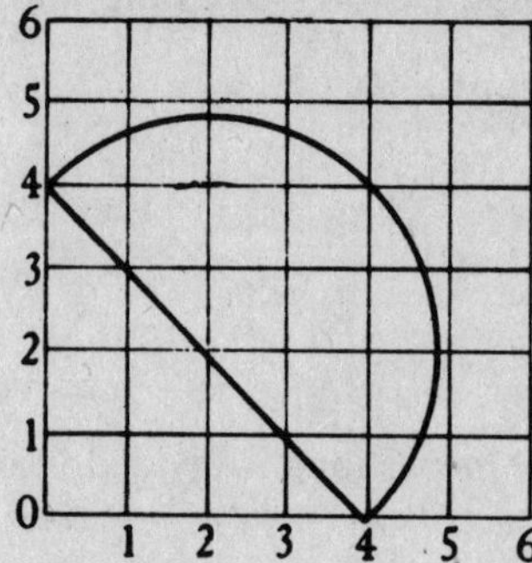

21. The sum of three consecutive odd numbers is always divisible by

I. 2
II. 3
III. 5
IV. 6

A. only I
B. only IV
C. only I and II
D. only I and III
E. only II and IV

22. In the diagram, triangle ABC is inscribed in a circle and CD is tangent to the circle. If angle BCD is 40° how many degrees are there in angle A?

F. 20
G. 30
H. 40
J. 50
K. 60

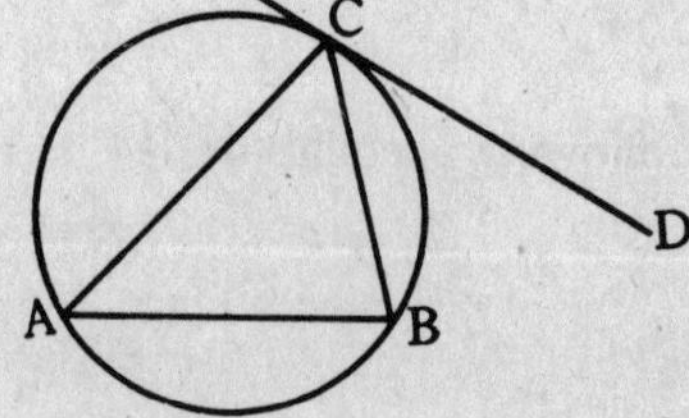

23. If a discount of 20% off the marked price of a suit saves a woman \$15, how much did she pay for the suit?

A. \$ 35
B. \$ 60
C. \$ 75
D. \$150
E. \$300

DO YOUR FIGURING HERE

24. Find the last number in the series: 8, 4, 12, 6, 18, 9, ?

F. 19
G. 20
H. 22
J. 24
K. 27

25. A 15-gallon mixture of 20% alcohol has 5 gallons of water added to it. The strength of the mixture, as a percent, is near

A. 15
B. $13\frac{1}{3}$
C. $16\frac{2}{3}$
D. $12\frac{1}{2}$
E. 20

26. In the figure below, QXRS is a parallelogram and P is any point on side QS. What is the ratio of the area of triangle PXR to the area of QXRS?

F. 1:4
G. 1:3
H. 2:3
J. 3:4
K. 1:2

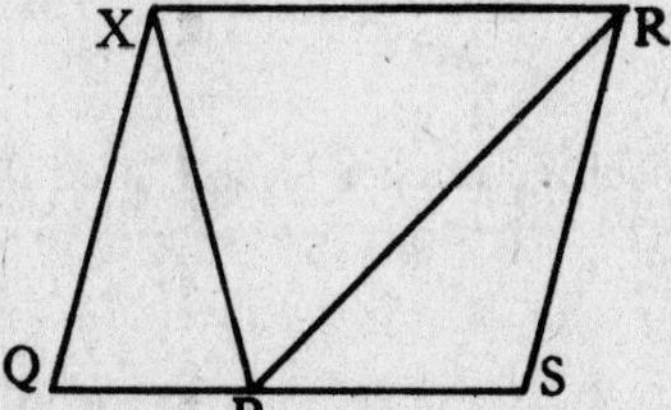

27. If x (p + 1) = M, then p =

A. M − 1
B. M
C. $\frac{M - 1}{x}$
D. M − x − 1
E. $\frac{M}{x} - 1$

28. If T tons of snow fall in 1 second, how many tons fall in M minutes?

F. 60 MT
G. MT + 60
H. MT
J. $\frac{60\ M}{T}$
K. $\frac{MT}{60}$

DO YOUR FIGURING HERE

29. If $\frac{P}{Q} = \frac{4}{5}$, what is the value of $2P + Q$?

A. 14
B. 13
C. -1
D. 3
E. cannot be determined from the information given

30. The figure shows one square inside another and a rectangle of diagonal T. The best approximation to the value of T, in inches, is given by which of the following inequalities?

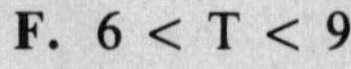

F. $6 < T < 9$
G. $11 < T < 12$
H. $12 < T < 13$
J. $9 < T < 11$
K. $10 < T < 11$

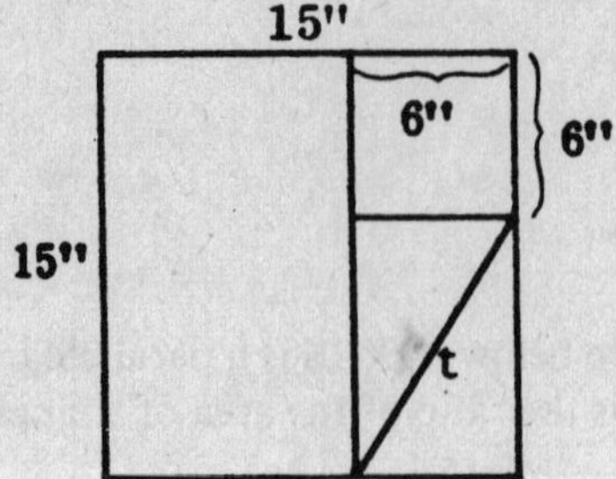

31. What is the smallest positive integer $K > 1$ such that $R^2 = S^3 = K$, for some integers R and S?

A. 4
B. 8
C. 27
D. 64
E. 81

32. The number of square units in the area of triangle RST is

F. 10
G. 12.5
H. 15.5
J. 17.5
K. 20

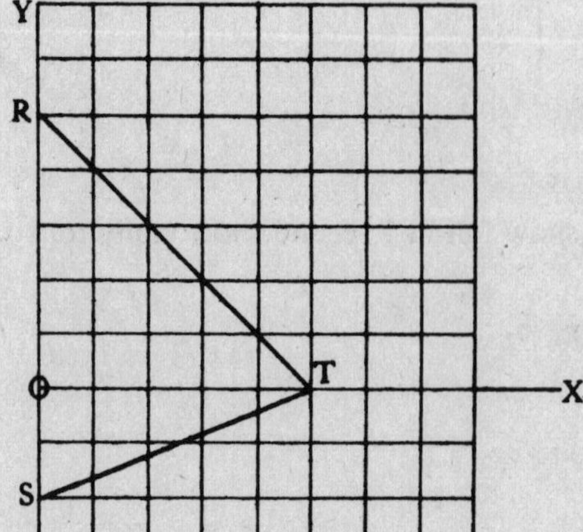

DO YOUR FIGURING HERE

33. In the figure, PQR is an equilateral triangle of side 10 inches. At each vertex, a small equilateral △ of side X is cut off to form a regular hexagon. What is the length of X, in inches?

A. 3
B. $3\frac{1}{3}$
C. $3\frac{1}{2}$
D. 4
E. $4\frac{1}{2}$

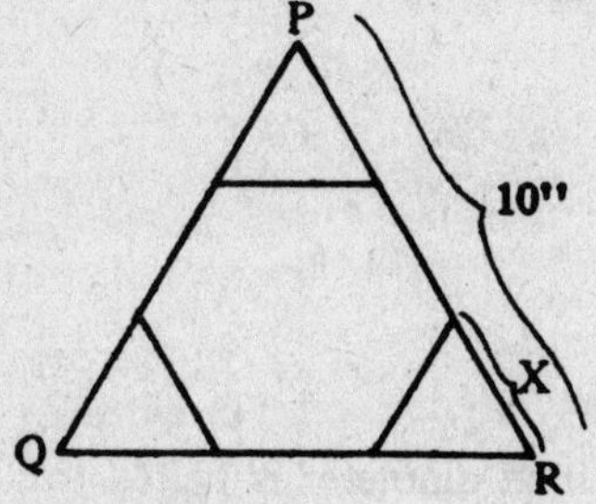

34. Which of the following has the same value as $\frac{P}{Q}$?

F. $\frac{P-2}{Q-2}$

G. $\frac{1+P}{1+Q}$

H. $\frac{P^2}{Q^2}$

J. $\frac{3P}{3Q}$

K. $\frac{P+3}{Q+3}$

35. A woman travels a certain distance at 60 miles per hour and returns over the same road at 40 miles per hour. What is her average rate for the round trip in miles per hour?

A. 42
B. 44
C. 46
D. 48
E. 50

36. As shown in the figure, a circular metal disc wears down to one-half of its original radius. What percent of the original area remains?

F. 50
G. 25
H. 75
J. 40
K. 60

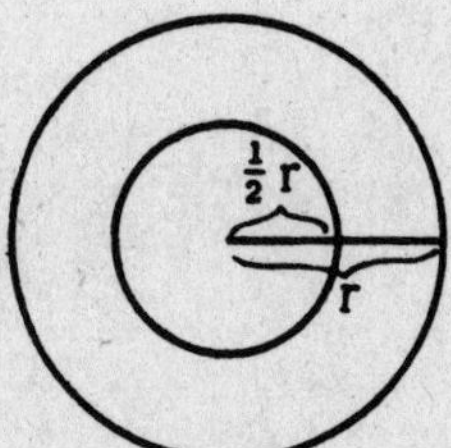

DO YOUR FIGURING HERE

37. A girl takes a 25-question test and answers all questions. Her percent score is obtained by giving her 4 points for each correct answer, and then subtracting 1 point for each wrong answer. If she obtains a score of 70%, how many questions did she answer correctly?

A. 17
B. 18
C. 19
D. 20
E. 21

38. A pulley having a 9 inch diameter is belted to a pulley having a 6 inch diameter, as shown in the figure. If the large pulley runs at 120 rpm, how fast does the small pulley run, in revolutions per minute?

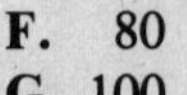

F. 80
G. 100
H. 160
J. 180
K. 240

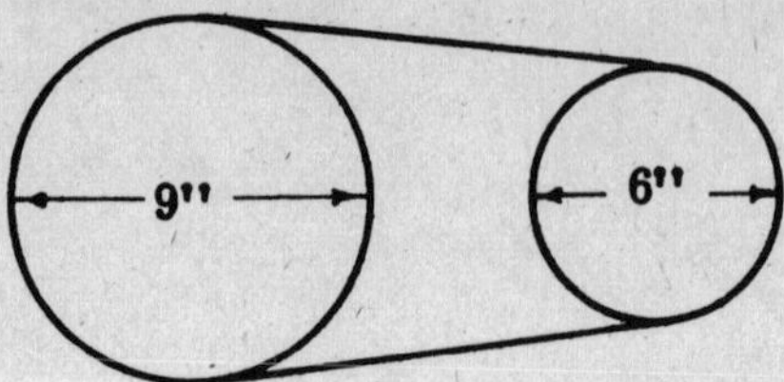

39. In the figure below, the side of the large square is 14. The four smaller squares are formed by joining the mid-points of opposite sides. Find the value of Y.

A. 5
B. 6
C. $6\frac{2}{3}$
D. $6\frac{5}{8}$
E. 6.8

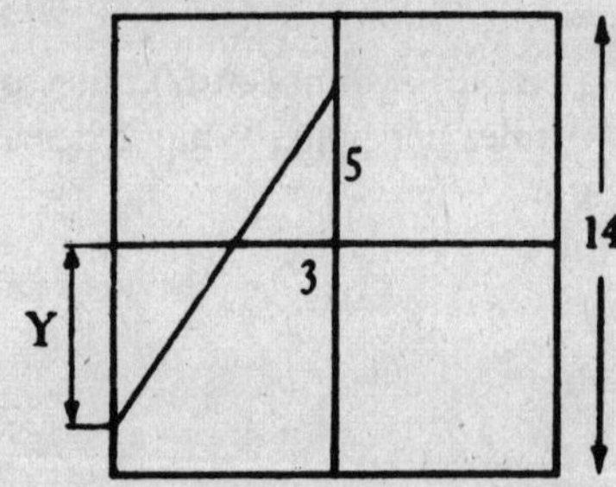

DO YOUR FIGURING HERE

40.

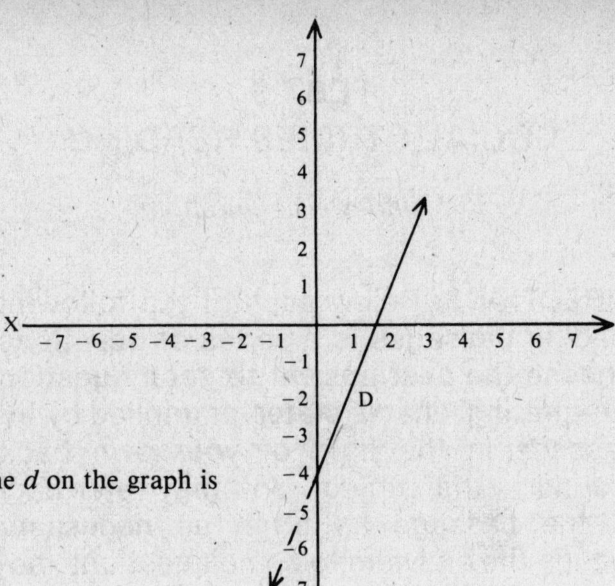

The equation for line *d* on the graph is

F. $y = \frac{2}{5}x - 4$

G. $y = \frac{5}{2}x - 4$

H. $y = \frac{5}{2}x + 4$

J. $y = -\frac{2}{5}x + 4$

K. $y = -\frac{2}{5}x - 4$

END OF TEST

If you complete this test before the time limit is up, check back over the questions on this test only. Do not go back to the previous test. Do not proceed to the next test until you are told to do so.

TEST 3
SOCIAL STUDIES READING

35 Minutes—52 Questions

DIRECTIONS: Below each of the following reading passages is a series of questions. Choose the *best* answer to each question, interpreting what is stated or implied by the passage in the light of your own background in the subject. You may refer back to the passage as often as necessary, though the answers to some questions may not be found expressly in the passage.

From the *Daily Newsprint:*

"To hear some generals tell it, the concept of an all-volunteer Army is an unrealistic dream that has already been shattered by the enlistment statistics of the past months. It is true that since the draft was suspended the Army has failed to meet its enlistment quotas. The shortfall, however, hardly endangers national security, since the Army has managed to fill about 75 percent of its openings.

"With enlistment bonuses of up to $3,000, plus a starting salary of $448 a month, we feel that enlistments will increase. It's not just poster rhetoric to point out that the military can indeed be an honorable and attractive alternative to a dead-end civilian job. We feel that it would be premature to reinstitute the draft at this time."

From the *News of Today:*

"Last night's *Daily Newsprint* (an offshoot of the radical *This Week's News*) blatantly suggests that it is unnecessary to ensure a strong army by using the draft. They state that manpower requirements are down 'only' 25%. This alone should be sufficient reason to reinstitute the draft, for our country cannot afford to be weak at any time and much less in times when our enemy's strengths are increasing. To do so would only invite attack and lead to our possible destruction.

"Our Constitution makes provisions for the draft because our forefathers realized the need for a strong, democratic army. The all-volunteer army will become a 'salt and pepper' army—white officers and black enlisted men. It will become an army of the poor, those to whom $5,400 a year looks attractive. The draft does not prevent volunteers, but it does help to guarantee a strong democratic army and it should be reinstated to keep us from becoming a second-class power."

1. The tone of the *News of Today* can best be described as

   A. emotional
   B. indifferent
   C. restrained
   D. impartial

2. Which branch of the government is responsible for creating draft laws?

   F. legislative
   G. executive
   H. judicial
   J. military

3. Why does *News of Today* mention that the *Daily Newsprint* is connected with *This Week's News?*

   A. so that the readers will have all the facts
   B. to prove that *Daily Newsprint* is a radical paper
   C. to associate *Daily Newsprint* with a paper they hope their own readers will not like
   D. to strengthen the arguments made by the *Daily Newsprint*

4. What does the *Daily Newsprint* think should be done to improve Army enlistments?

   F. army life should be made more attractive
   G. more money should be offered to those who enlist
   H. the present program should be given time to prove itself
   J. army jobs should be more like civilian jobs

5. Why does the *News of Today* mention the Constitution in its editorial?

   A. to show that its main purpose is support of the Constitution
   B. to prove that the *Daily Newsprint*'s stand is unconstitutional
   C. to add a feeling of authority to its own position
   D. to show that the Constitution is the law of the land

6. A fear that continued suspension of the draft laws may have a harmful effect on our country was implied

   F. only by the editor of the *Daily Newsprint*
   G. only by the editor of the *News of Today*
   H. by both editors
   J. by neither editor

7. The statement "Our nation needs a strong army" would be agreed to by

   A. only the editor of the *Daily Newsprint*
   B. only the editor of the *News of Today*
   C. both editors
   D. neither editor

8. Which of the following groups would be most likely to agree with the position of the *News of Today?*

   F. the generals of the Army
   G. college students who want to avoid the draft
   H. the United Nations
   J. the Congress of the United States

9. According to the opinion of *News of Today,* which of the following was NOT mentioned as a problem resulting from dropping the draft?

   A. a drop in total army inductees
   B. a racial imbalance in the army
   C. a danger to our freedom
   D. an infringement on personal freedom

10. The *Daily Newsprint* mentioned the viewpoint of the Army generals in order to

    F. show that the military is prejudiced
    G. make sure that the public knew all the facts
    H. place anti-military people on their side
    J. show that they support the Army

11. What was the major reason for dropping the draft as a means of raising an army?

    A. to reduce the turnover rate of the Army
    B. to improve the pay of the soldiers
    C. to reduce the cost of maintaining an army
    D. the reason was not given in these editorials

12. According to the Constitution, the draft

    F. is not constitutional
    G. is the only way the size of the Army may legally be increased
    H. is one legal means of raising an army
    J. can only be used if volunteers do not meet the demands of the Army

According to Hegel, a conflict between a thesis and its antithesis produces a synthesis which partakes of the natures of both. The general councils of the Church, which so far number twenty-one, may serve as an illustration of this philosophy. The Council of Trent (1545–63) was a reaction to the Lutheran revolt. The first Ecumenical Council of the Vatican (1869–70) was held in the shadow of the French Revolution of 1789, of the revolutions in 1848 and of the rationalist movement. The First Session of the Second Ecumenical Council of the Vatican (1963) was against the atheistic movement, mainly represented by communism, the new scientific irreligious trends and the fact that "The World was too strong for a divided Christianity." The Second Session of this Council, which began on September 29, 1963, and culminated in Pope Paul's visit to the Holy Land in January 1964, is mainly a unitive Council, to try to bring together the various churches in Christendom and to try to have dialogues with other religions for a united stand against disruptive forces in the world. This is the meaning of "ecumenism" in its Christian sense and in its wider and world-wide sense. Islam is only concerned with the latter sense. The thaw which is taking place at the Vatican, a new synthesis, may be regarded as a prelude to a wider thaw with the world religions through continuous dialogue with Islam, Judaism, and other religions.

The dialogue with Islam has a long history. In its beginning, the conflict between Christianity and Islam was violent. One could cite here the Muslim conquests in the seventh and eighth centuries, the Crusades, the Inquisition in Spain, religious persecution and the missionary movements. But throughout this long period there were sometimes peaceful and more rational dialogues and debates. Peter the Venerable in the twelfth century, for instance, wrote in his first book of *Adversus Nefandum Sectum Saracenorum* (against the unspeakable sect of the Saracens) as follows, addressing Muslims: "It appears odd and perhaps is actually so that a man so removed from you by great distance, speaking another language, and having a profession and customs and a manner of life so different from your own, should write from the furthest West to men who live in the countries of the Orient, and should direct his attacks against a people whom he has never seen, and that he assails you not with weapons, as Christians have often done, but by word, not by force but with reasons, not with hate but with love." Peter then pleads with the Saracens to enter into discussion. He was indignant that the Latins were living in ignorance of a religion so widespread as Islam. A century later, Roger Bacon condemned the method of the crusade and wanted to see the intellectuals taking part in discussions. He gave an illustration from the King of Tartary, who gathered before him people of differing beliefs in order that he might thereby come to a knowledge of the truth. Thomas Aquinas wrote his book *Summa Contra Gentiles* in order to use reason and discussion, especially with Muslims in Spain.

But what has been the attitude of the Muslims to all such approaches? It is one which stems from the Prophet's example given in his dealings with Christians and Jews in Arabia. He used to enjoin his followers not to enter into polemics with their adversaries, but to content themselves with saying to them that they (the Muslims) neither believed nor disbelieved what the others claimed in their Scriptures, but only believed in what was contained in the Quran. A verse in the Quran says: "Our Lord, we believe in what thou hast revealed and we follow the Apostle." Another verse says: "O followers of the Bible! Come to an equitable proposition between us and you that we shall not serve any but God and that we shall not associate anyone with Him, and that some of us shall not take others for Lords besides God: but if they [the Scriptuaries] turn back, then say: bear witness that we are muslims." A third verse says: "And do not dispute with the people of the Scriptures except by what is best, except those of them who act unjustly, and say: We believe in that which has been revealed to us and revealed to you, and our God and your God is one, and to him do we submit."

13. The "rationalist movement" refers to

A. the procedure of fixing allowances of food and other goods in time of scarcity
B. the reorganization of religion in accordance with up-to-date methods and practices
C. the explanation of behavior on grounds ostensibly rational but not in accord with the actual motives
D. the reliance upon reason alone, independently of authority or of revelation

14. The leaders of Islam

F. have traditionally been averse to religious discussions with the Catholics
G. are planning ecumenical councils of their own
H. have had a continuously friendly relationship with the Christians
J. were responsible for conducting the Spanish Inquisition

15. The work, *Adversus Nefandum Sectum Saracenorum,*

A. urged a final victory, bloody if necessary, over the followers of Islam
B. favored talks with the Saracens in order to arrive at a peaceful settlement of their differences
C. presented ideas that could be employed in the conversion of the Muslims
D. commended the religious beliefs of the Islamites

16. Synonyms for *Muslim* and *Quran* are

F. Mussel and Querin
G. Muslin and Quorum
H. Islam and Queries
J. Mohammedan and Koran

17. A major function of the ecumenical councils has been

A. to discuss religious persecution and missionary movements
B. to determine how to rid the world of evils such as poverty, disease, and war
C. to find common ground with the churches other than Catholic
D. to arrive at the most efficient means of eliminating atheism

18. The article does *not* make reference to a part of the following area:

F. the Iberian peninsula
G. Italy
H. Southwest Asia
J. the United States

19. The passage mentions the following conflicts between Christianity and Islam:

I. Muslim conquests of the 8th and 9th centuries
II. The Crusades
III. The Spanish Inquisition
IV. missionary movements

Those conflicts instigated by the Christians are

A. I, II, and III
B. II, III, and IV
C. II and III
D. III and IV

20. Moslems believe

F. that the Bible is false
G. that Christianity is evil
H. in one God
J. that conflict among adherents of various religions is inevitable

The culture of China two thousand years ago was somewhat similar to that of the ancient Mayas. Both cultures had made great advances in medicine and religion. They both had highly developed social and political structures. Today China remains one of the great cultures of the world, while the Mayan culture has all but disappeared. Yet, during those twenty centuries, the geographical conditions around which these cultures developed have not shown much change. It does not seem that their cultures were dependent upon geography for their development, for their existence, or for their survival.

There are many instances in which peoples living in the same geographical area have developed different cultures. Athens and Sparta, both city-states in the same peninsula, are a case in point. Sparta was known for its disciplined soldiers and its slavery. There was little interest in improving business, government or the arts. Although Athens also conquered many smaller communities, Athens absorbed the inhabitants and made them citizens. The Athenians were one of the most forward of all peoples and welcomed change and improvement. Since Sparta and Athens both developed under similar geographic conditions, it does not seem that the direction of a culture is determined nor retarded by climate.

21. As used in this passage the word *culture* means

A. the habits that individuals have developed
B. those traits for which a society is known
C. the everyday conduct that shows a good heritage
D. those understandings and actions which a formal education can teach

22. Judging from this passage, Spartan education was concerned primarily with

F. broadening understandings
G. business and commerce
H. developing arts and crafts
J. the military

23. Judging from this passage, Athenian education was concerned primarily with

A. broadening understanding
B. business and commerce
C. developing arts and crafts
D. the military

24. The best title for the passage would be

F. Ancient Cultures and How They Developed
G. The Differences Between Chinese and Other Ancient Cultures
H. The Role of Geography on Social Development
J. How Climate Causes Social Development

25. Both Athens and Sparta were parts of what is now known as

A. Asia
B. Greece
C. China
D. Persia

26. The author's main purpose is to

F. try to prove a theory of cultural determination
G. try to discredit a theory of cultural determination
H. describe some ancient culture patterns
J. show how culture patterns develop

27. The Mayan civilization developed in what is now

A. Central America
B. Asia
C. Africa
D. Europe

28. The author's attitude toward a theory that cultures are creations of geographical conditions is one of

F. agreement
G. disagreement
H. impartiality
J. a lack of sufficient knowledge

DIRECTIONS: The following questions are not based upon a reading passage. Read each questions and choose the *best* answer, drawing on your background in social studies.

29. Two weeks after the Treaty of Ghent was signed, a major battle was fought in

A. Detroit
B. Quebec
C. New Orleans
D. the area of Lake Erie

30. The protest put forth by the Seneca Falls Convention of 1848 took the form of a document modeled on

F. the Bible
G. the Constitution
H. the Declaration of Independence
J. *Common Sense*

31. Which of these international agencies of the United Nations did not exist under the League of Nations?

A. Trusteeship Council
B. International Labor Office
C. International Court of Justice
D. Educational, Scientific and Cultural Council

32. After the Civil War, Confederate President Jefferson Davis was

F. convicted of treason
G. impeached and acquitted
H. impeached and convicted
J. imprisoned

33. Assume that as the price of product A decreases, the demand for product B increases. It can then be concluded that

A. A and B are substitute goods
B. A and B are complementary goods
C. A is an inferior good
D. B is a superior good

34. The turn-of-the-century Prohibitionists and pre-Civil War abolitionists exemplify which type of social movement?

F. Expressive
G. Reform
H. Revolutionary
J. Resistance

35. The Emancipation Proclamation freed the slaves in all

A. territory controlled by the Union Army
B. territory resisting the Union Army
C. states and territories
D. southern states

36. To which of the following groups were the high tariffs of the late nineteenth century most injurious?

F. large industrial corporations
G. domestic manufacturers with small factories
H. Midwestern farmers selling agricultural products
J. new businesses that had begun after the Civil War

37. Which of the following was most characteristic of the depression period of the 1930s?

A. rapid growth of labor unions
B. successful international collaboration in currency stabilization
C. rising prices of raw materials and consumer goods throughout the world
D. the existence of prohibitive tariffs in western Europe and the United States

38. Which of the following statements about the North Atlantic Treaty Organization (NATO) are true?

I. Originally, it was an outgrowth of the Brussels Treaty organization for defense against Soviet encroachment
II. It had the effect of bringing the United States and a number of additional nations—not all European—into association for the purpose of Western European defense.
III. For the United States, membership was a drastic reversal of foreign policy in that, for the first time in history, the United States entered into a European military alliance in peacetime.
IV. Aside from its military implications, NATO has also been intended as a major means for the advancement of European political unity.

F. I, II, III, and IV
G. II, III, and IV
H. I, II, and IV
J. I, II, and III

39. The Gentlemen's Agreement of 1907 between the United States and Japan provided for

A. mutual recognition of the Open Door policy in China
B. establishment of a specific quota for Japanese immigration to the United States
C. United States restrictions on Japanese immigration
D. Japanese restriction of Japanese emigration to the United States

40. A historian studying demographic patterns in the American colonies would be most interested in examining

F. diaries and journals

G. bank records
H. census reports
J. church records

41. The procedure of *gerrymandering,* or altering the borders of election districts for political purposes, was

A. an electoral reform introduced by the Jacksonians
B. a technique first used by Tammany Hall
C. named after a popular dance of the 1920s
D. named after a delegate to the Constitutional Convention

"*We hold this truth to be self-evident*—that the test of a representative government is its ability to promote the safety and happiness of the people.

"*We hold this truth to be self-evident*—that twelve years of Republican leadership left our nation sorely stricken in body, mind and spirit; and that three years of Democratic leadership have put it back on the road to restored health and prosperity.

"*We hold this truth to be self-evident*—that twelve years of Republican surrender to the dictatorship of a privileged few have been supplanted by a Democratic leadership which has returned the people themselves to the place of authority, and has revived in them new faith and restored the hope which they had almost lost.

"*We hold this truth to be self-evident*—that this three-year recovery in all the basic values of life and the reestablishment of the American way of living has been brought about by humanizing the policies of the Federal Government as they affect the personal, financial, industrial and agricultural well-being of the American people.

"*We hold this truth to be self-evident*—that government in a modern civilization has certain inescapable obligations to its citizens, among which are:

(1) Protection of the family and the home
(2) Establishment of a democracy of opportunity for all the people
(3) Aid to those overtaken by disaster.

"These obligations, neglected through twelve years of the old leadership, have once more been recognized by American Government. Under the new leadership they will never be neglected . . . . We have built foundations for the security of those who are faced with the hazards of unemployment and old age; for the orphaned, the crippled and the blind. On the foundation of the Social Security Act we are determined to erect a structure of economic security for all our people, making sure that this benefit shall keep step with the ever-increasing capacity of America to provide a high standard of living for all its citizens.

"We will act to secure to the consumer fair value, honest sales and a decreased spread between the price he pays and the price the producer receives.

"This administration has fostered power rate yardsticks in the Tennessee Valley and in several other parts of the nation. As a result electricity has been made available to the people at a lower rate. We will continue to promote plans for rural electrification and for cheap power by means of the yardstick method . . .

"We believe that unemployment is a national problem . . . Where business fails to supply such employment, we believe that work at prevailing wages should be provided in cooperation with State and local governments on useful public projects, to the end that the national wealth may be increased, the skill and energy of the worker may be utilized, his morale maintained, and the unemployed assured the opportunity to earn the necessities of life.

"The Republican platform proposes to meet many pressing national problems solely by action of the separate States. We know that drought, dust storms, floods, minimum wages, maximum hours, child labor and working conditions in industry, monopolistic and unfair business practices cannot be adequately handled exclusively by 49 separate State legislatures, 49 separate administrations and 49 separate State courts. Transactions and activities which inevitably overflow State boundaries call for both State and Federal treatment . . .

"For the protection of government itself and promotion of its efficiency, we pledge the immediate extension of the merit system through the classified civil service—which was first established and fostered under Democratic auspices—to all non-policymaking positions in the Federal service.

"We shall subject to the civil service law all continuing positions which, because of the emergency, have been exempt from its operation . . .

"We have faith in the destiny of our nation. We are sufficiently endowed with natural resources and with productive capacity to provide for all a quality of life that meets the standards of real Americanism.

"Dedicated to a government of liberal American principles, we are determined to oppose equally the despotism of Communism and the menace of concealed Fascism.

"*We hold this final truth to be self-evident*—that the interests, the security and the happiness of the people of the United States of America can be perpetuated only under the democratic government as conceived by the founders of our nation."

42. The style of the opening paragraphs of this selection brings to mind the

F. Declaration of Independence
G. Preamble to the Constitution
H. Articles of Confederation
J. Gettysburg Address

43. The first portion of this document should be accepted as

A. a series of factual statements
B. a series of self-serving statements
C. a program for the future
D. the beginning of an indictment

44. The second portion of this document consists of

F. a general program of action
G. an outline of specific steps to be taken
H. no promises
J. more complaints about the Republicans

45. Built into this document are suggestions that
I. social security benefits be tied to the cost of living
II. electricity should be measured in yards
III. the government will institute wage and price controls

A. none of these
B. I only
C. I and II
D. I, II, and III

46. The ideals voiced in this document reflect

F. The Great Society
G. The Fair Deal
H. The Square Deal
J. The New Deal

47. A point of major disagreement between the Democrats and the Republicans is

A. which authority should charter banks
B. procedures for slum clearance
C. placement of responsibility for dealing with problems which transcend state lines
D. attitude toward Communism

48. Implicit in this document is an admission that

F. the Federal Government has usurped the powers of the States
G. public works projects are unconstitutional
H. the civil-service system had been bypassed in recent years
J. farmers have been given too many privileges

49. The date of this document is probably

A. 1884
B. 1912
C. 1936
D. 1948

50. This document is probably

F. a bill originating in the House
G. a bill originating in the Senate
H. a Presidential letter accompanying his signature on a piece of legislation
J. a party platform

51. The following are statements which appear in this document:
I. ". . . we are determined to oppose equally, the despotism of Communism and the menace of concealed Fascism."
II. ". . . the interests, the security and the

happiness of the people of the United States of America can be perpetuated only under the democratic government . . ."

III. "Transactions and activities which inevitably overflow State boundaries call for both State and Federal treatment."

The Republicans would wholeheartedly concur with

A. I only
B. II only
C. I and II
D. I and III

52. The ticket which rode to victory on this platform was

F. Roosevelt and Wilkie
G. Roosevelt and Garner
H. Roosevelt and Landon
J. Wilson and Marshall

END OF TEST

If you complete this test before the time limit is up, check back over the questions on this test only. Do not return to any of the previous tests. Do not proceed to the next test until you are told to do so.

TEST 4
NATURAL SCIENCE READING

35 Minutes—52 Questions

DIRECTIONS: Below each of the following reading passages is a series of questions. Choose the *best* answer to each question, interpreting what is stated or implied by the passage in the light of your own background in the subject. You may refer back to the passage as often as necessary, though the answers to some questions may not be found expressly in the passage.

Many important scientific developments came out of World War II, and one of the most important was radar. The word is a contraction of "radio detection and ranging." Radar works in much the same way as an echo. When you shout toward a cliff or a large building, part of the sound bounces back. In radar, short beams are sent out. When they strike an object they bounce back and are picked up by a receiver. The direction of the returning signal indicates the direction of the object, and the time it takes to return indicates how far away the object is. Because different objects reflect radar waves at different densities, objects can be detected in any kind of weather, day or night. Radar waves are not deflected by atmospheric layers and therefore always travel in a straight line.

Radar waves are electromagnetic waves, as are light waves, electric waves, x-rays, cosmic rays and radio waves. All electromagnetic waves travel at 186,000 miles per second, the speed of light. They differ from each other in the number of vibrations per second; this is known as their frequency. They also differ in their wave length. To find the wave length of an electromagnetic wave, the following formula is used:

$\text{wave length} = \frac{186{,}000}{\text{frequency}}$. Thus, a radio station broadcasting at 500 kilocycles (500,000 vibrations per second) would have a wave length of 0.3720 mile or about 1960 feet. If the frequency should go to 1,000 kilocycles the wave length would be 980 feet.

More and more research is developing other uses for electromagnetic waves. Radar operates at 10 million kilocycles (a wave length of just over 1 inch). Other inventions operate at even lower frequencies. As transmitters are developed which can transmit shorter and shorter wave lengths we will have more uses for electromagnetic waves.

Below is a table giving the range of the approximate wave length of some better known electromagnetic waves.

Type of Wave	**Wave Length**
electric waves	from $\frac{1}{8}$ mile—over 600 miles
radio broadcast waves	$\frac{1}{10}$ mile—15 feet
UHF, television and radar	15 feet—less than 1 inch
infrared heat	0.04—0.00004 inch
visible light	0.00001 inch (red)—0.000001 inch (violet)
x-rays	0.0000004 inch—0.000000004 inch
cosmic rays	0.00000000003 inch—0.000000000000003 inch

1. Radio waves and radar waves have the same

A. frequency
B. wave length
C. strength
D. speed

2. A beam having the frequency of 4,000 kilocycles would have a wave length of about

F. 1960 feet
G. 980 feet
H. 490 feet
J. 245 feet

3. A radar set could not locate an aircraft if the aircraft was flying

A. faster than the speed of sound
B. above a heavy storm
C. above the atmosphere
D. below the horizon

4. It is possible to find the distance an object is located from a radar set because the

F. wave length of radar is known
G. frequency of radar is known
H. speed of radar is 186,000 miles per second
J. power of each set is known

5. Does all visible light have the same frequency?

A. Yes; all light is electromagnetic
B. Yes; all light travels at the same speed
C. No; red has a higher frequency than violet
D. No; violet has a higher frequency than red

6. If an airplane altimeter uses a wave length of 2 inches, it is using

F. sound waves
G. Ultra High Frequency waves
H. light waves
J. x-rays

7. Radio waves will not penetrate the ionosphere, but UHF waves will. Would you expect x-rays to penetrate the ionosphere?

A. Yes, because they have a shorter wave length than UHF and radio waves
B. Yes, because they have a lower frequency than UHF and radio waves
C. No, because they travel more slowly than UHF and radio waves
D. No, because they have a different frequency and wave length from either radio or UHF waves.

8. Compared to cosmic rays the frequency of visible light waves is

F. higher
G. lower
H. the same
J. unable to be told from the information given

9. A kilocycle is

A. one thousand cycles per second
B. one hundred vibrations per second
C. a metric measure of volume
D. the speed of light

10. Practical uses of radar today include
I. an early warning system
II. transistors
III. computers
IV. traffic control

F. I and II
G. III and IV
H. I and IV
J. I, III, and IV

Recent scientific discoveries are throwing new light on the basic nature of viruses and on the possible nature of cancer, genes and even life itself. These discoveries are providing evidence for relationships among these four subjects which indicate that one may be dependent upon another to an extent not fully appreciated heretofore. Too often one works and thinks within too narrow a range and hence fails to recognize the significance of certain facts for other areas. Sometimes the important new ideas and subsequent fundamental discoveries come from the borderline areas between two well-established fields of investigation. This will result in the synthesis of new ideas regarding viruses, cancer, genes and life. These ideas in turn will result in the doing of new experiments, which may provide the basis for fundamental discoveries in these fields.

There is no doubt that of the four topics, life is the one most people would consider to be of the greatest importance. However, life means different things to different people and it is in reality difficult to define just what we mean by life. There is no difficulty in recognizing an agent as living so long as we contemplate structures like a man, a dog or even a bacterium, and at the other extreme, a piece of iron or glass or an atom of hydrogen or a molecule of water. The ability to grow or reproduce and to change or mutate has long been regarded as a special property characteristic of living agents along with the ability to respond to external stimuli. These are properties not shared by bits of iron or glass or even by a molecule of hemoglobin. Now if viruses had not been discovered, all would have been well. The organisms of the biologist would have ranged from the largest of animals all the way down to the smallest of the bacteria which are about 200 millimicra. There would have been a definite break with respect to size; the largest molecules known to the chemist were less than 20 millimicra in size. Thus life and living agents would have been represented by those structures which possessed the ability to reproduce themselves and to mutate and were about ten times larger than the largest known molecule. This would have provided a comfortable area of separation between living and non-living things.

Then came the discovery of the viruses. These infections, disease-producing agents are characterized by their small size, by their ability to grow or reproduce within specific living cells, and by their ability to change or mutate during reproduction. This was enough to convince most people that viruses were merely still smaller living organisms. When the sizes of different viruses were determined, it was found that some were actually smaller than certain protein molecules. When the first virus was isolated in the form of a crystallizable material it was found to be a nucleoprotein. It was found to possess all the usual properties associated with protein molecules yet was larger than any molecule previously described. Here was a molecule that possessed the ability to reproduce itself and to mutate. The distinction between living and non-living things seemed to be tottering. The gap in size between 20 and 200 millimicra has been filled in completely by the viruses, with some actual overlapping at both ends. Some large viruses are larger than some living organisms, and some small viruses are actually smaller than certain protein molecules.

Let us consider the relationship between genes and viruses, since both are related to life. Both genes and viruses seem to be nucleoproteins and both reproduce only within specific living cells. Both possess the ability to mutate. Although viruses generally reproduce many times within a given cell, some situations are known in which they appear to reproduce only once with each cell division. Genes usually reproduce once with each cell division, but here also the rate can be changed.

Actually the similarities between genes and viruses are so remarkable that viruses were referred to as "naked genes" or "genes on the loose."

Despite the fact that today viruses are known to cause cancer in animals and in certain plants, there exists a great reluctance to accept viruses as being of importance in human cancer. Basic biological phenomena generally do not differ strikingly as one goes from one species to another. It should be recognized that cancer is a biological problem and not a problem that is unique for man. Cancer originates when a normal cell suddenly becomes a cancer cell which multiplies widely and without apparent restraint. Cancer may originate in many different kinds of cells, but the cancer cell usually continues to carry certain traits of the cell of origin. The transformation of a normal cell into a cancer cell may have more than one kind of cause, but there is good reason to consider the relationships that exist between viruses and cancer.

Since there is no evidence that human cancer, as generally experienced, is infectious, many persons believe that because viruses are infectious agents they cannot possibly be of importance in human cancer. However, viruses can mutate and examples are known in which a virus that never kills its host can mutate to form a new strain of virus that always kills its host. It does not seem unreasonable to assume that an innocuous latent virus might mutate to form a strain that causes cancer. Certainly the experimental evidence now available is consistent with the idea that viruses as we know them today, could be the causative agents of most, if not all cancer, including cancer in man.

11. People were convinced that viruses were small living organisms, because viruses

A. are smaller than protein molecules
B. reproduce within living cells
C. could be grown on artificial media
D. consist of nucleoproteins

12. Scientists very often do not apply the facts learned in one subject area to a related field of investigation because

F. the borderline areas are too close to both to give separate facts
G. scientists work in a very narrow range of experimentation
H. new ideas are synthesized only as a result of new experimentation
J. fundamental discoveries are based upon finding close relationships in related sciences

13. Before the discovery of viruses, it might have been possible to distinguish living things from non-living things by the fact that

A. animate objects can mutate
B. non-living substances cannot reproduce themselves
C. responses to external stimuli are characteristic of living things
D. living things were greater than 20 millimicra in size

14. The size of viruses is presently known to be

F. beween 20 and 200 millimicra
G. smaller than any bacterium
H. larger than any protein molecule
J. larger than most nucleoproteins

15. That genes and viruses seem to be related might be shown by the fact that

A. both are ultra-microscopic
B. each can mutate but once in a cell
C. each reproduces but once in a cell
D. both appear to have the same chemical structure

16. Viruses were called "genes on the loose" because they

F. are able to reproduce very freely
G. like genes, seem to be able to mutate
H. seemed to be genes without cells
J. can loosen genes from cells

17. Cancer should be considered to be a biological problem rather than a medical one because

A. viruses are known to cause cancers in animals

B. at present, human cancer is not believed to be contagious
C. there are many known causes for the transformation of a normal cell to a cancer cell
D. results of experiments on plants and animals do not vary greatly from species to species

18. The possibility that a virus causes human cancer is indicated by

F. the fact that viruses have been known to mutate
G. the fact that a cancer-immune individual may lose his immunity
H. the fact that reproduction of human cancer cells might be due to a genetic factor
J. the fact that man is host to many viruses

19. The best title for this passage is

A. New Light on the Cause of Cancer
B. The Newest Theory on the Nature of Viruses
C. Viruses, Genes, Cancer and Life
D. On the Nature of Life

20. According to the passage, cancer cells are

F. similar to the cell of origin
G. mutations of viruses
H. unable to reproduce
J. among the smallest cells known

21. The need for basic research, as opposed to the obvious need for research into the cause and cure of specific diseases, is highlighted by

I. the rapid increase in the incidence of cancer
II. the narrowness of most experimentation
III. the need to understand interrelationships
IV. the possibility that there are still unknown forms of life

A. I, II, and III
B. II, III, and IV
C. II and III
D. I, II, and IV

DIRECTIONS: The following questions are not based upon a reading passage. Use your knowledge of the natural sciences to choose the *best* answer to each question.

22. In the equation $MnO_4^- + 8H^+(\ \ ) \rightleftharpoons Mn^{++} + 4H_2O$, the term that should be inserted in the parentheses is

F. $+ 3e^-$
G. $+ 5e^-$
H. $- 2e^-$
J. $- 8e^-$

23. Chemically pure water is prepared by

A. distillation
B. aeration
C. filtration
D. chlorination

24. A gravitational field is a conservative field. The work done in this field by transporting an object from one point to another

F. depends on the end points only
G. depends on both the end points and the path between these points
H. is not zero when the object is brought back to its initial position
J. is a function of velocity

25. Of the following, the structure that undergoes the *least* amount of change during mitosis is the

A. ribosomes
B. nucleus
C. centriole
D. mitochondria

26. The biome containing the greatest number of species is the

F. tundra
G. taiga
H. tropical rain forest
J. northern rain forest

27. Which one of the following metals is always in an amalgam?

A. tin
B. lead
C. zinc
D. mercury

28. When a lighted match is thrust into a bottle containing pure oxygen, the match

F. burns more rapidly
G. explodes
H. ignites the oxygen
J. goes out

29. On the basis of placement in the electromotive force series, it is possible to predict that in a chemical reaction

A. copper will displace lead from lead salts
B. gold is more readily oxidized than aluminum
C. copper will replace hydrogen from an acid
D. tin will displace copper from salts

30. The radiant energy we receive from the sun is believed to result chiefly from a process called

F. nuclear fusion
G. nuclear fission
H. combustion
J. photosynthesis

31. Under natural conditions large quantities of organic matter decay after each year's plant growth has been completed. As a result of such conditions

A. many animals are deprived of adequate food supplies
B. soil erosion is accelerated
C. soils maintain their fertility
D. earthworms are added to the soil

32. A new species was discovered living in salt water. It possessed five pairs of jointed legs, a hard exoskeleton and filter-feeding apparatus. The species was most likely a/an

F. insect
G. mammal
H. crustacean
J. echinoderm

33. Since the atomic weight of sulfur is *twice* that of oxygen, the percentage by weight of sulfur in sulfur dioxide is

A. 25 percent
B. 33 percent
C. 50 percent
D. 67 percent

On a sunny day in August bees are found in great abundance, feeding on flowers and annoying picnickers. The bees are voracious and feed almost constantly, remaining within a relatively small area while going about this business.

Experiment I. On such a sunny day a group of experimenters spread a large blue tablecloth on the grass and in its center put a dish of sugar water. They observed as many bees discovered this easy source of food and congregated on the dish of sugar water. Then these experimenters took away the blue cloth and the sugar water, substituting for it a black, gray and white checkered tablecloth with one blue square. Randomly placed on the tablecloth were empty glass dishes. The bees zeroed in directly on the empty dish on the blue square, avoiding all others.

Experiment II. On another day, in a different garden, the experimenters repeated the experiment, this time using a pure red tablecloth. Once more the bees discovered the dish of sugar water. However, when the red cloth was removed and the black, white and gray checkerboard with one pure red square was substituted, the bees showed utter confusion. They flew randomly to the empty dishes.

Experiment III. The third experiment was identical to the second except that the red of the red tablecloth and the red of the red square on the checkered tablecloth was a mixed red rather than a pure red. In phase two of this experiment, the bees went directly to the empty dish on the mixed red square.

Experiment IV. In the fourth experiment the experimenters established a larger initial feeding station. There were three tablecloths side by side, one blue, one pure red and one mixed red. On each tablecloth was a dish of sugar water. All three dishes drew large numbers of bees. When the three tablecloths and food were removed and the black, white and gray checkered tablecloth with one blue square, one pure red square and one mixed red square and only empty dishes substituted, the bees went to the empty dishes on the blue square and on the mixed red square only.

34. These four experiments in conjunction were designed to show that bees

F. like sugar water
G. cannot tell when a dish is empty
H. are easily confused
J. have some color vision

35. In Experiment I, the bees probably went to the empty cup on the one blue square because

A. blue is their favorite color
B. they had learned that blue is where the food is
C. blue appears as red to bees
D. grays are repulsive to bees

36. In Experiment II, the bees did not swarm to the empty cup on the pure red square because

F. they were less intelligent bees and had not learned that red is where the food is
G. bees prefer blue to red
H. they were unable to distinguish the red square from the various shades of gray
J. they were not hungry

37. In Experiment III the bees probably went to the empty cup on the mixed red square

A. because they were a different type of bee, and could see red
B. because the mixed color reflected blues and ultraviolets as well as red
C. because these were very hungry bees
D. purely by chance

38. The results of this series of experiments imply that plants with pure red flowers are pollinated by

F. insects other than bees
G. birds
H. the wind
J. sources other than bees

39. In Experiment IV, the bees which went to the empty cups on red squares

A. thought they were going to blue squares
B. saw those squares as blue
C. could tell the difference between the two reds
D. were trying to fool the experimenters

40. In which experiments did the bees demonstrate that they had learned to find food?

F. I and IV
G. I, II, and IV
H. I, III, and IV
J. I, II, III, and IV

41. In which experiments did the bees demonstrate some degree of color blindness?

A. I and II
B. II and III
C. III and IV
D. II and IV

42. It is most likely that a red-blind bee sees pure red as

F. blue
G. gray
H. yellow
J. none of these

The modern concept of matter holds that there are two particles that make up the nuclei of atoms. They are protons and neutrons. The proton has a positive charge while the neutron, as its name implies, has no charge. There are ninety-two naturally occurring elements, and these differ from one another in the number of protons present in the nucleus. The number of protons in an element is the *atomic number*.

The protons and neutrons together determine the mass of the nucleus. Since the electrons are outside of the nucleus and weigh almost nothing as compared with the nuclear weight, the mass of the nucleus is roughly that of the atom as a whole.

The characteristics exhibited by a nucleus depend on the relative number of particles (protons and neutrons) present in it. It is the number of protons present that determines which element it is. "Elements" with a common number of protons, regardless of the number of neutrons present, are but a single element. When the number of protons is the same but the number of neutrons is different, the substances are called *isotopes*. Since two isotopes of one element have the same number of protons but different numbers of neutrons, the two isotopes will be different in mass.

Within the nucleus there is a force whose function it is to bind the nuclear components together.

The nuclear mass is always less than the sum of the protons and neutrons that compose it. This difference in mass is called the *mass defect*, and represents mass that was converted into energy in order to hold the protons and neutrons together. This energy is called the *binding energy*. When a nucleus disintegrates into its components, the binding energy is no longer present. Instead it has become converted into mass, resulting in an increased total mass for the particles included in the nucleus.

Apparently energy and mass can be converted into one another, and this constitutes the basis of Einstein's formula, $E = mc^2$, where E equals energy, *m* equals mass, and *c* equals the velocity of light or 186,000 miles per second.

In the space around the nucleus, an element contains a number of electrons equal to the number of its protons. These electrons account for the chemical nature and activity of an element, but they are unable to effect any nuclear changes.

Some substances are *radioactive*. This means that their nuclei emit particles or radiation. As a result, these atoms break down into other atoms, at the same time liberating energy.

Natural radiation cannot be controlled by any means, either chemical or physical. As a result, naturally radioactive substances change into other substances. In some cases, the changes are extraordinarily rapid; in others, extremely slow.

The rate at which a radioactive substance disintegrates is measured by its *half-life*. Essentially, half-life means the length of time it takes for half of a mass of radioactive isotope to disintegrate. Thus, if the half-life of a substance (carbon-14) is approximately 5000 years, one half of a mass of carbon-14 will disintegrate in 5000 years. The portion which does not disintegrate will be reduced by one half within the *next* 5000 years. Thus, within approximately 10,000 years (two half-lives) three-quarters of a piece of carbon-14 will disintegrate.

In a living organism, the rate of assimilation of cosmic radiation and the rate of disintegration of radiocarbon are in precise equilibrium. At death, however, assimilation ceases and disintegration proceeds at the known immutable rate. The rate of disintegration of radioactive bodies is independent of the nature of the chemical compound in which the radioactive body resides and of the temperature, pressure, and other physical characteristics of its environment. Radiocarbon dating, the process by which the age of long-preserved organic remains is determined, is derived from this knowledge.

43. The atomic number of an element is based upon

A. the number of atoms in the element
B. the number of electrons in its shell
C. the number of protons in its nucleus
D. the number of neutrons and protons in the element

44. Different isotopes of the same element

F. have the same mass, but a different number of electrons
G. have different mass, but the same number of neutrons
H. are in reality different elements
J. have different mass, but the same number of protons

45. The term *mass defect* refers to

A. atomic imperfections
B. the difference between the sum of the protons and neutrons and the mass of the nucleus
C. atomic irregularities
D. the radiation emited by the nucleus

46. Einstein's formula, $E = mc^2$, is

F. consistent with the first law of thermodynamics because the speed of light is squared
G. an exception to the first law of thermodynamics; every law must have its exception
H. disproof of the first law of thermodynamics; scientific laws can breach no exceptions. If there is an exception, then the law is not true.
J. consistent with the first law of thermodynamics because energy is not created nor mass destroyed, there is simply a conversion

47. Natural radiation is best controlled by

A. Geiger counters and ionization chambers
B. chemical and physical measures in combination
C. all of the above
D. none of these means

48. The half-life of carbon-14 is

F. 5000 years
G. one-half of 5000 years
H. twice 5000 years
J. carbon-7

49. Radiocarbon dating is

A. imprecise because it does not account for the effects of pressure upon the sample
B. utilized by archeologists
C. an important factor in the development of nuclear warheads
D. a safety measure used at nuclear power plants

50. The electrons in the shell of an element

I. combine with the protons to effect nuclear change
II. are responsible for the chemical activity of the element
III. are equal in number to the number of neutrons in the element
IV. affect the weight of the element

F. none of these statements is true
G. all of these statements are true
H. II only
J. I, II, and IV

51. When an organism dies, it

A. ceases to assimilate cosmic radiation
B. continues to assimilate cosmic radiation at the same rate as when it was alive
C. assimilates cosmic radiation at a known reduced rate
D. assimilates cosmic radiation in half-lives

52. Development of an atomic bomb would have been impossible before

F. invention of a particle accelerator
G. understanding of the disintegration rate of carbon-14
H. discovery of massive defects in nuclei
J. isolation of isotopes

END OF EXAM

If you complete this test before the time limit is up, check over the questions on this test only. Do not return to any previous tests.

CORRECT ANSWERS
MODEL EXAM II

TEST 1. ENGLISH USAGE

1. C.	11. C.	21. C.	31. A.	40. J.	49. D.	58. J.	67. H.
2. G.	12. J.	22. G.	32. J.	41. C.	50. J.	59. C.	68. B.
3. D.	13. A.	23. D.	33. C.	42. G.	51. B.	60. G.	69. J.
4. J.	14. H.	24. J.	34. F.	43. B.	52. G.	61. B.	70. A.
5. B.	15. D.	25. D.	35. B.	44. J.	53. A.	62. D.	71. H.
6. H.	16. G.	26. J.	36. H.	45. B.	54. J.	63. H.	72. B.
7. A.	17. C.	27. D.	37. D.	46. H.	55. B.	64. B.	73. J.
8. G.	18. F.	28. F.	38. J.	47. B.	56. H.	65. H.	74. C.
9. D.	19. D.	29. D.	39. B.	48. H.	57. D.	66. A.	75. G.
10. H.	20. H.	30. H.					

TEST 2. MATHEMATICS USAGE

1. D.	6. K.	11. C.	16. F.	21. B.	26. K.	31. D.	36. G.
2. F.	7. A.	12. G.	17. D.	22. H.	27. E.	32. J.	37. C.
3. E.	8. G.	13. A.	18. K.	23. B.	28. F.	33. B.	38. J.
4. G.	9. C.	14. H.	19. C.	24. K.	29. E.	34. J.	39. C.
5. B.	10. F.	15. B.	20. J.	25. A.	30. K.	35. D.	40. G.

TEST 3. SOCIAL STUDIES READING

1. A.	8. F.	15. B.	22. J.	29. C.	35. B.	41. D.	47. C.
2. F.	9. D.	16. J.	23. A.	30. H.	36. H.	42. F.	48. H.
3. C.	10. H.	17. C.	24. H.	31. D.	37. D.	43. B.	49. C.
4. H.	11. D.	18. J.	25. B.	32. J.	38. F.	44. F.	50. J.
5. C.	12. H.	19. B.	26. G.	33. B.	39. D.	45. B.	51. C.
6. G.	13. D.	20. H.	27. A.	34. G.	40. J.	46. J.	52. G.
7. C.	14. F.	21. B.	28. G.				

TEST 4. NATURAL SCIENCE READING

1. D.	8. G.	15. D.	22. G.	29. D.	35. B.	41. D.	47. D.
2. J.	9. A.	16. G.	23. A.	30. F.	36. H.	42. G.	48. F.
3. D.	10. H.	17. D.	24. F.	31. C.	37. B.	43. C.	49. B.
4. H.	11. B.	18. F.	25. A.	32. H.	38. J.	44. J.	50. H.
5. D.	12. G.	19. C.	26. H.	33. C.	39. B.	45. B.	51. A.
6. G.	13. D.	20. F.	27. D.	34. J.	40. J.	46. J.	52. F.
7. A.	14. F.	21. C.	28. F.				

EXPLANATORY ANSWERS
MODEL EXAM II
TEST 1. ENGLISH USAGE

1. **C.** A comma is needed between adjectives that apply equally to the noun. (If you can insert "and" between the adjectives without changing the sense of the sentence, a comma is needed.) A *criticizer* is by implication one who seeks to find fault; a *critic* is one who makes a reasoned analysis and evaluation.

2. **G.** Avoid the split infinitive if possible.

3. **D.** The correct phrase to indicate opposing evidence is *to the contrary.*

4. **J.** *None* is singular and therefore takes the singular verb *is.*

5. **B.** Use the present perfect tense of the verb (*has . . . achieved*) for action which began in the past and is still going on in the present or for action completed at some indefinite past time.

6. **H.** A question must end with a question mark.

7. **A.** This is correct.

8. **G.** The possessive of Shakespeare is Shakespeare's. The long introductory prepositional phrase should be set off by a comma.

9. **D.** The correct word for the overcoming of an enemy is *victory,* not *win.*

10. **H.** *Less* refers to quantity; *fewer* is used for things that can be counted (as gladiators). *Than,* a conjunction, is used after the comparative degree of an adjective or adverb. *Then,* an adverb, means "at that time" or "next."

11. **C.** The noun form needed to serve as subject of this sentence is *threat,* not *threatening.*

12. **J.** *It would seem* is used here as a parenthetical expression and should, therefore, be set off from the main part of the sentence by commas.

13. **A.** This is correct.

14. **H.** The comparative degree is formed either by adding *-er* to the adjective or by using an expression such as "more and more" before the adjective. Use one or the other of these comparative methods, but not both.

15. **D.** It is necessary to begin a new sentence after *leisure hours* because a new thought is being introduced.

16. **G.** A comma is needed to separate the term *Sunday Neurosis* from the appositional phrase that follows. The appositional phrase does not express a complete thought and therefore is not a sentence.

17. **C.** This sentence requires the verb *afflict* meaning to "trouble," not *inflict* which means to "impose." Because *people* is the subject of the verb *become, who,* not *whom,* is correct.

18. **F.** This is correct.

19. **D.** When using a direct quotation, use a comma to separate the beginning of the quotation from the preceding phrase. Except in rare cases, the first word of a quotation is capitalized.

20. **H.** The phrase *surmount over* is repetitive, because surmount means "to overcome." To avoid a switch in verb tense, use the present, *surmounts.*

21. **C.** *Sometimes* is written as one word.

22. **G.** All other choices are double negatives.

23. **D.** All that is needed is a simple present tense.

24. **J.** The general rule for the verbs *to lie* and *to lay* is: Use *lay* when you can substitute *put*. One would *put down* a goal.

25. **D.** No capitalization or punctuation is necessary.

26. **J.** *That will permit* is the beginning of the final item in a list. *And* precedes the last item in an inclusive list.

27. **D.** The possessive form of *you* is *your. You're* is the contraction for *you are.* The capital form, as in B., is used only when referring to a deity.

28. **F.** One lives in only one environment.

29. **D.** D. is the correct idiom.

30. **H.** F. constitutes the double negative. *Cannot* would be correct, but it must be written as one word.

31. **A.** No punctuation or capitalization is necessary.

32. **J.** Mellon Art Gallery is the name of an art gallery. Each word of a name must begin with a capital letter.

33. **C.** *The Capitol* is the domed building in Washington, D.C. All other uses of *capital* are spelled *al.*

34. **F.** Because this sentence contrasts in tone with the previous sentence, *but* is the correct transition word.

35. **B.** C. and D. change the meaning of the sentence. A. is verbose.

36. **H.** F. is correct but confusing in its repeated use of *and.* J. would be correct, but a comma would be needed after *also.*

37. **D.** *Them* refers to *these amenities.* One does not "urge" or "encourage" amenities, nor can one introduce a new pronoun, *it,* without an antecedent. Therefore D. is the only correct answer.

38. **J.** This last clause provides only confusion and verbosity.

39. **B.** Unless you are referring to a specific dictionary, there is no need to capitalize. Also, no punctuation is needed.

40. **J.** Because there are many words other than *gadfly, gadfly* is a restrictive appositive and should not be set off by commas or dashes.

41. **C.** When referring to a specific word as a word, italicize it. In manuscript, underlining is tantamount to italicizing.

42. **G.** The clauses must be separated by either a period or a comma. A comma is ALWAYS inside the quotation marks. A semicolon NEVER precedes a coordinating conjunction.

43. **B.** *Which* refers only to things. *Who* is the subject of the adjective clause modifying *person. Whom* can only be used as an object.

44. **J.** J. is the most parallel form.

45. **B.** *It's* is the contraction for *it is. 'Tis* is colloquial. *Its* is the possessive form of *it. Its'* is an incorrect form.

46. **H.** F. is unclear; J. is stilted; one is not searching for the definition G.

47. **B.** The name of the organization is the *Great Books Foundation;* therefore each word of the name must begin with a capital letter. No punctuation is needed.

48. **H.** Skimming ahead, one clearly finds that only H. expresses the intent of the passage.

49. **D.** D. is simple, direct and clear.

50. **J.** Avoid the passive voice when possible.

51. **B.** Numbers under 100 should be written out. No punctuation is needed.

52. **G.** *Thursday evening* is a compound adjective.

53. **A.** *P.M.* is correctly written. No further punctuation is necessary.

54. **J.** One abbreviates *Street, Road, Avenue,* etc. only when addressing envelopes.

55. **B.** The name of the city is either *New York* or *New York City.* The abbreviation rule stated in Question 54 applies.

56. **H.** *Associate Professor* is the man's title. Both words must begin with capital letters. "Associate Professor at Oriental College" is a nonrestrictive appositive and must be set apart by commas.

57. **D.** *Oriental College* is a proper name both words of which must begin with capital letters. The comma is needed here to mark the end of the nonrestrictive appositive, as above.

58. **J.** J. states most clearly that in addition to his professorship and his work as program director, Dr. Daniels is actively involved as a coleader of Great Books groups.

59. **C.** *In each group* is the beginning of a direct quotation and must be enclosed in quotation marks. A comma ALWAYS is contained within the quotation marks. This quotation must be closed because the next words, *he explains,* are not a part of the quotation.

60. **G.** The clause must begin with quotation marks because it is a direct quotation immediately follow-

ing words which were not part of a quotation. The quotation marks need not be closed because the next sentence is a continuation of the same quotation.

61. **B.** *Other* is the last quoted word, so the quotation must be closed after *other* and before any words which are not quoted. The comma ALWAYS goes inside the quotation marks.

62. **D.** *The gadfly* is not a true appositive; therefore it is better set off by dashes.

63. **H.** When a portion of a sentence set off by a dash ends the sentence, the dashed-off portion is considered closed. *He's* is the contraction for *he is*. No quotation marks are needed because this sentence is a continuation of the quote of the previous sentence.

64. **B.** *Corners them* is clear and is the least verbose.

65. **H.** H. is the least verbose.

66. **A.** This is correct.

67. **H.** Don't confuse the homonyms *to, two* and *too*. *To* means "in the direction of." *Two* is the numeral 2. *Too* means "more than" or "also."

68. **B.** Use a singular verb (*is*) after two singular subjects (*training, experience*) joined by *or* or *nor*.

69. **J.** The relative pronoun *who* refers to persons; *which*, to animals or things; *that*, to persons, animals or things.

70. **A.** This is correct. *Individual* is singular and therefore takes the singular verb form *has had*. *Type* is also singular and therefore takes the singular verb *is*.

71. **H.** The preposition *of* is needed after the word *kind*. It is incorrect to say "what kind education."

72. **B.** To eliminate the comma splice, add a period after *difficult* and start a new sentence with *Many*. Choice D. is incorrect because *being* is a participle, not a conjunction.

73. **J.** Capitalize only the name of a specific medical school, not medical schools in general.

74. **C.** There is a change in emphasis from persons who do not find career decisions difficult to those who do. Such a subject change indicates the need for a new paragraph.

75. **G.** The *not only . . . but also* construction should connect words or phrases of equal rank, in this case two nouns (*information* and *knowledge*).

TEST 2. MATHEMATICS USAGE

1. **D.** $\frac{3}{4} = .75$

$\frac{35}{71}$ is slightly less than $\frac{35}{70} = .5$

$\frac{13}{20} = \frac{13 \times 5}{20 \times 5} = \frac{65}{100} = .65$

$\frac{71}{101}$ is very close to $\frac{7}{10}$ or .7

$\frac{15}{20} = \frac{15 \times 5}{20 \times 5} = \frac{75}{100} = .75$

$$\frac{19}{24} = 24\overline{)19.00}\ \text{.79}$$
$$\begin{array}{r} 168 \\ \hline 220 \\ 216 \\ \hline \end{array}$$

2. **F.**
$$\begin{aligned} 820 + RTS - 610 &= 342 \\ R + S + 210 &= 342 \\ R + S &= 132 \\ \text{If } R = 2\,S, \text{ then } 2S + S &= 132 \\ 3S &= 132 \\ S &= 44 \end{aligned}$$

3. **E.**

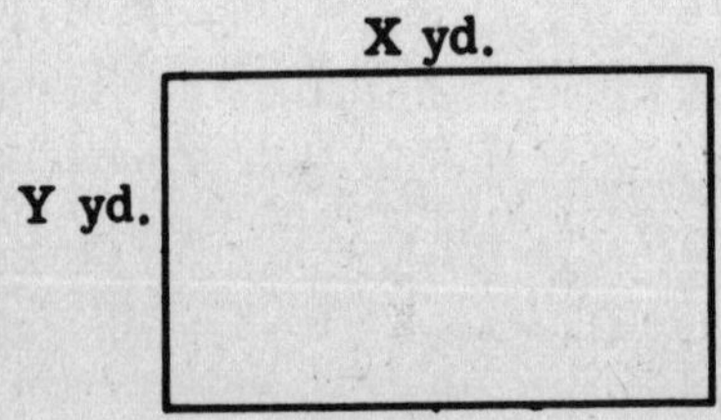

Area = xy sq. yd.
= 9 xy sq. ft
$9\,xy \cdot 2 = 18\,xy$

4. **G.**
$$\begin{aligned} 7\,M &= 3\,M - 20 \\ 4\,M &= -20 \\ M &= -5 \\ M + 7 &= -5 + 7 = 2 \end{aligned}$$

5. **B.** Arc EA = 85° and arc BD = 15°, since a central angle is measured by its arc. Then
$$\begin{aligned} \text{angle ECA} &= 1\,(AE - BD) \\ &= 1\,(85 - 15) \\ &= \frac{1}{2} \cdot 70 \\ &= 35^\circ \end{aligned}$$

6. **K.** If we know only the hypotenuse of a right triangle, we cannot determine its legs. Hence, the area of the rectangle cannot be determined from the data given.

7. **A.** If angle P > angle Q, then $\frac{1}{2}$ angle P > $\frac{1}{2}$ angle Q; then angle SPQ > angle SQP. Since the larger side lies opposite the larger angle, it follows that SQ > SP.

8. **G.** Since Z is equidistant from X and Y, it must lie on the Y − axis. Then △ OZY is a 30° − 60° − 90° triangle with YZ = 8. Hence OZ = $\frac{8}{2}\sqrt{3} = 4\sqrt{3}$. Coordinates of Z are $(0, 4\sqrt{3})$.

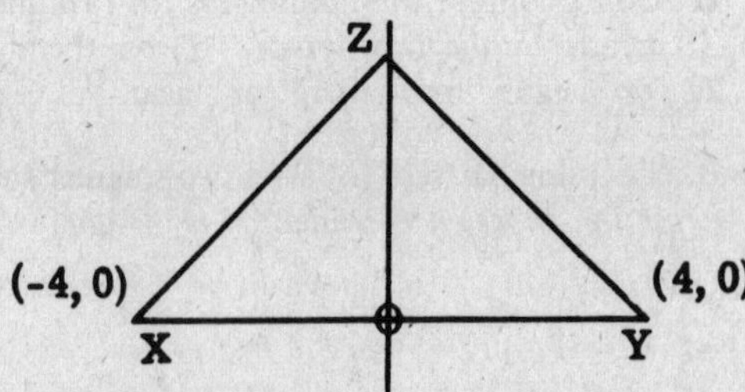

9. **C.** A. is a converse and not necessarily true
B. is also based on the truth of the converse
C. is based on the contrapositive, which is logically equivalent to the given statement
D. is based on the converse; not necessarily true
E. does not necessarily follow
Hence C.

10. **F.** Since ACB is a straight angle and angle DCE is a right angle, then angle ACD and angle BCE are complementary. Hence BCE = 90 − x.

11. **C.** The smallest positive number divisible by 3, 4, or 5 is $3 \cdot 4 \cdot 5 = 60$. Hence the desired number is 60 + 2 = 62.

12. **G.** Since there are 4d quarter miles in d miles, the charge = 90 + 65(4d − 1).

13. **A.** Assume that there are 100 draftees on the post; then 30 are from New York State and $\frac{1}{10} \times$

30 = 3 are from New York City.

$\frac{3}{100} = 3\%$

14. **H.** Rise in temp. = 36 − (−14) = 36 + 14 = 50°
$\frac{50}{5} = 10°$ (hourly rise)
Hence, at noon,
temp. = −14 + 3 (10) = −14 + 30 = +16°

15. **B.** 9 = 8 + 1 = 7 + 2 = 6 + 3 = 5 + 4
Thus, 4 ways.

16. **F.** $\frac{7\text{ ft. }9\text{ in.}}{3} = \frac{6\text{ ft. }21\text{ in.}}{3} = 2\text{ ft. }7\text{ in.}$

17. **D.** Area of Square = $2^2 = 4$
Area of Circle = $\pi \cdot 1^2 = \pi$
Difference = $4 - \pi = 4 - 3.14 = .86$

18. **K.** $3.14 \times 10^6 = 3.14 \times 1{,}000{,}000$
$= 3{,}140{,}000$

19. **C.** $\frac{36}{29 - \frac{4}{0.2}} = \frac{36}{29 - 20} = \frac{36}{9} = 4$

20. **J.** Diameter = $4\sqrt{2}$, since it is the hypotenuse of a right isosceles △ of leg 4
Then the radius = $2\sqrt{2}$
Area of semicircle = $1 \times \pi (2\sqrt{2})^2$
$= 1 \times \pi \cdot 8 = 4\pi$

21. **B.** Consecutive odd numbers may be represented as
2n + 1
2n + 3
2n + 5
Sum = 6n + 9
Always divisible by 3. Thus, only II.

22. **H.** Angle BCD is formed by tangent and chord and is equal to one-half arc BC. Angle A is inscribed angle and also equal to one-half of arc BC. Hence angle A = angle BCD = 40°

23. **B.** Let x = amount of marked price. Then
$\frac{1}{5}x = 15$
x = 75
75 − 15 = $60

24. **K.** There is a double recurring pattern here as indicated: Multiply by .5; then multiply by 3. Hence, the last term is 27.

25. **A.** The new solution is $\frac{3}{20}$ pure alcohol or 15%.

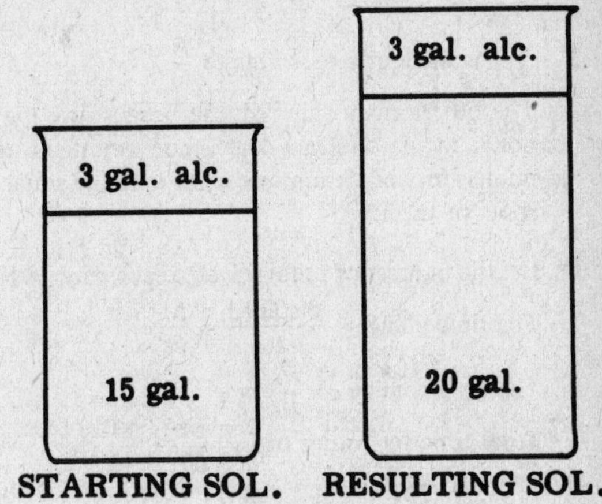

26. **K.** Area of ▭P = XR × altitude from P to XR.
Area of △XPR = $\frac{1}{2}$ XR × altitude from P to XR.
Hence, ratio of area of △ to ▭P = 1:2

27. **E.** x(p + 1) = M. Divide both sides by x.
$p + 1 = \frac{M}{x}$
or $p = \frac{M}{x} - 1$

28. **F.** $\frac{1}{1} = \frac{x}{60M}$
x = 60 MT

29. **E.** If $\frac{P}{Q} = \frac{4}{5}$ then 5P = 4Q.
However, there is no way of determining from this the value of 2P + Q.

30. **K.** The right triangle of which T is the hypotenuse has legs which are obviously 6 inches and 9 inches.
Hence, $T^2 = 6^2 + 9^2$
$T^2 = 36 + 81 = 117$
$T = \sqrt{117}$
or $10 < T < 11$

31. **D.** Since K is an integer and R and S are integers, K must be a perfect square and perfect cube. The smallest such number listed is $64 = 8^2 = 4^3$

32. **J.** The △ RST has a base of 7 and an altitude of 5.
Hence the area = $\frac{1}{2} \cdot 7 \cdot 5 = 17\frac{1}{2}$

33. **B.** Since the small triangles are also equilateral,

their sides must also equal X. Hence, PR is divided into three equal parts, so that X = $\frac{1}{3} \cdot 10 = 3\frac{1}{3}$

34. **J.** $\frac{3P}{3Q}$ is obviously reducible to $\frac{P}{Q}$.
The others cannot be reduced because we may not add or subtract the same numbers to numerator and denominator, or take the square roots of them.

35. **D.** Let the number of miles traveled each way = M

The time going = $\frac{\text{distance}}{\text{rate}} = \frac{M}{60}$

The time coming = $\frac{M}{40}$

Total time for round trip = $\frac{M}{60} + \frac{M}{40}$

$= \frac{2M + 3M}{120} = \frac{5M}{120} = \frac{M}{24}$

Average rate =

$\frac{\text{total distance}}{\text{total time}} = \frac{2M}{\frac{M}{24}}$ = 48 miles per hour.

36. **G.** Original area $-\pi r^2$

Reduced area $-\pi(\frac{1}{2}r)^2 - \frac{1}{4}\pi r^2$

Hence, 25% of original area remains.

37. **C.** Let x = number of questions correct.
25 − x = number of questions wrong.
Then 4x − 1(25 − x) = 70
4x − 25 + x = 70
5x = 95
x = 19

38. **J.** This is an inverse proportion; that is:

$\frac{9}{6} = \frac{x}{120}$

6x = 1080
x = 180

39. **C.** The similar triangles in the configuration produce the proportion

$\frac{3}{5} = \frac{4}{Y}$

3Y = 20
Y = $6\frac{2}{3}$

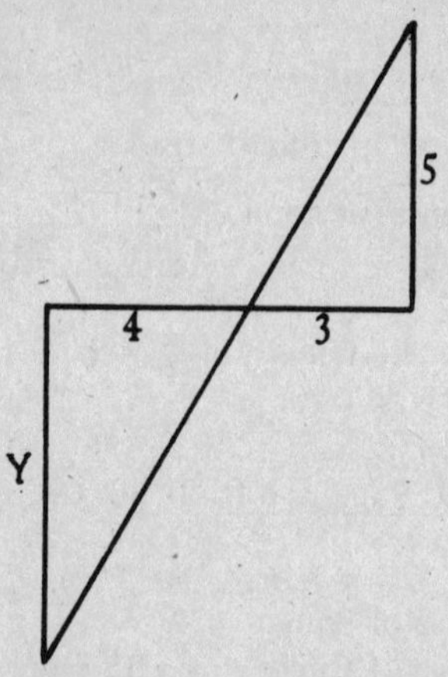

5
4
3
Y

40. **G.** To find the coordinates of a line, one must mark and label any point at which the line intercepts the intersection of any two whole units. The point which we will use in this explanation is (2,1). The point at which the line intercepts the Y axis must also be marked. On this graph, that point can plainly be seen to be (0, − 4). The slope of a line equals the *rise* over the *run* from the point at which the line intercepts the Y axis, therefore, the slope of line *d* = $\frac{5}{2}$. The equation of a line is y = mx + b. Since *m* is the slope of the line which we have already proven to be $\frac{5}{2}$, and since *b* is the line's Y intercept, (− 4), the equation of line *d is y* = $\frac{5}{2}$x − 4.

TEST 3. SOCIAL STUDIES READING

1. **A.** The editors of the *News of Today* are obviously very defense conscious. Their point of view and their choice of words combine to give this editorial an emotional tone.

2. **F.** The Legislative branch of government is charged with creating all laws.

3. **C.** The *News of Today* is attempting to rally instant sympathy with its point of view by spotlighting the relationship of the *Daily Newsprint* with the radical *This Week's News.* If the *News of Today* has a more conservative readership, this "guilt by association" may be a very effective device.

4. **H.** The second paragraph of the *Daily Newsprint* editorial implies that the $3,000 bonus and $5,400 annual salary are fairly new inducements. It suggests that time is all that is needed for manpower quotas to be fulfilled.

5. **C.** The editors of *News of Today* are very effective writers. By harking back to the Constitution and the forethought of the founding fathers as to the need for conscripting an army, the *News of Today* puts itself on very authoritative footing.

6. **G.** The editor of the *Daily Newsprint* is perfectly satisfied with the suspension of the draft and is optimistic that the all-volunteer army will soon have filled its ranks. The editor of the *News of Today,* on the other hand, is fearful for our national security should our enemies discover that our army is not at full strength.

7. **C.** That the editor of the *News of Today* would agree with the statement is obvious. The editor of the *Daily Newsprint* would not disagree with the statement, only with the means for attaining this army. The optimism he shows, that we soon will have our strong army again, certainly does not imply opposition to that army.

8. **F.** Draft age citizens might be more likely to agree with the *Daily Newsprint.* Army professionals would like to be reassured of a full complement of recruits at all times, so would favor the position of the *News of Today.* The first sentence of the *Daily Newsprint* editorial spells out the disillusionment of the generals with the all-volunteer army.

9. **D.** Personal freedom is not an issue in either of these editorials.

10. **H.** Since the *Daily Newsprint* is opposed to the draft, it assumes that most of its readership is in agreement. While there are many reasons for opposing the draft, many of those who do oppose it are antagonistic towards the military as a matter of principle. Mention that the army generals are upset at the absence of a draft is enough to arouse the sympathies of these anti-militaristic people.

11. **D.** The reason for suspension of the draft is not given.

12. **H.** The Constitution makes provisions for a draft but does not specify when and how it is to be used. The actual draft laws are a matter for legislation.

13. **D.** Rationalism is the reliance on reason as the basis for establishment of religious truth. A. is the definition of *rationing.* D. is the definition of *rationalization.*

14. **F.** The last paragraph tells us that Mohammed discouraged dialogue of any sort, but rather adopted a *live and let live* philosophy. Following this approach of Mohammed, there had been a long period of tolerance by the Moslems of their Christian and Jewish neighbors. Conflicts have been based upon factors other than religion. Catholics are singled out in option F. because through most of the history of Christianity the dominant Christian group has been the Catholics.

15. **B.** Peter the Venerable was an intellectual and somewhat of an anachronism in his violent time. He advocated dialogue and discussion, exchange of ideas and true understanding of others in place of armed conflict.

16. **J.** The Muslims are followers of the prophet Mohammed, hence Mohammedans. Koran is simply an alternative spelling of Quran, the Holy Book of the Muslims, revealed to and inspired by Mohammed.

17. **C.** The thrust of the first paragraph is that the ecumenical councils have sought to find common ground so that the churches might unite in a stand

against common dangers to their faith, recently and most specifically, Communism.

18. **J.** The United States is not mentioned in this article. Spain is on the Iberian peninsula, the Vatican and Sicily are in Italy, and Arabia is in Southwest Asia.

19. **B.** Obviously the Muslim conquests were instigated by Moslems. Islam is basically a tolerant faith. All conflicts based upon religion and with conversion as their goal were instigated by Christians.

20. **H.** Moslems believe in one God. They accept the Bible and the New Testament as true, though subject to their own interpretation rather than that of the Jews' or the Christians'. They consider that their own religion is *the true faith* but have no quarrel with other religions.

21. **B.** This passage uses the word *culture* to refer to the dominant traits of a society. Example of traits which might be subsumed under *culture* are belligerence, scientific advancement, development of the arts, physical development, etc. Within a culture any of these or other traits might be highly developed or might be nearly nonexistent; it is the proportion which makes each society distinct.

22. **J.** Since Spartan life was centered about the military, it stands to reason that the youth was educated to take its place in this society.

23. **A.** Athenian life appears to have been broad-based, so education was probably broad-based as well. The passage suggests that the Athenians were eager to accept change and improvement, hence the basis of their education must have been development of understanding and insight.

24. **H.** The passage discusses the role of geography on social development. This role, or lack thereof, is the theme of both paragraphs.

25. **B.** Athens and Sparta were Greek city-states.

26. **G.** The author does not appear to give much credence to the theory of geographical determination of cultural patterns. The purpose in writing this passage is to cite examples disproving this theory.

27. **A.** The Mayan civilization developed in the isthmus containing Guatemala and the southernmost part of Mexico.

28. **G.** The author's mind is fully made up. Further information is not sought. The author is fully convinced that geography and culture are not causally related.

29. **C.** Two weeks after the signing of the Treaty of Ghent, ending the War of 1812, Andrew Jackson defeated the British at the Battle of New Orleans.

30. **H.** The women's rights convention at Seneca Falls in 1848 adopted a *Declaration of Human Rights and Sentiments* based in form on the Declaration of Independence; instead of protesting the oppression of the colonies by George III, the document listed women's grievances against Man.

31. **D.** The United Nations Educational, Scientific and Cultural Council (UNESCO) was established in November 1946. No comparable agency existed under the League of Nations.

32. **J.** Former Confederate President Jefferson Davis was imprisoned under custody of the military from 1865 to 1867. A federal court indictment against him for treason was dropped and the case against him was closed in 1869, when he was granted amnesty. Davis was neither impeached nor convicted of treason.

33. **B.** Complementary goods are goods often used together—for example, hot dogs and mustard. If the price of hot dogs falls, more will be purchased and the demand for mustard will naturally increase.

34. **G.** In general, neither the turn-of-the-century Prohibitionists nor the pre-Civil War abolitionists challenged the basic foundations of the existing social order in any violent way. Rather, they sought to change by peaceful and legal means certain existing practices in such a way as to make them conform more closely to their own ideals.

35. **B.** The Emancipation Proclamation of 1863, a war measure, freed slaves in all areas resisting the Union Army, that is, in those territories under Confederate control (and hence unaffected by the Proclamation). Slaves in the loyal border states and in Confederate states controlled by federal troops were not emancipated by the Proclamation. *All* slaves were freed by the Thirteenth Amendment.

36. **H.** High tariffs of the late nineteenth century were favorable to business and industry but injurious to western farmers who received low prices for their agricultural products and were compelled to pay high prices for manufactured goods in a market without competition from foreign manufacturers.

37. **D.** Prior to and during the Depression, high protective tariff barriers were erected throughout the Western world in futile attempts to protect and stimulate domestic industries. In 1930 the United

States enacted the Hawley Smoot tariff, which was the highest in the history of the country.

38. **F.** All four statements apply to NATO. The nonEuropean members of NATO, all of whom were members at the formation of the organization in April 1949, are the United States, Canada, Iceland and Turkey (which is largely in Asia).

39. **D.** In response to opposition to Oriental immigration, particularly on the West Coast, President Theodore Roosevelt entered into a Gentlemen's Agreement with Japan, whereby Japan agreed to limit emigration to the United States.

40. **J.** An historian studying population changes (demographic patterns) of the colonial era would find church records the most reliable and complete of the sources mentioned. There was no government census in colonial times. The census was mandated by the Constitution in Article I, Section 2, Paragraph 3.

41. **D.** The procedure is named after Elbridge Gerry, delegate to the Constitutional Convention and fourth Vice-President of the United States, who, as Governor of Massachusetts, oversaw changes in the state's senatorial districts that were to the political advantage of Republicans. Gerry's Federalist opponents called the technique *gerrymandering,* based upon the reptilian shape of one of the newly formed senatorial districts.

42. **F.** The second paragraph of the Declaration of Independence, as justification for the action being taken by the colonists, begins, "We hold these Truths to be self-evident, that all men are created equal, that they are endowed by their Creator with certain unalienable Rights, that among these are Life, Liberty, and the Pursuit of Happiness."

43. **B.** The tone of the first portion of this document is too self-congratulatory to be accepted as objectively factual.

44. **F.** The second portion of the document continues describing progress made and states an intent to extend the progress already made. The language is vague and sweeping, mentioning no specifics.

45. **B.** The sentence, "On the foundation of the Social Security Act we are determined to erect a structure of economic security for all our people, making sure that this benefit shall keep step with the ever-increasing capacity of America to provide a high standard of living for all its citizens," implies that benefits will rise as the national standard of living and cost of living increase. The stated desire to hold down the cost of consumer goods does not imply the imposition of price controls. *Yardsticks* in regard to the price of electricity means *guidelines.* Electricity is measured in kilowatt-hours.

46. **J.** The vast social welfare program proposed in this document is consonant with President Roosevelt's New Deal.

47. **C.** The document states, "The Republican platform proposes to meet many pressing national problems solely by action of the separate States." It then proceeds to explain why this policy is not wise and in what instances Federal-State cooperation is warranted.

48. **H.** In stating, "We shall subject to the civil service law all continuing positions which, because of the emergency, have been exempt from its operation," the document is making the admission that appointments have been made outside of the legally mandated merit system.

49. **C.** The reference to twelve years of Republican leadership followed by three years of Democratic leadership, along with the social programs described, pinpoints the writing of this document at 1936.

50. **J.** The exceptionally partisan nature of this document along with the broad range of topics touched upon identifies it as the Democratic Platform of 1936.

51. **C.** The Republicans are certainly opposed to both Communism and Fascism, and they are staunch supporters of democratic (with a small *d*) government. The Republican platform, however, calls for handling most problems at the state level, holding Federal involvement to a minimum.

52. **G.** Franklin Roosevelt and John Garner were together reelected in 1936. Alfred Landon was the unsuccessful Republican challenger in that election, Wilkie was the Republican candidate in 1940, and Wilson and Marshall were elected together in 1912 and 1916.

TEST 4. NATURAL SCIENCE READING

1. **D.** Both radio waves and radar waves are electromagnetic waves. All electromagnetic waves travel at the speed of light, about 186,000 miles per second.

2. **J.** $\frac{186{,}000}{4{,}000{,}000 \text{ vibrations per second}} = .0465 \text{ miles}$

   $= 245 \text{ feet}$

3. **D.** Since radar waves travel only in a straight line, they could not bend to strike an object below the horizon, hence would return no signals. An aircraft flying below the horizon is effectively out of radar range.

4. **H.** Since the speed of the radar waves is 186,000 miles per second, the distance of an object may be easily calculated by considering the travel time of the signal. The time elapsed between the transmission of a signal and its return represents twice the distance between the transmitter and the object.

5. **D.** As can be seen on the table, violet light has a shorter wave length, hence a higher frequency than red light.

6. **G.** A wave length of two inches falls into the range shared by Ultra High Frequency (UHF), television and radar.

7. **A.** Since radio waves are longer than UHF waves, and radio waves will not penetrate the ionosphere but UHF waves will, one can assume that shorter wave lengths will penetrate the ionosphere whereas longer waves will not. Since x-rays are still shorter than UHF waves, one can reasonably expect x-rays to penetrate the ionosphere.

8. **G.** Frequency is inversely proportional to wave length. Thus, the lower the frequency the greater the wave length and the greater the frequency the shorter the wave length. Since visible light has a greater wave length than cosmic rays, visible light has the lower frequency.

9. **A.** The prefix *kilo* stands for one thousand. A kilocycle is a measure of speed of vibration.

10. **H.** Radar is extensively used today along the DEW Line (Distant Early Warning Line), a continuous series of radar installations along the Arctic Circle from Barrow, Alaska, to Iceland, designed to give advance warning of hostile aircraft approaching over the North Pole. Radar is also used by highway police to determine the speed of moving cars. While transistors and computers have both grown from the rapid advances in electronic technology, neither is dependent on radar.

11. **B.** Only living structures possess the ability to reproduce themselves. Since viruses reproduce within specific living cells, they must be classified as living things.

12. **G.** Scientists tend to work and think within a very narrow range, hence they often do not recognize the significance to others of the facts they discover nor the possible applications of their discoveries to related fields.

13. **D.** Before the discovery of viruses, four criteria were applied to distinguish living from non-living things. There were: (A) the fact that only animate objects can mutate; (B) the face that non-living substances cannot reproduce; (C) that only living things respond to external stimuli; and (D) that all known living things were greater than 20 millimicra in size. A., B. and C. are still valid means for distinguishing living from non-living things. Only the discovery of viruses much smaller than 200 millimicra has made it impossible to use size as a distinguishing factor.

14. **F.** Most known viruses are between 20 and 200 millimicra in size. Bacteria tend to be larger than viruses, while many protein molecules are smaller.

15. **D.** Genes and viruses are both nucleoproteins. A nucleoprotein is a compound that consists of a protein conjugated with a nucleic acid.

16. **G.** Many cells reproduce freely, but a specific characteristic of genes is that they mutate and then reproduce the mutations. In this respect, viruses behave in a manner similar to that of genes. The chief difference between them is that genes are contained within chromosomes while viruses are *on the loose.*

17. **D.** The term *medical problem* is commonly used in reference to the health status of animals. Since the

mechanism of cancer in plants is similar to that in animals, the more encompassing term *biological problem* is more appropriate.

18. **F.** The fact that viruses are infectious agents is irrelevant to the causation of cancer. However, viruses do mutate and new mutants do have new properties and new effects upon their host organisms. It is quite possible that a benign virus could mutate into a form that causes cancer.

19. **C.** The first sentence states the topic of the passage, and the development of the passage is true to the topic sentence.

20. **F.** The passage states, "Cancer originates when a normal cell suddenly becomes a cancer cell which multiplies widely and without apparent restraint. Cancer may originate in many different kinds of cells, but the cancer cell usually continues to carry certain traits of the cell of origin."

21. **C.** The first paragraph of the passage raises the problem created by "single issue" research. Basic research, that is research intended only to learn the nature and relationships of various organisms and processes, is necessary in order to suggest new possibilities for research specific to problems of a biological nature. Basic research may, indeed, uncover some hitherto unknown form of life, but there is no real need for such a search.

22. **G.** $MnO_4^- + 8H^+ (+5e^-) \rightarrow Mn^{++} + 4H_2O$
The total charge on the left is + 7, and the total charge on the right is + 2. Five electrons have to be added to go from + 7 to + 2.

23. **A.** Chemically pure water is generally produced by distillation. Distillation involves the evaporation of the water followed by condensation of the vapor to form pure water.

24. **F.** By definition, a conservative field is one in which energy is conserved. That is, if you return to the same point you have the same energy at that point. This implies that the work done must be independent of the paths and dependent only upon the end points.

25. **A.** Ribosomes are unchanged by cell division. The nucleus, nucleolus, chromosome and nuclear membrane all change drastically during mitosis.

26. **H.** Tropical rain forests contain greater diversity and abundance of organisms than any other biome.

27. **D.** By definition, an amalgam is a mixture of metals containing mercury.

28. **F.** Oxygen supports combustion, it does not in itself burn. A match will burn more rapidly in a bottle of pure oxygen.

29. **D.** Tin is above copper on the electromotive series. Tin will replace copper from copper salts as follows:
tin + copper sulfate → tin sulfate + copper

30. **F.** The energy produced on the sun is a result of the nuclear fusion of hydrogen atoms to form helium. Fusion produces a great deal of energy, some of which eventually reaches the earth.

31. **C.** The organic matter contained within the topsoil restores the natural minerals to this soil layer, thereby enabling its fertility to continue.

32. **H.** The characteristics described are those of a crustacean.

33. **C.** The formula for sulfur dioxide is SO_2. The weight of sulfur is 32, and the weight of the oxygen in this compound is $16 \times 2 = 32$. The weight of the sulfur equals the weight of the oxygen, so the percentage of sulfur is 50 percent.

34. **J.** The experiments show that bees have some color vision.

35. **B.** The bees obviously could discriminate blue from gray. Having eaten on the blue cloth in the first phase of the experiment, they went directly to the dish on the blue square expecting to find food there.

36. **H.** When food was to be found on the one red square, the bees discovered and enjoyed it. However, since bees are red-blind, they were unable to distinguish red from gray in phase two of the experiment, so flew randomly to all dishes.

37. **B.** A mixed color reflects wave lengths of various colors. Evidently the mixed red reflected some color which the bees were able to see, allowing them to discriminate between red and gray.

38. **J.** The experiment deals specifically with the color vision of bees. It makes no mention of the color vision of other insects, nor of birds. It is clear, however, that if color is the chief cue as to source of food, then pure red flowers are largely pollinated by sources other than bees.

39. **B.** The results can be explained in terms of visual discrimination and conditioned learning. The mixed red squares reflected the blues and ultraviolets which the bees could see, so the bees sought food there on the basis of their previous experience.

40. **J.** Food does not naturally occur in little glass

dishes. In the initial phase of the experiment the bees learned that food is found in little glass dishes. Their subsequent return to empty dishes confirms the fact of this learning. The errors made in experiments II and IV were not due to the absence of learning but to the failure of visual cues.

41. **D.** In experiments II and IV the bees demonstrated an inability to see pure red.

42. **G.** We must assume that it is not the nature of blue which makes the bee go to the blue square, but rather the ability to distinguish it from gray. If the bees were to see red as yellow, they would be able to distinguish it from gray and would thus be able to find the target square in the experiment. If, however, as is the known case, bees see red as gray, then discrimination is impossible.

43. **C.** The number of protons gives an element its atomic number.

44. **J.** Different isotopes of the same element have the same number of protons but a different number of neutrons. Since the mass of the nucleus is affected by both the number of protons and the number of neutrons, different isotopes will have different mass.

45. **B.** The nuclear mass is always less than the sum of the protons and neutrons that compose it. This difference, called *mass defect,* is explained by the conversion of some mass into *binding energy,* the energy that holds the protons and neutrons together in the nucleus.

46. **J.** The first law of thermodynamics states that in any system energy is neither created nor destroyed. In Einstein's equation, energy is not created but rather converted from mass by the action of speed upon that mass.

47. **D.** Natural radiation cannot be controlled by any means, neither chemical nor physical.

48. **F.** The half-life of carbon-14 is approximately 5000 years. This means that one half of a mass of carbon-14 will disintegrate in 5000 years.

49. **B.** Radiocarbon dating is extremely accurate because the decay rate of carbon-14 is not affected by pressure, temperature or the nature of the organism in which the carbon-14 resides. For this reason, radiocarbon dating is extensively used by archeologists to determine the age of samples and civilizations which they are unearthing.

50. **H.** The electrons in the shell of an element, by their attempts to gain electrons from other elements, are responsible for the chemical activity of the element. The electrons are almost weightless and exist and act quite independently of the nucleus of the element.

51. **A.** When an oganism dies it ceases to assimilate cosmic radiation, but continues to emit radiation at a constant rate. The amount of radioactive decay dates back to the moment of death when assimilation of cosmic radiation ceased and the system lost its radioactive equilibrium.

52. **F.** Invention of a particle accelerator which moves atomic particles at speeds near the speed of light was a prerequisite to achieving nuclear fission. Nuclear fission is basic to the atomic bomb.

PART V

MODEL EXAM III

ANSWER SHEET—MODEL EXAM III

ENGLISH USAGE

1 Ⓐ Ⓑ Ⓒ Ⓓ	12 Ⓕ Ⓖ Ⓗ Ⓙ	23 Ⓐ Ⓑ Ⓒ Ⓓ	34 Ⓕ Ⓖ Ⓗ Ⓙ	45 Ⓐ Ⓑ Ⓒ Ⓓ	56 Ⓕ Ⓖ Ⓗ Ⓙ	67 Ⓐ Ⓑ Ⓒ Ⓓ
2 Ⓕ Ⓖ Ⓗ Ⓙ	13 Ⓐ Ⓑ Ⓒ Ⓓ	24 Ⓕ Ⓖ Ⓗ Ⓙ	35 Ⓐ Ⓑ Ⓒ Ⓓ	46 Ⓕ Ⓖ Ⓗ Ⓙ	57 Ⓐ Ⓑ Ⓒ Ⓓ	68 Ⓕ Ⓖ Ⓗ Ⓙ
3 Ⓐ Ⓑ Ⓒ Ⓓ	14 Ⓕ Ⓖ Ⓗ Ⓙ	25 Ⓐ Ⓑ Ⓒ Ⓓ	36 Ⓕ Ⓖ Ⓗ Ⓙ	47 Ⓐ Ⓑ Ⓒ Ⓓ	58 Ⓕ Ⓖ Ⓗ Ⓙ	69 Ⓐ Ⓑ Ⓒ Ⓓ
4 Ⓕ Ⓖ Ⓗ Ⓙ	15 Ⓐ Ⓑ Ⓒ Ⓓ	26 Ⓕ Ⓖ Ⓗ Ⓙ	37 Ⓐ Ⓑ Ⓒ Ⓓ	48 Ⓕ Ⓖ Ⓗ Ⓙ	59 Ⓐ Ⓑ Ⓒ Ⓓ	70 Ⓕ Ⓖ Ⓗ Ⓙ
5 Ⓐ Ⓑ Ⓒ Ⓓ	16 Ⓕ Ⓖ Ⓗ Ⓙ	27 Ⓐ Ⓑ Ⓒ Ⓓ	38 Ⓕ Ⓖ Ⓗ Ⓙ	49 Ⓐ Ⓑ Ⓒ Ⓓ	60 Ⓕ Ⓖ Ⓗ Ⓙ	71 Ⓐ Ⓑ Ⓒ Ⓓ
6 Ⓕ Ⓖ Ⓗ Ⓙ	17 Ⓐ Ⓑ Ⓒ Ⓓ	28 Ⓕ Ⓖ Ⓗ Ⓙ	39 Ⓐ Ⓑ Ⓒ Ⓓ	50 Ⓕ Ⓖ Ⓗ Ⓙ	61 Ⓐ Ⓑ Ⓒ Ⓓ	72 Ⓕ Ⓖ Ⓗ Ⓙ
7 Ⓐ Ⓑ Ⓒ Ⓓ	18 Ⓕ Ⓖ Ⓗ Ⓙ	29 Ⓐ Ⓑ Ⓒ Ⓓ	40 Ⓕ Ⓖ Ⓗ Ⓙ	51 Ⓐ Ⓑ Ⓒ Ⓓ	62 Ⓕ Ⓖ Ⓗ Ⓙ	73 Ⓐ Ⓑ Ⓒ Ⓓ
8 Ⓕ Ⓖ Ⓗ Ⓙ	19 Ⓐ Ⓑ Ⓒ Ⓓ	30 Ⓕ Ⓖ Ⓗ Ⓙ	41 Ⓐ Ⓑ Ⓒ Ⓓ	52 Ⓕ Ⓖ Ⓗ Ⓙ	63 Ⓐ Ⓑ Ⓒ Ⓓ	74 Ⓕ Ⓖ Ⓗ Ⓙ
9 Ⓐ Ⓑ Ⓒ Ⓓ	20 Ⓕ Ⓖ Ⓗ Ⓙ	31 Ⓐ Ⓑ Ⓒ Ⓓ	42 Ⓕ Ⓖ Ⓗ Ⓙ	53 Ⓐ Ⓑ Ⓒ Ⓓ	64 Ⓕ Ⓖ Ⓗ Ⓙ	75 Ⓐ Ⓑ Ⓒ Ⓓ
10 Ⓕ Ⓖ Ⓗ Ⓙ	21 Ⓐ Ⓑ Ⓒ Ⓓ	32 Ⓕ Ⓖ Ⓗ Ⓙ	43 Ⓐ Ⓑ Ⓒ Ⓓ	54 Ⓕ Ⓖ Ⓗ Ⓙ	65 Ⓐ Ⓑ Ⓒ Ⓓ	
11 Ⓐ Ⓑ Ⓒ Ⓓ	22 Ⓕ Ⓖ Ⓗ Ⓙ	33 Ⓐ Ⓑ Ⓒ Ⓓ	44 Ⓕ Ⓖ Ⓗ Ⓙ	55 Ⓐ Ⓑ Ⓒ Ⓓ	66 Ⓕ Ⓖ Ⓗ Ⓙ	

MATHEMATICS USAGE

1 Ⓐ Ⓑ Ⓒ Ⓓ Ⓔ	7 Ⓐ Ⓑ Ⓒ Ⓓ Ⓔ	13 Ⓐ Ⓑ Ⓒ Ⓓ Ⓔ	19 Ⓐ Ⓑ Ⓒ Ⓓ Ⓔ	25 Ⓐ Ⓑ Ⓒ Ⓓ Ⓔ	31 Ⓐ Ⓑ Ⓒ Ⓓ Ⓔ	37 Ⓐ Ⓑ Ⓒ Ⓓ Ⓔ
2 Ⓕ Ⓖ Ⓗ Ⓙ Ⓚ	8 Ⓕ Ⓖ Ⓗ Ⓙ Ⓚ	14 Ⓕ Ⓖ Ⓗ Ⓙ Ⓚ	20 Ⓕ Ⓖ Ⓗ Ⓙ Ⓚ	26 Ⓕ Ⓖ Ⓗ Ⓙ Ⓚ	32 Ⓕ Ⓖ Ⓗ Ⓙ Ⓚ	38 Ⓕ Ⓖ Ⓗ Ⓙ Ⓚ
3 Ⓐ Ⓑ Ⓒ Ⓓ Ⓔ	9 Ⓐ Ⓑ Ⓒ Ⓓ Ⓔ	15 Ⓐ Ⓑ Ⓒ Ⓓ Ⓔ	21 Ⓐ Ⓑ Ⓒ Ⓓ Ⓔ	27 Ⓐ Ⓑ Ⓒ Ⓓ Ⓔ	33 Ⓐ Ⓑ Ⓒ Ⓓ Ⓔ	39 Ⓐ Ⓑ Ⓒ Ⓓ Ⓔ
4 Ⓕ Ⓖ Ⓗ Ⓙ Ⓚ	10 Ⓕ Ⓖ Ⓗ Ⓙ Ⓚ	16 Ⓕ Ⓖ Ⓗ Ⓙ Ⓚ	22 Ⓕ Ⓖ Ⓗ Ⓙ Ⓚ	28 Ⓕ Ⓖ Ⓗ Ⓙ Ⓚ	34 Ⓕ Ⓖ Ⓗ Ⓙ Ⓚ	40 Ⓕ Ⓖ Ⓗ Ⓙ Ⓚ
5 Ⓐ Ⓑ Ⓒ Ⓓ Ⓔ	11 Ⓐ Ⓑ Ⓒ Ⓓ Ⓔ	17 Ⓐ Ⓑ Ⓒ Ⓓ Ⓔ	23 Ⓐ Ⓑ Ⓒ Ⓓ Ⓔ	29 Ⓐ Ⓑ Ⓒ Ⓓ Ⓔ	35 Ⓐ Ⓑ Ⓒ Ⓓ Ⓔ	
6 Ⓕ Ⓖ Ⓗ Ⓙ Ⓚ	12 Ⓕ Ⓖ Ⓗ Ⓙ Ⓚ	18 Ⓕ Ⓖ Ⓗ Ⓙ Ⓚ	24 Ⓕ Ⓖ Ⓗ Ⓙ Ⓚ	30 Ⓕ Ⓖ Ⓗ Ⓙ Ⓚ	36 Ⓕ Ⓖ Ⓗ Ⓙ Ⓚ	

SOCIAL STUDIES READING

1 Ⓐ Ⓑ Ⓒ Ⓓ	8 Ⓕ Ⓖ Ⓗ Ⓙ	15 Ⓐ Ⓑ Ⓒ Ⓓ	22 Ⓕ Ⓖ Ⓗ Ⓙ	29 Ⓐ Ⓑ Ⓒ Ⓓ	36 Ⓕ Ⓖ Ⓗ Ⓙ	43 Ⓐ Ⓑ Ⓒ Ⓓ Ⓔ	50 Ⓕ Ⓖ Ⓗ Ⓙ Ⓚ
2 Ⓕ Ⓖ Ⓗ Ⓙ	9 Ⓐ Ⓑ Ⓒ Ⓓ	16 Ⓕ Ⓖ Ⓗ Ⓙ	23 Ⓐ Ⓑ Ⓒ Ⓓ	30 Ⓕ Ⓖ Ⓗ Ⓙ	37 Ⓐ Ⓑ Ⓒ Ⓓ	44 Ⓕ Ⓖ Ⓗ Ⓙ Ⓚ	51 Ⓐ Ⓑ Ⓒ Ⓓ Ⓔ
3 Ⓐ Ⓑ Ⓒ Ⓓ	10 Ⓕ Ⓖ Ⓗ Ⓙ	17 Ⓐ Ⓑ Ⓒ Ⓓ	24 Ⓕ Ⓖ Ⓗ Ⓙ	31 Ⓐ Ⓑ Ⓒ Ⓓ	38 Ⓕ Ⓖ Ⓗ Ⓙ	45 Ⓐ Ⓑ Ⓒ Ⓓ Ⓔ	52 Ⓕ Ⓖ Ⓗ Ⓙ Ⓚ
4 Ⓕ Ⓖ Ⓗ Ⓙ	11 Ⓐ Ⓑ Ⓒ Ⓓ	18 Ⓕ Ⓖ Ⓗ Ⓙ	25 Ⓐ Ⓑ Ⓒ Ⓓ	32 Ⓕ Ⓖ Ⓗ Ⓙ	39 Ⓐ Ⓑ Ⓒ Ⓓ	46 Ⓕ Ⓖ Ⓗ Ⓙ Ⓚ	
5 Ⓐ Ⓑ Ⓒ Ⓓ	12 Ⓕ Ⓖ Ⓗ Ⓙ	19 Ⓐ Ⓑ Ⓒ Ⓓ	26 Ⓕ Ⓖ Ⓗ Ⓙ	33 Ⓐ Ⓑ Ⓒ Ⓓ	40 Ⓕ Ⓖ Ⓗ Ⓙ	47 Ⓐ Ⓑ Ⓒ Ⓓ Ⓔ	
6 Ⓕ Ⓖ Ⓗ Ⓙ	13 Ⓐ Ⓑ Ⓒ Ⓓ	20 Ⓕ Ⓖ Ⓗ Ⓙ	27 Ⓐ Ⓑ Ⓒ Ⓓ	34 Ⓕ Ⓖ Ⓗ Ⓙ	41 Ⓐ Ⓑ Ⓒ Ⓓ	48 Ⓕ Ⓖ Ⓗ Ⓙ Ⓚ	
7 Ⓐ Ⓑ Ⓒ Ⓓ	14 Ⓕ Ⓖ Ⓗ Ⓙ	21 Ⓐ Ⓑ Ⓒ Ⓓ	28 Ⓕ Ⓖ Ⓗ Ⓙ	35 Ⓐ Ⓑ Ⓒ Ⓓ	42 Ⓕ Ⓖ Ⓗ Ⓙ	49 Ⓐ Ⓑ Ⓒ Ⓓ Ⓔ	

NATURAL SCIENCE READING

1 Ⓐ Ⓑ Ⓒ Ⓓ	8 Ⓕ Ⓖ Ⓗ Ⓙ	15 Ⓐ Ⓑ Ⓒ Ⓓ	22 Ⓕ Ⓖ Ⓗ Ⓙ	29 Ⓐ Ⓑ Ⓒ Ⓓ	36 Ⓕ Ⓖ Ⓗ Ⓙ	43 Ⓐ Ⓑ Ⓒ Ⓓ Ⓔ	50 Ⓕ Ⓖ Ⓗ Ⓙ Ⓚ
2 Ⓕ Ⓖ Ⓗ Ⓙ	9 Ⓐ Ⓑ Ⓒ Ⓓ	16 Ⓕ Ⓖ Ⓗ Ⓙ	23 Ⓐ Ⓑ Ⓒ Ⓓ	30 Ⓕ Ⓖ Ⓗ Ⓙ	37 Ⓐ Ⓑ Ⓒ Ⓓ	44 Ⓕ Ⓖ Ⓗ Ⓙ Ⓚ	51 Ⓐ Ⓑ Ⓒ Ⓓ Ⓔ
3 Ⓐ Ⓑ Ⓒ Ⓓ	10 Ⓕ Ⓖ Ⓗ Ⓙ	17 Ⓐ Ⓑ Ⓒ Ⓓ	24 Ⓕ Ⓖ Ⓗ Ⓙ	31 Ⓐ Ⓑ Ⓒ Ⓓ	38 Ⓕ Ⓖ Ⓗ Ⓙ	45 Ⓐ Ⓑ Ⓒ Ⓓ Ⓔ	52 Ⓕ Ⓖ Ⓗ Ⓙ Ⓚ
4 Ⓕ Ⓖ Ⓗ Ⓙ	11 Ⓐ Ⓑ Ⓒ Ⓓ	18 Ⓕ Ⓖ Ⓗ Ⓙ	25 Ⓐ Ⓑ Ⓒ Ⓓ	32 Ⓕ Ⓖ Ⓗ Ⓙ	39 Ⓐ Ⓑ Ⓒ Ⓓ	46 Ⓕ Ⓖ Ⓗ Ⓙ Ⓚ	
5 Ⓐ Ⓑ Ⓒ Ⓓ	12 Ⓕ Ⓖ Ⓗ Ⓙ	19 Ⓐ Ⓑ Ⓒ Ⓓ	26 Ⓕ Ⓖ Ⓗ Ⓙ	33 Ⓐ Ⓑ Ⓒ Ⓓ	40 Ⓕ Ⓖ Ⓗ Ⓙ	47 Ⓐ Ⓑ Ⓒ Ⓓ Ⓔ	
6 Ⓕ Ⓖ Ⓗ Ⓙ	13 Ⓐ Ⓑ Ⓒ Ⓓ	20 Ⓕ Ⓖ Ⓗ Ⓙ	27 Ⓐ Ⓑ Ⓒ Ⓓ	34 Ⓕ Ⓖ Ⓗ Ⓙ	41 Ⓐ Ⓑ Ⓒ Ⓓ	48 Ⓕ Ⓖ Ⓗ Ⓙ Ⓚ	
7 Ⓐ Ⓑ Ⓒ Ⓓ	14 Ⓕ Ⓖ Ⓗ Ⓙ	21 Ⓐ Ⓑ Ⓒ Ⓓ	28 Ⓕ Ⓖ Ⓗ Ⓙ	35 Ⓐ Ⓑ Ⓒ Ⓓ	42 Ⓕ Ⓖ Ⓗ Ⓙ	49 Ⓐ Ⓑ Ⓒ Ⓓ Ⓔ	

SCORE SHEET

	Number Correct								
English Usage	_____	÷	75	=	_____	×	100	=	_____ %
Mathematics Usage	_____	÷	40	=	_____	×	100	=	_____ %
Social Studies Reading	_____	÷	52	=	_____	×	100	=	_____ %
Questions based on reading	_____	÷	39	=	_____	×	100	=	_____ %
Questions not based on reading	_____	÷	13	=	_____	×	100	=	_____ %
Natural Science Reading	_____	÷	52	=	_____	×	100	=	_____ %
Questions based on reading	_____	÷	38	=	_____	×	100	=	_____ %
Questions not based on reading	_____	÷	14	=	_____	×	100	=	_____ %
Total Score	_____	÷	219	=	_____	×	100	=	_____ %

PROGRESS CHART

	Exam I	Exam II	Exam III
English Usage	%	%	%
Mathematics Usage	%	%	%
Social Studies Reading	%	%	%
Natural Science Reading	%	%	%
Total	%	%	%

TEST 1
ENGLISH USAGE

40 Minutes—75 Questions

DIRECTIONS: In each of the following passages, some portions are underlined and numbered. Corresponding to each numbered portion are three alternative ways of saying the same thing. Read through each passage quickly to determine the sense of the passage, then return to the underlined portions. If you feel that an underlined portion is correct and is stated as well as possible, mark NO CHANGE, **A** or **F.** If you feel that there is an error in grammar, sentence structure, punctuation or word usage, choose the correct answer. If an underlined portion appears to be correct, but you believe that one of the alternative choices would be more effective, mark that choice. Remember, you are to choose the *best* answer.

Passage I

Everyone has at one time or another (1) felt the need to express himself (2). What must you (3) do in order to learn to

1. **A.** NO CHANGE
   B. the other
   C. an other
   D. one other

2. **F.** NO CHANGE
   G. theirself
   H. themself
   J. theirselves

3. **A.** NO CHANGE
   B. they
   C. he
   D. one

say exactly what you want to say. You will have to study
4 5 6

4. F. NO CHANGE
G. we want
H. one wants
J. everyone wants

5. A. NO CHANGE
B. say?
C. say!
D. say:

6. F. NO CHANGE
G. They ought to
H. We should
J. One must

very careful the English language and especially it's
7 8

7. A. NO CHANGE
B. with care
C. carefully (inserted after language)
D. OMIT

8. F. NO CHANGE
G. its
H. its'
J. their

grammer. Some people think that Good English is fancy
9 10

9. A. NO CHANGE
B. grammer. Some
C. grammar. (begin a new paragraph with Some)
D. grammer. (begin a new paragraph with Some)

10. F. NO CHANGE
G. good english
H. good English
J. English that is good

English, but this contention isnt true. Just because a
11

11. A. NO CHANGE
B. isn't
C. aint
D. aren't

person uses long words it does not mean that
12

12. F. NO CHANGE
G. words, it does not mean that
H. words, you don't know that
J. words, he does not necessarily

he speaks good. The person whom uses simple words
13 14

and phrases which say exactly what he means is using
15

better English than the individual who shows off with
16

hard-to understand expressions.
17

13. **A.** NO CHANGE
B. he speaks well.
C. speak correct.
D. speak well.

14. **F.** NO CHANGE
G. who
H. what
J. which

15. **A.** NO CHANGE
B. what say
C. which says
D. who say

16. **F.** NO CHANGE
G. from
H. then
J. instead of

17. **A.** NO CHANGE
B. hard to understand expressions.
C. hard-to-understand expressions.
D. hard-to-understand-expressions.

Passage II

I have received your letter informing me that I am
18
now to be charged an extra dollar per month

for not publishing my telephone number. In other words
19 20
you propose to charge me for a non-service.

18. **F.** NO CHANGE
G. had received
H. received
J. am receiving

19. **A.** NO CHANGE
B. for not having published
C. for you not listing
D. for your not listing

20. **F.** NO CHANGE
G. In other words,
H. However,
J. Moreover,

You give as your reason the fact that not publishing my
21 22
number incurs additional expense requiring special
22 23
record keeping and the personal handling of requests

21. **A.** NO CHANGE
B. The fact is that the reason is
C. You claim that
D. You say that

22. **F.** NO CHANGE
G. by not publishing my number
H. when you don't publish my number it
J. an unpublished number

23. **A.** NO CHANGE
B. expense, requiring
C. expense, because of requiring
D. expense, because of the requirement for

for these numbers. It seems obvious that by not
24 25
publishing my number you get several hundred percent
25 26

24. **F.** NO CHANGE
G. for my number.
H. for it.
J. such a number.

25. **A.** NO CHANGE
B. an unpublished number receives
C. when you don't publish my number you get
D. if you do not publish my number you will not get

26. **F.** NO CHANGE
G. hundred %
H. hundred per centum
J. hundred per-cent

less calls to my number and it is therefore less costly to
27 28 29
your company to service an unpublished number than
the listed kind.

27. **A.** NO CHANGE
B. smaller calls
C. fewer calls
D. lesser calls

28. **F.** NO CHANGE
G. to it
H. to that number
J. OMIT

29. **A.** NO CHANGE
B. , and it is therefore
C. and, it is therefore
D. and, it is, therefore

Your charge is an outrage and (30) your reasoning is an insult to normal intelligence but (31) I am forced to pay since there is no other outfit I can take my business to (32). Its (33) a cheap and shabby bit of stealing by a company that has been getting (34) away with murder for as many years as (35) we have (36) an anti-trust law in this country. Yet, less (37) you get the impression that we the consumer (38) are completely helpless against such exploitation (39) I hereby inform you

30. F. NO CHANGE
G. outrage! and
H. outrage, and
J. outrage; and

31. A. NO CHANGE
B. intelligence! But
C. intelligence, But
D. intelligence; but

32. F. NO CHANGE
G. I can bring my business to.
H. I can give my orders to.
J. to which I can give my business.

33. A. NO CHANGE
B. It's
C. This is
D. The charge is

34. F. NO CHANGE
G. has got
H. got
J. gets

35. A. NO CHANGE
B. ever since
C. even though
D. because

36. F. NO CHANGE
G. we had
H. we have had
J. we had had

37. A. NO CHANGE
B. lest
C. least
D. unless

38. F. NO CHANGE
G. we, the consumer,
H. us consumers
J. we consumers

39. A. NO CHANGE
B. exploitation,
C. exploitations
D. exploitations,

that I intend to bring this matter up with the civil service
40
commission. I am sure they have a grievance committee
40 41

40. F. NO CHANGE
    G. at the Civil Service Commission
    H. to the Civil Service Commission
    J. with the Better Business Bureau

41. A. NO CHANGE
    B. there is
    C. that it has
    D. that there are

to hear complaints against this sort of thing.
42

42. F. NO CHANGE
    G. about this sort of thing.
    H. against unfair practice.
    J. about unfair practices.

Passage III

Do you know its not necessary to always travel to
43 44

43. A. NO CHANGE
    B. that its not
    C. that it is'nt
    D. that it isn't

44. F. NO CHANGE
    G. to travel
    H. to travel always
    J. to always go traveling

distant lands to bring back things of scientific value?
45 46 47

45. A. NO CHANGE
    B. lands of great distance
    C. distant land's
    D. distance lands

46. F. NO CHANGE
    G. take back
    H. bring
    J. take

47. A. NO CHANGE
    B. values?
    C. valuability?
    D. valuableness?

Right here in the good old U.S.A. you can find hidden
48

48. F. NO CHANGE
    G. U.S. of A.
    H. US
    J. United states of America

treasures. Not every inch of space in our's country have
49 50

49. A. NO CHANGE
B. ours
C. ours'
D. our

50. F. NO CHANGE
G. countries have
H. countries has
J. country has

been explored, there are some spots still unknown to
51

51. A. NO CHANGE
B. explored; there
C. explored, they're
D. explored; they're

American's. Consider the Atlantic seaboard and the
52 53 54

52. F. NO CHANGE
G. Americans.
H. Americans!
J. American citizens.

53. A. NO CHANGE
B. For example,
C. In some areas of
D. Along

54. F. NO CHANGE
G. Atlantic-seaboard
H. Atlantic seabored
J. Atlantic Seaboard

Mississippi valley, where there are beautiful wild-birds
55 56

55. A. NO CHANGE
B. Mississippi-valley
C. Mississippi Valley
D. Mississippi's valley

56. F. NO CHANGE
G. wildbirds
H. Wildbirds
J. wild birds

never captured by man.
57

57. A. NO CHANGE
B. never before captured
C. never even seen
D. never, captured

Passage IV

It was lack of power and speed that once again brings
58

58. F. NO CHANGE
G. bring
H. brung
J. brought

about the Yankees' defeat. They couldn't run fast
59

enough to break up the Ranger's double plays; and in
60
the field they were unable to get to drives that in the past

years would have been turned into outs.
61

The flashy style of Buddy Bell at third, making
62

plays as clean as though he is using a broom, was only a
63 64 65
part of the Rangers' play. They came on strong and were

as hard to catch as the lawmen for whom they were
66
named. Each time the Yankees threatened to score, the

Rangers came up with the big play. And when a man like
67
Jackson of the Yankees strikes out three times you can

figure upon the strength of Ranger pitching. Jackson is
68

59. **A.** NO CHANGE
B. Yankee's defeat.
C. Yankees defeat!
D. Yankees' defeat!

60. **F.** NO CHANGE
G. Rangers' double-plays
H. Rangers' double plays,
J. Ranger's double plays

61. **A.** NO CHANGE
B. have been turned out.
C. have been out.
D. have been certain outs.

62. **F.** NO CHANGE
G. The flashy third baseman Buddy Bell
H. Buddy Bell's flashy style at third
J. Buddy Bell's flash and style at third

63. **A.** NO CHANGE
B. plays, cleanly
C. plays as cleanly
D. plays, as cleanly

64. **F.** NO CHANGE
G. as if
H. like as if
J. like as though

65. **A.** NO CHANGE
B. uses
C. has used
D. were using

66. **F.** NO CHANGE
G. for who
H. for what
J. for which

67. **A.** NO CHANGE
B. When
C. And if
D. If

68. **F.** NO CHANGE
G. sort of figure
H. estimate
J. be sure of

one of the game's best hitters, but yesterday finding (69) nothing that he could touch.

69. **A.** NO CHANGE
B. he has found
C. he found
D. he founded

A strong point in the Yankee teams' favor was its (70) refusal to give up even when the Rangers were well on there (71) way to a third straight victory.

70. **F.** NO CHANGE
G. it's
H. there
J. their

71. **A.** NO CHANGE
B. their
C. our
D. its

New York is (72) a better team than it had last year. So has Texas. We doubt, though, that any team in the American League could have beaten the Rangers yesterday afternoon—Eastern or Western Division (73). The Yankee team hasn't no (74) cause for despair over its showing (75) against those odds.

72. **F.** NO CHANGE
G. are
H. was
J. has

73. **A.** NO CHANGE
B. (place this after League, set off by dashes)
C. (place this after team, set off by commas)
D. (place this after Tigers, set off within parentheses)

74. **F.** NO CHANGE
G. have no
H. has no
J. hasn't got any

75. **A.** NO CHANGE
B. its showing,
C. it's showing
D. it's showing,

END OF TEST

If you complete this test before the time limit is up, look back over the questions. Do not proceed to the next test until you are told to do so.

TEST 2
MATHEMATICS USAGE

50 Minutes—40 Questions

DIRECTIONS: Solve each problem and mark the letter of the correct answer on your answer sheet.

DO YOUR FIGURING HERE

1. What is 40% of $\frac{10}{7}$?

A. $\frac{2}{7}$

B. $\frac{4}{7}$

C. $\frac{10}{28}$

D. $\frac{1}{28}$

E. $\frac{28}{10}$

2. A prime number is one which is divisible only by itself and 1. Which of the following are prime numbers?

I. 17
II. 27
III. 51
IV. 59

F. I only
G. I and II only
H. I, III, and IV only
J. I and IV only
K. III and IV only

3. As shown in the diagram, AB is a straight line and angle BOC = 20°. If the number of degrees in angle DOC is 6 more than the number of degrees in angle x, find the number of degrees in angle x.

A. 77
B. 75
C. 78
D. $22\frac{6}{7}$
E. 87

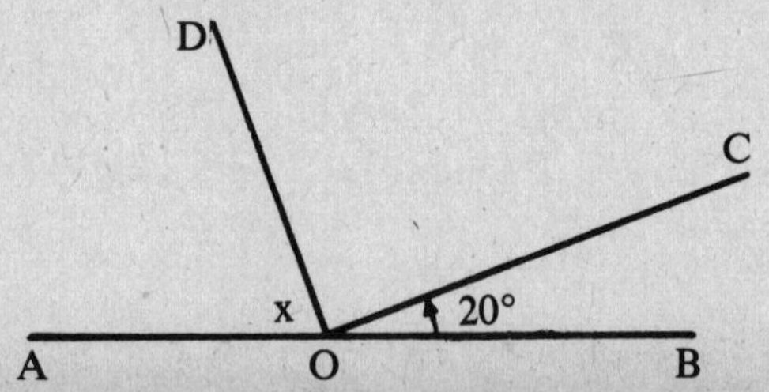

D
C
x
20°
A
O
B

4. As shown in the figure, a cylindrical oil tank is $\frac{1}{3}$ full. If 3 more gallons are added, the tank will be half-full. What is the capacity, in gallons, of the tank?

DO YOUR FIGURING HERE

F. 15
G. 16
H. 17
J. 18
K. 19

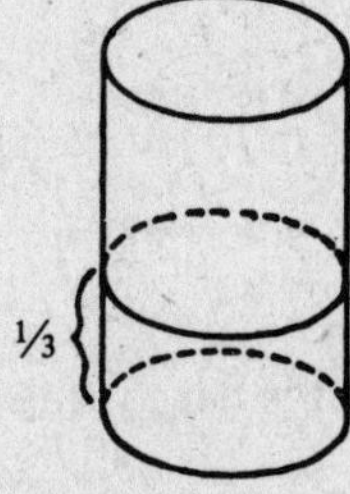

5. A girl receives grades of 91, 88, 86, and 78 in four of her major subjects. What must she receive in her fifth major subject in order to average 85?

A. 86
B. 85
C. 84
D. 83
E. 82

6. If a steel bar is 0.39 feet long, its length in inches is

F. less than 4
G. between 4 and $4\frac{1}{2}$
H. between $4\frac{1}{2}$ and 5
J. between 5 and 6
K. more than 6

7. In the figure, PS is perpendicular to QR. If PQ = PR = 26 and PS = 24, then QR =

A. 14
B. 16
C. 18
D. 20
E. 22

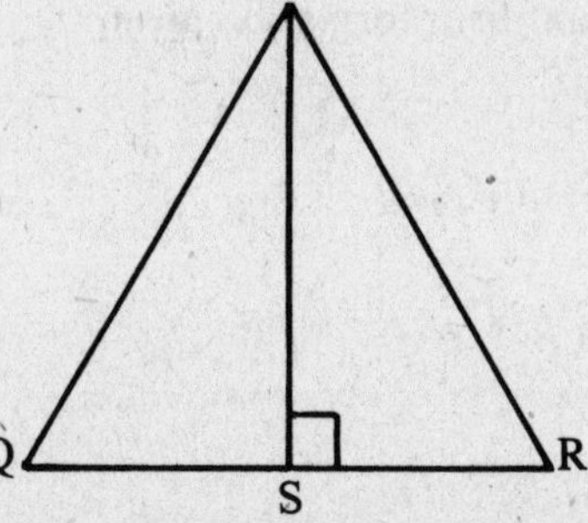

8. If $x = 0$, for what value of y is the equation $5x^3 + 7x^2 - (4y + 13)x - 7y + 15 = 0$ valid?

F. $-2\frac{1}{7}$
G. 0
H. $+2\frac{1}{7}$
J. $\frac{15}{11}$
K. $3\frac{1}{7}$

DO YOUR FIGURING HERE

9. A woman spends exactly \$81 buying some shirts and string ties. If the shirts cost \$7 and the string ties cost \$3 each, what is the ratio of shirts to string ties purchased when more shirts than ties are purchased?

A. 5:3
B. 4:3
C. 5:2
D. 4:1
E. 3:2

10. If a woman walks $\frac{2}{5}$ mile in 5 minutes, what is her average rate of walking in miles per hour?

F. 4
G. $4\frac{1}{2}$
H. $4\frac{4}{5}$
J. $5\frac{1}{5}$
K. $5\frac{3}{4}$

11. One end of a dam has the shape of a trapezoid with the dimensions indicated. What is the dam's area in square feet?

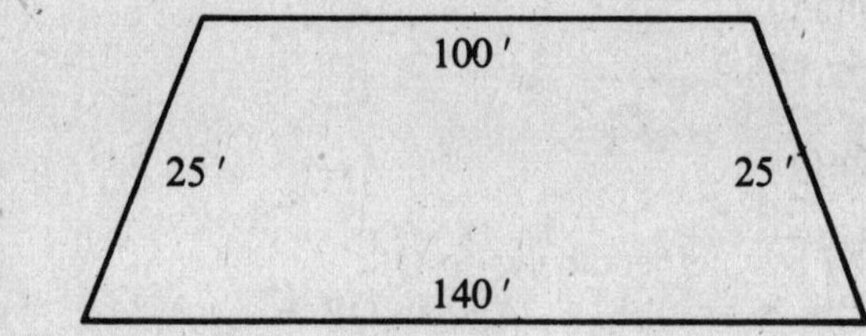

A. 1000
B. 1200
C. 1500
D. 1800
E. cannot be determined from the information given

12. If $1 + \frac{1}{t} = \frac{t+1}{t}$, what does t equal?

F. + 2 only
G. + 2 or − 2 only
H. + 2 or − 1 only
J. − 2 or + 1 only
K. T is any number except 0.

13. Point A is 3 inches from line b as shown in the diagram. In the plane that contains point A and line b, what is the total number of points which are 6 inches from A and also 1 inch from b?

A. 0
B. 1
C. 2
D. 3
E. 4

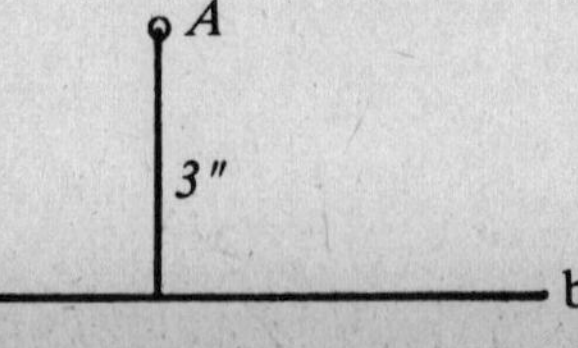

14. If R and S are different integers, both divisible by 5, then which of the following is *not necessarily* true?

DO YOUR FIGURING HERE

F. R − S is divisible by 5
G. RS is divisible by 25
H. R + S is divisible by 5
J. $R^2 + S^2$ is divisible by 5
K. R + S is divisible by 10

15. If a triangle of base 7 is equal in area to a circle of radius 7, what is the altitude of the triangle?

A. 8π
B. 10π
C. 12π
D. 14π
E. cannot be determined from the information given

16. If the following numbers are arranged in order from the smallest to the largest, what will be their correct order?

I. $\frac{9}{13}$

II. $\frac{13}{9}$

III. 70%

IV. $\frac{1}{.70}$

F. II, I, III, IV
G. III, II, I, IV
H. III, IV, I, II
J. II, IV, III, I
K. I, III, IV, II

17. The coordinates of the vertices of quadrilateral PQRS are P (0, 0), Q (9, 0), R (10, 3) and S (1, 3) respectively. The area of PQRS is

A. $9\sqrt{10}$
B. $\frac{9}{2}\sqrt{10}$
C. $\frac{27}{2}$
D. 27
E. not determinable from the information given

18. In the circle shown, AB is a diameter. If secant AP = 8 and tangent CP = 4, find the number of units in the diameter of the circle.

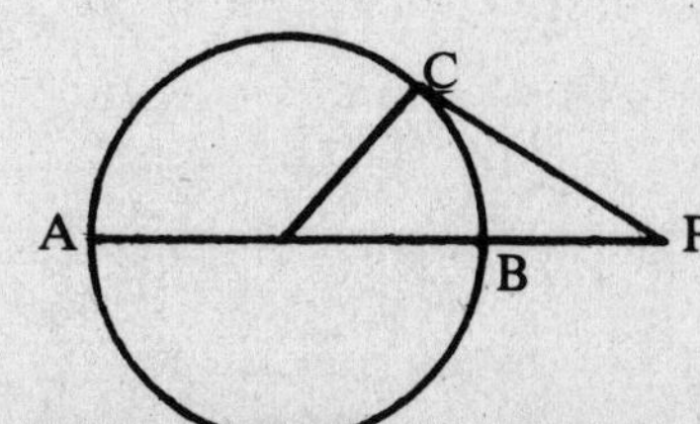

F. 6
G. $6\frac{1}{2}$
H. 8
J. $3\sqrt{2}$
K. cannot be determined from the information given

DO YOUR FIGURING HERE

19. A certain type of siding for a house costs \$10.50 per square yard. What does it cost for the siding of a wall 4 yards wide and 60 feet long?

A. \$ 800
B. \$ 840
C. \$2520
D. \$3240
E. \$5040

20. A circle whose radius is 7 has its center at the origin. Which of the following points are outside the circle?

I. (4, 4)
II. (5, 5)
III. (4, 5)
IV. (4, 6)

F. I and II only
G. II and III only
H. II, III, and IV only
J. II and IV only
K. III and IV only

21. A merchant sells a radio for \$80, thereby making a profit of 25% of the cost. What is the ratio of cost to selling price?

A. $\frac{4}{5}$

B. $\frac{3}{4}$

C. $\frac{5}{6}$

D. $\frac{2}{3}$

E. $\frac{3}{5}$

22. How many degrees are between the hands of a clock at 3:40?

F. 150°
G. 140°
H. 130°
J. 125°
K. 120°

DO YOUR FIGURING HERE

23. Two fences in a field meet at 120°. A cow is tethered at their intersection with a 15 foot rope, as shown in the figure. Over how many square feet may the cow graze?

A. 50π
B. 75π
C. 80π
D. 85π
E. 90π

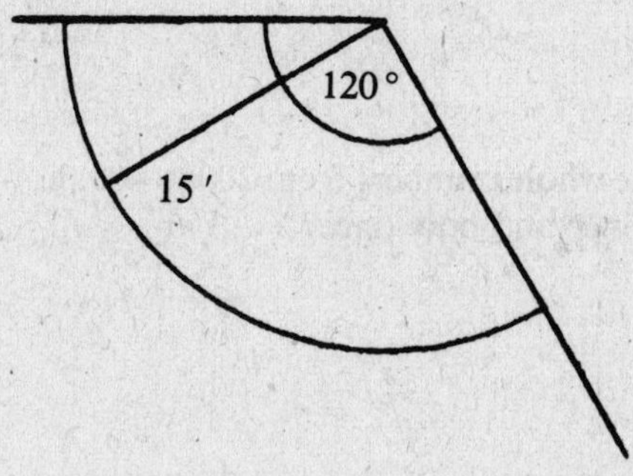

24. If $\frac{17}{10}$ y = 0.51, then y =

F. 3
G. 1.3
H. 1.2
J. .3
K. .03

25. A junior class of 50 girls and 70 boys sponsored a dance. If 40% of the girls and 50% of the boys attended the dance, approximately what percent attended?

A. 40
B. 42
C. 44
D. 46
E. 48

26. In the figure below, *r, s,* and *t* are straight lines meeting at point P, with angles formed as indicated; y =

F. 30°
G. 120°
H. 3x
J. 180 − x
K. 180 − 3x

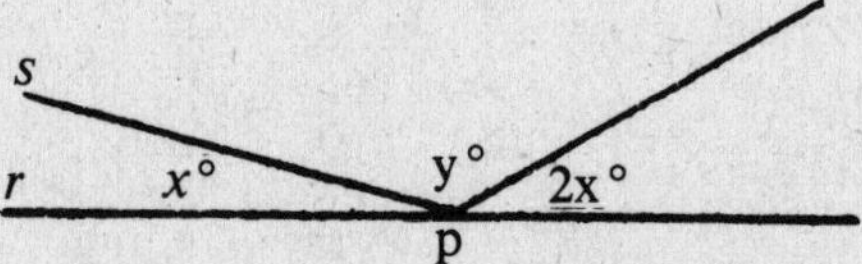

DO YOUR FIGURING HERE

27. $\frac{18}{33} = \frac{\sqrt{36}}{\sqrt{?}}$

A. 11
B. 121
C. 66
D. 144
E. 1089

28. If we write all the whole numbers from 200 to 400, how many of these contain the digit 7 once and only once?

F. 32
G. 34
H. 35
J. 36
K. 38

29. $(r + s)^2 - r^2 - s^2 = (?)$

A. $2rs$
B. rs
C. rs^2
D. 0
E. $2r^2 + 2s^2$

30. In the figure, angle S is obtuse, PR = 9, PS = 6 and Q is any point on RS. Which of the following inequalities expresses possible values of the length of PQ?

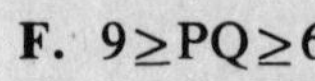

F. $9 \geq PQ \geq 6$
G. $9 \geq 6 \geq PQ$
H. $6 \geq PQ \geq 9$
J. $PQ \geq 9 \geq 6$
K. $9 \leq PQ \leq 6$

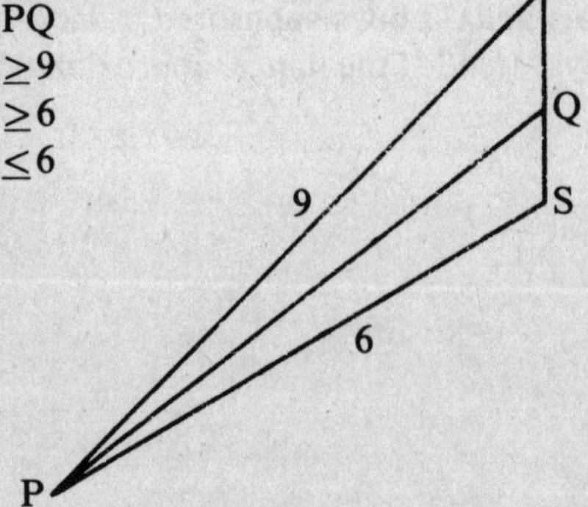

31. If a woman buys several articles for K cents per dozen and sells them for $\frac{K}{8}$ cents per article, what is her profit, in cents, per article?

A. $\frac{K}{48}$

B. $\frac{K}{12}$

C. $\frac{3K}{4}$

D. $\frac{K}{18}$

E. $\frac{K}{24}$

32. If all P are S and no S are Q, it necessarily follows that

DO YOUR FIGURING HERE

F. all Q are S
G. all Q are P
H. no P are Q
J. no S are P
K. some Q are P

33. The average of four numbers is 45. If one of the numbers is increased by 6, the average will remain unchanged if each of the other three numbers is reduced by

A. 1
B. 2
C. $\frac{3}{4}$
D. 4
E. $\frac{4}{3}$

34. In the series 3, 12, 21, 30, 39, 48 . . . ., which of the following will be a number?

F. 10,000
G. 10,002
H. 9,999
J. 101,000
K. none of these

35. A set of papers is arranged and numbered from 1 to 40. If the paper numbered 4 is drawn first and every seventh paper thereafter is drawn, what will be the number of the last paper drawn?

A. 36
B. 37
C. 38
D. 39
E. 40

36. If the angles of a triangle are in the ratio of 2:3:5, the triangle is

F. obtuse
G. acute
H. isosceles
J. right
K. equilateral

37. In the figure, a rectangular piece of cardboard 18 inches by 24 inches is made into an open box by cutting a 5-inch square from each corner and building up the sides. What is the volume of the box in cubic inches?

A. 560
B. 1233
C. 1560
D. 2160
E. 4320

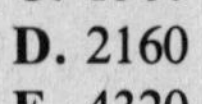

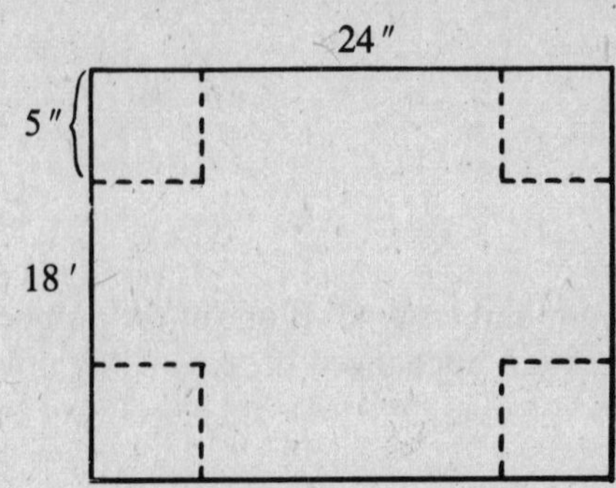

38. The figure below represents the back of a house. Find, in feet, the length of one of the equal rafters PQ or QR, if each extends 12 inches beyond the eaves.

F. 19
G. 21
H. 23
J. 25
K. 43

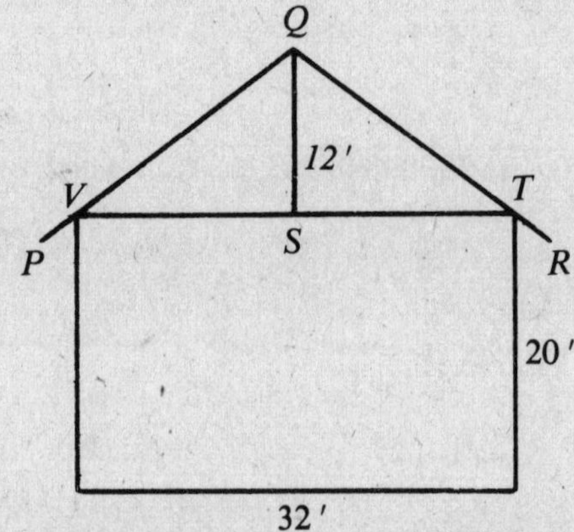

39. The scale of a certain map is $\frac{3}{4}$ inch = 9 miles. Find in square miles the actual area of a park represented on the map by a square whose side is $\frac{7}{8}$ inch.

A. $10\frac{1}{2}$
B. 21
C. $110\frac{1}{4}$
D. 121
E. $125\frac{2}{3}$

40. A relationship that holds for all waves is expressed by the formula $V = fL$, where V is the velocity, f is the frequency, and L the wave length. Express the wave length L in terms of V and f.

F. $L = \frac{V}{f}$
G. $L = V - f$
H. $L = Vf$
J. $L = V + f$
K. $L = \frac{f}{V}$

END OF TEST

If you complete this test before the time limit is up, check back over the questions on this test only. Do not return to the previous test. Do not proceed to the next test until you are told to do so.

TEST 3
SOCIAL STUDIES READING

35 Minutes—52 Questions

DIRECTIONS: Below each of the following reading passages is a series of questions. Choose the *best* answer to each question, interpreting what is stated or implied by the passage in the light of your own background in the subject. You may refer back to the passage as often as necessary, though the answers to some questions may not be found expressly in the passage.

Although most high school students lead active lives through involvement in extra-curricular activities, many students, especially girls, spend much time watching soap operas.

Regular soap opera viewers watch soaps anywhere from one to five times per week. Although the reasons why *soapoperatics* watch soaps differ, most viewers agree that they "get hooked on them." One disparager of this trend suggests that watching soap operas is addictive, somewhat like using drugs; it dulls the mind and becomes habit-forming.

Supporting this claim, one student who regularly watches "General Hospital," the most popular soap, explains that she watches because she "must see what is happening to Laura and Scotty," two of the program's characters.

Other students are attracted to soap operas for emotional reasons. Many find the soaps "hysterical" or "ridiculous." A sophomore boy devotee watches "General Hospital" daily because "I love to see people with so many problems!"

Still other students, mainly girls, claim that they watch soap operas because the soaps provide a source for conversation with peers. As one girl puts it, "It isn't nice to gossip about people you know, but it is socially acceptable to talk about the characters in the soaps." A disgusted boy comments, "All you hear girls talking about nowadays are soap operas—they watch all of them."

Some students watch soaps to "pass the time," especially while they babysit. Others agree with the senior who refuses to watch soaps because they are "inane, stupid, and a waste of time." While many soap opera viewers are attracted by the element of pathos in soaps, nonviewers may be repelled by this same aspect. One nonviewer says that soaps are too "emotional," while another, who hates suspense, says "They drive me up the wall."

Still, many students obviously watch soaps. In a paper on the good and evil effects of wealth, reports an English teacher, students used more examples from soap operas than from literature. This teacher regards the viewing of soaps as a "fashion that spreads like a new style of clothing," which acts as a "pollutant of the intellectual environment."

Speaking of the effects of soap opera viewing on students, the English teacher asserts, "It makes their brains soggy—the soap opera doesn't challenge their thinking." The teacher also views this "indulgence" as a waste of time. He agrees that we all need occasional retreats from routine and responsibility, but suggests that a carefully planned regimen of intellectual exercise is sometimes better than this type of indulgence.

Adapted from an article in the Scarsdale H.S. *Maroon*, with permission of the editor.

1. The writer of this article is

   A. objective
   B. approving
   C. judgmental
   D. disapproving

2. The phenomenon of soap opera addiction should be of scientific interest to
   I. psychologists
   II. sociologists
   III. English teachers
   IV. historians

   F. I only
   G. I and II
   H. I, II, and III
   J. I, II, III, and IV

3. Addiction to soap operas among teenagers is mostly

   A. an emotional outlet
   B. a social outlet
   C. an intellectual exercise
   D. a new fad

4. An example of rationalization in this article is the statement

   F. "I love to see people with so many problems!"
   G. "It isn't nice to gossip about people you know, but it is socially acceptable to talk about the characters in the soaps."
   H. "All you hear girls talking about nowadays are soap operas—they watch all of them."
   J. ". . . students used more examples from soap operas than from literature."

5. If one could claim that watching soaps is governed by an *instinct,* that *instinct* would be

   A. inertia—the instinctive need to sit and do nothing
   B. sexual—sublimation of this instinct into vicarious stimulation through the soap opera characters
   C. social—the instinct to conform and to belong to the *in group*
   D. mental stimulation—the instinctive need to have something to think about

6. Objections to habitual watching of soap operas include the
   I. narcotic effect on the mind
   II. heavy emotional content
   III. time wasted
   IV. gossip engendered

   F. I and III
   G. II and IV
   H. I, II, and IV
   J. I, II, and III

7. Soap operas are so named because

   A. they serve as emotional catharsis or cleansing
   B. the situations portrayed are contrived and "frothy"
   C. they were once watched mainly by housewives as a respite from cleaning house
   D. they are traditionally sponsored by soap companies

8. The English teacher feels that

   F. it is good that students are able to use examples from soap operas in their written work
   G. studying the soaps is a good intellectual exercise
   H. there are better forms of recreation
   J. the latest fads in clothing are disgraceful

"Each State shall appoint, in such Manner as the Legislature thereof may direct, a Number of Electors, equal to the whole Number of Senators and Representatives to which the State may be entitled in the Congress; but no Senator or Representative, or Person holding an Office of Trust or Profit under the United States, shall be appointed an Elector.

"The Electors shall meet in their respective States, and vote by Ballot for two Persons, of whom one at least shall not be an inhabitant of the same State with themselves. And they shall make a List of all the Persons voted for, and of the Number of Votes for each; which List they shall sign and certify, and transmit sealed to the Seat of the Government of the United States, directed to the President of the Senate. The President of the Senate shall, in the Presence of the Senate and House of Representatives, open all the Certificates, and the Votes shall then be counted. The Person having the greatest Number of Votes shall be the President, if such Number be a Majority of the whole Number of Electors appointed; and if there be more than one who have such Majority, and have an equal Number of Votes, then the House of Representatives shall immediately chuse by Ballot one of them for President; and if no person have a Majority, then from the five highest on the List the said House shall in like manner chuse the President. But in chusing the President, the Votes shall be taken by States, the Representation from each State having one Vote; A quorum for this Purpose shall consist of a Member or Members from two thirds of the States, and a Majority of the States shall be necessary to a Choice. In every Case, after the Choice of the President, the Person having the greatest Number of Votes of the Electors shall be the Vice President. But if there should remain two or more who have equal Votes, the Senate shall chuse from them by Ballot the Vice President.

"The Congress may determine the Time of chusing the Electors, and the Day on which they shall give their Votes; which Day shall be the same throughout the United States."

9. The people who actually elect the President are known as the

A. electorate
B. Congress
C. majority
D. electors

10. If a state has 27 members in the House of Representatives, its total number of electoral votes would be

F. 27
G. 29
H. 54
J. dependent on the number of people who voted in the state

11. The person responsible for opening the electoral ballots is the

A. President of the Congress
B. Vice President of the United States
C. majority leader of the House
D. Chairman of the election committee

12. Of the following, which one could qualify as an elector?

F. A United States Senator
G. The Secretary of State of the U.S.
H. The Governor of N.Y. State
J. The Vice President of the U.S.

13. If a presidential candidate receives 45 percent of the popular vote

A. he cannot become the next President
B. he may still win the election
C. he will receive 45 percent of the electoral vote
D. his election would be dependent on the Senate

14. The votes of the electors must be sent to

F. Washington, D.C.
G. the state capitols
H. the headquarters of the leading candidates
J. the Republican and Democratic party chairmen

15. People who consider this plan "undemocratic" would rather see the President elected by

A. the electoral college
B. Congress
C. popular vote
D. written ballot

16. According to the electoral system, the number of people who may be nominated to become President

F. allows for only a two-party system
G. is limited to three people

H. is limited to the candidates of majority parties
J. is not limited to a set number

17. At no time in the history of the United States have we had a President and a Vice President from the same state. This is because

A. talent is naturally geographically distributed, so the best-qualified persons are never from the same state
B. the nominating conventions hope that people will vote for a candidate from their own state; therefore they nominate candidates from more than one state
C. it is unconstitutional for both President and Vice President to come from the same state
D. some electors would be disenfranchised if presidential and vice-presidential candidates were from the same state

18. The document here quoted is, of course, the United States Constitution (Article II, Section 1). The Twelfth Amendment has altered the prescribed method for choosing the Vice President. The purpose of the change was to

F. allow the President to choose his own Vice President
G. permit voting for a "ticket"
H. avoid the too likely possibility that the President and Vice President might be of opposing parties and politically incompatible
J. allow the Vice President to come from the same state as the President

19. The framers of the Constitution were intelligent men with great vision, but their education left them poorly prepared in

I. spelling
II. capitalization and punctuation
III. mathematics

A. none of these
B. I and II
C. III
D. I, II, and III

20. According to the Constitution, if the Electors fail to elect a President, the House of Representatives must do so

F. at the time the ballots are counted
G. on a date set by mutual agreement of both houses
H. by March 4
J. by January 20

21. The Electoral College is

A. in Washington, D.C.
B. a creation of the press
C. a fictional body
D. a semantic term

22. The Constitution provides that the electors be

F. appointed by the Legislature of each state
G. appointed by the congressional delegation of each state
H. elected by the people of each state
J. appointed according to the directions of each state legislature

SPEAKER NUMBER ONE

Many schemes have been devised to strengthen our economy and raise our standard of living. The irony of the situation is that nothing needs to be done. The best method of improving our economy is to rely on human instinct: on the ability of people to pay to have their own wants satisfied and to profit from satisfying the wants of others. The Constitution guarantees the pursuit of happiness, but many of the collectivist schemes try to guarantee happiness itself by the use of handouts. We do not need a super-government dictating what both management and labor need to do to be productive.

If we go back to the old-fashioned competition upon which the country has prospered we will find that the cost of government will drop and we can lower taxes. This will increase the amount of money available for investment and production.

The increase in activity is what our economy needs to prosper and give all our people a chance to strive for happiness.

SPEAKER NUMBER TWO

We all agree that it is important to improve our economy and to end the social and economic crises resulting from a faltering economy. Past experience has shown that unless definite controls are placed upon concentrations of economic power the economy will not properly regulate itself. We must not allow monopolies to destroy the freedom of the marketplace. We must protect the purchasing power of our senior citizens through continuation of social security programs. We must control the flow of currency through the use of a graduated income tax. In short, we must use those tools which the science of economics has developed to control our own economy. Only in that way will everyone be able to share in its growth.

23. What is the most basic difference between the two points of view presented here?

- **A.** whether or not our economy should be made stronger
- **B.** how much government control should be used in our economic system
- **C.** whether or not we should have competition in our economy
- **D.** the place of democracy in our economic system

24. How would Speaker Number One feel about strengthening the Sherman Anti-Trust Act? The speaker would

- **F.** like it because it strengthens competition
- **G.** agree only if it proved to be constitutional
- **H.** oppose it as unnecessary government interference
- **J.** oppose it because he feels it is undemocratic

25. How would Speaker Number One feel about strikes which bring industry to a halt?

- **A.** The speaker would want them settled through government-sponsored mediation
- **B.** The speaker would feel strikes should not be allowed if they interrupt our economy
- **C.** Strikes are a natural way for differences to be worked out between labor and management
- **D.** Strikes are the result of large companies' refusing to treat their workers fairly

26. Which of the following taxes would Speaker Number Two most likely oppose? A/An

- **F.** Corporate Tax
- **G.** Inheritance Tax
- **H.** Income Tax
- **J.** Sales Tax

27. The more complex our economy becomes, the more necessary government controls become.

- **A.** both speakers would agree
- **B.** neither speaker would agree
- **C.** only Speaker Number One would agree
- **D.** only Speaker Number Two would agree

28. The philosophy espoused by Speaker Number One is

- **F.** laissez-faire
- **G.** protectionism
- **H.** patriotism
- **J.** democracy

29. Ups and downs in business cycles are not desirable.

- **A.** both speakers would agree
- **B.** neither speaker would agree
- **C.** only Speaker Number One would agree
- **D.** only Speaker Number Two would agree

30. On the basis of the stated views, we may assume that Speaker Number One would be opposed to the

I. OSHA
II. CIA

III. FHA
IV. FDIC

F. I and III
G. II and IV
H. I, III, and IV
J. none of these

31. On the basis of the stated views, we may assume that Speaker Number Two would be opposed to the
I. OSHA
II. CIA
III. FHA
IV. FDIC

A. I and III
B. II and IV
C. I, III, and IV
D. none of these

DIRECTIONS: The following group of questions is not based upon a reading passage. Choose the *best* answer to each question in accordance with your background and understanding in the social studies.

32. The Northwest Ordinance of 1787 provided for the

F. admission of new states to the Union as equals to the original states
G. admission of new states to the Union with popular sovereignty on slavery
H. creation of self-governing territories independent of Congress
J. creation of new states governed by Congressional Committees

33. The 3/5 Compromise at the Constitutional Convention of 1787 provided that

A. for purposes of representation and taxation, the votes of three free men were equal to those of five slaves
B. for purposes of representation and taxation, five slaves would be counted as three free persons
C. the votes of 3/5 of the slave-holding states would be needed to pass any legislation affecting slavery
D. the votes of 3/5 of the southern states would be needed to pass any legislation affecting representation or taxation

34. One reason why the United States declared war on England rather than on France in 1812 was that

F. Napoleon had respected American rights as neutrals
G. New England shipowners and merchants had clamored for war with England
H. western expansionists in Congress wished to annex Canada
J. the French had great naval power in the Caribbean

35. The following problems were all common to the post-war settlements of both World War I and World War II *except*

A. the Italo-Yugoslav boundary
B. the Polish boundaries
C. Russian intransigence at post-war conferences
D. reparations from the defeated countries

36. Of the following, which one constitutes an implicit cost to a firm?

F. payments made on leased equipment
G. taxes paid to a local municipality for real estate
H. salaries paid to its legal consultants
J. depreciation of company-owned equipment

37. Most members of delinquent juvenile gangs are

A. mentally retarded
B. psychopaths
C. paranoid
D. normal except for their delinquency

38. The independent territory of Texas was annexed in 1845 by

F. executive order
G. a joint resolution of Congress
H. a formal treaty between the United States and Texas
J. the Treaty of Guadalupe Hidalgo

39. Which of the following statements most accurately describes Union policy toward black troops?

A. former slaves were not permitted to serve in the Union Army
B. former slaves were allowed to join the Union Army but were not permitted to become officers
C. the 13th Amendment guaranteed blacks admission into the Union Army
D. 170,000 black troops served in the Union Army after the first combat year

40. Immigrants in the late nineteenth century established their own self-help organizations in the form of

F. settlement houses
G. political parties
H. burial and insurance societies
J. public schools

41. The Supreme Court decided that separate facilities for blacks were legally equal to those provided for whites in

A. *Brown* v. *Board of Education*
B. *Muller* v. *Oregon*
C. *Plessy* v. *Ferguson*
D. *Gibbons* v. *Ogden*

42. Which one of the following was *not* a cause of controversy between the United States and England in the period immediately following the Treaty of Paris of 1783?

F. debts owed to English merchants
G. the impressment of American seamen
H. the treatment of Loyalists
J. the northern boundary of the new nation

43. Which one of the following was *not* a cause for rivalry between England and the Netherlands in the 17th century?

A. competition for fisheries in the North Sea
B. rivalry for commercial posts in the East Indies
C. control of settlements in America
D. antagonism arising from religious differences

44. The League of Nations was established in 1919 by

F. the "Fourteen Points"
G. a joint vote of Congress
H. the Versailles Treaty
J. the recommendation of the Senate Foreign Relations Committee

The development of voting laws in England is important to us because they were the basis of voting laws in colonial America. As England began to change from an agricultural country to an industrial country, the absolute power of the King began to dissolve. Those who began to have economic power also began to have political power. This political power was recognized by the English "Bill of Rights" passed in 1689. In order that this power would not become further diluted, early English voting laws were based on requirements of land ownership and formal education.

While these same restrictions were followed in colonial America, the effect was different. In England the poor could not own land, but in America land could be acquired by simply clearing and working it. This new political power, coupled with independent economic power, resulted in a new kind of democracy which eventually led to the Declaration of Independence and the U.S. Constitution.

45. The main purpose of this article is to

A. describe the parliamentary law of 1689
B. show why voting laws are necessary
C. explain the voting laws of England
D. explain the background of voting laws in America

46. What does the author cite as an important factor in the changes in voting laws?

F. changes in economic situations
G. colonization
H. modern ideas of government
J. the growth of world population

47. Which one of the following is the best example of the economic power mentioned in this article? The ability to

A. buy land
B. pay the costs of government
C. bribe public officials
D. buy votes

48. Judging from this passage, which one of the following qualifications probably became the most important factor in voting as a result of the 1689 "Bill of Rights"?

F. religion
G. money
H. education
J. ancestry

49. The first people allowed to vote in England probably gained this right as the result of

A. religion
B. money
C. education
D. ancestry

50. The purpose of the "Bill of Rights" of 1689 was to

F. furnish a pattern for colonial America
G. outlaw tyranny of any kind
H. guard the voting rights of all citizens
J. formalize the sharing of political power

51. What would be the most likely reason for the King of England's signing the 1689 "Bill of Rights"? He

A. received a great deal of money for doing so
B. was forced to sign in order to retain his position
C. wanted to share his responsibilities
D. felt democracy was the best form of government

52. The United States Bill of Rights

F. is patterned closely on the English "Bill of Rights"
G. was passed shortly after the "English Bill of Rights"
H. completely rejects the English "Bill of Rights"
J. is unrelated to the "English Bill of Rights"

END OF TEST

If you complete this test before the time limit is up, check back over the questions on this test only. Do not go back to any previous tests. Do not proceed to the next test until you are told to do so.

TEST 4
NATURAL SCIENCE READING

35 Minutes—52 Questions

DIRECTIONS: Below each of the following reading passages is a series of questions. Choose the *best* answer to each question, interpreting what is stated or implied by the passage in the light of your own background in the subject. You may refer back to the passage as often as necessary, though the answers to some questions may not be found expressly in the passage.

An action of apparent social significance among animals is that of migration. But several different factors are at work causing such migrations. These may be concerned with food-getting, with temperature, salinity, pressure and light changes, with the action of sex hormones and probably other combinations of these factors.

The great aggregations of small crustaceans, such as copepods found at the surface of the ocean, swarms of insects about a light, or the masses of unicellular organisms making up a part of the plankton in the lakes and oceans, are all examples of nonsocial aggregations of organisms brought together because of the presence or absence of certain factors in their environment, such as air currents, water currents, food or the lack of it, oxygen or carbon dioxide, or some other contributing causes.

Insects make long migrations, most of which seem due to the urge for food. The migrations of the locust, both in this country and elsewhere, are well known. While fish, such as salmon, return to the same stream where they grew up, such return migrations are rare in insects, the only known instance being in the monarch butterfly. This is apparently due to the fact that it is long-lived and has the power of strong flight. The mass migrations of the Rocky Mountain and the African species of locust seem attributable to the need for food. Locusts live, eat, sun themselves and migrate in groups. It has been suggested that their social life is in response to the two fundamental instincts, aggregation and imitation.

Migrations of fish have been studied carefully by many investigators. Typically, the migrations are from deep to shallow waters, as in the herring, mackerel and many other marine fish. Fresh-water fish in general exhibit this type of migration in the spawning season. Spawning habits of many fish show a change in habitat from salt to fresh water. Among these are the shad, salmon, alewife and others. In the North American and European eels, long migrations take place at the breeding season. All these migrations are obviously not brought about by a quest for food, for the salmon and many other fish feed only sparingly during the spawning season, but are undoubtedly brought about by metabolic changes in the animal initiated by the interaction of sex hormones. If this thesis holds, then here is the beginning of social life.

Bird migrations have long been a matter of study. The reasons for the migration of the golden plover from the Arctic regions to the tip of South America and return in a single year are not fully explainable. Several theories have been advanced, although none have been fully proved. The reproductive "instinct," food scarcity, temperature and light changes, the metabolic changes brought about by the activity of the sex hormones and the length of the day, all have been suggested, and ultimately several may prove to be factors. Aside from other findings, it is interesting to note that bird migrations take place year after year on about the same dates. Recent studies in the biochemistry of metabolism, showing that there is a seasonal cycle in the blood sugar that has a definite relation to activity and food, seem to be among the most promising leads.

In mammals the seasonal migrations that take place, such as those of the deer, which travel from the high mountains in summer to the valleys in the winter, or the migration of the caribou in the northern areas of Canada, are based on the factor of temperature which regulates the food supply. A real mystery is the migration of the lemming, a small ratlike animal found in Scandinavia and Canada. The lemming population varies greatly from year to year, and, at times when it greatly increases, a migration occurs in which hordes of lemmings march across the country, swimming rivers and even plunging into the ocean if it bars their way. This again cannot be a purely social association of animals. The horde is usually made up entirely of males, as the females seldom migrate.

1. The migration of the lemmings cannot be considered as a simple instance of social association since

A. only males migrate
B. the migrants do not return
C. the migration appears to be purposeful
D. it occurs only when the community appears to be thriving

2. A characteristic of migration is the return of the migrants to their former home areas. This is, however, not true of

F. birds
G. insects
H. mammals
J. fish

3. The reproductive instinct is probably not a factor in the actual migration of

A. shad
B. lemming
C. golden plover
D. monarch butterfly

4. In paragraph 1, several probable factors causing migrations are given. None of these seems to explain the migrations of

F. lemming
G. caribou
H. salmon
J. locusts

5. The reasons for the migrations of birds may ultimately be determined by scientists working in the field of

A. population studies
B. ecology
C. metabolism chemistry
D. reproduction

6. According to the passage, the reproductive process seems to be the main factor in the migration of many

F. fish
G. mammals
H. insects
J. birds

7. Animals which migrate back and forth between the same general areas are

A. locusts and salmon
B. salmon and golden plover
C. golden plover and lemming
D. monarch butterfly and honey bee

8. One-way migrations are usually associated with animals that

F. make long migrations
G. are long-lived
H. have short lives
J. make short migrations

9. The main purpose of the passage is to

   A. show how a natural event effects change in different species
   B. present a new theory in regard to biological evolution
   C. describe a phenomenon that has not yet been satisfactorily explained
   D. show how species behave similarly under the same conditions

10. The migration of the lemmings into the sea is an example of

   F. survival of the fittest
   G. population control
   H. self-preservation
   J. natural selection

11. The migration of the nomadic Lapps of Norway is most similar to the migration of

   A. European eels
   B. locusts
   C. Norwegian lemmings
   D. caribou

12. The swallows return each year to the Mission of San Juan Capistrano on St. Joseph's Day because

   I. they are religious
   II. they are natural *hams* and know that there are throngs of tourists waiting for them
   III. this is the northern terminus of their migration
   IV. of a combination of factors

   F. I and III
   G. II, III, and IV
   H. III and IV
   J. I, II, III, and IV

A colored transparent object, such as a piece of red glass, transmits red light and absorbs all or most of the other colors that shine on it. But what about opaque (non-transparent) objects? Why is one piece of cloth red, for example, while another is blue? The answer is that we see only the light that is reflected from such an object. White light, which contains all colors, shines on our piece of cloth. The dye in the cloth is of such a nature that it pretty well absorbs all colors except red. The red is then reflected, and that is what we see. If some other color or combination of colors is reflected, then we may get any hue or tint. Incidentally, this gives us a hint as to why many fabrics seem to have one color under artificial light and another color in daylight. The artificial light is of a different composition from daylight, and therefore the amount of each color reflected is different.

Light from an incandescent lamp, for example, contains proportionately more red and yellow than does sunlight, and hence emphasizes the red and yellow hues, weakening the blues and violets by contrast. Strangely enough, though, yellow may appear quite white under an incandescent lamp. This comes about because our eyes, being accustomed to the yellowish light from the lamp, no longer distinguish the lamplight from the real white of sunlight. Therefore, a piece of yellow cloth or paper, reflecting all the colors contained in the lamplight, appears to be white.

13. If an object were manufactured so that all light rays that hit it were reflected away from it, the color of the object would be

   A. white
   B. black
   C. iridescent
   D. transparent

14. If an object absorbed all of the light that strikes it, the color of the object would be

   F. white
   G. black
   H. iridescent
   J. transparent

15. If an object were made in such a way that the light striking it was neither reflected nor absorbed, the object would be

A. white
B. black
C. translucent
D. transparent

16. If the light from a blue mercury lamp which contains no red light waves were to illuminate a pure red tie, the tie would appear to be

F. white
G. black
H. red
J. transparent

17. The author implies that for an object to be visible

A. all of the received light must be reflected
B. some of the received light must be reflected
C. some of the received light must be absorbed
D. some of the received light must pass through

18. The phenomenon of seeing an object as its usual color even though the color is distorted by artificial light is called

F. transformation
G. compensation
H. transmutation
J. assimilation

19. Artificial light
I. is different from sunlight
II. contains more red and yellow than sunlight
III. appears more like sunlight with a green shade
IV. makes glass transparent

A. I only
B. I and II
C. I, II, and III
D. I, II, III, and IV

DIRECTIONS: The following questions are not based upon a reading passage. Choose the *best* answer to each question on the basis of your scientific knowledge.

20. A crystal of anhydrous KNO_3 is made up of

F. atoms of potassium, nitrogen and three atoms of oxygen alternately spaced in the crystal
G. molecules of KNO_3
H. a geometrical pattern of potassium ions and nitrate ions in the crystal
J. potassium nitrate molecules alternately spaced with water molecules

21. The loss of a neutron from the nucleus of an atom

A. changes the chemical nature of the atom
B. changes a physical property of the atom
C. causes the subsequent loss of an electron
D. reduces the atomic number of the atom

22. The number of atoms in $(NH_4)_2CrO_4$ is

F. 10
G. 15
H. 3
J. 4

23. A block of mass *m* at the end of a string is whirled around in a vertical circle of radius *R*. Find the critical speed of the block at the top of its swing below which the string would become slack as the block reaches the top of its swing.

A. $(Rg)^{\frac{1}{2}}$
B. Rg
C. $(Rg)^2$
D. $\frac{R}{g}$

24. A cell part *not* containing any DNA is the

F. nucleolus
G. cell vacuole
H. spindle
J. mitochondrion

25. Two animals belong to the same species if they

   A. can live together in a similar environment
   B. can mate and produce fertile descendants
   C. show a very close resemblance
   D. come from a common ancestor

26. Which of the following is *not* a colloidal dispersion?

   F. mineral oil
   G. protoplasm
   H. paint
   J. muddy water

27. Seawater can be made suitable for drinking by

   A. coagulation
   B. chlorination
   C. distillation
   D. filtration

28. If 25 ml of an acid are needed to neutralize exactly 50 ml of a 0.2N solution of a base, the normality of the acid is

   F. 0.2
   G. 0.4
   H. 2.0
   J. 4.0

29. Which of the following does *not* belong with the others?

   A. bat
   B. whale
   C. horse
   D. alligator

30. A student in the laboratory tossed two pennies from a container 100 times and recorded these results: both heads, 25, one head and one tail, 47; both tails, 28. Which cross between plants would result in approximately the same ratio?

   F. Aa × AA
   G. Aa × Aa
   H. AA × aa
   J. Aa × aa

31. A girl examining her finger under a microscope could detect no epidermal cells because

   A. these cells are located under the skin
   B. the nail blocked her view
   C. each single cell is larger than the area of the microscope field
   D. a finger is about one-half inch thick

32. Of the following, the physical property *least* frequently used in chemistry instruction is

   F. taste
   G. odor
   H. solubility
   J. density

33. Sodium is placed on water. The gas given off

   A. supports combustion
   B. turns moist litmus red
   C. burns
   D. has an irritating odor

Sixty high school sophomores were recruited to assist in a learning experiment. Each subject was interviewed and was able to satisfy the experimenters that he or she had had no previous experience in the learning of nonsense syllables. The nonsense syllables were to be learned in pairs as MYP—BUB.

The subjects were divided into two types of learning groups. Groups I, II, and III were each handed a long sheet which contained all the pairs of syllables to be learned. In three separate rooms, under close supervision, the students were instructed to silently learn all the pairs. The proctor enforced the silence rule.

The subjects in Group I studied the list for a full hour. The subjects in Group II studied the list for a half hour, then engaged in conversation for a half hour. The subjects in Group III studied the list for ten minutes, then took ten minutes off, studied the list for ten more minutes, alternating study and rest periods of ten minutes for the hour.

Subjects in Groups IV, V, and VI learned the syllables in a very different manner. In three rooms (because of the time variations) they sat before a screen. The first member of a nonsense pair was flashed upon the screen, and all subjects read it aloud. Then the second syllable appeared on the screen with the first, and the subjects read both aloud, in unison.

Subjects in Group IV spent a full hour in this

fashion. Subjects in Group V learned the pairs for one half hour and were free to chat for the other half hour. Subjects in Group VI alternated ten minutes of learning with ten minutes of relaxation. There was a ten minute break after the hour in which coffee was served to all subjects.

For the test of learning, all subjects sat in the same room before the screen. The first member of each pair of nonsense syllables was flashed upon the screen, and the subjects were required to write on a piece of paper the second member of each pair.

The results were as follows:
Subjects in groups IV, V, and VI all learned better than any subject in groups I, II and III. The superiority of groups IV, V, and VI collectively was highly significant. Within each type of learning group, the group that alternated ten minute periods performed best, while the group which learned for one-half hour and talked for one-half hour turned in the poorest results.

In summary, in order of proficiency of learning the groups may be ranked: VI, IV, V, III, I, II.

34. The effects of forgetting were demonstrated by groups

F. II and III
G. V and VI
H. II and V
J. III and VI

35. The procedure followed with groups IV, V, and VI is called

A. active learning
B. visual learning
C. learning through audio-visual technique
D. passive learning

36. The ten minute break between learning and testing was offered to all subjects because

F. the groups learning for a full hour needed a break
G. the investigators were interested in the effects of coffee upon the learning process
H. all experiments have a ten minute break
J. the coffee was ready

37. The finding that groups III and VI learned better than groups I and IV, even though groups I and IV had a full hour of study as opposed to the total of one half hour for groups III and VI shows that

A. too much practice is harmful
B. people need practice in "not forgetting"
C. ten minutes is the maximum length of time in which people can concentrate
D. distributed practice is more effective than massed practice

38. The most important control in this experiment was

F. the use of nonsense syllables
G. giving everyone the same amount of time from the first exposure to the syllables until the test
H. correlating the learning times of groups IV, V, and VI with the learning times of groups I, II, and III
J. the serving of coffee

39. An important uncontrolled factor was

A. the possibility that some subjects might prefer tea
B. how loudly the subjects in groups IV, V, and VI pronounced the syllables
C. the possibility of subvocalization by subjects in groups I, II, and III
D. the intelligence of the subjects

40. The purpose of this experiment was to

I. determine the best way to teach nonsense syllables
II. find out which nonsense syllables are easiest to learn
III. discover the effects of massed versus distributed learning
IV. find out what kind of learning procedure is best

F. I and II
G. III and IV
H. I, III, and IV
J. II, III, and IV

41. If schools were to utilize the information presented by the superior learning of groups IV, V, and VI, they would

A. show more movies
B. offer regular coffee breaks
C. have teachers read aloud to the students
D. schedule more periods per student in the science labs

42. The results of this experiment imply that passive rote memorization of whole units is

F. good
G. bad
H. inefficient
J. totally useless

43. Occasional breaks from study

A. are good because they allow time to assimilate and integrate that which was learned
B. are bad because they give time to forget
C. are good because they give time to drink coffee, which is an aid to studying
D. are bad because they just waste valuable time

44. The student who takes these results seriously will

F. go to the movies the night before an exam
G. cram for the last 24 hours before an exam
H. study and review periodically throughout the term
J. read all materials aloud

Throughout the history of our planet, natural phenomena have played an important role in determining the contours of the earth, the distribution of the waters and the nature of life supported in the various regions.

Within known history, natural catastrophes have affected the lives of millions of people. Some of these catastrophes have caused widespread death and destruction. Others have forced us to alter our ways to conform to the demands of nature.

Despite all of our advanced technologies, we have not devised any method for reversal of natural phenomena. We cannot prevent or halt an earthquake or a volcanic eruption. We cannot cause rain to fall in a period of severe drought, nor cause the rain to stop when floods rampage over the land.

Since, much as we may try, we seem unable to alter natural phenomena, we have diverted our energies into learning to cope with them. These efforts have met with varying degrees of success. Irrigation systems have given relief in areas of consistent drought, but are of no use where sudden, unexpected drought strikes for a prolonged number of years. Hurricanes are predicted and tracked so that people in their paths may scurry to safety, but the hurricane may shift its path erratically and strike unprepared areas. Seismographic reports of suboceanic earth shifts may help to predict tsunamis, but the warning may come too late.

The recent eruption of Mount St. Helens in the state of Washington has led to renewed research into the nature of volcanos, the causes of their eruptions after hundreds of years of dormancy, and the possibilities of preventing such eruptions. Consideration has been given to procedures for rupturing the plugs in the throats of volcanos, thus relieving pressure before it builds to a violent explosion. Innovative scientists are also giving thought to the feasibility of opening volcanic arteries in the sides of such mountains, if those arteries can be identified, and allowing the lava to flow harmlessly down a predetermined path.

A more frightening outgrowth of our advanced technology is our ability to induce natural phenomena, not to simulate these events, but to actually create them. The building of dams with the subsequent creation of huge artificial lakes has caused earthquakes in Colorado, Africa and India. These earthquakes, in areas which had never before experienced such phenomena, were probably caused by the weight of water in areas unaccustomed to such weight. Man-made earthquakes are not necessarily insignificant tremors. The 1967 earthquake near the Koyna Dam in India killed 177 people.

Earthquakes have also been triggered by nuclear explosions, and by the drilling of very deep (two or more miles) wells and then pumping into them large quantities of water polluted with toxic wastes. The fact that pumping water deep into the earth can cause earthquakes has led scientists to explore the possibility of using carefully placed injections of water for earthquake control.

With our new technological capabilities, we have even created a geyser. In 1955, an operation in Oregon working for geothermal power bored through a layer of sand and brought up a jet of hot water. This geyser, named Crump Well, has continued to this date to spout a jet of water one hundred feet into the air precisely once every nine hours.

45. The natural phenomena which have determined the contours of the earth have included
I. movement of ice caps
II. travelling of continents
III. death of the dinosaurs
IV. erosion

A. I only
B. I and II
C. I, II, and IV
D. I, II, III, and IV

46. A tsunami is a/an

F. tidal wave
G. earthquake
H. typhoon
J. tornado

47. A seismograph measures

A. wind velocity
B. hurricane intensity
C. earth tremors
D. earth temperature

48. A major difference between a volcano and a geyser is that

F. the steam produced by a volcano is hotter
G. eruption of geysers is predictable and rhythmic
H. geysers are in uninhabited areas
J. volcanos are releases of built-up pressure

49. The eruption of a geyser consists of

A. distilled water
B. cool mineral water and spray
C. hot water and steam
D. water and pebbles

50. Earthquakes are caused by
I. artificial water pressure
II. water pollution
III. natural forces not completely understood
IV. volcanic eruptions

F. I and III
G. II and IV
H. I, II, and III
J. II, III, and IV

51. The tone of this article is

A. ebullient and optimistic
B. pessimistic
C. cautionary but optimistic
D. neutral

52. A tidal wave is

F. caused by action of the moon
G. very swift-moving
H. affected by the action of sun spots
J. usually caused by underwater nuclear explosions

END OF EXAM

If you complete this test before the time limit is up, check back over the questions on this test only. Do not return to any previous tests.

CORRECT ANSWERS
MODEL EXAM III

TEST 1. ENGLISH USAGE

1. A.	11. B.	21. C.	31. B.	40. J.	49. D.	58. J.	67. A.
2. F.	12. J.	22. J.	32. J.	41. C.	50. J.	59. A.	68. J.
3. D.	13. D.	23. D.	33. D.	42. J.	51. B.	60. H.	69. C.
4. H.	14. G.	24. J.	34. J.	43. D.	52. G.	61. D.	70. F.
5. B.	15. A.	25. B.	35. C.	44. G.	53. A.	62. G.	71. B.
6. J.	16. F.	26. F.	36. F.	45. A.	54. F.	63. C.	72. J.
7. D.	17. C.	27. C.	37. B.	46. F.	55. A.	64. G.	73. B.
8. G.	18. F.	28. J.	38. J.	47. A.	56. J.	65. D.	74. H.
9. C.	19. D.	29. B.	39. B.	48. F.	57. A.	66. J.	75. A.
10. H.	20. G.	30. H.					

TEST 2. MATHEMATICS USAGE

1. B.	6. H.	11. D.	16. K.	21. A.	26. K.	31. E.	36. J.
2. J.	7. D.	12. K.	17. D.	22. H.	27. B.	32. H.	37. A.
3. A.	8. H.	13. E.	18. F.	23. B.	28. J.	33. B.	38. G.
4. J.	9. E.	14. K.	19. B.	24. J.	29. A.	34. G.	39. C.
5. E.	10. H.	15. D.	20. J.	25. D.	30. F.	35. D.	40. F.

TEST 3. SOCIAL STUDIES READING

1. A.	8. H.	15. C.	22. J.	29. A.	35. C.	41. C.	47. A.
2. G.	9. D.	16. J.	23. B.	30. F.	36. J.	42. G.	48. G.
3. D.	10. G.	17. D.	24. H.	31. D.	37. D.	43. D.	49. D.
4. G.	11. B.	18. H.	25. C.	32. F.	38. G.	44. H.	50. J.
5. C.	12. H.	19. A.	26. J.	33. B.	39. D.	45. D.	51. B.
6. F.	13. B.	20. F.	27. D.	34. H.	40. H.	46. F.	52. J.
7. D.	14. F.	21. D.	28. F.				

TEST 4. NATURAL SCIENCE READING

1. C.	8. H.	15. C.	22. G.	29. D.	35. A.	41. D.	47. C.
2. G.	9. C.	16. G.	23. A.	30. G.	36. F.	42. H.	48. G.
3. B.	10. G.	17. A.	24. C.	31. D.	37. D.	43. A.	49. C.
4. F.	11. D.	18. G.	25. B.	32. F.	38. F.	44. H.	50. F.
5. C.	12. H.	19. A.	26. F.	33. C.	39. C.	45. C.	51. C.
6. F.	13. A.	20. H.	27. C.	34. H.	40. G.	46. F.	52. G.
7. B.	14. G.	21. B.	28. G.				

EXPLANATORY ANSWERS
MODEL EXAM III
TEST 1. ENGLISH USAGE

1. **A.** The idiom is correctly written. *Another* is always one word.

2. **F.** *Everyone* is singular; therefore the pronoun must be singular. Furthermore, none of the incorrect choices is a legitimate word.

3. **D.** Avoid use of the word *you* when not addressing a specific person or group of people.

4. **H.** As in question 3, avoid the use of *you*.

5. **B.** A question must end with a question mark.

6. **J.** Again, see question 3.

7. **D.** The sentence is incorrect as written because *careful* is an adjective and what is needed is an adverb to modify the verb *study*. Choices B. and C. are correct but awkward. Since studying implies care, no modifying adverb is required.

8. **G.** The possessive form of *it* is *its*. *It's* is the contraction for *it is*. *The English language* is singular.

9. **C.** The author is introducing a new idea, so a new paragraph is required.

10. **H.** *English* is the name of the language, so must be capitalized. There is no reason to capitalize the adjective *good*. Choice J. is verbose.

11. **B.** *This contention* is singular, so the singular verb *is* must be used. The correct contraction for *is not* is *isn't*.

12. **J.** *It* is an expletive (a pronoun subject with no antecedent). An expletive is always weak, but especially when it occurs in the middle of a sentence. Unless a sentence is compound, try to maintain the same subject throughout the sentence, as in J.

13. **D.** Because the passage continues from choice J. of question 12, the subject *he* has already been stated. *Correct* is an adjective and thus cannot modify the verb *speak*.

14. **G.** *Who* is the subject of the verb *to speak*. *Which* cannot apply to people.

15. **A.** The subject, *words and phrases,* is plural, requiring use of the plural verb *say*. *Who* cannot refer to things. *What* is not a relative pronoun.

16. **F.** *Than* is a pronoun expressing comparison. *Then* is an adverb expressing progression in time.

17. **C.** *Hard-to-understand* is a made-up adjective, and its parts must be connected by hyphens.

18. **F.** The author is speaking of his present state; he is not recounting a past event. The present perfect tense is the tense suited for the situation.

19. **D.** One does not publish one's own telephone number. *Listing* is a gerund and therefore acts as a noun and should be modified by the adjective *your*.

20. **G.** Normally an introductory prepositional phrase need not be separated by a comma unless it contains five or more words. In this sentence, however, *in other words* has a somewhat parenthetical sense and should be set off by a comma.

21. **C.** *Claim* is a clearer verb than the general *say*. A. and B. are extremely verbose.

22. **J.** is most succinct.

23. **D.** The additional expense is a result of the special record keeping and handling of requests, not vice-versa as implied in A. and B.

24. **J.** The phrase is referring to *an unpublished number* (see question 22 J). F. is incorrect because it does not maintain agreement in number. The pronoun in H. is an unwise choice, for the antecedent is too distant.

25. **B.** All other choices are verbose.

26. **F.** The term *percent* (also *per cent*) is derived from the Latin term *per centum*. Use of the Latin term is technically correct but is quite stilted in ordinary use. The percent sign is used only in technical writing.

27. **C.** Since calls are discrete events that can be counted, *fewer* is the correct adjective.

28. **J.** The phrase is unnecessary.

29. **B.** When two independent clauses are separated by a coordinating conjunction, the conjunction should be preceded by a comma. Setting off *therefore* with commas is optional.

30. **H.** See explanation for question 29.

31. **B.** A semicolon NEVER precedes a coordinating conjunction. A comma may not be followed by a capital letter (unless the word is a proper noun). A. is incorrect because a comma would be required before the coordinating conjunction. The strong statement may legitimately be punctuated with an exclamation point. The subsequent new sentence begins with a capital letter.

32. **J.** A written sentence should not end with a preposition.

33. **D.** Because the word *charge* is so far away, the antecedent of the pronoun is unclear; therefore repeat the noun. Unless the desired antecedent is the last noun stated, the best policy is usually to repeat the noun.

34. **J.** This answer requires looking ahead. The company "gets away with murder" in *spite* of the antitrust law, not because of it; therefore 35 C. is correct. In conjunction with 35 C., 34 J. is the only logical answer.

35. **C.** See question 34.

36. **F.** in question 35 we eliminated a time frame; therefore, use a simple present tense as in question 34.

37. **B.** *Lest* is the correct word in this construction.

38. **J.** *We consumers* is the subject of the verb *are. Us* can only be an object. *We, the consumer,* lacks agreement in number.

39. **B.** An introductory subordinate clause is followed by a comma.

40. **J.** The sentence must make sense.

41. **C.** *Better Business Bureau* is a singular noun and therefore the correct pronoun is *it.* Expletive construction as in B. should be avoided whenever possible.

42. **J.** F. and G. are unclear. *Against* is the wrong preposition.

43. **D.** All other choices have missing or misplaced apostrophes.

44. **G.** All other choices are verbose and awkward.

45. **A.** B. has a different meaning. C. and D. are grammatically incorrect.

46. **F.** One *brings* something *here*; one *takes* it *there. Bring* requires an indirect object or a word acting in that capacity.

47. **A.** C. and D. are not words. B. implies that *things* acquire their values from science.

48. **F.** *U.S.A.* is a correct abbreviation. *US* would require periods. If the name of the country is spelled out, all the major words must begin with capital letters.

49. **D.** *Our* is the possessive adjective form of *we.*

50. **J.** We have only one country and it is singular.

51. **B.** The two independent clauses must be separated by a semicolon. *They're* is the contraction for *they are.*

52. **G.** There is no reason for a possessive form. Citizenship is irrelevant in the context of the sentence.

53. **A.** All other choices would leave the main clause of the sentence without a verb.

54. **F.** There is no reason for a hyphen or for a capital *S.* The sea has no feelings, so cannot be bored.

55. **A.** There is no need for a hypen nor for a capital *V.* The apostrophe is unnecessary as *Mississippi valley* is an acceptable term.

56. **J.** *Wild* is an adjective modifying *birds.* The word *wildbird* does not exist.

57. **A.** If the birds were *never seen,* the author would not know about them. The phrase *never before captured* implies that they recently were.

58. **J.** The past tense of the verb *to bring* is *brought.*

59. **A.** the *Yankees* as a team were defeated, not any particular Yankee. The statement is not an exclamation.

60. **H.** The *Rangers* create double plays as a team. *Double play* is two words. A comma is needed before a coordinating conjunction separating complete clauses.

61. **D.** D. is more succinct than A. B. and C. change the meaning.

62. **G.** All other choices are incorrect because *style* does not *make plays.*

63. **C.** No punctuation is needed, but an adverb is.

64. **G.** The idiom is *as if.*

65. **D.** A statement contrary to fact (he was not using a broom) requires the subjunctive.

66. **J.** *Who* and *whom* refer only to people. *What* is not a relative pronoun.

67. **A.** *When* is a better word than *if* because it puts the sentence into a time frame. The word *and* provides necessary transition.

68. **J.** One *figures upon* an abacus or calculator. *Estimate* is the wrong word; if *Jones* strikes out, you are *sure of* the pitching strength.

69. **C.** The past tense of the verb *to find* is *found.* As the author is recounting a past incident, the past tense, not the present perfect, is correct.

70. **F.** The *team* is a collective noun taking the singular pronoun *it.* The possessive form of *it* is *its. It's* is the contraction for *it is.*

71. **B.** The *Rangers* are referred to as a group of individuals, so the correct pronoun is *their. There* refers to place.

72. **J.** The verb must be parallel. Since New York *had* a team last year, it *has* a team this year.

73. **B.** Eastern or Western Division refers to the American League and should therefore be placed directly after it.

74. **H.** The *team* is singular, thus *has.* F. constitutes use of a double negative. J. is verbose.

75. **A.** No punctuation is needed. *Its* is the possessive form of *it. It's* is the contraction for *it is.*

TEST 2. MATHEMATICS USAGE

1. **B.** $40\% = \frac{2}{5}$

   $\frac{2}{5} \times \frac{10}{7} = \frac{4}{7}$

2. **J.** 27 and 51 are each divisible by 3. 17 and 59 are prime numbers.

3. **A.** Angle DOC = 6 + x

   $$\begin{aligned} \text{Angle AOC} &= (6 + x) + x = 180 - 20 \\ 6 + 2x &= 160 \\ 2x &= 154 \\ x &= 77 \end{aligned}$$

4. **J.** Let C = the capacity in gallons.

   Then $\frac{1}{3}C + 3 = \frac{1}{2}C$

   Multiplying through by 6, we obtain

   $$\begin{aligned} 2C + 18 &= 3C \\ \text{or } C &= 18 \end{aligned}$$

5. **E.** $$\begin{aligned} \frac{91 + 88 + 86 + 78 + x}{5} &= 85 \\ 343 + x &= 425 \\ x &= 82 \end{aligned}$$

6. **H.** $12 \times .39 = 4.68$ inches; that is, between $4\frac{1}{2}$ and 5.

7. **D.**

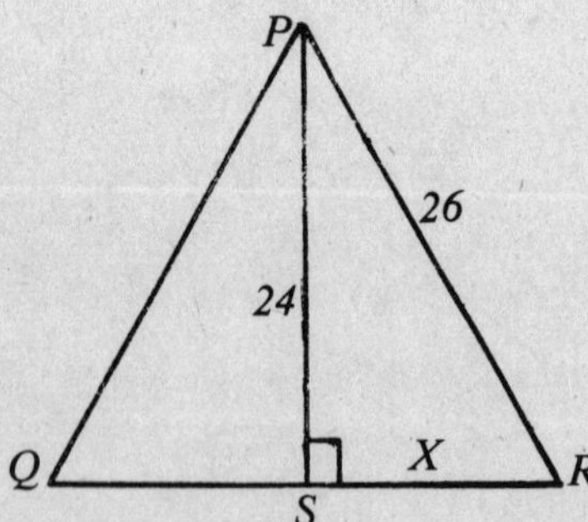

   In the figure above, PS⊥QR. Then, in right triangle PSR,

   $$\begin{aligned} x^2 + 24^2 &= 26^2 \\ x^2 &= 26^2 - 24^2 \\ &= (26 + 24)(26 - 24) \\ x^2 &= 50 \cdot 2 = 100 \\ x &= 10 \end{aligned}$$

   Thus, QR = 20

8. **H.** All terms involving x are 0.

   Hence, the equation reduces to

   $$\begin{aligned} 0 - 7y + 15 &= 0 \\ \text{or } 7y &= 15 \\ y &= 2\tfrac{1}{7} \end{aligned}$$

9. **E.** Let s = number of shirts and t = number of string ties, where s and t are integers.

   $$\begin{aligned} \text{Then } 7s + 3t &= 81 \\ 7s &= 81 - 3t \\ s &= \frac{81 - 3t}{7} \end{aligned}$$

   Since s is an integer, t must have an integral value such that 81 − 3t is divisible by 7. Trial shows that t = 6 is the smallest such number,

   making $s = \frac{81 - 18}{7} = \frac{63}{7} = 9$

   $$\begin{aligned} s : t &= 9 : 6 \\ &= 3 : 2 \end{aligned}$$

10. **H.** $\text{rate} = \frac{\text{distance}}{\text{time}} = \frac{\frac{2}{5}\text{ mile}}{\frac{5}{60}\text{ hour}} = \frac{\frac{2}{5}}{\frac{1}{12}}$

    $\text{rate} = \frac{2}{5} \cdot \frac{12}{1} = \frac{24}{5} = 4\frac{4}{5}$ miles per hour

11. **D.** Draw the altitudes indicated. A rectangle and two right triangles are produced. From the figure, the base of each triangle is 20 feet. By the Pythagorean theorem, the altitude is 15 feet. Hence, the area

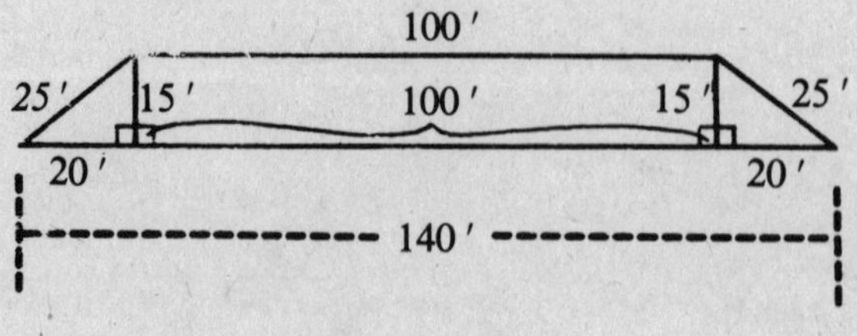

$$\begin{aligned} K &= \frac{1}{2} \cdot 15\,(100 + 140) \\ &= \frac{1}{2} \cdot 15 \cdot 240 \\ &= 15 \cdot 120 \\ &= 1800 \text{ square feet} \end{aligned}$$

12. **K.** If $1 + \frac{1}{t} = \frac{t+1}{1}$, then the right hand fraction can also be reduced to $1 + \frac{1}{t}$, and we have an identity, which is true for all values of t except 0.

13. **E.** All points 6 inches from A are on a circle of radius 6 with the center at A. All points 1 inch from b are on 2 straight lines parallel to b and 1 inch from it on each side. These two parallel lines intersect the circle in 4 points.

14. **K.** Let R = 5P and S = 5Q where P and Q are integers.
Then $R - S = 5P - 5Q = 5(P - Q)$ is divisible by 5
$RS = 5P \cdot 5Q = 25PG$ is divisible by 25
$R + S = 5P + 5Q = 5(P + Q)$ is divisible by 5
$R^2 + S^2 = 25P^2 + 25Q^2 = 25(P^2 + Q^2)$ is divisible by 5
$R + S = 5P + 5Q = 5(P + Q)$, which is not necessarily divisible by 10

15. **D.** $\frac{1}{2} \cdot 7 \cdot h = \pi \cdot 7^2$
Dividing both sides by 7, we get
$\frac{1}{2}h = 7\pi$
or $h = 14\pi$

16. **K.** $\frac{9}{13} = \overline{)9.00}$ = .69

$$\begin{array}{r} .69 \\ 13\overline{)9.00} \\ \underline{78} \\ 120 \\ \underline{117} \end{array}$$

$$\frac{13}{9} = \begin{array}{r} 1.44 \\ \overline{)13.00} \\ \underline{9} \\ 40 \\ \underline{36} \\ 40 \\ \underline{36} \end{array}$$

70% = .7

$$\frac{1}{.70} = \frac{1}{\frac{7}{10}} = \frac{10}{7} \begin{array}{r} 1.42 \\ \overline{)10.00} \\ \underline{7} \\ 30 \\ \underline{28} \\ 20 \end{array}$$

Correct order is $\frac{9}{13}$, 70%, $\frac{L}{.70}$, $\frac{13}{9}$
or I, III, IV, II.

17. **D.**

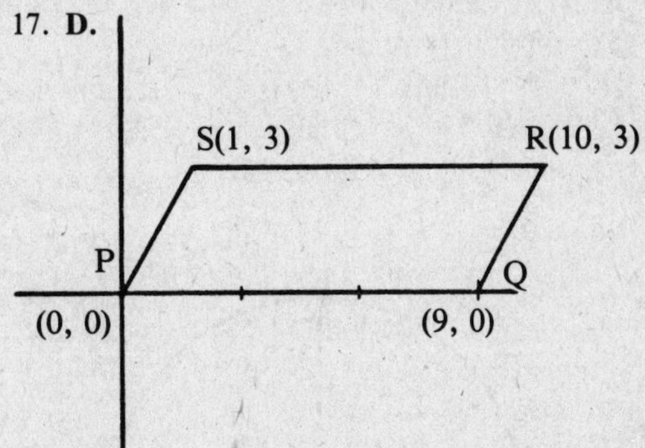

Since PQ and RS are parallel and equal, the figure is a parallelogram of base = 9 and height = 3. Hence, area $= 9 \cdot 3 = 27$

18. **F.**

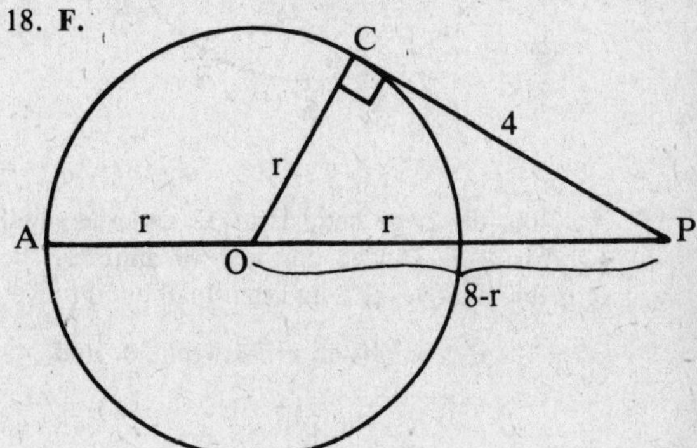

From the figure, in right △ PCO,
$PO^2 = r^2 + 4^2$
$(8 - r)^2 = r^2 + 16$
$64 - 16r + r^2 = r^2 + 16$
$48 = 16r$
$r = 3$
$6 = \text{Diameter}$

19. **B.** Area of wall $= 4 \cdot \frac{60}{3} = 4 \cdot 20 = 80$ sq. yd.
Cost $= 80 \times \$10.50 = \$840.00$

20. **J.** Distance of (4, 4) from origin =
$\sqrt{16 + 16} = \sqrt{32} < 7$
Distance of (5, 5) from origin =
$\sqrt{25 + 25} = \sqrt{50} > 7$
Distance of (4, 5) from origin =
$\sqrt{16 + 25} = \sqrt{41} < 7$
Distance of (4, 6) from origin =
$\sqrt{16 + 36} = \sqrt{52} > 7$
Hence, only II and IV are outside circle.

21. **A.** Let x = the cost.

Then $x + \frac{1}{4}x = 80$

$4x + x = 320$

$5x = 320$

$= \$64$ (cost)

$\frac{\text{Cost}}{\text{S.P.}} = \frac{64}{80}$

$= \frac{4}{5}$

22. **H.**

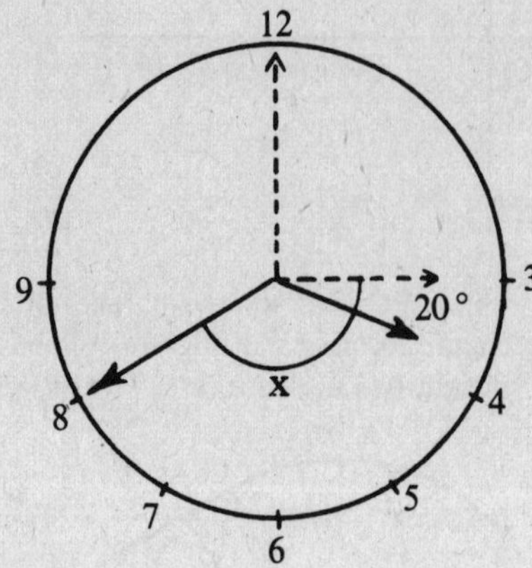

At 3:00, the large hand is at 12 and the small hand is at 3. During the next 40 minutes, the large hand moves to 8 and the small hand moves $\frac{40}{60} = \frac{2}{3}$ of the distance between 3 and 4; $\frac{2}{3} \times 30° = 20°$. Since there are 30° between two numbers of a clock $\measuredangle x = 5(30°) - 20° = 150° - 20° = 130°$.

23. **B.** Area of sector $= \frac{120}{360} \cdot \pi \cdot 15^2$

$= \frac{1}{3} \cdot \pi \cdot 15 \cdot 15$

$= 75\pi$

24. **J.** $\frac{17}{10}y = 0.51$

Multiplying both sides by 10, we get

$17y = 5.1$

$y = .3$

25. **D.** $40\% = \frac{2}{5} \times 50 = 20$ girls attended

$50\% = \frac{1}{2} \times 70 = 35$ boys attended

Total attended = 55

$\frac{55}{50 + 70} = \frac{55}{120} =$

$\frac{11}{24}$ $\quad 11.000 \div 24 = .458 = 45.8\%$

```
     .458
24 )11.000
     96
     140
     120
      200
      192
```

26. **K.** Since $x + 2x + y = 180°$, it follows that

$3x + y = 180$

$y = 180 - 3x$

27. **B.** $\frac{18}{33} = \frac{6}{11}$.

$6^2 = 36$, $11^2 = 121$. Therefore

$\frac{\sqrt{6^2}}{\sqrt{11^2}} = \frac{\sqrt{36}}{\sqrt{121}}$

28. **J.** There are 20 numbers that contain 7 in the one's place. There are 20 more that contain 7 in the ten's place. Thus, there are 40 numbers with 7 in either the one's or ten's place. But the numbers 277 and 377 must be rejected, and they have each been counted twice. 40 − 4 = 36.

29. **A.** $(r + s)^2 - r^2 - s^2 =$

$r^2 + 2rs + s^2 - r^2 - s^2 =$

$2rs$

30. **F.** As Q moves from R to S, PQ gets smaller. Its largest possible value would be 9. Hence $9 \geq PQ \geq 6$

31. **E.** selling price per article $= \frac{K}{8}$

cost per article $= \frac{K}{12}$

profit per article $= \frac{K}{8} - \frac{K}{12} = \frac{3K - 2K}{24}$

$= \frac{K}{24}$

32. **H.** Analyze this by means of the diagram below

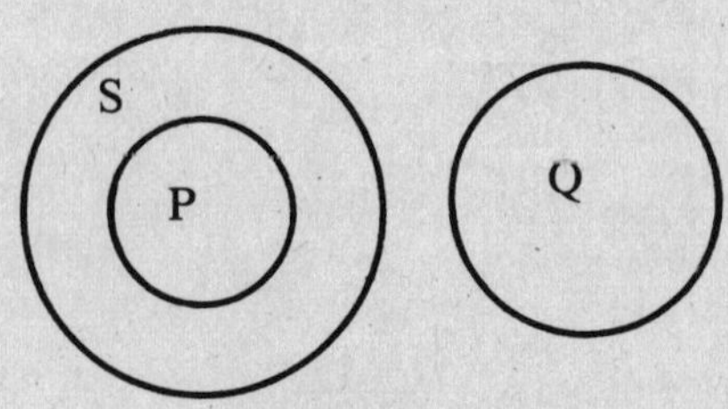

From the figure, we readily see that no P are Q.

33. **B.** The sum of the four numbers is 45 × 4 = 180.

For the average to remain the same, the sum must remain unchanged. If one number is increased by 6, then each of the other three must be reduced by 2.

34. **G.** The general term of this arithmetic progression is 3 + 9(n − 1) where n = 1, 2, 3, ... etc. Thus, any member must equal 3 + 9(n − 1) where n is an integer. Try A, B, C, D in turn. We see that, if 9 + 3(n − 1) = 10002

$$\begin{aligned} \text{Then } 3(n-1) &= 9993 \\ \text{and } n-1 &= 3331 \\ \text{or } n &= 3332 \end{aligned}$$

Thus, 10,002 will be a number.

35. **D.** The papers drawn will be numbered 4, 11, 18, 25, 32, 39. Number 39 will be the last.

36. **J.** Let the angles be 2x, 3x, and 5x

$$\begin{aligned} \text{Then } 2x + 3x + 5x &= 180^\circ \\ 10x &= 180^\circ \\ x &= 18 \end{aligned}$$

5x = 90° and the triangle is right.

37. **A.** The dimensions of the open box become:
length = 24 − 10 = 14 in.
width = 18 − 10 = 8 in.
height = 5 in.
Hence, V = 14 • 8 • 5 = 560 cu. in.

38. **G.** VT = 32 feet, so ST = $\frac{1}{2}$ VT = 16 feet.

Therefore, in right triangle QST, the legs are 12 and 16. Right triangles can be expressed in a 3-4-5 ratio. 12 = 4 • *3*, 16 = 4 • *4*, and therefore hypotenuse QT equals 4 • *5*, 20. Adding 1 foot for the over hang yields 21 feet.

39. **C.** Form the proportion

$$\frac{\frac{3}{4}}{9} = \frac{\frac{7}{8}}{x}, \text{ where x is the side in miles.}$$

Then $\frac{3}{4}x = \frac{7}{8} \cdot 9$. Multiply both sides by 8.

$$6x = 7 \cdot 9 = 63$$
$$x = 10\tfrac{1}{2} \text{ miles}$$
$$\text{Area} = x^2 = \frac{21}{2} \cdot \frac{21}{2} = \frac{441}{4} =$$
$$110\tfrac{1}{2} \text{ square miles}$$

40. **F.** Given V = fL, divide both sides by f.

$$L = \frac{V}{f}$$

TEST 3. SOCIAL STUDIES READING

1. **A.** The author of this article is stating both sides of a controversial matter in an objective manner.

2. **G.** While English teachers certainly notice the effects of television upon the reading habits and the thoughts of their students, the specific phenomenon of the soaps is not of scientific interest to them. Likewise, historians might take notice of the phenomenon, but not out of scientific interest. Sociologists would be interested in the nature of a society which produces this type of activity. Social psychologists would probe the needs served by collective watching of soap operas.

3. **D.** Again, since many reasons are given for watching soap operas, the one certain factor is that teenage fascination with the soaps is a new fad.

4. **G.** Rationalization is providing plausible, reasonable, but untrue reasons for one's behavior. It is unlikely that people watch soap operas so that they may avoid gossiping about each other.

5. **C.** This question takes liberties with the definition of *instinct.* The instinct served by the watching of soap operas is *aggregation,* the instinct to be part of the group.

6. **F.** The objections to *habitual* watching of soap operas center about the dulling effect on the mind and the wasted time which might be better spent on extra-curricular activities or individual mind-stretching occupations.

7. **D.** The first soap operas were on radio, sponsored by laundry products, and the name has come to be applied to all serialized melodramas.

8. **H.** The English teacher feels that relaxation and recreation are necessary, but there are more constructive outlets available than the mindless watching of soaps.

9. **D.** Actual election of the President is by the electors according to provision of the Constitution.

10. **G.** The Constitution provides that the total number of electors to which a state is entitled is the combined number of Representatives and Senators.

11. **B.** The Constitution provides that the ballots of the electors be opened by the President of the Senate. The Vice President of the United States is the President of the Senate.

12. **H.** The Constitution provides that ". . . no Senator or Representative, or Person holding an Office of Trust or Profit under the United States, shall be appointed an Elector." A state's governor is an official of that state only.

13. **B.** It is possible for the popular vote to be so distributed that a candidate might win the majority of the electoral votes while winning only 45 percent of the popular vote. This might happen if the candidate were to earn the electoral votes of some of the most populous states by very slim margins while losing many other states very decisively.

14. **F.** The Constitution requires that the ballots be sent to "the Seat of the Government of the United States." The seat of government is Washington, D.C.

15. **C.** There are people who consider the electoral system undemocratic, mainly because of the possibility of a *minority President,* that is, a President who was not chosen by a majority of the people. Electing the President by popular vote would eliminate this criticism.

16. **J.** The Constitution sets no limits on the number of candidates for the presidency, nor does it make any mention of political parties.

17. **D.** The Constitution provides that an elector must vote for at least one candidate from a state other than his own. If candidates for both President and Vice President were to come from the same state, the electors from that state would be disenfranchised, prohibited from voting for both of them. The Constitution does not actually prohibit one state from monopolizing the White House and, theoretically it might have happened before 1804, at which time President and Vice President were winner and runner-up rather than candidates for two positions. B. is also correct, but it is not the *best* answer.

18. **H.** The problems created by having President and Vice President of opposing parties and often in

philosophical disagreement on crucial issues led to the Twelfth Amendment. Under this Amendment, electors vote separately for a President and a Vice President and are expected to have the good sense to not put political rivals into office together. The Twelfth Amendment restates the requirement that an elector must vote for one candidate from a state other than his own.

19. **A.** The spelling, capitalization and punctuation of the Constitution were all correct at the time of writing (in 1787). The apparent anomaly of more than one person's having a majority of the vote is clarified when one remembers that the Constitution provides that each elector cast separate votes for two people. Since the passage of the Twelfth Amendment, which requires that each elector cast one vote for a President-Vice President slate, it is no longer possible for more than one candidate to win a majority of the votes.

20. **F.** ". . . then the House of Representatives shall immediately chuse by Ballot one of them for President." The implication is that this should be done at the time of the counting of the ballots.

21. **D.** The Electoral College is the semantic term referring to all of the electors in their role as electors.

22. **J.** The Constitution grants discretion to each state legislature to direct that electors be appointed according to rules of its own making.

23. **B.** The basic quarrel between these two speakers has to do with government control, the need for it or its excessive use with regard to our economy.

24. **H.** While Speaker Number One believes in free competition, his antipathy toward government interference is so great that he most certainly would be opposed to regulation of industry by the Sherman Anti-Trust Act. In fact, with his attitude that "business will do what is best," he would accept monopolies as being in the best interests of business.

25. **C.** While Speaker Number One would certainly not be happy with strikes which interfered with business, he would accept them as being part of the natural process and would oppose government efforts to settle them.

26. **J.** Speaker Number Two is concerned with the economic plight of the aged and the poor. The Sales Tax is a regressive tax in that it falls equally upon the poor and the rich, thus constituting a greater burden to the poor. Speaker Two specifically proposes the Income Tax, which ostensibly falls more heavily upon those more able to pay.

27. **D.** Speaker Two feels that government controls are necessary in a complex economy. Speaker One feels that government controls are never the answer.

28. **F.** Laissez-faire, a French term meaning "let the people do as they please," is a doctrine opposing government interference in economic affairs beyond the minimum necessary for maintaining property rights.

29. **A.** The speakers would not agree as to the means for avoiding swings in business cycles, but both would agree that ups and downs in the economy are not desirable.

30. **F.** OSHA (Occupational Safety and Health Administration) is responsible for the health and safety of workers on their jobs. The FHA (Federal Housing Administration) grants low-cost guaranteed mortgages to certain people who might otherwise be unable to purchase houses. Both of these agencies would represent government interference to Speaker Number One. There is no reason to assume that Speaker One would oppose the CIA (Central Intelligence Agency), an intelligence gathering agency, or the FDIC (Federal Deposit Insurance Corporation), which provides insurance for bank deposits in national and state banks that are members of the Federal Reserve system.

31. **D.** Speaker Number Two would consider both OSHA and the FHA to be useful, humanitarian organizations. There is no reason to believe that Speaker Two would oppose the security efforts of the CIA, or the insurance provided by the FDIC.

32. **F.** The Northwest Ordinance, passed by Congress in 1787, provided for the administration of United States territories in what is now the Midwest, and provided for the eventual creation by Congress of three to five states in this area; the new states were to be admitted to the Union as equals to the original states.

33. **B.** The 3/5 Compromise provided that five slaves would be considered equal to three white persons in determining the representation of the states in the House of Representatives and also for apportioning taxes. This compromise was a concession to the southern states.

34. **H.** In 1811–1812 a group of Congressmen representing the West gained control of the House of Representatives. Their two most important leaders were Henry Clay and John C. Calhoun. Clay and Calhoun advocated a war with England to have the opportunity to annex Canada.

35. **C.** Russia was not involved in post-World War I peace conferences.

36. **J.** Depreciation, while not a visible cost to a firm, must be written off during each fiscal period in order to record accurately the expense of capital deterioration. All the others are explicit, visible costs.

37. **D.** Delinquent gangs arise chiefly out of informal childhood play groups, following roughly the same dynamics that affect the development of non-delinquent gangs. The nature of a gang is determined by its leadership and is influenced by social and economic circumstances. Membership is based upon geographical contiguity rather than on shared abnormalities of the members.

38. **G.** Texas was annexed by a joint resolution of Congress in 1845, several days before President Tyler left office. The resolution was signed by President Polk in December 1845. The Treaty of Guadalupe Hidalgo ended the Mexican War, February 2, 1848.

39. **D.** From 1862 to 1865, 170,000 blacks served in the Union Army. Former slaves were not prevented from joining the army nor from entering combat. The 13th Amendment did not affect black troops during the Civil War since it did not come about until the war was over. During the first year of the war, the Union Army rejected black troops; Lincoln feared that the arming of blacks would not be well-received. Black soldiers were accepted in the army in 1862 and thereafter were formed into black regiments, generally led by white officers; blacks could and did, however, attain officer rank during the war.

40. **H.** Immigrants in urban areas organized burial and insurance societies. Public schools, political parties, and settlement houses were not self-help organizations initiated by immigrants themselves, but were institutions established by society.

41. **C.** The *Plessy* v. *Ferguson* decision of 1896 upheld a Louisiana statute to enforce racial segregation in railroad cars; the decision supported the "separate but equal" doctrine and encouraged further legislation to enforce segregation of blacks in public facilities. The court contended that the 14th Amendment was intended to enforce equality but not to abolish social distinctions. The case of *Brown* v. *Board of Education* in 1954 effectively reversed the decision in *Plessy* v. *Ferguson,* at least insofar as education is concerned, by declaring that separate is by its nature unequal. *Muller* v. *Oregon* was a case concerning the constitutionality of labor laws which apply solely to women. *Gibbons* v. *Ogden* was a case in interstate commerce regulation.

42. **G.** The United States and England continued to disagree about many issues even following the Treaty of Paris, but the impressment of American seamen was not one of those issues at that time. England began seizing American ships and impressing seamen into service of the Crown during the Napoleanic Wars, at which time England hoped to suppress American trade with France.

43. **D.** England and the Netherlands were both Protestant nations, hence religious differences never presented a problem. The two seafaring nations were rivals in all areas concerning fishing, trade and colonialism.

44. **H.** The League of Nations was established in 1919 under the terms of the Versailles Treaty. The formula for the League had first been presented by President Wilson in his "Fourteen Points" speech before Congress in 1918. The Treaty and American membership in the League of Nations were defeated by the Senate in 1919 and 1920, much to the chagrin of President Wilson.

45. **D.** The first sentence states the theme and purpose of the passage. English voting laws were the basis for American voting laws.

46. **F.** Loss of power by the King led to increased power in the hands of the people, initially the landed gentry. The shift from an agricultural, somewhat feudal, economy to an industrial economy caused further change in the seat of power.

47. **A.** In England land ownership was prerequisite to political power. All land not inherited could be obtained only through purchase, thus economic means led to political power.

48. **G.** With industrialization the economy ceased being based upon exchange of goods and services and became instead based upon money. It was money that enabled citizens to buy the land and obtain the education necessary for acquiring voting rights as defined in the 1689 bill.

49. **D.** Prior to industrialization and the money economy, land ownership was strictly hereditary.

50. **J.** The 1689 English "Bill of Rights" was passed just as the King began to lose his absolute power. Without an orderly means for distributing this power, anarchy might have prevailed. Further, this Bill was still highly restrictive, granting some share of power to only a privileged few. By signing the Bill, the King hoped to maintain control and keep dilution of royal power to a minimum.

51. **B.** It seems unlikely that the King willingly gave up his absolute power. Undoubtedly he signed in order to maintain his throne and to limit the extent of the power he would relinquish.

52. **J.** The United States Bill of Rights (the first ten amendments to the Constitution) is in no way related to the English "Bill of Rights." The United States document makes no mention of qualifications for voting. Rather, it sets forth specific rights and privileges offered to American citizens and to the individual states.

TEST 4. NATURAL SCIENCE READING

1. **C.** The migration of the lemmings appears to be purposeful. It consists of a relentless drive to the sea and an apparent urge to commit suicide. Many animals do form social groups of males from time to time, but these males do not permanently absent themselves from the company of females.

2. **G.** The passage tells us that return migrations of insects are unknown, with the outstanding exception of the monarch butterfly.

3. **B.** While the full influence of the reproductive instinct upon migration is not fully understood in most animals, it clearly is not a factor in the one-way migration of male lemmings. If anything, the factor operative with the lemmings is a self-destructive instinct.

4. **F.** The migrations of caribou and locusts are motivated by the desire for better living conditions, specifically to search for food. Migration of salmon has to do with reproductive needs. None of the reasons suggested in the first paragraph seems to account for the behavior of lemmings.

5. **C.** "Recent studies in the biochemistry of metabolism, showing that there is a seasonal cycle in the blood sugar (of birds) that has a definite relation to activity and food, seems to be among the most promising leads."

6. **F.** The fourth paragraph explains the reproduction-linked migration of fish.

7. **B.** Salmon live in the ocean, but at spawning time travel upstream to the fresh water rivers in which they were born. Golden plovers make an annual round trip between the Arctic and the tip of South America. Locusts, lemmings and honey bees are all one-way migrants.

8. **H.** The passage tells us that return migrations in insects are rare. The exception to this generalization is the monarch butterfly, which is long-lived. The implication is that those animals that do not return migrate are short-lived.

9. **C.** The purpose of this passage is to discuss migration and its various possible causes. The known facts are presented and various theories posited, with many questions raised but not answered.

10. **G.** Since the migration of the lemmings occurs only in years when the population is very great, the migration of the adult males is evidently a means for reducing the size of the population, immediately and for the near future as well. This act could hardly be considered self-preservation, for the migrants perish, but controlling the population by this means is a form of species-preservation, for if the population were to grow unchecked, the food supply might be exhausted and all would perish.

11. **D.** The migrations of the Lapps to the mountains in the summer and to the warmer valleys in the winter, are based upon temperature and the availability of food supply, as are the migrations of caribou. In fact, the caribou is part of the food supply which the Lapps are following.

12. **H.** San Juan Capistrano in southern California is the northern terminus of the swallows' migration. Their return there on the same date each year is governed by the same unknown factors that govern the very regular migrations of other birds —biochemistry, sex needs, length of days, etc.

13. **A.** White light contains rays of all colors. If all the light hitting a piece of cloth is reflected, then all the color rays will also be reflected. We will see all the color rays together as white.

14. **G.** We can see only colors whose rays are reflected; if no rays are reflected we can see only the absence of color, which is black.

15. **C.** The word *translucent* comes from the Latin and means *to shine through.* If light is neither absorbed nor reflected it must shine through. A translucent object may also be transparent, but light shining through does not automatically denote transparency. The object may diffuse the light which passes through so that objects beyond cannot be clearly distinguished.

16. **G.** If the tie, which reflects only red light, were to have no red light waves to reflect, it would absorb all other colors and appear to be black.

17. **A.** We see objects only by the light that is reflected by them. An object perceived as black reflects no colors, but still reflects some light.

18. **G.** Compensation is the process by which the eye and the brain accommodate for and neutralize the effects of artificial variations.

19. **A.** The only entirely true statement is that artificial light is different from sunlight. Incandescent light contains more red and yellow than sunlight, but other types of artificial light, fluorescent for example, do not. The transparency of glass has to do with its manufacture and with the way light is passed through the glass; it has nothing to do with the nature of the light that shines upon it.

20. **H.** Potassium nitrate is an ionic compound containing the potassium ion and the nitrate ion. In the solid state the ions are in a definite geometrical pattern forming the crystal.

21. **B.** The loss of a neutron from the nucleus of an atom will decrease its atomic weight by one. The weight of an atom is a physical property. The atomic number is not the same as the atomic weight; it is based upon the number of protons in the atom. The chemical nature of an atom is influenced by the number of electrons, not the number of neutrons.

22. **G.** $(NH_4)_2CrO_4$

N:	$2 \times 1 =$	2
H:	$2 \times 4 =$	8
Cr:		1
O:		4
		15

23. **A.** A critical speed would be that speed at which the centrifugal force is equal to the gravitational force exerted on the block.

$$\frac{mv^2}{R} = mg$$

$$v = \sqrt{Rg}$$

24. **G.** The cell vacuole is solely a storage compartment. A mitochondrion does contain a small amount of DNA.

25. **B.** Living things belonging to the same species exhibit the ability to mate with one another, producing fertile offspring. This definition is applicable to most members of the same species. However, due to geographical isolation, many organisms have evolved separate and distinct methods of reproduction which may prevent them from mating with their counterparts found in other areas or locations. This variation on the species level has resulted in the formation of sub-species.

26. **F.** A colloidal dispersion is composed of very small particles in a solvent. The solvent particles are larger than the molecular particles in a solution. Mineral oil is not a colloidal dispersion.

27. **C.** Distillation is the process of separating soluble salts from a liquid by evaporating the liquid and then condensing it. Since the salt in seawater is in solution, it cannot be removed by filtration. Chlorination might serve to counter bacterial impurities in seawater, but would not reduce salinity.

28. **G.** The volume of the acid times the normality of the acid is equal to the volume of the base times the normality of the base. $25(N) = (50)(.2)$ The normality of the acid $= 0.4$.

29. **D.** All choices except D. are members of the order *Mammalia*. The alligator is a reptile.

30. **G.** The results approximate a 1:2:1 ratio which illustrates the genotypic ratio of Mendel's law of segregation. Aa × Aa results in 25 percent AA, 50 percent Aa and 25 percent aa, the characteristic 1:2:1 ratio.

31. **D.** Any material undergoing microscopic examination must be thin enough to enable light rays to pass through and be deflected upward through the body tube into the eyepiece. The finger, because of its thickness, is opaque.

32. **F.** It is dangerous to taste an unknown substance; it may be poison.

33. **C.** When sodium reacts with water, the gas produced is hydrogen. Hydrogen gas burns.

34. **H.** Groups II and V had the same one-half hour of practice as groups III and VI, but they had it massed in the first half hour, followed by distracting idleness of long duration.

35. **A.** While the presentation of the material to the subjects in groups IV, V, and VI was audiovisual in nature, the actual learning procedure, the reading aloud of the syllables, was an instance of participatory or active learning.

36. **F.** The groups which had been learning for a full hour were tired, and the experimenters did not want their results to be contaminated by fatigue.

37. **D.** The most reasonable interpretation of these results is that distributed practice is more effective than massed practice.

38. **F.** The most important control in this experiment was the use of subject matter that was unfamiliar to all subjects. Students rapidly invent mnemonic devices and devise private methods of learning, so

that a true test of the efficacy of the two methods would have been impossible had students had previous experience with the type of material being learned.

39. **C.** In light of the superiority of groups IV, V, and VI, it is unlikely that subvocalization was an important factor in the learning of groups I, II, and III. Had it been a factor, it might have influenced the results in ways unknown to the investigators.

40. **G.** Nonsense syllables were the medium, not the object of this research. The investigators wanted to learn about the effects of massed and distributed practice and about the relative efficiency of private rote versus active learning.

41. **D.** Since active participation in the learning process seems to produce more efficient learning, it follows that there should be greater results from more work in the science labs.

42. **H.** One should not make a value judgment based on this experiment alone, but here active verbalization of the connection between two members of a pair produced more efficient learning than passive learning of the pair as a given unit.

43. **A.** Since the students who interrupted their study with short breaks performed best, we conclude that breaks are beneficial.

44. **H.** H. is analogous to the conditions of groups III and VI. G. is analogous to the experimental condition of groups I and IV. F. is analogous to the condition of groups II and V.

45. **C.** The death of the dinosaurs resulted from the same factors that determined the contours of the earth, namely changing temperatures, the movement of earth by ice caps, the rearrangement of land masses through the travel of continents, and to a lesser degree, erosion.

46. **F.** *Tsunami* is the Japanese word for tidal wave. A typhoon is a hurricane that takes place in the Orient.

47. **C.** A seismograph is an instrument that measures the intensity of earth tremors and earthquakes, expressed in degrees on the Richter scale.

48. **G.** Eruptions of volcanos and geysers are each produced by the build-up of pressure deep in the earth and the subsequent release of this very hot material through a relatively small opening. While geysers erupt on a predictable and rhythmic schedule, volcanos are erratic.

49. **C.** The eruption of a geyser releases hot water and steam.

50. **F.** Naturally occurring earthquakes are caused by natural forces which are under study but which are so far not well understood. Those earthquakes caused by humans have been caused by the pressure of huge artificial lakes and by the pumping of water into holes bored deep into the earth.

51. **C.** The author of this article appears wary lest we create major disasters with our new but uncontrolled technology. On the other hand, the author appears to be optimistic that with greater understanding of natural phenomena we may someday be able to control them and avert catastrophe.

52. **G.** A tidal wave, despite its name, has nothing to do with tides, hence is not under the control of the moon. A naturally occurring tidal wave is the result of suboceanic earthquakes or massive shifts in the ocean floor. It travels across oceans with extreme speed, inundating land masses in its path.

PART VI

MODEL EXAM IV

ANSWER SHEET—MODEL EXAM IV

ENGLISH USAGE

1 Ⓐ Ⓑ Ⓒ Ⓓ	12 Ⓕ Ⓖ Ⓗ Ⓙ	23 Ⓐ Ⓑ Ⓒ Ⓓ	34 Ⓕ Ⓖ Ⓗ Ⓙ	45 Ⓐ Ⓑ Ⓒ Ⓓ	56 Ⓕ Ⓖ Ⓗ Ⓙ	67 Ⓐ Ⓑ Ⓒ Ⓓ
2 Ⓕ Ⓖ Ⓗ Ⓙ	13 Ⓐ Ⓑ Ⓒ Ⓓ	24 Ⓕ Ⓖ Ⓗ Ⓙ	35 Ⓐ Ⓑ Ⓒ Ⓓ	46 Ⓕ Ⓖ Ⓗ Ⓙ	57 Ⓐ Ⓑ Ⓒ Ⓓ	68 Ⓕ Ⓖ Ⓗ Ⓙ
3 Ⓐ Ⓑ Ⓒ Ⓓ	14 Ⓕ Ⓖ Ⓗ Ⓙ	25 Ⓐ Ⓑ Ⓒ Ⓓ	36 Ⓕ Ⓖ Ⓗ Ⓙ	47 Ⓐ Ⓑ Ⓒ Ⓓ	58 Ⓕ Ⓖ Ⓗ Ⓙ	69 Ⓐ Ⓑ Ⓒ Ⓓ
4 Ⓕ Ⓖ Ⓗ Ⓙ	15 Ⓐ Ⓑ Ⓒ Ⓓ	26 Ⓕ Ⓖ Ⓗ Ⓙ	37 Ⓐ Ⓑ Ⓒ Ⓓ	48 Ⓕ Ⓖ Ⓗ Ⓙ	59 Ⓐ Ⓑ Ⓒ Ⓓ	70 Ⓕ Ⓖ Ⓗ Ⓙ
5 Ⓐ Ⓑ Ⓒ Ⓓ	16 Ⓕ Ⓖ Ⓗ Ⓙ	27 Ⓐ Ⓑ Ⓒ Ⓓ	38 Ⓕ Ⓖ Ⓗ Ⓙ	49 Ⓐ Ⓑ Ⓒ Ⓓ	60 Ⓕ Ⓖ Ⓗ Ⓙ	71 Ⓐ Ⓑ Ⓒ Ⓓ
6 Ⓕ Ⓖ Ⓗ Ⓙ	17 Ⓐ Ⓑ Ⓒ Ⓓ	28 Ⓕ Ⓖ Ⓗ Ⓙ	39 Ⓐ Ⓑ Ⓒ Ⓓ	50 Ⓕ Ⓖ Ⓗ Ⓙ	61 Ⓐ Ⓑ Ⓒ Ⓓ	72 Ⓕ Ⓖ Ⓗ Ⓙ
7 Ⓐ Ⓑ Ⓒ Ⓓ	18 Ⓕ Ⓖ Ⓗ Ⓙ	29 Ⓐ Ⓑ Ⓒ Ⓓ	40 Ⓕ Ⓖ Ⓗ Ⓙ	51 Ⓐ Ⓑ Ⓒ Ⓓ	62 Ⓕ Ⓖ Ⓗ Ⓙ	73 Ⓐ Ⓑ Ⓒ Ⓓ
8 Ⓕ Ⓖ Ⓗ Ⓙ	19 Ⓐ Ⓑ Ⓒ Ⓓ	30 Ⓕ Ⓖ Ⓗ Ⓙ	41 Ⓐ Ⓑ Ⓒ Ⓓ	52 Ⓕ Ⓖ Ⓗ Ⓙ	63 Ⓐ Ⓑ Ⓒ Ⓓ	74 Ⓕ Ⓖ Ⓗ Ⓙ
9 Ⓐ Ⓑ Ⓒ Ⓓ	20 Ⓕ Ⓖ Ⓗ Ⓙ	31 Ⓐ Ⓑ Ⓒ Ⓓ	42 Ⓕ Ⓖ Ⓗ Ⓙ	53 Ⓐ Ⓑ Ⓒ Ⓓ	64 Ⓕ Ⓖ Ⓗ Ⓙ	75 Ⓐ Ⓑ Ⓒ Ⓓ
10 Ⓕ Ⓖ Ⓗ Ⓙ	21 Ⓐ Ⓑ Ⓒ Ⓓ	32 Ⓕ Ⓖ Ⓗ Ⓙ	43 Ⓐ Ⓑ Ⓒ Ⓓ	54 Ⓕ Ⓖ Ⓗ Ⓙ	65 Ⓐ Ⓑ Ⓒ Ⓓ	
11 Ⓐ Ⓑ Ⓒ Ⓓ	22 Ⓕ Ⓖ Ⓗ Ⓙ	33 Ⓐ Ⓑ Ⓒ Ⓓ	44 Ⓕ Ⓖ Ⓗ Ⓙ	55 Ⓐ Ⓑ Ⓒ Ⓓ	66 Ⓕ Ⓖ Ⓗ Ⓙ	

MATHEMATICS USAGE

1 Ⓐ Ⓑ Ⓒ Ⓓ Ⓔ	7 Ⓐ Ⓑ Ⓒ Ⓓ Ⓔ	13 Ⓐ Ⓑ Ⓒ Ⓓ Ⓔ	19 Ⓐ Ⓑ Ⓒ Ⓓ Ⓔ	25 Ⓐ Ⓑ Ⓒ Ⓓ Ⓔ	31 Ⓐ Ⓑ Ⓒ Ⓓ Ⓔ	37 Ⓐ Ⓑ Ⓒ Ⓓ Ⓔ
2 Ⓕ Ⓖ Ⓗ Ⓙ Ⓚ	8 Ⓕ Ⓖ Ⓗ Ⓙ Ⓚ	14 Ⓕ Ⓖ Ⓗ Ⓙ Ⓚ	20 Ⓕ Ⓖ Ⓗ Ⓙ Ⓚ	26 Ⓕ Ⓖ Ⓗ Ⓙ Ⓚ	32 Ⓕ Ⓖ Ⓗ Ⓙ Ⓚ	38 Ⓕ Ⓖ Ⓗ Ⓙ Ⓚ
3 Ⓐ Ⓑ Ⓒ Ⓓ Ⓔ	9 Ⓐ Ⓑ Ⓒ Ⓓ Ⓔ	15 Ⓐ Ⓑ Ⓒ Ⓓ Ⓔ	21 Ⓐ Ⓑ Ⓒ Ⓓ Ⓔ	27 Ⓐ Ⓑ Ⓒ Ⓓ Ⓔ	33 Ⓐ Ⓑ Ⓒ Ⓓ Ⓔ	39 Ⓐ Ⓑ Ⓒ Ⓓ Ⓔ
4 Ⓕ Ⓖ Ⓗ Ⓙ Ⓚ	10 Ⓕ Ⓖ Ⓗ Ⓙ Ⓚ	16 Ⓕ Ⓖ Ⓗ Ⓙ Ⓚ	22 Ⓕ Ⓖ Ⓗ Ⓙ Ⓚ	28 Ⓕ Ⓖ Ⓗ Ⓙ Ⓚ	34 Ⓕ Ⓖ Ⓗ Ⓙ Ⓚ	40 Ⓕ Ⓖ Ⓗ Ⓙ Ⓚ
5 Ⓐ Ⓑ Ⓒ Ⓓ Ⓔ	11 Ⓐ Ⓑ Ⓒ Ⓓ Ⓔ	17 Ⓐ Ⓑ Ⓒ Ⓓ Ⓔ	23 Ⓐ Ⓑ Ⓒ Ⓓ Ⓔ	29 Ⓐ Ⓑ Ⓒ Ⓓ Ⓔ	35 Ⓐ Ⓑ Ⓒ Ⓓ Ⓔ	
6 Ⓕ Ⓖ Ⓗ Ⓙ Ⓚ	12 Ⓕ Ⓖ Ⓗ Ⓙ Ⓚ	18 Ⓕ Ⓖ Ⓗ Ⓙ Ⓚ	24 Ⓕ Ⓖ Ⓗ Ⓙ Ⓚ	30 Ⓕ Ⓖ Ⓗ Ⓙ Ⓚ	36 Ⓕ Ⓖ Ⓗ Ⓙ Ⓚ	

SOCIAL STUDIES READING

1 Ⓐ Ⓑ Ⓒ Ⓓ	8 Ⓕ Ⓖ Ⓗ Ⓙ	15 Ⓐ Ⓑ Ⓒ Ⓓ	22 Ⓕ Ⓖ Ⓗ Ⓙ	29 Ⓐ Ⓑ Ⓒ Ⓓ	36 Ⓕ Ⓖ Ⓗ Ⓙ	43 Ⓐ Ⓑ Ⓒ Ⓓ Ⓔ	50 Ⓕ Ⓖ Ⓗ Ⓙ Ⓚ
2 Ⓕ Ⓖ Ⓗ Ⓙ	9 Ⓐ Ⓑ Ⓒ Ⓓ	16 Ⓕ Ⓖ Ⓗ Ⓙ	23 Ⓐ Ⓑ Ⓒ Ⓓ	30 Ⓕ Ⓖ Ⓗ Ⓙ	37 Ⓐ Ⓑ Ⓒ Ⓓ	44 Ⓕ Ⓖ Ⓗ Ⓙ Ⓚ	51 Ⓐ Ⓑ Ⓒ Ⓓ Ⓔ
3 Ⓐ Ⓑ Ⓒ Ⓓ	10 Ⓕ Ⓖ Ⓗ Ⓙ	17 Ⓐ Ⓑ Ⓒ Ⓓ	24 Ⓕ Ⓖ Ⓗ Ⓙ	31 Ⓐ Ⓑ Ⓒ Ⓓ	38 Ⓕ Ⓖ Ⓗ Ⓙ	45 Ⓐ Ⓑ Ⓒ Ⓓ Ⓔ	52 Ⓕ Ⓖ Ⓗ Ⓙ Ⓚ
4 Ⓕ Ⓖ Ⓗ Ⓙ	11 Ⓐ Ⓑ Ⓒ Ⓓ	18 Ⓕ Ⓖ Ⓗ Ⓙ	25 Ⓐ Ⓑ Ⓒ Ⓓ	32 Ⓕ Ⓖ Ⓗ Ⓙ	39 Ⓐ Ⓑ Ⓒ Ⓓ	46 Ⓕ Ⓖ Ⓗ Ⓙ Ⓚ	
5 Ⓐ Ⓑ Ⓒ Ⓓ	12 Ⓕ Ⓖ Ⓗ Ⓙ	19 Ⓐ Ⓑ Ⓒ Ⓓ	26 Ⓕ Ⓖ Ⓗ Ⓙ	33 Ⓐ Ⓑ Ⓒ Ⓓ	40 Ⓕ Ⓖ Ⓗ Ⓙ	47 Ⓐ Ⓑ Ⓒ Ⓓ Ⓔ	
6 Ⓕ Ⓖ Ⓗ Ⓙ	13 Ⓐ Ⓑ Ⓒ Ⓓ	20 Ⓕ Ⓖ Ⓗ Ⓙ	27 Ⓐ Ⓑ Ⓒ Ⓓ	34 Ⓕ Ⓖ Ⓗ Ⓙ	41 Ⓐ Ⓑ Ⓒ Ⓓ	48 Ⓕ Ⓖ Ⓗ Ⓙ Ⓚ	
7 Ⓐ Ⓑ Ⓒ Ⓓ	14 Ⓕ Ⓖ Ⓗ Ⓙ	21 Ⓐ Ⓑ Ⓒ Ⓓ	28 Ⓕ Ⓖ Ⓗ Ⓙ	35 Ⓐ Ⓑ Ⓒ Ⓓ	42 Ⓕ Ⓖ Ⓗ Ⓙ	49 Ⓐ Ⓑ Ⓒ Ⓓ Ⓔ	

NATURAL SCIENCE READING

1 Ⓐ Ⓑ Ⓒ Ⓓ	8 Ⓕ Ⓖ Ⓗ Ⓙ	15 Ⓐ Ⓑ Ⓒ Ⓓ	22 Ⓕ Ⓖ Ⓗ Ⓙ	29 Ⓐ Ⓑ Ⓒ Ⓓ	36 Ⓕ Ⓖ Ⓗ Ⓙ	43 Ⓐ Ⓑ Ⓒ Ⓓ Ⓔ	50 Ⓕ Ⓖ Ⓗ Ⓙ Ⓚ
2 Ⓕ Ⓖ Ⓗ Ⓙ	9 Ⓐ Ⓑ Ⓒ Ⓓ	16 Ⓕ Ⓖ Ⓗ Ⓙ	23 Ⓐ Ⓑ Ⓒ Ⓓ	30 Ⓕ Ⓖ Ⓗ Ⓙ	37 Ⓐ Ⓑ Ⓒ Ⓓ	44 Ⓕ Ⓖ Ⓗ Ⓙ Ⓚ	51 Ⓐ Ⓑ Ⓒ Ⓓ Ⓔ
3 Ⓐ Ⓑ Ⓒ Ⓓ	10 Ⓕ Ⓖ Ⓗ Ⓙ	17 Ⓐ Ⓑ Ⓒ Ⓓ	24 Ⓕ Ⓖ Ⓗ Ⓙ	31 Ⓐ Ⓑ Ⓒ Ⓓ	38 Ⓕ Ⓖ Ⓗ Ⓙ	45 Ⓐ Ⓑ Ⓒ Ⓓ Ⓔ	52 Ⓕ Ⓖ Ⓗ Ⓙ Ⓚ
4 Ⓕ Ⓖ Ⓗ Ⓙ	11 Ⓐ Ⓑ Ⓒ Ⓓ	18 Ⓕ Ⓖ Ⓗ Ⓙ	25 Ⓐ Ⓑ Ⓒ Ⓓ	32 Ⓕ Ⓖ Ⓗ Ⓙ	39 Ⓐ Ⓑ Ⓒ Ⓓ	46 Ⓕ Ⓖ Ⓗ Ⓙ Ⓚ	
5 Ⓐ Ⓑ Ⓒ Ⓓ	12 Ⓕ Ⓖ Ⓗ Ⓙ	19 Ⓐ Ⓑ Ⓒ Ⓓ	26 Ⓕ Ⓖ Ⓗ Ⓙ	33 Ⓐ Ⓑ Ⓒ Ⓓ	40 Ⓕ Ⓖ Ⓗ Ⓙ	47 Ⓐ Ⓑ Ⓒ Ⓓ Ⓔ	
6 Ⓕ Ⓖ Ⓗ Ⓙ	13 Ⓐ Ⓑ Ⓒ Ⓓ	20 Ⓕ Ⓖ Ⓗ Ⓙ	27 Ⓐ Ⓑ Ⓒ Ⓓ	34 Ⓕ Ⓖ Ⓗ Ⓙ	41 Ⓐ Ⓑ Ⓒ Ⓓ	48 Ⓕ Ⓖ Ⓗ Ⓙ Ⓚ	
7 Ⓐ Ⓑ Ⓒ Ⓓ	14 Ⓕ Ⓖ Ⓗ Ⓙ	21 Ⓐ Ⓑ Ⓒ Ⓓ	28 Ⓕ Ⓖ Ⓗ Ⓙ	35 Ⓐ Ⓑ Ⓒ Ⓓ	42 Ⓕ Ⓖ Ⓗ Ⓙ	49 Ⓐ Ⓑ Ⓒ Ⓓ Ⓔ	

SCORE SHEET

	NUMBER CORRECT								
ENGLISH USAGE	____	÷	75	=	____	× 100	=	____%
MATHEMATICS USAGE	____	÷	40	=	____	× 100	=	____%
SOCIAL STUDIES READING	____	÷	52	=	____	× 100	=	____%
Questions based on reading	____	÷	39	=	____	× 100	=	____%
Questions not based on reading	____	÷	13	=	____	× 100	=	____%
NATURAL SCIENCE READING	____	÷	52	=	____	× 100	=	____%
Questions based on reading	____	÷	40	=	____	× 100	=	____%
Questions not based on reading	____	÷	12	=	____	× 100	=	____%
TOTAL SCORE	____	÷	219	=	____	× 100	=	____%

PROGRESS CHART

	Exam I	Exam II	Exam III	Exam IV
ENGLISH USAGE	%	%	%	%
MATHEMATICS USAGE	%	%	%	%
SOCIAL STUDIES READING	%	%	%	%
NATURAL SCIENCE READING	%	%	%	%
TOTAL	%	%	%	%

TEST 1
ENGLISH USAGE

40 Minutes—75 Questions

DIRECTIONS: In each of the following passages, some portions are underlined and numbered. Corresponding to each numbered portion are three alternative ways of saying the same thing. Read through each passage quickly to determine the sense of the passage, then return to the underlined portions. If you feel that an underlined portion is correct and is stated as well as possible, mark NO CHANGE, A or F. If you feel that there is an error in grammar, sentence structure, punctuation or word usage, choose the correct answer. If an underlined portion appears to be correct, but you believe that one of the alternative choices would be more effective, mark that choice. Remember, you are to choose the *best* answer.

These numbered paragraphs may or may not be arranged in the most logical sequence. The last item will ask you to select the most logical sequence.

(1)

For an employer, the most difficult aspect of the hiring process is the lining up by suitable candidates (1) for a

1. **A.** NO CHANGE
   B. by suited candidates
   C. of suitable candidates
   D. suitable candidates

specific job, doing this is indispensable to good selection.
2

2. F. NO CHANGE
G. job; so that
H. job, but
J. job, except

It is better to seek and select rather than waiting for
3
applications. You can find new employees running want
4
ads in local newspapers, employment agencies, or placement bureaus of high schools, business schools, and colleges. Of course, these are only some of the potential sources of employees, there are many another effective
5 6
ways to find personnel.

3. A. NO CHANGE
B. awaiting for
C. awaiting
D. wait for

4. F. NO CHANGE
G. listing
H. in
J. through

5. A. NO CHANGE
B. employees, their
C. employees; there
D. employees. Their

6. F. NO CHANGE
G. another affective
H. other effective
J. other affective

(2)

Careful choice of personnel is essential to protect the reputation of any small business. Selecting the right em-
7
ployee, you should have planned in advance what you
8
want the applicant to do, and then look for the one to fill your particular needs.
9

7. A. NO CHANGE
B. In the selection of
C. Selection of
D. To select

8. F. NO CHANGE
G. should have planned ahead
H. should plan in advance
J. should have made a plan in advance

9. A. NO CHANGE
B. one for filling
C. one who fill
D. one who filled

(3)

Often one of the major mistakes in choosing an employee is to hire an individual; without a clear knowl-
10
edge beforehand of exactly what his or her duties will be. Although it is true that in a small business you will
11
need flexible employees who can shift from task to task

10. F. NO CHANGE
G. an individual: without
H. an individual. Without
J. an individual without

11. A. NO CHANGE
B. It being true that
C. It is true that
D. While it is true that

and who may be called upon to perform unexpected and unforeseen 12 tasks. Nevertheless, you should plan your

12. **F.** NO CHANGE
    G. unexpecting
    H. unexpected
    J. OMIT

hiring to assure an organization capable of performing 13 every essential function. Write down the job descrip-

13. **A.** NO CHANGE
    B. for performing
    C. for the performance of
    D. of the performance of

tions. For example, you should answer these kind of questions 14 before hiring; if 15 you are running a retail store, will a salesperson also do stockkeeping or bookkeeping? In a restaurant, will a waitress also perform some of the duties of a hostess?

14. **F.** NO CHANGE
    G. such kind of questions
    H. such kinds of a question
    J. such questions as these

15. **A.** NO CHANGE
    B. hiring; "If
    C. hiring: "If
    D. hiring: If

(4)

By securing 16 applicants you must screen them. Applica-

16. **F.** NO CHANGE
    G. Once you have secured
    H. Once you had secured
    J. By obtaining

tion forms, filled out 17 by the prospective employees will help. Some applicants may be eliminated right away by studying the forms. For each of the others, the applica-

17. **A.** NO CHANGE
    B. forms—filled in
    C. forms; filled in
    D. forms filled out

tion will serve as a basis for the interview. Each interview is for being 18 conducted in private. Put the applicant at ease by describing your business in general and the job in particular. But once you have done this, encourage the applicant to talk. Do not make the mistake of doing

18. **F.** NO CHANGE
    G. Each interview should be
    H. START NEW PARAGRAPH
    J. START NEW PARAGRAPH; substitute "interviewing" for "interview"

all or most of the talking. Selection 19 the right person is extremely important to you and you must learn

19. **A.** NO CHANGE
    B. In the selection of
    C. Selecting
    D. For you to select

everything you can about them 20 that is pertinent to the job.

20. **F.** NO CHANGE
    G. about the applicant
    H. regarding them
    J. concerning them

21. Choose the sequence that represents the most logical order for this essay's structure.

A. NO CHANGE
B. 2, 1, 4, 3
C. 3, 1, 2, 4
D. 2, 3, 1, 4

Passage II

Alice was beginning to get very tired of sitting by her sister on the <u>bank, and having</u>[22] nothing to <u>do: once</u>[23] or twice she had peeped into the book her sister was reading, but it had no pictures or conversation in <u>it, "and</u>[24] what is the use of a <u>book thought Alice,</u>[25] <u>without</u>[26] pictures or <u>conversations?"</u>[27] So she was <u>considering, in her own mind</u>[28], whether the pleasure of making a <u>daisy-chain</u>[29] would be worth the trouble of getting up and picking the

22. **F.** NO CHANGE
G. bank and having
H. bank, with
J. bank with

23. **A.** NO CHANGE
B. do; once
C. do, once
D. do. Once

24. **F.** NO CHANGE
G. it. "And
H. it, "And
J. it: "And

25. **A.** NO CHANGE
B. book?" thought Alice,
C. book"? thought Alice,
D. book," thought Alice,

26. **F.** NO CHANGE
G. "without
H. "Without
J. Without

27. **A.** NO CHANGE
B. conversations."
C. conversations!"
D. conversations"?

28. **F.** NO CHANGE
G. thinking
H. wondering
J. considering

29. **A.** NO CHANGE
B. daisy chain
C. daisychain
D. Daisy-chain

daisies, when suddenly a White Rabbit with pink eyes ran close by her. There was nothing remarkable in that.
30 31

30. **F.** NO CHANGE
G. daisies when
H. daisys, when
J. daisys when

31. **A.** NO CHANGE
B. "White Rabbit"
C. white rabbit
D. "white rabbit"

Nor did Alice think of it to be so very unusual to hear
32

32. **F.** NO CHANGE
G. of the unusualness of it
H. of it to be so unusual
J. it so unusual

the rabbit say to himself "Oh dear! Oh dear! I shall be
33 34

33. **A.** NO CHANGE
B. himself, "Oh dear!"
C. himself, "Oh dear!
D. himself, oh dear!

34. **F.** NO CHANGE
G. "Oh dear!
H. "Oh dear!"
J. Oh dear!"

too late!" but, when the rabbit actually took a watch
35 36

35. **A.** NO CHANGE
B. to late!"
C. so late!"
D. too late"!

36. **F.** NO CHANGE
G. ; but, when
H. But, when,
J. But, when

out of its waistcoat pocket, looked at it and then hurried
37

37. **A.** NO CHANGE
B. it's
C. its'
D. his

on, Alice started to her feet; for it flashed across her
38

38. **F.** NO CHANGE
G. feet for it
H. feet, for it
J. feet. For it

mind that she had never before seen a rabbit with either
39

39. **A.** NO CHANGE
B. never seen before
C. never seen
D. never ever seen

a waistcoat pocket or a watch to take out of it, and,
40 41
burning with curiosity, she ran across the field after him
41
and was just in time to see him pop down a large rabbit-hole under a hedge. Alice followed, giving no
42
consideration to how she might not ever come up. The
43
rabbit-hole went straight on like a tunnel for some way, then dipped down so suddenly that Alice had not a moment to think about stopping herself before she found
44
herself falling down what ought to be a very, deep well.
45 46

I guess the well was very deep, or else she fell
47
very slow, for she had plenty of time as she went down
48 49

40. **F.** NO CHANGE
G. pocket, or
H. pocket nor
J. pocket, nor

41. **A.** NO CHANGE
B. it; and, burning
C. it. And burning
D. it. Burning

42. **F.** NO CHANGE
G. rabbit hole
H. rabbit's hole
J. rabbits' hole

43. **A.** NO CHANGE
B. the possibility that there might be no way up.
C. not coming up.
D. how she might get back up.

44. **F.** NO CHANGE
G. on stopping
H. of stopping
J. while stopping

45. **A.** NO CHANGE
B. should
C. ought to have been
D. appeared to be

46. **F.** NO CHANGE
G. very deep
H. real deep
J. really deep

47. **A.** NO CHANGE
B. She thought
C. Because
D. Either

48. **F.** NO CHANGE
G. very slow
H. very slowly,
J. very slowly

49. **A.** NO CHANGE
B. for, she
C. and she
D. before she

to look about her and to wonder what was going to
50

50. **F.** NO CHANGE
G. about her; and
H. about it, and
J. about; and

happen next. First, she tried to look down and make out
51
what she was coming to, but it was too dark to see

51. **A.** NO CHANGE
B. find out
C. search out
D. determine out

anything: then, she looked at the sides of the well and
52
noticed that they were filled with cupboards and

52. **F.** NO CHANGE
G. anything; then, she
H. anything. Then, she
J. anything. She

book-shelves; here and there she saw maps and pictures
53

53. **A.** NO CHANGE
B. bookshelves, here
C. book shelfs. Here
D. bookshelves. Here

hung by pegs.
54

54. **F.** NO CHANGE
G. hung below
H. hung from
J. hanging from

Passage III

Some people choose one way of solving their personal problems. While others choose other ways. You can get
55

55. **A.** NO CHANGE
B. problems, while
C. problems, at the same time that
D. problems while

a good idea of a persons character by the way he tries
56 57

56. **F.** NO CHANGE
G. person's
H. persons'
J. persons's

57. **A.** NO CHANGE
B. in
C. from
D. taking notice of

to solve his problems. If an individual gets real mad at life and gives all kinds of nonsensical excuses, you may conclude that he is living in an unreal world. He needs help to get back to the real world—the world of
58 59

58. F. NO CHANGE
G. at solving
H. in the solution of
J. for the solution of

59. A. NO CHANGE
B. very mad at
C. angry with
D. angry at

thinkers' and scientists'. Maybe he is trying to accomplish the impossible and needs a task that is
60

60. F. NO CHANGE
G. thinkers' and scientists.'
H. thinkers and scientists.
J. thinker's and scientist's.

possible to be performed. That person is wise if he can learn to develop realistic expectations.
61 62

61. A. NO CHANGE
B. for performing
C. to perform
D. for performance

62. F. NO CHANGE
G. wise who
H. knowledgeable if
J. knowledgable who

Passage IV

Dear Sirs:

In reply to your ad in the Sunday Times, I should like to apply for the opening on your magazine.
63 64

63. A. NO CHANGE
B. In response to
C. Replying to
D. As an answer to

64. F. NO CHANGE
G. *Sunday Times*
H. "Sunday Times"
J. Sunday *Times*

May I inform you that I am seventeen years of age,
65

65. A. NO CHANGE
B. I hereby inform you that
C. I want you to know that
D. OMIT

a current graduate of Brookford High and was the
66 67

66. **F.** NO CHANGE
G. a recent graduate of
H. a senior at
J. a member of the current graduating class of

67. **A.** NO CHANGE
B. a former
C. used to be
D. am

editor of our school paper here. I desire to pursue a
68

68. **F.** NO CHANGE
G. our here school paper.
H. the school paper here.
J. the school paper.

career in journalism after graduation and my
69

69. **A.** NO CHANGE
B. graduation. And my
C. graduation. My
D. graduation, and my

teachers have complimented me on my literary work.
70

70. **F.** NO CHANGE
G. teacher's have complemented
H. teachers' have complemented
J. teachers have complemented

Your ad interested me since it holds forth promise of
71
a good future. I am certainly interested in that

71. **A.** NO CHANGE
B. holds interest for me
C. is interesting to me
D. interests me

at my age I can type, do the technical work in a
72

72. **F.** NO CHANGE
G. as old as I am.
H. as young as I am.
J. (begin the sentence with this phrase)

publishing office, and also know stenography.
73

73. **A.** NO CHANGE
B. take stenography.
C. also take stenography.
D. in addition also know stenography.

I await your prompt reply, I am
74

74. **F.** NO CHANGE
G. As I wait for your prompt reply, I am
H. I await your prompt reply.
J. Thanking you in advance for the courtesy of an early reply, I am

Very respectfully yours
75
Wallace Carter

75. **A.** NO CHANGE
B. Respectfully yours,
C. Very Respectfully Yours,
D. Respectfully:

END OF TEST

If you complete this test before the time limit is up, look back over the questions. Do not proceed to the next test until you are told to do so.

TEST 2
MATHEMATICS USAGE

50 Minutes—40 Questions

DIRECTIONS: Solve each problem and mark the letter of the correct answer on your answer sheet.

DO YOUR FIGURING HERE

1. In two hours, the minute hand of a clock rotates through an angle of

A. 60°
B. 90°
C. 180°
D. 360°
E. 720°

2. Which of the following fractions is less than one-third?

F. $\frac{22}{63}$
G. $\frac{4}{11}$
H. $\frac{15}{46}$
J. $\frac{33}{98}$
K. $\frac{102}{303}$

3.

The length of each side of the square above is $\frac{2x}{3} + 1$. The perimeter of the square is

A. $\frac{8x + 4}{3}$
B. $\frac{8x + 12}{3}$

DO YOUR FIGURING HERE

C. $\frac{2x}{3} + 4$

D. $\frac{2x}{3} + 16$

E. $\frac{4x}{3} + 2$

4. A motorist travels 120 miles to a destination at the average speed of 60 miles per hour and returns to the starting point at the average speed of 40 miles per hour. The average speed for the entire trip is

F. 53 miles per hour
G. 50 miles per hour
H. 48 miles per hour
J. 45 miles per hour
K. 52 miles per hour

5. A snapshot measures $2\frac{1}{2}$ inches by $1\frac{7}{8}$ inches. It is to be enlarged so that the longer dimension will be 4 inches. The length of the enlarged shorter dimension will be

A. $2\frac{1}{2}$ inches
B. 3 inches
C. $3\frac{3}{8}$ inches
D. $2\frac{5}{8}$ inches
E. none of these

6. From a piece of tin in the shape of a square 6 inches on a side, the largest possible circle is cut out. Of the following, the ratio of the area of the circle to the area of the original square is closest in value to

F. $\frac{4}{5}$

G. $\frac{2}{3}$

H. $\frac{3}{5}$

J. $\frac{1}{2}$

K. $\frac{3}{4}$

7. The approximate distance s in feet that an object falls in t seconds when dropped from a height is obtained by use of the formula $s = 16t^2$. In 8 seconds the object will fall

A. 15,384 feet
B. 1,024 feet
C. 256 feet
D. 2,048 feet
E. none of these

8. In the figure, AB = BC and angles BAD and BCD are right angles. Which one of the following conclusions may be drawn?

DO YOUR FIGURING HERE

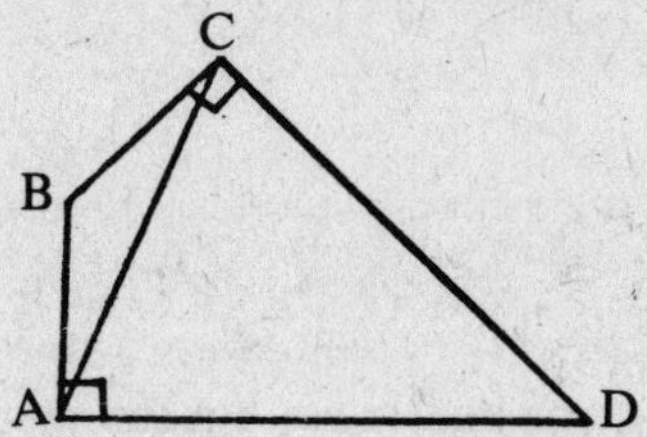

F. ∡ BCA = ∡ CAD
G. ∡ B > ∡ D
H. AC = CD
J. AD = CD
K. BC < CD

9. A pound of water is evaporated from 6 pounds of sea water containing 4% salt. The percentage of salt in the remaining solution is

A. $3\frac{1}{3}$
B. 4
C. $4\frac{4}{5}$
D. 5
E. none of these

10. The product of 75^3 and 75^7 is

F. $(75)^{10}$
G. $(150)^{10}$
H. $(75)^{21}$
J. $(5625)^{10}$
K. $(75)^5$

11. The scale of a map is: $\frac{3}{4}$ of an inch = 10 miles. If the distance on the map between two towns is 6 inches, the actual distance is

A. 45 miles
B. 60 miles
C. 80 miles
D. 75 miles
E. none of these

12. If $d = m - \frac{50}{m}$, and *m* is a positive number that increases in value, *d*

F. increases in value
G. decreases in value
H. remains unchanged
J. increases, then decreases
K. decreases, then increases

DO YOUR FIGURING HERE

13. If a cubic inch of a metal weighs 2 pounds, a cubic foot of the same metal weighs

A. 8 pounds
B. 24 pounds
C. 288 pounds
D. 96 pounds
E. none of these

14. Of the following, the one that is *not* a meaning of $\frac{2}{3}$ is

F. 1 of the 3 equal parts of 2
G. 2 of the 3 equal parts of 1
H. 2 divided by 3
J. a ratio of 2 to 3
K. 4 of the 6 equal parts of 2

15. If the average weight of girls of Judy's age and height is 105 lbs. and if Judy weighs 110% of average, then Judy weighs

A. 110 lbs.
B. 110.5 lbs.
C. 106.5 lbs.
D. 126 lbs.
E. $115\frac{1}{2}$ lbs.

16. On a house plan on which 2 inches represents 5 feet, the length of a room measures $7\frac{1}{2}$ inches. The actual length of the room is

F. $12\frac{1}{2}$ feet
G. $15\frac{3}{4}$ feet
H. $17\frac{1}{2}$ feet
J. $18\frac{3}{4}$ feet
K. $13\frac{3}{4}$ feet

17. ABCD is a parallelogram, and DE = EC

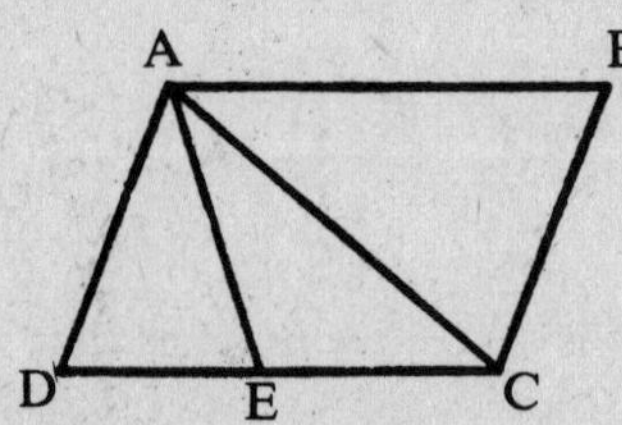

What is the ratio of triangle ADE to the area of the parallelogram?

A. 1:2
B. 1:3
C. 2:5
D. 1:4
E. cannot be determined from the given information

18. If pencils are bought at 35 cents per dozen and sold at 3 for 10 cents, the total profit on $5\frac{1}{2}$ dozen is

DO YOUR FIGURING HERE

F. 25 cents
G. $27\frac{1}{2}$ cents
H. $28\frac{1}{2}$ cents
J. $31\frac{1}{2}$ cents
K. 35 cents

19. Of the following, the one which may be used correctly to compute $26 \times 3\frac{1}{2}$ is

A. $(26 \times 30) + (26 \times \frac{1}{2})$
B. $(20 \times 3) + (6 \times 3\frac{1}{2})$
C. $(20 \times 3\frac{1}{2}) + (6 \times 3)$
D. $(20 \times 3) + (26 \times \frac{1}{2}) + (6 \times 3\frac{1}{2})$
E. $(26 \times \frac{1}{2}) + (20 \times 3) + (6 \times 3)$

20. It costs 31 cents a square foot to lay linoleum. To lay 20 square yards of linoleum it will cost

F. \$16.20
G. \$18.60
H. \$62.80
J. \$62.00
K. \$55.80

21. 10 to the fifth power may correctly be expressed as

A. 10×5
B. 5^{10}
C. $5\sqrt{10}$
D. $10 \times 10 \times 10 \times 10 \times 10$
E. $10^{10} \div 10^{2}$

22. The total cost of $3\frac{1}{2}$ pounds of meat at \$1.10 a pound and 20 oranges at \$.60 a dozen will be

F. \$4.65
G. \$4.85
H. \$5.05
J. \$4.45
K. none of these

DO YOUR FIGURING HERE

23. A recipe for a cake calls for $2\frac{1}{2}$ cups of milk and 3 cups of flour. With this recipe, a cake was baked using 14 cups of flour. How many cups of milk were required?

A. $10\frac{1}{3}$
B. $10\frac{3}{4}$
C. 11
D. $11\frac{3}{5}$
E. $11\frac{2}{3}$

24. A certain type of board is sold only in lengths of multiples of 2 feet from 6 ft. to 24 ft. A builder needs a large quantity of this type of board in $5\frac{1}{2}$-foot lengths. For minimum waste, the lengths to be ordered should be

F. 6 ft.
G. 12 ft.
H. 24 ft.
J. 22 ft.
K. 18 ft.

25. The tiles in the floor of a bathroom are $\frac{15}{16}$ inch squares. The cement between the tiles is $\frac{1}{16}$ inch. There are 3240 individual tiles in this floor. The area of the floor is

A. 225 sq. yds.
B. 2.5 sq. yds.
C. 250 sq. ft.
D. 22.5 sq yds.
E. 225 sq ft.

26. A group of 15 children received the following scores in a reading test: 36, 36, 30, 30, 30, 29, 27, 27, 27, 26, 26, 26, 26, 18, 13. What was the median score?

F. 25.4
G. 26
H. 27
J. 30
K. 24.5

27. Two rectangular boards each measuring 5 feet by 3 feet are placed together to make one large board. How much shorter will the perimeter be if the two long sides are placed together than if the two short sides are placed together?

A. 2 feet
B. 4 feet
C. 6 feet
D. 8 feet
E. the perimeter will remain the same

DO YOUR FIGURING HERE

28. A jacket that normally sells for $35 can be purchased on sale for 2,975 pennies. What is the rate of discount represented by the sale price?

F. 5%
G. 10%
H. 15%
J. 20%
K. 25%

29. Two cars start from the same point at the same time. One drives north at 20 miles an hour and the other drives south on the same straight road at 36 miles an hour. How many miles apart are they after 30 minutes?

A. less than 10
B. between 10 and 20
C. between 20 and 30
D. between 30 and 40
E. more than 40

30. A sportswriter claims that his football predictions are accurate 60% of the time. During football season, a fan kept records and found that the writer was inaccurate for a total of 16 games, although he did maintain his 60% accuracy. For how many games was the sportswriter accurate?

F. 15
G. 24
H. 40
J. 5
K. 60

31. A stock clerk has on hand the following items:
500 pads worth four cents each
130 pencils worth three cents each
50 dozen rubber bands worth two cents per dozen
If, from this stock, she issued 125 pads, 45 pencils, and 48 rubber bands, the value of the remaining stock would be

A. $ 6.43
B. $ 8.95
C. $17.63
D. $18.47
E. none of these

32. A jet pilot wishes to cover a certain distance in 25% less time than he had previously taken to cover that distance. What percent must he increase his speed in order to accomplish this?

F. 25%
G. $33\frac{1}{3}$%
H. 40%
J. $66\frac{2}{3}$%
K. 100%

DO YOUR FIGURING HERE

33. As a train departs from station A, it has 12 empty seats, 14 seated passengers and 4 standing passengers. At the next stop, 8 passengers get off, 13 passengers get on and everyone takes a seat. How many empty seats are there?

A. 1
B. 2
C. 3
D. 4
E. 5

34. In a group of 4000 people, $\frac{1}{4}$ are married and single men and $\frac{2}{3}$ are married women. Of the unmarried women, $\frac{1}{5}$ are unemployed and $\frac{1}{8}$ of the employed unmarried women are teachers. What fractional part of the original group of people are single women teachers?

F. $\frac{1}{10}$
G. $\frac{1}{20}$
H. $\frac{1}{30}$
J. $\frac{1}{40}$
K. none of these

35. In 1976 a company purchased 500 dozen pencils at 40 cents per dozen. In 1978, only 75 percent as many pencils were purchased as were purchased in 1976, but the price was 20 percent higher than the 1976 price. What was the total cost of pencils purchased by the company in 1978?

A. $180.00
B. $187.50
C. $240.00
D. $250.00
E. $257.40

36. A certain highway intersection has had A accidents over a ten-year period, resulting in B deaths. What is the yearly average death rate for the intersection?

F. $A + B - 10$
G. $\frac{B}{10}$
H. $10 - \frac{A}{B}$
J. $\frac{A}{10}$
K. $\frac{AB}{12}$

37. In the diagram chord TU =

DO YOUR FIGURING HERE

A. $(TY + UY)^2$

B. $\sqrt{TY + TU}$

C. $\sqrt{TY^2 + UY^2}$

D. $\frac{TY \times UY}{2}$

E. $\sqrt{(TY + UY)^2}$

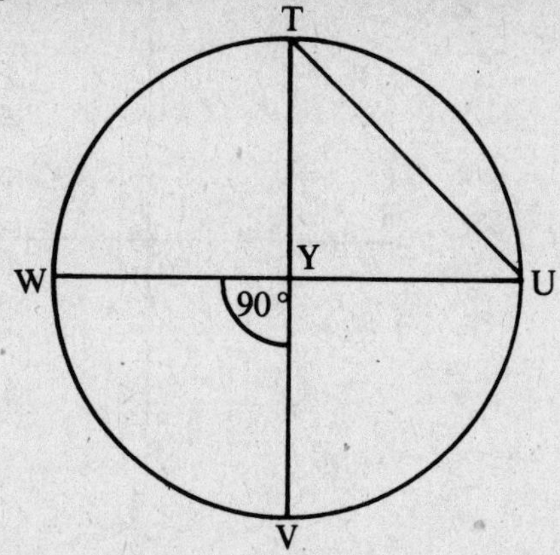

38. A is older than B. With the passage of time

F. the ratio of the ages of A and B remains unchanged
G. the ratio of the ages of A and B increases
H. the ratio of the ages of A and B decreases
J. the difference in their ages varies
K. the ratio varies

39. The formula $y = \frac{3}{4}x + 2$ is represented by which one of the following graphs?

A.

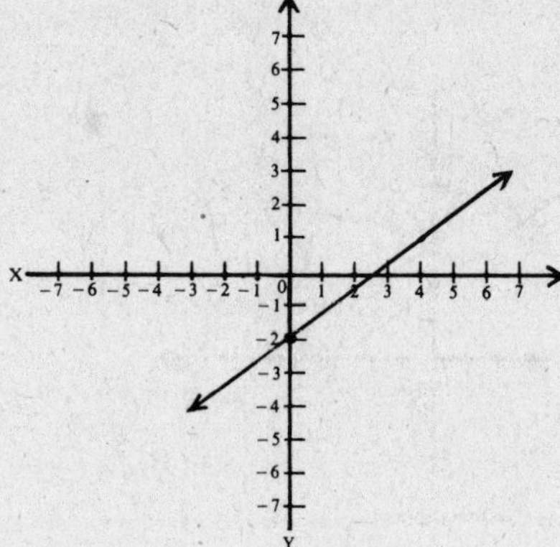

B.

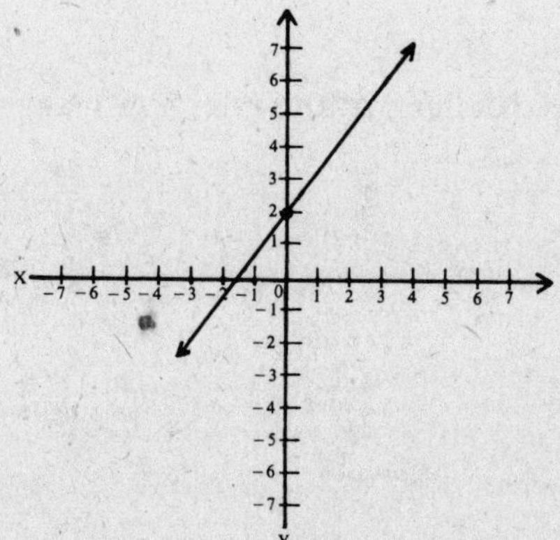

DO YOUR FIGURING HERE

C.

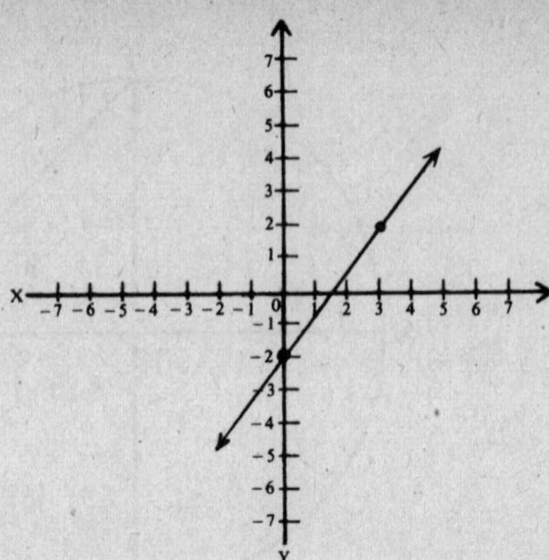

D.

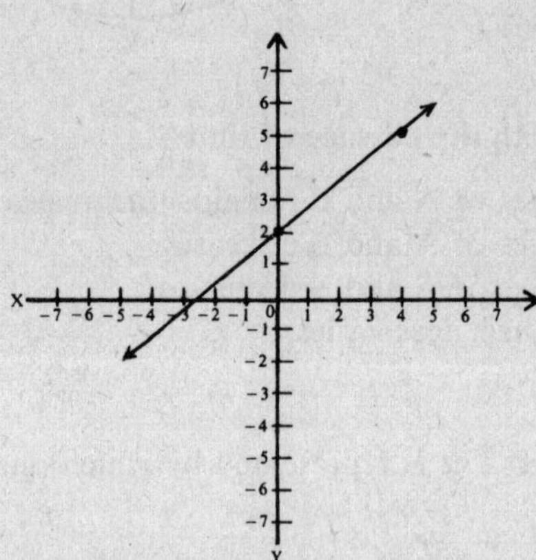

E.

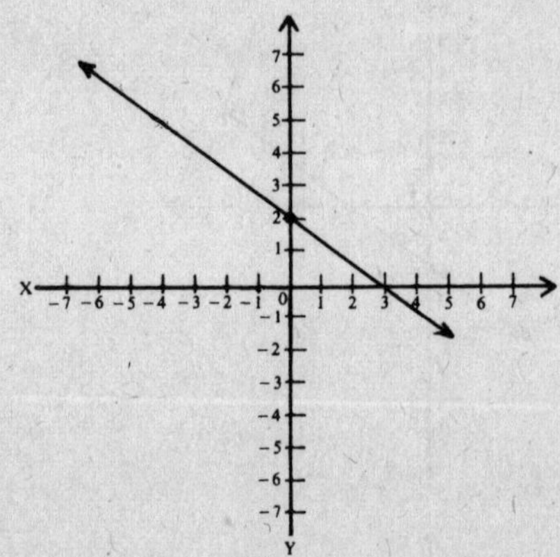

40. The cost of 30 melons is *d* dollars. At this rate, how many melons can you buy for 80 cents?

F. $\frac{24}{d}$

G. $\frac{240}{d}$

H. $24d$

J. $\frac{3d}{8}$

K. $\frac{8d}{3}$

END OF TEST

If you complete this test before the time limit is up, go back over the questions on this test only. Do not return to the previous test. Do not proceed to the next test until you are told to do so.

TEST 3
SOCIAL STUDIES READING

35 Minutes—52 Questions

DIRECTIONS: Below each of the following reading passages is a series of questions. Choose the *best* answer to each question, interpreting what is stated or implied by the passage in the light of your own background in the subject. You may refer back to the passage as often as necessary, though the answers to some questions may not be found expressly in the passage.

"The United Kingdom, the United States and the Soviet Union have received from many quarters evidence of atrocities, massacres and cold-blooded mass executions which are being perpetrated by Hitlerite forces in the many countries they have overrun, and from which they are now being steadily expelled. The brutalities of Hitlerite domination are no new thing, and all peoples or territories in their grip have suffered from the worst form of government by terror. What is new is that many of these territories are now being redeemed by the advancing armies of the liberating powers and that in their desperation the recoiling Hitlerite Huns are redoubling their ruthless cruelties. This is now evidenced with particular clearness by monstrous crimes of the Hitlerites on the territory of the Soviet Union which is being liberated from the Hitlerites, and on French and Italian territory.

"Accordingly, the aforesaid three Allied powers, speaking in the interests of the thirty-two United Nations, hereby solemnly declare and give full warning of their declaration as follows:

"At the time of the granting of any armistice to any government which may be set up in Germany, those German officers and men and members of the Nazi party who have been responsible for or have taken a consenting part in the above atrocities, massacres and executions will be sent back to the countries in which their abominable deeds were done in order that they may be judged and punished according to the laws of these liberated countries and of the free governments which will be created therein. Lists will be compiled in all possible detail from all these countries, having regard especially to the invaded parts of the Soviet Union, to Poland and Czechoslovakia, to Yugoslavia and Greece, including Crete and other islands, to Norway, Denmark, the Netherlands, Belgium, Luxembourg, France and Italy.

"Thus, the Germans who take part in wholesale shooting of Italian officers or in the execution of French, Dutch, Belgian or Norwegian hostages or of Cretan peasants, or who have shared in slaughters inflicted on the people of Poland or in territories of the Soviet Union which are now being swept clear of the enemy, will know they will be brought back to the scene of their crimes and judged on the spot by the peoples whom they have outraged. Let those who have hitherto not imbrued their hands with innocent blood beware lest they join the ranks of the guilty, for most assuredly the three Allied powers will pursue them to the uttermost ends of the earth and will deliver them to their accusers in order that justice may be done.

"The above declaration is without prejudice to the case of the major criminals whose offenses have no particular geographical localization and who will be punished by the joint decision of the governments of the Allies."

1. The single word which best describes the attitude of the signatories to this document is

A. outrage
B. despair
C. disgust
D. resignation

2. The term "Hitlerite Huns" refers to

F. Hitler's real name
G. Hitler's ancestry
H. German racial stock
J. the German national religion

3. The group or groups of victims about which the signatories of this document do not concern themselves at this time are

I. prisoners of war
II. noncombatants
III. German citizens
IV. Ionians

A. none of these
B. I and II
C. III only
D. IV only

4. According to the statement

F. all war criminals are to be tried at Nuremburg
G. all war criminals are to be tried at the site of their crimes
H. the victims themselves will sit in judgment
J. the governments of countries in which crimes were committed will try some criminals

5. Not mentioned specifically in this statement are the genocidal activities of the Germans against the Jews. This is probably because

A. the three powers did not care about the Jews
B. the three powers did not think that the Jews required individual treatment beyond that offered other residents of the specified countries
C. the death camps had not yet been liberated
D. one of the signatory nations was anti-semitic

6. The thirty-two United Nations mentioned in the second paragraph are

F. the Allies
G. the countries invaded by Germany
H. the charter nations of the U.N.
J. the members of the League of Nations

7. The Japanese were also known to have committed certain atrocities during the course of the war, yet they are nowhere mentioned in this statement. This is probably because

A. they were scheduled to be dealt with by the atomic bomb
B. the document is specific to Europe and the Germans
C. the Japanese committed no atrocities on the British
D. no one really cared about the Chinese

8. The three nations which prepared this statement learned about German atrocities from

F. eyewitness reports of the victims
G. broadcasts of the Voice of America
H. smuggled letters
J. reports of the liberating armies

9. German behavior towards subjugated peoples was most vicious in

A. the first weeks after overrunning the countries
B. the face of defeat
C. Russia
D. territories of the Soviet Union

10. This paper is a/an

F. warning
G. plea
H. ultimatum
J. reprimand

11. The atrocities detailed by this document include

I. public floggings
II. torture
III. mass executions

A. I and II
B. II and III
C. III only
D. I, II, and III

Section 1. Equality of rights under the law shall not be denied or abridged by the United States or by any State on account of sex.
Section 2. The Congress shall have the power to enforce, by appropriate legislation, the provisions of this article.
Section 3. This amendment shall take effect two years after the date of ratification.

Speaker 1. "Any man who notices the fine nuances while raising a daughter has got to be for it. I'm less concerned about my daughter being drafted or operating a jack hammer or using a co-educational john than being a second-class citizen all her life. . . Why should my daughter be treated differently under the law than my son?"
Speaker 2. "Family life is the nuclear substance of every known society. Destroy or weaken the family and society itself is the target. The ramifications and implementation of this so-called 'Equal Rights Amendment' will require changing the laws that have been developed to safeguard family life and protect children. If society won't protect its own children, it destroys its own future."
Speaker 3. "By marriage, the husband and wife are one person in law . . . the very being or legal existence of the woman is suspended during the marriage. . . For this reason a man cannot grant anything to his wife, or enter into covenant with her, for the grant would be to suppose her separate existence, and to convenant with her would be only to convenant with himself."
Speaker 4. "Should widows be deprived of preferential tax, property and homestead benefits? Should homosexual 'marriages' be legalized and such couples be permitted to adopt children and get tax and homestead benefits now given to husbands and wives? Should wives not employed outside the home be deprived of their present right to receive Social Security benefits based on their husband's earnings? Should wives not employed outside the home be denied their present right to get credit in their husband's name? Should all colleges, schools, military academies and physical education classes be required to become 50/50 co-ed?"
Speaker 5. "Despite advances, differential enlistment standards and quotas still hinder career opportunities for women in the military. The Army continues to maintain higher enlistment and test score standards for women. In addition, all of the Armed Services maintain quotas which limit the number of women allowed to hold jobs in the military. As things now stand, women are denied equal access to the escape route from poverty, vocational training, advancement possibilities, veterans' benefits and opportunities to serve their country which are offered to their male counterparts."
Speaker 6. "The ERA amendment has nothing in its vague and innocuous wording to insure the extension of any benefits. It mandates only that treatment of men and women be the same. This means that women will lose all benefits of protective legislation."

12. The legal passage quoted here is

F. the Fourteenth Amendment
G. the proposed Twenty-sixth Amendment
H. the Twenty-sixth Amendment
J. the proposed Twenty-seventh Amendment

13. Speaker 1

A. agrees with the ERA because he wants his daughter to operate a jack hammer
B. agrees in principle

C. disagrees because his daughter is a second-class citizen
D. disagrees because he is afraid his daughter will become a second-class citizen

14. Speaker 2

F. advocates use of nuclear power to generate electricity
G. expects Congress to pass laws which discriminate against children
H. is reading more into the Amendment than can reasonably be found there
J. is entirely rational in his argument

15. Speaker 3

A. is quoted for the purpose of describing the current status of married women
B. is quoted to demonstrate what would happen if ERA were to be adopted
C. is making a statement about his own feelings with regard to women
D. agrees with Speaker 2

16. Speaker 4

F. is for the ERA
G. is opposed to the ERA
H. is objectively raising questions about the ERA
J. believes that women should not work

17. Speaker 5

A. believes that women should be drafted
B. objects to the peacetime draft
C. would send women into combat
D. would allow women to go into combat

18. Speaker 6

F. raises a legitimate problem
G. totally misreads the Amendment
H. interprets the Amendment correctly
J. has doubts but supports the Amendment

19. Fear of change is a potent argument against change. Those speakers who use this argument are

I. Speakers 1 and 3
II. Speakers 2 and 4
III. Speakers 1 and 5
IV. Speakers 4 and 6

A. I and II
B. III and IV
C. I and III
D. II and IV

20. Speaker 5 would probably respond to Speaker 4.

I. Your questions are irrelevant.
II. I still think that if men are drafted women should be drafted.
III. In addition, women should not be thwarted from obtaining credit in their own name.
IV. Physical education classes are already 50-50 co-ed.

F. I only
G. I and III
H. II and III
J. I, II, III, and IV

21. The arguments of which speaker would have been most easily understood by delegates to the women's rights convention at Seneca Falls?

A. Speaker 2
B. Speaker 3
C. Speaker 4
D. Speaker 5

22. ERA was first introduced in Congress in

F. 1848
G. 1923
H. 1954
J. 1972

23. With regard to homosexual marriages, the ERA will

A. make them legal
B. make them illegal
C. have no effect whatsoever
D. make the laws apply equally so that if, by law, men cannot marry men, then women cannot marry women, but if the law should permit men to marry men, then equally women would be permitted to marry women

24. The ERA was not ratified by 3/4 of the states within seven years of the date it was submitted to the states by Congress. This means that

F. since the Constitutional time limit has expired, the Amendment is dead and the entire amending procedure must be repeated in order to revive it

G. ERA automatically becomes a law rather than an Amendment

H. since the time limit was legislative rather than constitutional, Congress had an opportunity to grant a time extension, but did not

J. since the time limit was legislatively imposed, Congress voted to grant the states a time extension

To say the parliament is absolute and arbitrary, is a contradiction. The parliament cannot make 2 and 2, 5; omnipotency cannot do it. The supreme power in a state as *jus dicere* only;—*jusdare,* strictly speaking, belongs along to G-d. Parliaments are in all cases to declare what is for the good of the whole; but it is not the declaration of the parliament that makes it so. There must be in every instance, a higher authority, viz. G-d. Should an act of parliament be against any of His natural laws, which are immutably true, their declaration would be contrary to eternal truth, equity and justice, and consequently void: and so it would be adjudged by the parliament itself when convinced of their mistake. Upon this great principle, parliaments have repealed such acts as soon as they find they have been mistaken in having declared them to be for the public good, when in fact they were not so. See here the grandeur of the British Constitution! See the wisdom of our ancestors! The supreme legislative, and the supreme executive, are a perpetual check and balance to each other. If the supreme executive errs, it is informed by the supreme legislative in parliament: If the supreme legislative errs, it is informed by the King's courts of law—here the King appears, as represented by his judges, in the highest lustre and majesty as supreme executor of the commonwealth; and he never shines brighter, but on his Throne at the head of the supreme legislative. This is government! This is a Constitution! To preserve which, either from foreign or domestic foes, has cost oceans of blood and treasure in every age, and the blood and the treasure have upon the whole been well spent.

25. The title of this article should be

A. Divine Right of Kings
B. Balance of Power
C. Limited Government
D. Kings and Parliaments

26. Parliament is not absolute because

F. it has certain limitations
G. there is a higher authority than parliament
H. both of these
J. neither of these

27. The author states that Divine Law

A. is found in the Bible
B. was preached by Jesus
C. is immutably and eternally true
D. is inferior to common law

28. The check-and-balance system mentioned in the article differs from the same system used in the United States in that

F. the former has no judicial branch
G. the U.S. has no king
H. Parliament and Congress do not perform the same roles
J. the President is actually the head of state, while the King is only a figurehead

29. This article was written at approximately the same time as the

A. Magna Carta
B. Declaration of Independence
C. Emancipation Proclamation
D. Fourteen Points

30. The British Constitution was written

F. long before this article was written
G. shortly before this article was written
H. at the same time as this article was written
J. it is impossible to tell from this article when the British Constitution was written

31. The author

A. considers the Constitution unnecessary because Divine Law is supreme
B. asserts that in combination the King and the Parliament have wisdom equal to that of G-d's
C. is enamored of the British Constitution
D. is an innovative mathematician

DIRECTIONS: The questions in the following group are not based upon a reading passage. Choose the *best* answer to each question on the basis of your knowledge in social studies.

32. Which of the following best describes the effect of the 18th Amendment? It

F. had little effect on American political life
G. brought women into public life in the 1920s
H. marked the demise of old suffrage organizations
J. prohibited the manufacture and sale of intoxicating liquors

33. Education was of particular importance to the Puritans in Massachusetts Bay because it

A. provided knowledge of the Scriptures, needed for salvation
B. opened the door to economic opportunity
C. encouraged proper decorum among children
D. encouraged egalitarianism

34. The Sugar Act passed by Parliament in 1764

F. lowered the duties on molasses imports
G. favored the southern colonies unfairly
H. discriminated against the southern colonies
J. raised the duties on molasses imports

35. The British government differs from that of the United States in that its powers cannot be expanded by

A. laws passed by Parliament
B. customs and practices
C. judicial decisions
D. a specific process of amending the Constitution

36. Which question is worded in a clear and unslanted way?

F. "Have you stopped beating your wife?"
G. "Do you get your information from books, magazines, newspapers, or textbooks?"
H. "Do you agree that Red China should be admitted to the U.N.?"
J. "Are you in favor of higher taxes for education?"

37. Shays' Rebellion in western Massachusetts can be most accurately said to have been brought about by

A. boundary conflicts
B. high taxes and a decline in the value of paper money
C. objections to the presence of British troops
D. the issues that led to the "Great Compromise"

38. The American Colonization Society, formed in 1816, advocated

F. immediate emancipation and colonization of slaves
G. compensated emancipation and colonization of slaves
H. resettlement of blacks who were already freed
J. establishing Liberia as a territory of the United States

39. The leaders of the Women's Rights Movement in the antebellum period received their training in reform by

A. attending pioneer women's colleges
B. joining church and missionary societies
C. participating in politics on a local level
D. participating in the Temperance and Antislavery movements

40. Which one of the following was *not* a result of the Commercial Revolution?

F. the domestic system of production was introduced
G. some European merchants became wealthy enough to live like princes
H. the power of the absolute monarchs decreased
J. feudalism continued to disintegrate on the Continent

41. Which one of the following monarchs was *not* considered an enlightened or benevolent despot in the eighteenth century?

A. Catherine the Great of Russia
B. Frederick the Great of Prussia
C. Joseph II of Austria
D. Louis XV of France

42. "Fifty-four Forty or Fight" refers to the

F. dispute over Oregon
G. Mexican War
H. line above which President Truman would not allow General MacArthur to advance during the Korean War
J. election of 1848

43. The Knights of Labor, organized in 1869, attempted to

A. agitate for profit-sharing
B. organize white-collar workers
C. organize unskilled and black workers
D. wage an ideological war on capitalism

44. President Hoover responded to the Stock Market Crash of 1929 by

F. promoting business investment through the National Recovery Administration
G. promoting business investment through the Reconstruction Finance Corporation
H. promoting legislation aimed at a redistribution of the national income
J. concentrating on immediate relief measures such as unemployment insurance, welfare legislation, and aid to agriculture

". . . as your President, performing my constitutional duty to 'give to the Congress information of the state of the Union,' I find it necessary to report that the future and the safety of our country and of our democracy are overwhelmingly involved in events far beyond our borders.

"Armed defense of democratic existence is now being gallantly waged in four continents. If that defense fails, all the population and all the resources of Europe, Asia, Africa and Australasia will be dominated by the conquerors. The total of those populations and their resources greatly exceeds the sum total of the population and resources of the whole of the Western Hemisphere —many times over.

"In times like these it is immature—and incidentally untrue—for anybody to brag that an unprepared America, single-handed, and with one hand tied behind its back, can hold off the whole world . . .

"The first phase of the invasion of this Hemisphere would not be the landing of regular troops. The necessary strategic points would be occupied by secret agents and their dupes—and great numbers of them are already here, and in Latin America . . .

"Our most useful and immediate role is to act as an arsenal for them as well as for ourselves. They do not need manpower. They do need billions of dollars worth of weapons of defense . . .

"Let us say to the democracies: 'We Americans are vitally concerned in your defense of freedom. We are putting forth our energies, our resources and our organizing powers to give you the strength to regain and maintain a free world. We shall send you, in ever-increasing numbers, ships, planes, tanks, guns. This is our purpose and our pledge.'

". . . As men do not live by bread alone, they do not fight by armaments alone. Those who man our defenses, and those behind them who build our defenses, must have the stamina and courage which come from an unshakable belief in the manner of life which they are defending. The mighty action which we are calling for cannot be based on a disregard of all things worth fighting for . . .

"I have called for personal sacrifice. I am assured of the willingness of almost all Americans to respond to that call . . .

"In the future days, which we seek to make secure, we look forward to a world founded upon four essential human freedoms.

"The first is freedom of speech and expression—everywhere in the world.

"The second is freedom of every person to worship G-d in his own way—everywhere in the world.

"The third is freedom from want—which, translated into world terms, means economic understandings which will secure to every nation a healthy peacetime life for its inhabitants —everywhere in the world.

"The fourth is freedom from fear—which, translated into world terms, means a worldwide reduction of armaments to such a point and in such a thorough fashion that no nation will be in a position to commit an act of physical aggression against any neighbor—anywhere in the world.

"That is no vision of a distant millennium. It is a definite basis for a kind of world attainable in our own time and generation. That kind of world is the very antithesis of the so-called new order of tyranny which the dictators seek to create with the crash of a bomb."

45. This State of the Union message has been titled the

A. Declaration of War Speech
B. Four Freedoms Speech
C. Bread Alone Speech
D. International Friendship Speech

46. The year this speech was given must have been

F. 1917
G. 1937
H. 1941
J. 1945

47. In the speech, the President

I. asks for institution of the draft
II. commits American troops to fight in the Western Hemisphere
III. offers military hardware to threatened countries
IV. warns against a "Fifth Column"

A. I and II
B. II and III
C. III and IV
D. II, III, and IV

48. The President feels that there is

F. no danger to the United States because we are well prepared
G. no danger to the United States because we are so far from Europe
H. immediate danger and we are unprepared
J. potential danger and we must prepare

49. In suggesting that secret agents of foreign nations are already among us in strategic places, the President is setting the stage for

A. Japanese internment camps
B. flights of the U-2 spy planes
C. the CIA
D. the Army-McCarthy hearings

50. The bomb referred to in the last quoted sentence is

F. the atomic bomb
G. the hydrogen bomb
H. the neutron bomb
J. no specific bomb

51. Were this President alive today he would probably

A. favor the principle of the SALT talks
B. oppose the principle of the SALT talks
C. advocate that every country should choose its own national religion
D. brag about America's preparedness

52. The Constitutional duty to which the President alludes in the first quoted sentence is the duty of the President to

F. enter into foreign treaties
G. serve as Commander-in-Chief of the Army and the Navy
H. give reports to Congress
J. convene Congress in case of emergency

END OF TEST

If you complete this test before the time limit is up, check back over the questions on this test only. Do not return to any previous test. Do not proceed to the next test until you are told to do so.

TEST 4
NATURAL SCIENCE READING

35 Minutes—52 Questions

DIRECTIONS: Below each of the following reading passages is a series of questions. Choose the *best* answer to each question, interpreting what is stated or implied by the passage in the light of your own background in the subject. You may refer back to the passage as often as necessary, though the answers to some questions may not be found expressly in the passage.

As far back as 1936 surgeons were working out a way to treat a psychosis by an operation called prefrontal lobotomy—the last resort for schizophrenics and manic-depressives. Using a technique devised by the University of Lisbon's emeritus professor Dr. Antonio Caetano de Abreu Freire Egas Moniz, skilled neurosurgeons cut away important nerve connections in the prefrontal brain lobe (a seat of reasoning) and the thalamus in the rear of the brain (a way station for emotional responses). The operation's aim: helping the patient to a better adjustment with his environment.

Working in a similar field was a 68-year-old Swiss physiologist, Dr. Walter Rudolph Hess, Director of Zurich University's Physiological Institute. A specialist in the circulatory and nervous systems, Dr. Hess studied the reaction of animals to electric shocks. By applying electrodes to parts of a cat's brain he was able to make the animal do what it would normally do if it saw a dog, i.e., hiss, etc. By experiments, Dr. Hess was able to determine how parts of the brain control organs of the body.

In 1949 the Council of the Caroline Institute at the University of Stockholm awarded the Nobel Prize in Medicine and Physiology jointly to Dr. Hess and Dr. Moniz. His half of the $30,000 would come in handy to Dr. Hess. Said he: "It will simplify my work. I have certain plans and everything costs money. . . . Now I will be able to hire assistants."

Wealthy, 75-year-old Dr. Moniz, whose hands are badly deformed by long exposure to radioactivity, is the first Portuguese ever to win a Nobel Prize.

1. A prefrontal lobotomy is

A. a psychosis
B. an operation on the brain
C. a mental aberration
D. a schizophrenic

2. It is used on

F. skilled neurology surgeons
G. mild cases of schizophrenia
H. maladjusted people
J. extreme cases of mental disease

3. The prefrontal lobotomy involves

A. cutting the prefrontal brain lobe
B. severing nerve connections
C. destroying the thalamus
D. massaging brain tissues

4. As a result of a prefrontal lobotomy, doctors hope to

F. eliminate schizophrenia
G. regenerate injured nerve tissue
H. destroy germs which cause the disease
J. help the patient get along better in normal life

5. The operation is based on the theory that

A. people react to electric shock
B. certain parts of the brain control certain types of action
C. adjustment is a matter of proper reactions
D. a dog will hiss if certain spots are touched with an electric wire

6. Dr. Moniz is

F. the developer of the prefrontal lobotomy
G. a specialist in circulatory and nervous systems
H. a professor of technical sciences
J. a famous schizophrenic

7. Dr. Walter Rudolph Hess is

A. the inventor of the prefrontal lobotomy
B. a pioneer in electric shock therapy
C. a student of electrical disturbances
D. a physiologist doing research on brain control of body organs

8. Drs. Hess and Moniz jointly made news because

F. they did excellent work
G. they effected wonderful cures
H. they were awarded the Nobel Prize
J. they effected a revolution in medical techniques

9. Dr. Hess will use the money received for

A. a trip
B. medicine
C. assistants
D. the University

10. Dr. Moniz will use the money for

F. repairing his hands
G. Portugal
H. nothing determinable from the article
J. additional research expenditures

11. Dr. Moniz's hands became deformed by exposure to radioactivity from

A. brain waves
B. schizophrenics
C. electrodes
D. sources unrelated to brain surgery

12. Prefrontal lobotomy is no longer used as a treatment for schizophrenia and manic-depression because

I. it was too dangerous
II. it did not entirely serve the purpose for which it was intended
III. better results were achieved with newly invented drugs
IV. lobotomy was adjudged to be cruel and unusual punishment

F. I and II
G. I, III, and IV
H. I, II, and III
J. I, II, III, and IV

13. Dr. Hess' experiments were intended to

A. determine how to treat mental patients with electroshock therapy
B. reveal differentiation in the brain
C. devise a way to make cats like dogs
D. earn him the Nobel Prize

We know that a small permanent magnet, such as a compass needle, will set itself parallel to a magnetic line of force. But an unmagnetized piece of soft iron will do the same thing, and will, furthermore, be attracted to the pole of a permanent magnet just as a compass needle is. Suppose that a nail, for example, is brought near the south pole of a permanent magnet. A north pole is induced in the nail on the end nearer the south pole of a permanent magnet and it becomes, temporarily, a magnet. But it loses most of its induced magnetism as soon as it is removed from the field of the permanent magnet.

Nearly all materials have weak magnetic properties that can be detected and measured by delicate apparatus. But a very few materials—iron, cobalt, nickel and several alloys—show outstandingly large magnetic effects. They naturally contain a multitude of tiny magnets which are normally pointing in all the various directions, so that their individual magnetic effects cancel out. When the material is placed in a magnetic field, all the tiny magnets in it turn about and tend to line up with the field and so with one another. As a result, the sample is itself a good magnet, as long as it is in the magnetic field. Once it is removed, the tiny magnets again become disorganized, and the sample no longer acts as a magnet.

Permanent magnets are also made of ferromagnetic materials, but various tricks are employed to keep the tiny elementary magnets in them from getting out of alignment once they have been lined up in a magnetic field. In steel, for example, the elementary magnets are brought into cooperation only with difficulty, but they also find it hard to get out of line with one another after the magnetizing field is removed; a permanent magnet is the result. Even a steel magnet, however, will lose its magnetism if it is heated or severely jarred. In recent years, certain alloys have been used to make extremely powerful permanent magnets.

It is not known why iron, nickel and cobalt naturally contain these tiny magnets, while gold, lead and other metals do not have them. The electrons in metal continually whirl, teetotum-fashion. Both of these motions constitute electric currents, and the magnetic effects of these currents are presumably responsible for the magnetic behavior of the material. In fact, the weak magnetic properties of ordinary materials can be explained quite acceptably by considering in detail how these electron currents will interact with external magnetic fields. The ferromagnetic metals are more of a puzzle. How the travelling and spinning electrons in them cooperate to produce tiny magnetized domains is beginning to be understood, but the picture is not yet complete.

The magnetism of the earth remains essentially unexplained, despite the many theories that have been advanced. The magnetism of both sun and earth appears to be connected with the rotation of these bodies. For many reasons it seems unlikely that the earth's core actually contains a large iron magnet. But why aren't the magnetic poles located at the geographic poles? And why do the magnetic poles gradually shift their positions with the passage of years? At present, the north magnetic pole (that is, the place where a compass needle points vertically downward) is located north of Hudson Bay, well over a thousand miles from the north geographic pole. It is moving westward at the rate of a very few miles per year. The south magnetic pole is in the Antarctic, nearly opposite the north magnetic pole.

The behavior of the earth's magnetic poles is not only mysterious, but most annoying. Compass needles fail to point true north and, what is worse, their error, or declination, changes slightly from year to year in any one locality. In Maine the compass points as much as 23° to the west of true north, and in the state of Washington as much as 24° to the east of true north. There is one line in the United States (extending irregularly from South Carolina northward through the middle of Lake Superior) where the compass does point to the true north; but east or west of this line the declination varies between 0° and the maximum of 23° or 24°.

14. The south pole of a magnet attracts

F. the north pole of another magnet
G. the south pole of another magnet
H. both poles of another magnet
J. either pole, but not both poles of another magnet

15. In an ordinary piece of iron the atomic magnets are probably arranged

A. with all poles pointing in the same direction
B. with poles on either end pointing in the same direction

C. so that only the poles in the center neutralize each other
D. in a random order

16. The reason a temporary magnet loses its magnetism is that the atomic groups have

F. lost their magnetism
G. lost their alignment
H. become permanent magnets
J. become temporary magnets

17. In order to make a light alloy of aluminum that would be magnetic, it might be best to combine it with

A. helium
B. silver
C. gold
D. nickel

18. If two large magnets were placed together and heated

F. one magnet would increase in strength and one magnet would decrease
G. both magnets would increase in strength
H. both magnets would decrease in strength
J. both magnets would remain unchanged

19. The causes for the magnetic fields of the earth are probably connected with

A. materials at the earth's core
B. materials located at the earth's poles
C. the rotation of the moon around the earth
D. the daily rotation of the earth

20. If a sailor living in Washington corrects his compass so that it points to true north, and then he moves to Maine, his compass would

F. point 1° west of true north
G. point 23° west of true north
H. point 47° west of true north
J. point 1° east of true north

21. If the north poles of two separate magnets are brought together, their attraction is

A. negative
B. positive
C. zero
D. alternating

22. If a compass were corrected today for local use, when would it be necessary to correct it again if it is to be absolutely correct?

F. next month
G. next year
H. next century
J. never

23. The south pole is

A. at the south magnetic pole
B. almost 1000 miles north of the south magnetic pole
C. over 1000 miles west of the south magnetic pole
D. over 1000 miles east of the south magnetic pole

24. Which of the following materials would probably be best to use to protect a delicate instrument from magnetism?

F. iron
G. copper
H. rubber
J. paper

DIRECTIONS: The following questions are not based upon a reading passage. Choose the *best* answer to each question, drawing upon your own background in science.

25. Pound for pound, sodium carbonate, when compared with sodium bicarbonate, will provide

A. fewer sodium ions and less carbon dioxide
B. more sodium ions and less carbon dioxide
C. fewer sodium ions and more carbon dioxide
D. more sodium ions and more carbon dioxide

26. In the nuclear equation ${}_{52}Te^{130} + {}_{1}H^{2} \rightarrow {}_{53}I^{131}$ + _?_ the missing term is a/an

F. positron

G. alpha particle
H. neutron
J. beta particle

27. After 40 days, the weight in grams which remains of eight grams of a pure radioisotope with a half-life of 10 days is

A. 1.0
B. 2.0
C. 6.0
D. 0.5

28. In which group of organisms is sexual reproduction absent?

F. bacteria
G. blue-green algae
H. ciliated protozoa
J. fungi

29. Repeated rapid mitotic division of a fertilized egg is called

A. cleavage
B. reduction division
C. conjugation
D. gametogenesis

30. A piece of copper wire is cut into ten equal parts. These parts are connected in parallel. The joint resistance of the parallel combination will be equal to the original resistance of the single wire, multiplied by a factor of

F. .01
G. .10
H. 10
J. 100

31. In the nuclear reaction ${}_3Li^7 + {}_1H^1 \rightarrow {}_2He^4 + X$, the term X represents

A. ${}_2He^4$
B. ${}_1H^3$
C. ${}_3Li^6$
D. ${}_1H^2$

32. A wood splint dipped into concentrated H_2SO_4 turns black because H_2SO_4

F. has a high boiling point
G. is a dehydrating agent
H. is an oxidizing agent
J. is a strong acid

33. The primary reason why fungi are often found growing abundantly in the depths of the forest is that

A. it is cooler
B. it is warmer
C. they have little exposure to sunlight for photosynthesis
D. they have an abundant supply of organic matter

34. Why doesn't the pressure of the atmosphere crush animals? Because animals have

F. strongly built bodies
G. an inside pressure much greater than atmospheric pressure
H. an inside pressure equal to the atmospheric pressure
J. an inside pressure which is less than atmospheric pressure

35. Which of the following compounds is the most volatile?

A. ammonium hydroxide
B. calcium hydroxide
C. potassium hydroxide
D. sodium hydroxide

36. A chemical balance is calibrated in

F. cubic centimeters
G. grams
H. liters
J. inches

Thirty long-haired white rats were trained to a Y maze. In the training situation, Phase I, food was always to be found at the end of the right arm of the maze, and the rat which went to the left arm of the maze was always greeted with an electric shock. The rats soon learned to run down the right arm of the maze. When the experimenters were certain that all the rats would always choose the right arm, the conditions were changed.

In Phase II, food remained at the end of the right arm of the maze, but a shock was administered in the middle of that arm, en route to the food. At the end of the left arm there was no longer a shock nor was there food. Ten of the rats were then fed until they were satisfied and were placed, one by one, in the maze. After a few initial trips to the right arm, where they received an electric shock on their way to the food, the rats began to explore the left arm of the maze. Soon all of these rats were regularly choosing the left arm of the maze, even though they found nothing at its end. Ten more rats were fed a portion of their rations and were released into the maze. These rats too soon learned to choose the left arm of the maze rather than the right.

A third group of ten rats was allowed to become very hungry. These rats continued to run to the right arm of the maze, accepting the shock on the way to the food. Even after exploring the left arm, these rats continued to choose the right arm most often. Three of the rats, after many runs through the maze, began to leap over the shock area on the way to the food.

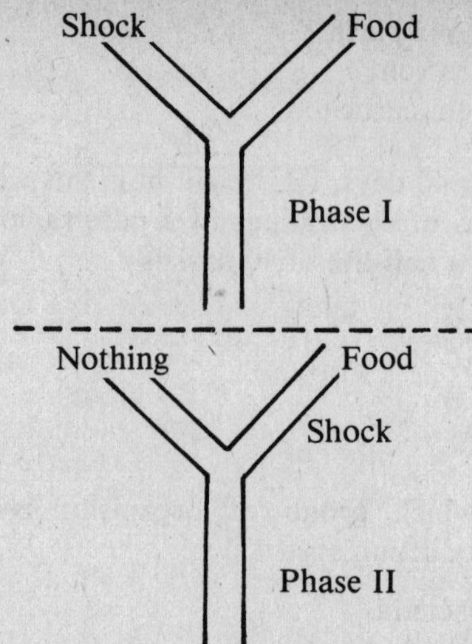

37. In Phase I of the experiment, all the rats quickly learned to run to the food. This shows that

 A. rats like to eat
 B. rats are right-handed
 C. when offered a choice between pain and reward, rats choose reward
 D. rats are eager to please experimenters

38. The somewhat hungry rats that in Phase II chose the left arm of the maze were proving that

 F. avoidance of pain may be a more powerful stimulus than reward
 G. they could discriminate right from left
 H. rats are not gluttonous
 J. they had forgotten where the food was

39. This experiment shows that

 A. learned behavior is immutable
 B. learned behavior is adaptive
 C. rats cannot learn from experience
 D. it is difficult to predict the behavior of rats

40. This experiment is worthwhile because it

 F. teaches the value of electric shock in rehabilitating criminals
 G. gives valuable clues as to how best to teach maze-running
 H. gives insight into the relative merits of pleasure and pain as stimuli in a learning situation
 J. suggests that the most efficient learning is done on an empty stomach

41. The very hungry rats that chose to accept the shock on the way to the food were showing that

 A. reward is a more powerful stimulus than the avoidance of pain
 B. they had gotten used to the shocks
 C. they were annoyed with finding nothing at the end of the left arm
 D. extreme hunger is more painful than the intensity of electric shock administered in this experiment

42. The fact that a few rats leaped over the area of shock while most rats submitted to shock en route to the food indicates that some rats

F. were hungrier than others
G. are more sensitive to shock than others
H. carefully considered the alternatives and decided that the shock was worth it
J. are more intelligent and innovative than others

43. We learn from this experiment that
I. it is not always easy to classify stimuli
II. rats do not like electric shocks
III. the intensity of a stimulus affects the animal's reaction to it

A. I and II
B. II only
C. II and III
D. I, II, and III

44. Rats are often used in laboratory experiments because
I. they are loyal and eager to please
II. they are inexpensive
III. their learning processes are similar in many respects to those of humans
IV. bringing the rats into the laboratory keeps them off the streets

F. I and III
G. II and IV
H. I and IV
J. II and III

Fluorine, chlorine, bromine and iodine constitute an active group of nonmetals known as the *halogens*. Their degree of activity in combining with metals and hydrogen to form salts and acids respectively is represented by the order in which they were just given. Fluorine is the most active and iodine the least active in the series. They are found widely distributed in nature as salts. Examples of such salts are sodium chloride and calcium fluoride.

A *binary acid* is one that contains only two elements, hydrogen and a nonmetal. Halogens form binary acids, such as hydrochloric acid and hydrofluoric acid. The halogens can be prepared for laboratory study by the oxidation of their binary acids. Thus, when concentrated hydrochloric acid is oxidized by manganese dioxide, chlorine is given off.

All of the halogens contain seven electrons in their outer shell. In attempting to complete this outer shell, they act in such a way as to gain an electron. Elements (including oxygen) that attempt to gain electrons are called *oxidizing agents*. The halogens act as oxidizing agents in reaction with metals, hydrogen, and water.

The individual halogens can be identified as follows:

- Chlorine is a green-yellow gas which produces a light yellow color when mixed with carbon tetrachloride.
- Bromine is a red-brown liquid. When bromine is mixed with carbon tetrachloride, it produces an amber-colored solution.
- Iodine is a grey-colored solid. When mixed with carbon tetrachloride, it produces a violet-colored solution.

When a halogen is combined with another element, it is known as a *halide*. The halides can be identified as follows:

- When silver nitrate is added to a chloride, a white precipitate is formed. This precipitate will dissolve in aluminum hydroxide but not in nitric acid.
- The test for a bromide is to dissolve the substance in water to which a small amount of chlorine water and carbon tetrachloride have been added. After the mixture is shaken and the layers have separated out, the carbon tetrachloride will settle to the bottom of the tube. If a bromide is present, the carbon tetrachloride layer will become orange in color.
- The procedure in testing for an iodide is the same as for a bromide. If an iodide is present, the carbon tetrachloride layer will become violet in color.

The halogens are of great importance in the modern world. Chlorine is used as a bleaching agent and a purifier of water. It is also used in antiseptic solutions, in gold extraction, and in the preparation of many organic compounds, such as DDT, chloroform, and synthetic rubber. Some of bromine's most important uses are in producing photographic paper, ethylene dibromide (used in making lead tetraethyl, the anti-knock ingredient in gasoline), and many kinds of drugs. Iodine is used in medicine, in the production of photographic film, and as an antiseptic. Fluorine's commercial uses include the etching of glass, the prevention of dental caries, and the production of refrigerants, plastics, insecticides and lubricants.

The most useful of the halogen acids are hydrochloric and hydrofluoric acids. Hydrochloric acid has a great array of industrial uses, including the cleaning of metals (called *pickling*) and the manufacture of dyes and textiles. Hydrofluoric acid is widely used in the etching of glass and in the making of cryolite, a substance used in the extraction of aluminum from its ore.

The commercial production of hydrogen chloride consists of the direct combination of hydrogen and chlorine. In the laboratory, hydrogen chloride is generally prepared by the action of sulfuric acid on sodium chloride.

Hydrogen fluoride, an extremely poisonous gas, is dissolved in water and kept in wax or plastic bottles (because of its etching effect on glass). It can be prepared by the action of concentrated sulfuric acid on calcium fluoride.

45. The halogens are all alike in that

I. they all have industrial uses
II. as individual elements they all occur as liquids
III. they all contain nine electrons in their outer shells
IV. they all occur abundantly in nature as salts

A. I and III
B. I and IV
C. I, III, and IV
D. I, II, III, and IV

46. Fluorine appears to be both caustic, as evidenced by its ability to eat through glass, and poisonous, yet it is used as a component of toothpaste. This is

F. an unsafe practice but worth it if the fluorine prevents dental caries
G. a safe practice because in different compounds fluorine behaves differently
H. an unwise practice because cavities should not be artificially prevented
J. all right because people do not eat toothpaste

47. A red-brown liquid is found in an unlabeled bottle. A few drops of carbon tetrachloride are added and the solution color turns amber. The liquid is

A. fluorine
B. chlorine
C. bromine
D. iodine

48. Binary acids are formed by

F. combining any two elements
G. combining oxygen and a liquid
H. combining hydrogen and a gas
J. combining hydrogen and any nonmetal

49. An oxidizing agent reacts with

A. metals, hydrogen and water
B. oxygen, halogen and water
C. electrons, metals and elements
D. carbon tetrachloride, nitric acid and white precipitates

50. Some of the uses of chlorine and bromine have fallen out of public favor because of the actions of

F. environmentalists
G. feminists
H. pacifists
J. artists

51. Aluminum is extracted from its ore by

A. a process called pickling
B. a substance named cryolite
C. hydrochloric acid
D. hydrofluoric acid

52. An oxidizing agent behaves as it does in an attempt to

F. gain an eighth electron
G. complete its inner core
H. complete its outer shell
J. get rid of as many electrons as possible

END OF EXAM

If you complete this test before the time limit is up, check back over the questions on this test only. Do not return to any of the previous tests.

CORRECT ANSWERS
MODEL EXAM IV

TEST 1. ENGLISH USAGE

1. C.
2. H.
3. D.
4. J.
5. C.
6. H.
7. D.
8. H.
9. A.
10. J.
11. C.
12. H.
13. A.
14. J.
15. D.
16. G.
17. D.
18. G.
19. C.
20. G.
21. D.
22. J.
23. D.
24. G.
25. D.
26. G.
27. A.
28. H.
29. B.
30. F.
31. C.
32. J.
33. C.
34. F.
35. A.
36. J.
37. D.
38. H.
39. A.
40. F.
41. D.
42. G.
43. D.
44. H.
45. D.
46. G.
47. D.
48. H.
49. A.
50. F.
51. B.
52. H.
53. D.
54. J.
55. D.
56. G.
57. C.
58. F.
59. D.
60. H.
61. C.
62. G.
63. B.
64. J.
65. D.
66. H.
67. B.
68. J.
69. D.
70. F.
71. D.
72. J.
73. B.
74. H.
75. B.

TEST 2. MATHEMATICS USAGE

1. E.
2. H.
3. B.
4. H.
5. B.
6. F.
7. B.
8. J.
9. C.
10. F.
11. C.
12. F.
13. E.
14. K.
15. E.
16. J.
17. D.
18. G.
19. E.
20. K.
21. D.
22. G.
23. E.
24. J.
25. B.
26. H.
27. B.
28. H.
29. C.
30. G.
31. D.
32. G.
33. C.
34. J.
35. A.
36. G.
37. C.
38. H.
39. D.
40. F.

TEST 3. SOCIAL STUDIES READING

1. A.
2. H.
3. C.
4. J.
5. C.
6. F.
7. B.
8. J.
9. B.
10. F.
11. C.
12. J.
13. B.
14. H.
15. A.
16. G.
17. D.
18. F.
19. D.
20. G.
21. B.
22. G.
23. D.
24. J.
25. C.
26. H.
27. C.
28. F.
29. B.
30. F.
31. C.
32. J.
33. A.
34. F.
35. D.
36. J.
37. B.
38. H.
39. D.
40. H.
41. D.
42. F.
43. C.
44. G.
45. B.
46. H.
47. C.
48. J.
49. A.
50. J.
51. A.
52. H.

TEST 4. NATURAL SCIENCE READING

1. B.
2. J.
3. B.
4. J.
5. B.
6. F.
7. D.
8. H.
9. C.
10. H.
11. D.
12. H.
13. B.
14. F.
15. D.
16. G.
17. D.
18. H.
19. D.
20. H.
21. A.
22. F.
23. C.
24. F.
25. B.
26. H.
27. D.
28. G.
29. A.
30. F.
31. A.
32. G.
33. D.
34. H.
35. A.
36. G.
37. C.
38. F.
39. B.
40. H.
41. D.
42. J.
43. D.
44. J.
45. B.
46. G.
47. C.
48. J.
49. A.
50. F.
51. B.
52. H.

EXPLANATORY ANSWERS
MODEL EXAM IV
TEST 1. ENGLISH USAGE

1. **C.** The construction of this sentence calls for a preposition following *lining up*. The context of this sentence requires the use of *of* rather than *by*.

2. **H.** Connect these run-on sentences correctly by placing the conjunction *but* after *job*. *But,* meaning "yet," is used here to link the discussion of two different characteristics of lining up suitable candidates—its difficulty and its necessity.

3. **D.** To keep the structure of this sentence parallel, use *walk* to correspond to *seek* and *select*.

4. **J.** The preposition *through* is needed here because it is the only choice that correctly connects all of the elements in the series.

5. **C.** A semicolon correctly separates these run-on sentences. The adverb *there* must be used rather than the possessive pronoun *their*.

6. **H.** Idiom requires the use of *other* in this sentence. *Effective,* meaning "producing the desired effect," not *affective,* meaning "emotional," is the appropriate adjective here.

7. **D.** This is the most concise and correct way to begin this sentence.

8. **H.** Avoid shifting tenses within a sentence. Since this sentence is giving general advice to the reader, the present tense is needed.

9. **A.** The infinitive *to fill* is the best choice here.

10. **J.** Don't separate a prepositional phrase from the main part of the sentence.

11. **C.** Correct this sentence fragment by using the indefinite subject *it*. *It being* is unacceptable. The use of *while* in choice D. does not correct the sentence fragment.

12. **H.** *Unexpected and unforeseen* is a redundant phrase. *Unexpecting* is not a word.

13. **A.** This is the most concise choice.

14. **J.** Choices F., G. and H. all contain errors in agreement concerning the singular and plural forms of the words *kind* and *question*. Only J. contains no conflict between the singular and the plural.

15. **D.** Quotation marks are not necessary because this is not a direct quotation of something that was said or written. These questions are listed here only as examples of what information about a specific job the employer should be able to supply. Use a colon to separate an introductory statement from an example when the example forms a complete sentence.

16. **G.** Choices F. and J. make no sense. The helping verb *have* must be used here instead of *had* because the rest of the sentence is in the present tense.

17. **D.** The modifier, "filled out by the prospective employees," should not be separated from its subject (application forms).

18. **G.** This is the most grammatical choice. There is no need to start a new paragraph because the main idea of this paragraph is screening job applicants, and conducting interviews is a part of this screening process.

19. **C.** The gerund form is the simplest and most correct of the selections.

20. **G.** This prepositional phrase refers to "selecting the right person." *Person* is singular; any word that refers back to *person* must also be singular. Choice B. gives the only singular alternative, *applicant*.

21. **D.** This is the most logical order for this essay. Paragraph 2 gives the essay's topic, the choice of personnel, and lists the two steps an employer should follow (deciding what the applicant must do on the job and looking for a qualified applicant). Paragraph 3 goes into detail about the first step (deciding what the applicant's duties will be). Paragraph 1 discusses where to look for applicants, and paragraph 4 explains what an employer should do once she or he has applicants for a job.

22. **J.** J. is simplest, and no comma is necessary.

23. **D.** A semicolon, as in B., would be correct, but the sentences are long enough. Separate them.

24. **G.** Alice is beginning a sentence in her thinking with the word *And.* The previous sentence must end with a period.

25. **D.** When breaking up a quote in the middle of a sentence, end the first part with a comma and close the quotes.

26. **G.** When continuing a quotation within a sentence, open quotes and use the lower case.

27. **A.** Alice is asking a question, so a question mark is necessary. When the actual quote is a question, the question mark goes inside the quotation marks.

28. **H.** One considers, thinks and wonders nowhere but in one's own mind. What Alice was doing was *wondering.*

29. **B.** *Daisy* is an adjective. It modifies the noun *chain.*

30. **F.** The plural of *daisy* is *daisies.* When a subordinate clause ends a sentence, a preceding comma is optional. In this sentence, because of the surprise element, a comma is effective.

31. **C.** There is no reason for capitalization or punctuation.

32. **J.** All other choices are excessively verbose.

33. **C.** A direct quote in the middle of a sentence must be preceded by a comma. Since the quote continues, do not close it.

34. **F.** A quote is neither beginning nor ending; therefore no quotation marks are needed.

35. **A.** *Too* is the adverb meaning "more than desired." Since the exclamation is part of the quote, the exclamation point goes inside the quotation marks.

36. **J.** *But* begins the sentence so must begin with a capital *B.* There is no reason for a coma after *when.*

37. **D.** One could refer to a male rabbit as either *it* or *him,* however since the author has already used the pronoun *he* (. . . *say to himself* . . .), consistency requires that the rabbit now be referred to as a *he.*

38. **H.** When a coordinating conjunction separates two independent clauses, it should be preceded by a comma, never a semicolon.

39. **A.** Alice has just seen the rabbit, so it would be incorrect to say that she had *never seen* one, C.

40. **F.** *Or* is the correlative of *either.* No punctuation is needed.

41. **D.** The sentence is too long. Start a new one. The transitional *and* is unnecessary because of the flowing tone.

42. **G.** Rabbit hole is a compound noun. It is not hyphenated.

43. **D.** B. and D. are both correct, but D. is more succinct.

44. **H.** Thinking *about* implies conscious thought. Thinking *of* implies spur-of-the-moment realization.

45. **D.** D. is the only meaningful choice.

46. **G.** No punctuation is needed between an adjective and its modifying adverb. *Real* and *really* are colloquialisms of *very.*

47. **D.** Reading ahead, one sees that the only logical choice is *either.*

48. **H.** The adverb is needed to modify the verb *fell.* The comma is needed before the coordinating conjunction which connects two independent clauses.

49. **A.** The cause-effect relationship requires the use of the conjunction *for* (or *because*). There is no reason for a comma.

50. **F.** No punctuation is needed. *It* has no reference.

51. **B.** *Make out* and *search out* are colloquial. *Determine* would be correct, but *determine out* is not.

52. **H.** To maintain parallel form, the *first* should be complemented by a *then.* G. is technically correct, but it is better in this case, to divide into two shorter sentences.

53. **D.** *Bookshelves* is one word. B. constitutes a run-on sentence.

54. **J.** What the pictures are doing now is *hanging.* They were *hung* a long time ago.

55. **D.** When a subordinate clause ends a sentence, it need not be preceded by a comma.

56. **G.** The possessive is established by the preposition *of.* An apostrophe, even if properly placed, is redundant.

57. **C.** The idiomatic expression is that one *gets a good idea from.*

58. **F.** All other choices are awkward.

59. **D.** *Mad* means "crazy." One is angry *with* a person, but angry *at* a thing or event.

60. **H.** The possessive is created by the preposition *of*. Additional use of apostrophes is incorrect.

61. **C.** The passive voice is unnecessary. B. and D. are awkward.

62. **G.** Knowledge is acquired learning; wisdom is innate. *If he* implies that *that person* is a specific person.

63. **B.** One *replies* to a question; one *responds* to an ad.

64. **J.** The name of a newspaper is italicized; days of the week are not. *Sunday* refers only to the issue.

65. **D.** All opening clauses are superfluous.

66. **H.** Later in the letter the author states that he desires to be a journalist "after graduation." He is therefore currently a senior. J. is correct but verbose.

67. **B.** The way the sentence is constructed, the verb *am* in "I am seventeen . . ." is made to apply to the entire sentence; therefore no other verbs can be used.

68. **J.** *Here* is unnecessary.

69. **D.** B. and C. are correct but create choppiness.

70. **F.** *To complement,* as in G., H. and J., means "to make complete" or "to supply a lack in." (That tie *complements* your jacket beautifully.) No possession is indicated.

71. **D.** The interest has not died out, so the past tense is incorrect. B. and C. are correct but verbose.

72. **J.** A modifier should be as close as possible to that which it modifies.

73. **B.** Only B. makes the structure parallel.

74. **H.** The closing of a letter should not be in the same sentence as the body.

75. **B.** The complimentary closing of a letter ends with a comma. Only the first letter of the complimentary closing is capitalized.

TEST 2. MATHEMATICS USAGE

1. **E.** Every hour, the minute hand of a clock goes around once, or 360°. In two hours, it rotates 720°.

2. **H.** $\frac{15}{45}$ would be $\frac{1}{3}$. With a larger denominator, the fraction $\frac{15}{46}$ is less than $\frac{1}{3}$.

3. **B.** Since the perimeter of a square is four times the length of a side, it is

$$4x\left(\frac{2x}{3} + 1\right), \text{ or } \frac{8x + 12}{3}$$

4. **H.** In the first trip, the motorist travels 120 miles at 60 m.p.h., which takes 2 hours. On the way back, she travels the same distance at 40 m.p.h., which takes 3 hours. Her average rate is the total distance (240 miles) divided by the total time (5 hours), which yields 48 m.p.h.

5. **B.** The proportion to be solved is $2\frac{1}{2}:4 = 1\frac{7}{8}:x$, where x is the length of the shorter dimension of the enlargement. Solving, x = 3.

6. **F.** The area of the circle is π times the square of the radius, or 9π. The area of the square is 36. Thus, the ratio is $\frac{9\pi}{36}$, or $\frac{\pi}{4}$. Approximating π as 3.14, we divide and obtain .785, which is closest to $\frac{4}{5}$.

7. **B.** By simple substitutions, $s = 16 \times 8 \times 8$, or 1024.

8. **J.** If angles BAD and BCD are right angles, they are equal. Angle BAC equals angle BCA, since they are base angles of an isosceles triangle. Subtracting equals from equals, angle DAC equals angle DCA. Therefore, ACD is an isosceles triangle, and AD = CD.

9. **C.** The original 6 pounds contained .24 pounds of salt. Now, the same .24 pounds are in 5 pounds of solution, so the percentage is $\frac{24}{5}$ or $4\frac{4}{5}$.

10. **F.** By the Law of Exponents, $(75)^3 \times (75)^7 = (75)^{3+7} = (75)^{10}$.

11. **C.** This is a proportion. $\frac{3}{4}$ in.:6 in. = 10 mi.:x. Solving, x = 80 miles.

12. **F.** If h is any positive quantity, then letting $d' = (m + h) - \left(\frac{50}{m + h}\right)$, we can see that d' is greater than d, since h is greater than zero and $\frac{50}{m}$ is greater than $\frac{50}{m + h}$. Therefore, d increases as m does.

13. **E.** One cubic foot equals 12^3 cubic inches, or 1728. Thus, one cubic foot of the metal would weigh 3456 pounds.

14. **K.** 4 of the 6 equal parts of 2 means $\frac{4}{6} \times 2$, or $\frac{4}{3}$.

15. **E.** 110% of 105 is 1.1×105, or 115.5

16. **J.** This is a proportion. 2 inches:$7\frac{1}{2}$ inches = 5 feet:x, so x = $18\frac{3}{4}$ feet.

17. **D.** The area of triangle ADE equals the area of triangle AEC, since they have the same base and altitude. The area of triangle ABC equals that of triangle ADC, since the diagonal of a parallelogram divides it equally.

18. **G.** At 3 for 10¢, one dozen pencils cost 40¢, so the profit on each dozen is 5¢. With $5\frac{1}{2}$ dozen, the profit is $27\frac{1}{2}$¢.

19. **E.** $26 \times 3\frac{1}{2} = (26 \times 3) + (26 \times \frac{1}{2})$ by the distributive law. $26 \times 3 = (20 \times 3) + (6 \times 3)$ by the distributive law. Therefore, $26 \times 3\frac{1}{2} = (26 \times \frac{1}{2}) + (20 \times 3) + (6 \times 3)$.

20. **K.** 20 square yards equals 180 square feet. At 31¢ per square foot, it will cost $55.80.

21. **D.** 10^5 is defined as $10 \times 10 \times 10 \times 10 \times 10$ or 100,000. $10 \times 5 = 50$; $5^{10} = 25^5$; $5\sqrt{10}$ is between 1 and 2; and $10^{10} \div 10^2 = 10^8$.

22. **G.** $3\frac{1}{2} \times \$1.10 = \$3.85$. At 60¢ a dozen, one orange costs 5¢, and 20 cost $1.00. The total is $4.85.

23. **E.** This is a proportion. $2\frac{1}{2}:3 = x:14$; $x = \frac{35}{3}$, or $11\frac{2}{3}$.

24. **J.** There will be no waste if the lengths are multiples of $5\frac{1}{2}$ feet. This occurs between 6 and 24 only for 22 feet.

25. **B.** Each tile, including half of the cement around it, has an area of 1 square inch. 3240 square inches equals 22.5 square feet, or 2.5 square yards.

26. **H.** A median score is the middle score when all scores are arranged in ascending or descending order. This is 27 here.

27. **B.** Perimeter = 2l + 2w
If the two long sides are together the perimeter will be
5 + 3 + 3 + 5 + 3 + 3 = 22

3 3
5 5

If the two short sides are together, the perimeter will be
3 + 5 + 5 + 3 + 5 + 5 = 26
26 − 22 = 4 feet shorter

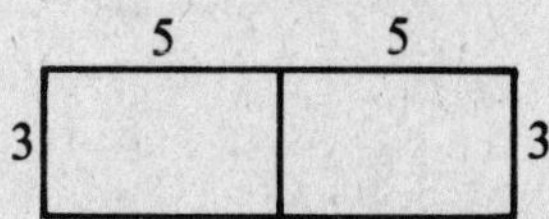

28. **H.** 2,975 pennies = \$29.75
\$35.00 − \$29.75 = \$5.25 saved
Rate of discount = $\frac{5.25}{35} \times 100 =$
.15 × 100 = 15%

29. **C.** One car went 20 mph for $\frac{1}{2}$ hour, or 10 miles. The other car went 36 mph for $\frac{1}{2}$ hour, or 18 miles. Since they went in opposite directions, add the two distances to find the total number of miles apart. 10 + 18 = 28

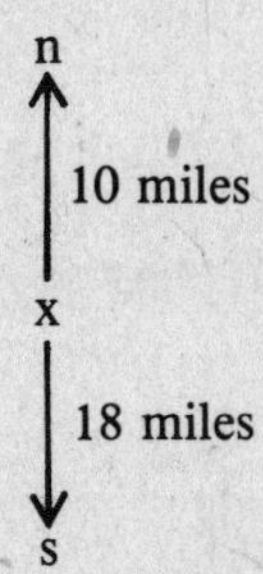

30. **G.** If 60% of the games were predicted accurately, then 40% of the games were predicted inaccurately.
Let x = games played
.40 x = 16
x = 40 games played
40 − 16 = 24 games won
Therefore, the sportwriter was accurate for 24 games.

31. **D.** 500 − 125 = 375 pads @ \$.04 = \$15.00
130 − 45 = 85 pencils @ \$.03 = \$2.55
50 dozen − 4 dozen = 46 dozen rubber bands @ \$.02 = \$.92
\$15.00 + \$2.55 + \$.92 = \$18.47

32. **G.** $\text{Rate} = \frac{\text{Distance}}{\text{Time}}$
Let D = 100 and T = 1

$$R = \frac{100}{1 - \frac{1}{4}}$$

$$R = \frac{100}{\frac{3}{4}}$$

$$R = 100 \times \frac{4}{3} = \frac{400}{3} = 133\tfrac{1}{3}$$

$133\frac{1}{3} - 100 = 33\frac{1}{3}\%$ increase

33. **C.** Number of seats = 12 + 14 = 26
Number of passengers at station A = 14 + 4 = 18
Number of passengers at next stop = 18 − 8 + 13 = 23
Number of empty seats = 26 − 23 = 3

34. **J.** $\frac{1}{4} \times 4000 = 1000$ men
4000 − 1000 = 3000 women
$\frac{2}{3} \times 3000 = 2000$ married women
3000 − 2000 = 1000 unmarried women
$\frac{1}{5}$ unemployed ∴ $\frac{4}{5}$ employed
$\frac{4}{5} \times 1000 = 800$ employed unmarried women
$\frac{1}{8} \times 800 = 100$ unmarried women teachers
$\frac{100}{4000} = \frac{1}{40}$

35. **A.** 500 dozen @ \$.40 per dozen = 1976 purchase
75% of 500 = 375 pencils purchased in 1978
20% of \$.40 = \$.08 increase in cost per dozen
375 × \$.48 = \$180 spent on pencils in 1978

36. **G.** The number of accidents is irrelevant to the question. B deaths occurred in 10 years, so each

year an average of one-tenth of B deaths occurred.

37. **C.** The angle formed by WYV is a right angle, therefore the angle opposite it, angle TYU, is also a right angle. Therefore triangle TYU is a right triangle. Chord TU is the hypotenuse of the triangle, since it is the side opposite the right angle. The formula $A^2 + B^2 = C^2$ determines the length of the hypotenuse. Substituting our own values in this formula:
$TY^2 + UY^2 = TU^2 \therefore TU = \sqrt{TY^2 + UY^2}$

38. **H.** The number of years by which A is older than B must remain constant. Thus, if A is 2 years older than B, A will always be 2 years older than B, but the ratio will decrease. For example, if A is 4 when B is 2, then four years later A will be 8 while B is 6. Thus, the ratio decreases from 2:1 to $\frac{4}{3}$:1.

39. **D.** The equation of a line is $y = mx + b$. When the given equation ($y = \frac{3}{4}x + 2$) is substituted in the formula, m (the slope of the line) $= \frac{3}{4}$ and b (the point at which the line intercepts the Y axis) = 2.

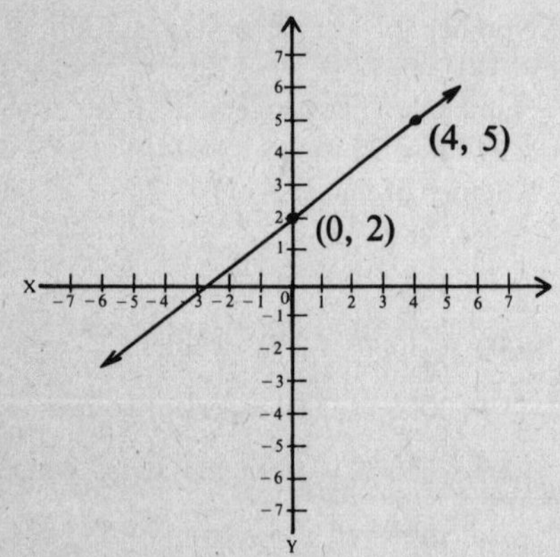

As the slope of a line equals the *rise* over the *run* from the point at which the line intercepts the Y axis, one must move three units vertically and four units horizontally from the Y intercept. Since the line has a positive slope, these movements must be upwards and to the right, to the point indicated on the graph above. Then the line is drawn connecting this point (4,5) with the Y intercept (0,2). The equation of this line is $y = \frac{3}{4}x + 2$.

The equations of the other graphs are:

(A) $y = \frac{3}{4}x - 2$; (B) $y = \frac{4}{3}x + 2$;

(C) $y = \frac{4}{3}x - 2$; (E) $y = -\frac{3}{4}x + 2$.

40. **F.** Let x = No. of melons for 80 cents.

Then $\frac{30}{100d} = \frac{x}{80}$

$100dx = 2400$

$x = \frac{24}{d}$

TEST 3. SOCIAL STUDIES READING

1. **A.** Their strong language and uncompromising tone make it quite clear that the signatories to this document are outraged at the information they have received.

2. **H.** The Huns were an exceptionally bellicose and warlike tribe which came from Asia and overran much of the area which is now Germany during the third to fifth centuries. Another wave of Huns swept into Germany during the tenth century. While the area was successively settled by Goths, Visigoths, Teutons and others, the Huns are a part of the German heritage. Because of the markedly uncivilized nature of the Huns, their name has become an epithet attached to particularly vicious persons or groups.

3. **C.** The document is concerned only with crimes committed in countries conquered by the Germans, not crimes committed within Germany. The crimes that it is concerned with are both military and civilian atrocities. Ionians are Greek islanders.

4. **J.** The statement specifies that war crimes committed at no specific geographical location will be centrally tried. (This later happened at Nuremburg.) Those Germans perpetrating crimes against a specific population in a single locale would be tried by the post-war governments of those areas. Since the crime detailed in the document is murder, the victims themselves cannot sit in judgment.

5. **C.** Judging from the horror of the entire world when the death camps were finally discovered and liberated, it can only be assumed that at the time of this statement the camps were not a subject of public knowledge. Most death camps were in Germany itself or in closed-in parts of Poland, and so were in the last areas to be liberated.

6. **F.** The League of Nations was defunct and the United Nations had not been formed at this time. Germany did not invade thirty-two countries, but thirty-two countries were united and allied in their war against Germany.

7. **B.** This is a specific, limited statement, not a general comment on all warfare of the time.

8. **J.** The liberating armies reported what they saw for themselves and what was reported by survivors, not by victims.

9. **B.** The document claims that in their retreat the Germans became more vicious and committed their most heinous crimes.

10. **F.** The second paragraph pronounces that this is a warning.

11. **C.** While the actual atrocities committed by the Nazis cover a wide range of tortures and forms of murder, this document limits itself to mass executions. This document is the statement on atrocities prepared at the Moscow Conference in October 1943.

12. **J.** The ERA, if and when ratified, will become the Twenty-seventh Amendment to the Constitution.

13. **B.** Speaker 1 cares less about the details of the ERA than about his daughter as a person. He fervently desires first-class citizenship and full equality for his daughter. (The statement of Speaker 1 is from an editorial by Frosty Troy, Editor, *The Oklahoma Observer.*)

14. **H.** A certain hysterical fear and negativism leads Speaker 2 to find in the words of the Amendment threats to the family, to society and to the rights and lives of children. (The statement of Speaker 2 is adapted from a flier of "Women for Honest Equality in our Nation," Merrick, N.Y.)

15. **A.** The legal status of married women in most states of the United States is still based upon English Common Law. (The statement of Speaker 3 is a summary of the status of married women under English Common Law, written by William Blackstone in 1775).

16. **G.** Speaker 4 asks generally irrelevant questions in a somewhat belligerent manner. The emotional charge is such that one comes out answering "no," then transferring that *no* to the ERA even though ERA is not connected to the questions. (The questions of Speaker 4 are excerpted from a flier by "Operation Wake Up," Harrison, N.Y.)

17. **D.** Speaker 5 makes no mention of the draft, but does, however, urge that women be offered all the

opportunities which are offered to men, including the opportunity to volunteer for combat duty. (The Statement of Speaker 5 was adapted from "In Pursuit of Equal Rights—Women in the '70s," a publication of the League of Women Voters.)

18. **F.** Speaker 6 is correct when branding the wording of the ERA Amendment as being vague and innocuous. The first sentence is a genuine concern and is entirely accurate. Speaker 6 is mistaken in the last sentence, wherein equality is interpreted to mean that women must lose. Nowhere is it written that protective legislation will be denied to women. It is equally likely that such protection will be extended to men. (The statement of Speaker 6 was compiled from literature of opponents of the ERA.)

19. **D.** Speakers 2, 4, and 6 all draw upon fear of the unknown in their arguments against the ERA and in their search for adherents to their cause.

20. **G.** Speaker 5 appears to be quite objective and would thus immediately recognize Speaker 4's questions as irrelevant. Since Speaker 5 advocates equal opportunity for women, surely Speaker 5 would agree that women should be able to get credit either through their husbands, or through their own credentials and assets. While Speaker 5 would probably agree with statement II, the argument is not likely to be raised with Speaker 4, since Speaker 4 did not raise the question of the draft. Title IX requires that physical education classes offer equal training and equal facilities to both men and women, but they need be coeducational only where appropriate to the physical activity involved. There is no mandated sex ratio in physical education classes.

21. **B.** The delegates to the women's rights convention at Seneca Falls, New York, in 1848, were acutely conscious of women's inferior status under the law.

22. **G.** The ERA was first introduced in Congress in 1923 by the National Women's Party. 1848 is the date of the women's rights convention. 1954 is the date of the Civil Rights Act. 1972 is the year the ERA was approved by Congress and sent to the states for ratification.

23. **D.** The ERA will simply assure that laws apply equally to women and men.

24. **J.** The Constitution makes no mention of a time limit within which the states must ratify an amendment. Congress itself imposed the seven-year limit on the ERA. In October 1978, Congress voted to extend the deadline until June 30, 1982.

25. **C.** The article is indeed about "Kings and Parliaments," yet "Limited Government" is a better, more descriptive title. The article discusses the interaction between Parliament and the King within the limits of the British Constitution and as subject to natural law.

26. **H.** Parliament is not absolute because it is constitutionally held in check by the King and the King's judges (F.), and because, even beyond constitutional limitations, the supreme power belong to G-d, G.

27. **C.** *Divine law* is the same thing as *His natural laws,* which, the author states, are immutably true and serve to automatically void any contrary manmade laws.

28. **F.** Under the British Constitution the legislative and the executive branches serve as check and balance to each other. There are judges, but the judges represent the King, hence they are an arm of the executive. In the United States there are three entirely independent branches of government—executive, legislative and judiciary—serving as check and balance to each other.

29. **B.** The spelling, construction and use of language indicate that this article was written a long time ago. There was no English Parliament at the time of the Magna Carta, so A. is incorrect. The other three choices might conceivably be correct, but it is most likely that a defense of the English system would have been written at the time that that system was under attack, namely during the American Revolution. The Declaration of Independence (B.) was written at the outset of the revolution; the Emancipation Proclamation (C.) was a Civil War document; the Fourteen Points (D.) were part of Woodrow Wilson's peace plan at the end of World War I.

30. **F.** In the last sentence the author states that preservation of this Constitution has cost well-spent oceans of blood and treasure in every age. Obviously, the Constitution had already been in existence for a long time before this article was written.

31. **C.** The author waxes ecstatic over the "grandeur of the British Constitution."

32. **J.** The 18th Amendment prohibited the manufacture and sale of intoxicating liquor and was a source of contention in American political life. It was repealed by the 21st Amendment, adopted in 1933. The "Women's Suffrage" Amendment was the 19th Amendment.

33. **A.** The Puritans believe that knowledge of Scripture was necessary to experience conversion and thereby the possibility of salvation. Every town with fifty families was required to establish a primary school and every town with one hundred families was required to establish a *grammar* school, the equivalent of a high school.

34. **F.** The Sugar Act of 1764, a revenue-raising measure imposed by Parliament, actually provided for a lowering of the duties on molasses imports, but insisted that the duties were to be collected and the Act enforced.

35. **D.** The power of the British government cannot be expanded by a specific constitutional amending process because Britain has no single document which is its Constitution.

36. **J.** F. is a leading question. G. limits options (there is, for example, no way to indicate that one gets information from television, lectures, or discussions). H. slants the question a bit by the use of the word *agree,* perhaps also putting the person being questioned on the defensive. J. presents its question clearly and in an unslanted way.

37. **B.** In 1787, Massachusetts farmers led by Daniel Shays protested against the refusal of the Massachusetts legislature to issue more paper money by closing the courts and attempting to seize an arsenal. The rebellion was suppressed and the rebels eventually pardoned. One ramification of the rebellion was that it caused uneasiness among many Americans about the effectiveness of the Articles of Confederation as a basis of government. Conservatives felt that a stronger central government was needed to preclude such outbursts.

38. **H.** The American Colonization Society raised funds for the purpose of transporting free blacks for resettlement in Africa. The movement was endorsed by such prominent statesmen as Thomas Jefferson, James Monroe and Henry Clay. Many supporters of colonization hoped that the movement would encourage slaveowners to free their slaves without fear of the eventual power of free blacks in the community. Abolitionists, however, criticized the movement for devoting its attention to the exportation of free blacks rather than to the emancipation of slaves.

39. **D.** Leaders of the antebellum Women's Rights Movement, Susan B. Anthony, Elizabeth Cady Stanton, Lucretia Mott and Lucy Stone, to name a few, received their training in reform through participation in the Temperance or Antislavery movements.

40. **H.** The power of the absolute monarchs *increased* as a result of the Commercial Revolution. The monarch and the rising merchant class found that it was to their mutual advantage to support each other against the old feudal aristocracy.

41. **D.** An enlightened despot must devote considerable time and energy to governing his nation efficiently. He must also show concern for the welfare of his subjects. Catherine the Great, Frederick the Great and Joseph II of Austria were all rulers of this genre. Louis XV was more interested in his own pleasures than in the welfare of his nation and subjects, thus contributing to the popular dissatisfaction which led to the French Revolution.

42. **F.** The United States and England had shared the Oregon Territory, which extended from northern California to Alaska, since 1818. Under the Oregon Treaty of 1846 they divided the area at the 49th parallel, the present northern boundary of the contiguous United States. American expansionists wished to claim the entirety of the territory up to the Alaskan boundary, the *fifty-four forty* line. The crucial line in the Korean War and the current boundary between North and South Korea is the 38th parallel.

43. **C.** The Knights of Labor was the first union to attempt to organize unskilled as well as skilled labor. At the peak of its power, between 1878 and 1887, it had over 700,000 members. The Haymarket Riot of 1886 contributed to its decline in power.

44. **G.** President Hoover hoped that the Reconstruction Finance Corporation would encourage business investment, that this would bolster the economy, and that benefits would *trickle down* to other segments of the population. He did not intend to redistribute the national income. The other responses to the Depression mentioned in the answer choices were actions taken by President Roosevelt under his New Deal program.

45. **B.** The address has come to be known as the "Four Freedoms" speech.

46. **H.** In 1941 the Nazis and the Italians were waging war on Europe and Africa while the Japanese were attacking China and threatening Australia. This is the scenario to which President Roosevelt refers in the second quoted paragraph. The First World War (1917) was confined to Europe and Africa. In 1937 the Axis aggression had not reached proportions suf-

ficient to alarm a depression-bound America. By 1945 the United States was an active participant in the war.

47. **C.** The President makes no mention of the draft and specifically states that our manpower is not needed. He does offer money, airplanes and assorted armor and ammunition. A *fifth column* is an indigenous population that is disloyal to the country in which it lives and which serves as a spy or sabotage network for an enemy power. The President warns that great numbers of secret agents are here.

48. **J.** The President suggests that while attack from abroad is not imminent it is a real potential danger and that the country must have the moral will to be alert to it and to prepare a defense machine.

49. **A.** Panic lest the Pacific Coast Japanese population represent a *Fifth Column* led to the relocation of all these Japanese to internment camps inland. The civil rights of all Japanese who had lived on the West Coast, immigrant and United States citizens alike, were disregarded, and these persons were forced to sit out the war in these camps, without due process of law. The U-2 spy planes were used to fly over Russia during the Cold War. The CIA is assigned to collect intelligence information abroad. The Army-McCarthy hearings had to do with corruption in the 1950s.

50. **J.** The Manhattan Project, which developed the atomic bomb, was not even conceived until December 1941, and the hydrogen and neutron bombs were still later developments. President Roosevelt is using the term "with the crash of a bomb" figuratively to refer to force and firepower.

51. **A.** The SALT talks and SALT agreements aim to establish a program for mutual arms reduction. The acronym stands for Strategic Arms Limitation Treaty. President Roosevelt suggests that freedom from fear can best be attained through a worldwide reduction in armaments and thus could be expected to be supportive of the principles espoused by SALT talks.

52. **H.** Article II, Section 3, of the Constitution begins: "He (the President) shall from time to time give to the Congress Information of the State of the Union, and recommend to their Consideration such Measures as he shall judge necessary and expedient . . ."

TEST 4. NATURAL SCIENCE READING

1. **B.** This is stated and described in the first paragraph.

2. **J.** The very first sentence in the passage states that this operation is the last resort for schizophrenia and manic-depression, both serious and advanced mental illnesses.

3. **B.** The second sentence of the first paragraph describing the prefrontal lobotomy states that surgeons cut away important nerve connections in both the prefrontal brain lobe and thalamus.

4. **J.** The last sentence of the first paragraph states that the operation's aim is to help the patient adjust better to the environment.

5. **B.** The second paragraph describes the work of Dr. Walter R. Hess and his experiments with electrodes implanted in a cat's brain. The last sentence of that paragraph summarizes that Dr. Hess was able to determine how parts of the brain control organs of the body.

6. **F.** The second sentence of the passage states that Dr. Antonio Moniz devised the prefrontal lobotomy technique.

7. **D.** Again, this is stated in the last sentence of the second paragraph.

8. **H.** The Nobel Prize in Medicine and Physiology was awarded jointly to Drs. Hess and Moniz.

9. **C.** The last sentence in the third paragraph quotes, "Now I will be able to hire assistants."

10. **H.** At no point in the passage is reference made to the way Dr. Moniz plans to spend the Nobel Prize money.

11. **D.** As a professor, physician and research scientist, Dr. Moniz undoubtedly was repeatedly exposed to radioactivity. This exposure was a result of his other activities, not a result of his work on the brain.

12. **H.** Prefrontal lobotomy has been all but abandoned and has been supplanted by many varieties of newly developed mind-altering and mood-altering drugs. While the drugs are not panaceas, are not universally successful, and do have side effects, they are not nearly as dangerous to the patient as prefrontal lobotomy. Despite the research of Dr. Hess, the brain is still basically uncharted and many necessary portions of patients' brains were destroyed in the expectation of severing the connections that led to the aberrant behavior. Since damage to the intellect so often accompanied prefrontal lobotomy, the operation did not achieve its goal, for the patients were not able to adjust to or function in society as brain-damaged individuals. Lobotomy was never used as a punishment in any civilized nation, so no ruling was ever made judging it to be cruel and unusual punishment.

13. **B.** Dr. Hess' experiments aimed to learn more about the brain, how it controls various organs and functions, and which portions of the brain are in charge of each organ and function.

14. **F.** So stated in the first paragraph. The aphorism *opposites attract* derives from this fact.

15. **D.** When a ferromagnetic substance is in the nonmagnetic state, its internal magnets are arranged in random fashion so as to induce no polarization.

16. **G.** When a ferromagnetic object is brought into a magnetic field, its atomic magnets automatically align themselves to create a magnetized object. One pole of that object is attracted to the magnet which created the magnetic field. The other pole in turn, may attract another ferromagnetic substance. When the object leaves the magnetic field, the atomic magnets lose the force that held them in alignment, so they return to their random positions, and the temporary magnet is no longer.

17. **D.** Nickel displays strong magnetic effects. In combination with lightweight, non-magnetic aluminum metal, it would form a lightweight magnetic alloy. Silver and gold do not have magnetic properties. Helium does not have a solid state, hence cannot be used to create a metallic alloy.

18. **H.** Heating reduces magnetism in a permanent magnet by increasing atomic activity, thus destroying rigid alignment. Two magnets heated together would be equally affected by the heat.

19. **D.** Rotation creates electric currents, and electric currents create magnetic fields. Since the earth

rotates, one can assume that the magnetic fields of the earth are connected with its rotation, though the precise mechanism is not fully understood.

20. **H.** Living in the state of Washington, where the compass points 24° east of true north, the sailor would correct his compass by moving it 24° to the west. If the sailor were then to move to Maine, his compass would register 23° west of true north plus the 24° west by which he had previously adjusted it, in all 47° west of true north.

21. **A.** A negative attraction is a repulsion. Like poles of a magnet repel each other.

22. **F.** The north magnetic pole is moving westward at a rate of a few miles per year. This movement is very slow and gradual, but it is constant. The more often a compass is corrected, the greater the accuracy.

23. **C.** The north magnetic pole is over 1000 miles west of the north geographic pole. The south magnetic pole is directly opposite the north magnetic pole, hence it is over 1000 miles east of the south geographic pole. The south geographic pole is, then, over 1000 miles west of the south magnetic pole.

24. **F.** Iron, which would absorb magnetism, is the most effective protection. The other substances all transmit the magnetism on the instrument. However, it is most important that the iron not come into direct physical contact with the instrument, lest, acting as a magnet, the iron itself might attract the instrument. For example, a ship's compass is *suspended* within an iron casing.

25. **B.** Sodium carbonate is Na_2CO_3. Sodium bicarbonate is $NaHCO_3$. They react with HCl as shown:
$Na_2CO_3 + 2HCl \rightarrow 2NaCl + H_2O + CO_2$
$NaHCO_3 + HCl \rightarrow NaCl + H_2O + CO_2$
You can see that mole for mole, Na_2CO_3 produces more NaCl and as much CO_2 as $NaHCO_3$. However, since Na_2CO_3 has a higher molecular weight than $NaHCO_3$ (106 compared to 82), there are proportionally more moles of the latter per pound, and so $NaHCO_3$ produces more CO_2 per pound (by a ratio of $\frac{106}{82}$). Na_2CO_3 produces more NaCl, by a ratio of 2 times $\frac{82}{106}$ or $\frac{164}{106}$.

26. **H.** In a nuclear equation the atomic numbers on the left must equal the atomic numbers on the right, and the mass numbers on the left must equal the mass numbers on the right.
${}_{52}Te^{130} + {}_{1}H^{2} \rightarrow {}_{53}I^{131} + ?$
numbers 52 + 1 = 53 + 0
weights 130 + 2 = 131 + 1
The number of the particle is 0 and the mass is 1. This is the neutron.

27. **D.** The half-life is the amount of time it takes for half the weight of a radioactive material to disintegrate. At the end of ten days 4 grams will remain, at the end of twenty days 2 grams will remain, at the end of thirty days 1 gram will remain, and at the end of forty days 0.5 grams will remain.

28. **G.** Blue-green algae may have been the first photosynthetic cells and have no sexual reproduction. They and Euglena are the only groups to reproduce *only* asexually.

29. **A.** The process of repeated mitotic cell divisions by which the fertilized egg develops into the multicellular embryo is known as cleavage.

30. **F.** If the original resistance of the single wire is R, each piece will have a resistance of 0.1 R. If these are then connected in parallel, the total resistance is
$\frac{1}{R_1} = 10\left(\frac{1}{0.1R}\right)$
$R_1 = 0.01R$
$\frac{R_1}{R} = 0.01$

31. **A.** In a nuclear reaction, the atomic weights and the atomic numbers on the left and right must be equal.
${}_{3}Li^{7} + {}_{1}H^{1} \rightarrow {}_{2}He^{4} + {}_{2}X^{4}$
numbers 3 + 1 = 2 + *2*
weights 7 + 1 = 4 + *4*
X is ${}_{2}He^{4}$

32. **G.** Sulfuric acid is a dehydrating agent. This means it removes water from compounds. When water is removed from the cellulose ($C_6H_{10}O_5$) in the wood, black carbon remains.

33. **D.** Fungi lack chlorophyll. They do not manufacture their own food and availability of sunlight is irrelevant to their existence. Fungi are saprophytes; they obtain their nourishment from dead organic matter which abounds in the forest.

34. **H.** In order to compensate for the outside pressure of the atmosphere, living things maintain within their bodies a pressure equal to that of the atmosphere.

35. **A.** The word *volatile* in chemisty means that the liquid will readily turn into a gas. If ammonium hydroxide is allowed to stand in an open vessel, the volatile gas ammonia will escape.

36. **G.** A chemical balance is used to obtain the weight of substances. In chemistry the universal system of measurement, the metric system, is used. The unit of weight in the metric system is the gram.

37. **C.** An electric shock is painful and food is a reward. Avoidance of pain and the desire for rewarding food gave twofold impetus to the rats' learning.

38. **F.** The somewhat hungry rats were choosing to avoid the pain of the shock at all costs, even though it meant that they missed out on the food. Discrimination of right from left had already been established in Phase I.

39. **B.** The rats first learned to run to the right arm of the maze for food and to shun the left arm to avoid shock. When the situation changed, the rats were able to learn to alter their behavior in accordance with their own physical conditions and the new circumstances in the maze.

40. **H.** This experiment is interesting in that it shows the relative merits of reward and punishment on the learning behavior of rats.

41. **D.** If A. were true, then all rats should have behaved in the same manner. The only reasonable conclusion is that the rats found their hunger to be so painful that they withstood the shocks in order to relieve the pain of hunger.

42. **J.** There are individual differences in intelligence even among rats.

43. **D.** Sometimes reward and punishment are clearly delineated, but sometimes it is hard to say whether an empty maze is rewarding because there is no punishment, or punishing because there is no reward, or whether food is itself a reward or simply the mitigation of pain. When hunger was only a mild stimulus, the rats ignored it in favor of the stronger stimulus to avoid the pain of shock. When the hunger became an intense stimulus, it became the dominant input into the rat's behavior.

44. **J.** Laboratory rats are bred specially for laboratory use; they are not domesticated wild rats. They are, however, relatively inexpensive and they learn very quickly, making them ideal subjects.

45. **B.** The halogens all have many industrial uses and all occur widely in nature as salts. The halogens contain seven electrons in their outer shells. As individual elements, chlorine is a gas, iodine is a solid and only bromine is a liquid.

46. **G.** The caries-preventive agent in toothpaste is stannous fluoride. In this compound, fluorine poses no health hazard.

47. **C.** When carbon tetrachloride is added to pure bromine, the original red-brown color of the liquid changes to amber.

48. **J.** A binary acid is one that contains only two elements, hydrogen and a nonmetal.

49. **A.** An oxidizing agent reacts with metals, hydrogen and water in its attempt to gain electrons to complete its outer shell.

50. **F.** Chlorine is used in the production of DDT and bromine in the production of lead tetraethyl for gasoline. Both of these substances are classified as pollutants.

51. **B.** Hydrofluoric acid is instrumental in the production of cryolite. Cryolite, not the hydrofluoric acid itself, is used in the extraction of aluminum from its ore.

52. **H.** The chemical activity of an element is governed by the number of electrons in its outer shell. Atoms are constantly striving to either gain or give up electrons. An element which strives to gain electrons serves as an oxidizing agent. The halogens, with their seven-electron shells, are searching to gain an eighth. Other oxidizing agents may have different numbers of electrons in their incomplete outer shells.